The Fire Below

The Fire Below

How the Caucasus Shaped Russia

Edited by
ROBERT BRUCE WARE

B L O O M S B U R Y
NEW YORK · LONDON · NEW DELHI · SYDNEY

Bloomsbury Academic
An imprint of Bloomsbury Publishing Plc

175 Fifth Avenue	50 Bedford Square
New York	London
NY 10010	WC1B 3DP
USA	UK

www.bloomsbury.com

First published 2013

Political-Administrative Map of the Caucasus based on an original map licensed to M.E. Sharpe, published in *Dagestan: Russian Hegemony and Islamic Resistance in the North Caucasus* by Robert Bruce Ware and Enver F. Kisriev (Armonk, NY: M.E. Sharpe, 2009), reproduced with kind permission.

Library of Congress Cataloging-in-Publication Data
A catalog record for this book is available from the Library of Congress

ISBN: HB: 978-1-4411-6086-7
PB: 978-1-4411-0793-0
ePDF: 978-1-4411-0648-3
ePub: 978-1-4411-6206-9

Typeset by Newgen Imaging Systems Pvt Ltd, Chennai, India
Printed and Bound in the United States of America

To the peoples of the Caucasus and Russia

CONTENTS

NOTES ON CONTRIBUTORS

Patrick Armstrong received a PhD from Kings College, University of London, in 1976 and served for 30 years as an analyst for the Canadian government, specializing in the former Union of Soviet Socialist Republic (USSR) and then Russia. He was a Political Counsellor in the Canadian Embassy in Moscow from 1993 to 1996.

First Lieutenant Andrei Doohovskoy received his MA from Harvard University, where he researched a variety of security topics related to Russian and Soviet counterinsurgency doctrine and practice. His dissertation integrated primary sources and subsequent analysis in an assessment of recent campaigns within the context of counterinsurgency theory. Andrei is currently serving as an Infantry officer in the US Army, and continues to research counterinsurgency and Russian security issues.

Andrew Foxall is Lecturer in Human Geography at Queen's University, Belfast, and ESRC Postdoctoral Fellow at the School of Geography and the Environment, University of Oxford. He holds a BSc (Hons) from the University of Plymouth, an MSc from the University of Birmingham, and a DPhil from the University of Oxford. His research encompasses two main areas—geopolitics of ethnicity and nationalism, and the political geographies of energy. He has worked both as an academic and a practitioner, specializing in conflict studies and developmental aspects of the environment, which are brought together through an empirical focus on post-Soviet Russia.

Anna Matveeva is an Honorary University Fellow at the Department of Politics, University of Exeter. She specializes in international peace-building. The geographical remit of her interests covers conflicts in the North and South Caucasus, and in Central Asia, where she lived in 2003–4 working as the United Nations Development Programme (UNDP) Regional Adviser on Peace and Development. Her recent publications on the North Caucasus include "The Caucasus: Views from Within. People's perspectives on peace and security" (research report for Saferworld, London, 2012); "The North Caucasus and Challenges of Minority Governance," in Oleh Protsyk and Benedikt Harzl (eds), *Managing Ethnic Diversity in Russia* (London:

Routledge, 2012), "Chechnya: Dynamics of War and Peace," *Problems of Post-Communism*, 54(3), May/June 2007. In 2010, Dr Matveeva headed the Research Secretariat of the international Kyrgyzstan Inquiry Commission. She consults for organizations, such as the United Nations (UN), the European Union (EU), and Organization for Security and Co-operation in Europe (OSCE), and for international nongovernmental organizations. Previously she was a Research Fellow at Chatham House, worked at the London School of Economics, and headed programs at International Alert and Saferworld. She writes for the *Guardian's Comment is Free* column on Russian politics and society.

Nicolai Petro is Professor of Political Science at the University of Rhode Island. He received his PhD in foreign affairs from the University of Virginia, and previously taught at the Monterey Institute of International Studies, the University of Pennsylvania, and Novgorod State University in Russia, where he was awarded an honorary doctorate in 1997. During the collapse of the Soviet Union he served as special assistant for policy in the US State Department. He is the author or editor of eight books and has written about Russia for the *Asia Times, Boston Globe, Christian Science Monitor, International Herald Tribune, Harvard International Review*, and *Wilson Quarterly*.

Walter Richmond received his PhD in Slavic Languages and Literatures from the University of Southern California in 1994. In 1995 he lived in Moscow and taught at the A. M. Gorky Literary Institute. He was invited to participate in the 1996 International Research and Exchanges Board (IREX) summer seminar on Russian history at Columbia University, and the 2004 IREX Regional Security Symposium. Specializing in the northwest Caucasus, he has published in scholarly venues including *The Journal of Muslim Minority Affairs* and *The Journal of Genocide Research*. In 2008, Routledge Press published his monograph, *The Northwest Caucasus: Past, Present, Future*. His new book, *The Circassian Genocide*, is forthcoming from Rutgers University Press. He is currently the director of the Russian Studies Program at Occidental College in Los Angeles.

Domitilla Sagramoso is a Lecturer in Security and Development at the Department of War Studies, King's College, London. She joined the Department of War Studies in 2005, having previously been the Principal Researcher at the Caucasus Policy Institute, within the International Policy Institute (KCL). From 1999 to 2004 she was a Research Fellow at the Centre for Defence Studies at King's College, London. She obtained an MA in War Studies (KCL) in 1992 and a PhD at the School of Slavonic and East European Studies, University College, London, in 1999. She specializes in issues of conflict, security, and development in Russia and the Caucasus, and is currently conducting research on Terrorism, Violence, and Islam in the Russian North Caucasus. Her recent publications include:

"The Radicalisation of Islamic Salafi *Jamaats* in the North Caucasus: Moving Closer to the Global *Jihad*ist Movement?," *Europe-Asia Studies*, 64(3), May 2012; "Islamic Radicalism in the North Western Caucasus," in Galina Yemelianova (ed.), *Islamic Radicalism in the Former Soviet Space*, Routledge, 2009; and "Violence and Conflict in the Russian North Caucasus," *International Affairs*, 83(4), July 2007.

Richard Sakwa is Professor of Russian and European Politics at the University of Kent and an Associate Fellow of the Russia and Eurasia Programme at the Royal Institute of International Affairs, Chatham House. He has published widely on Soviet, Russian, and post-communist affairs. Recent books include: *Postcommunism* (Buckingham: Open University Press, 1999), *Contextualising Secession: Normative Aspects of Secession Struggles* (Oxford: Oxford University Press, 2003), coedited with Bruno Coppieters; the edited volume *Chechnya: From Past to Future* (London: Anthem Press, 2005); *Russian Politics and Society* (London & New York: Routledge, 2008); and *Putin: Russia's Choice* (London & New York: Routledge, 2008). His book on *The Quality of Freedom: Khodorkovsky, Putin and the Yukos Affair* came out with Oxford University Press in 2009; and his study of contemporary Russian politics, *The Crisis of Russian Democracy: The Dual State, Factionalism, and the Medvedev Succession* was published by Cambridge University Press in 2011.

Lieutenant Colonel Robert Schaefer is a US Army Special Forces (Green Beret) and Eurasian Foreign Area Officer. For over 25 years he has served in a variety of special units and participated in almost every US overseas operation since 1990. He has extensive experience with counterinsurgency and counterterrorist operations around the world and has lived and worked in many countries of the former Soviet Union. His award-winning book, *The Insurgency in Chechnya and the North Caucasus; from Gazavat to Jihad* was named a "Best of 2011" by Kirkus Reviews and was named in the "Top 150 Books on Terrorism and Counterterrorism." LTC Schaefer is the 2001 recipient of the US Special Operations Command (SOCOM), and the OSS Society's Award of Excellence as the US Special Operations Command Person of the Year for his achievements with Russian airborne forces. He obtained his MA from Harvard University, and is the host of National Public Radio's Memorial Day Special 2007–12. He is a member of the Editorial Board for the Caucasus Survey and a frequent commentator for news programs and seminars focusing on the North Caucasus insurgency. He currently serves as the Chief of Central and South Asia Branch, International Military Affairs, and the Army Central Command.

Robert Bruce Ware since earning his doctorate at Oxford University, has conducted field research in the North Caucasus, publishing numerous articles on the region. He is the coauthor of *Dagestan: Russian Hegemony and Islamic Resistance in the North Caucasus*, and author of *Hegel: the Logic of Self-consciousness and the Legacy of Subjectivity Freedom.* His commentaries have appeared in *The Los Angeles Times, The San Francisco Chronicle, The Chicago Tribune, The St. Louis Post-Dispatch, The Boston Globe, The International Herald Tribune, The Moscow Times, The Hindu,* and *The Asian Times.* He is a Professor of Philosophy at Southern Illinois University, Edwardsville.

Akhmet Yarlykapov is Senior Researcher at the Institute of Ethnology and Anthropology at the Russian Academy of Sciences. He is also an Associate Professor at the Russian State University of Humanities in Moscow (RGGU), and has written extensively on Islamic radicalization in the North Caucasus. His publications include: *Islam u Stepnykh Nogaitsev,* Moscow, Russian Academy of Sciences, 2008; "Novoe islamskoe dvizhenie na Severnom Kavkaze: vzglyad etnografa," in *Rasy i narody: sovremennye etnicheskie i rasovye problemi* (Moscow: Nauka, 2006); and (edited with Irina Babich), *Islamskoe vozrozhdenie v sovremennoi Kabardino-Balkarii: perspektivy i posledstviya* (Moscow: RUDN, 2003).

Political-

Administrative

Map of the

Caucasus

(2013)

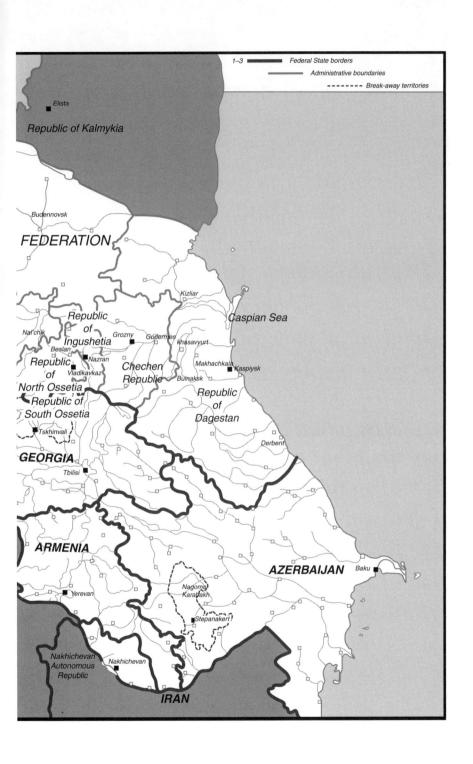

CHAPTER ONE

Introduction: How Has the Caucasus Shaped Russia?

Robert Bruce Ware

How has the Caucasus shaped Russia? Once I had asked it of myself that question seemed so natural and inevitable that I wondered whether I could hope to understand either Russia or the Caucasus without answering it. Yet an answer was not easy to find.

My initial search turned up a single study that seemed to address the question directly.[1] Whereas many publications have examined the effects that the Russian Federation has had upon events in the Caucasus, there has been much less attention to ways in which the causal relationship has also been reversed. Most of the articles, essays, and studies that I found seemed to presuppose the converse of my question: *how has Russia shaped the Caucasus?*[2] They thereby seemed to presuppose that Russians are naturally agents, that Caucasians are generally patients, and that somehow contrary to Newtonian physics the former affects the latter without the inconvenience of causal reciprocity.

Even at first glance, that seemed unlikely. For if the first Chechen conflict was the culmination of Boris Yeltsin's decentralizing strategies, the second conflict set the parameters for Vladimir Putin's recentralization of the Russian state, and for North Caucasian instabilities that have shaped the development of the Federation ever since:

- Putin became Russia's Prime Minister in August 1999, just one week after Chechnya-based militants invaded Dagestan, and his administrative style was cast in the opening months of the war.

- In May 2000, almost immediately after he was elected president, Putin announced the reorganization of the Russian Federation on the model of Russia's seven military districts.

- On September 13, 2004—barely one week after the Beslan hostage crisis, and in explicit response to "terrorist" threats—Putin announced the centralized appointment of Russia's regional governors, and an overhaul of the Russian electoral system that assured additional strength for the party in power.

- In January 2010, President Dmitri Medvedev announced the formation of the North Caucasus Federal District with a focus upon the relentless problems of the region.

- New pressures arrived as early as 2007 with preparations for the 2014 Winter Olympics in the North Caucasian city of Sochi.

- Meanwhile, the republics of this region—especially Dagestan, Chechnya, and Ingushetia—continued to deviate sharply from, and exercise disproportionate influence upon, the rest of the Russian Federation.

Yes, Russia has done much to shape the Caucasus, but as its most volatile region, the North Caucasus also has exerted a disproportionately strong influence upon the evolution of Russia's federal relations, as well as upon Russia's social, political, and religious cultures. These complex dynamics seemed to deserve attention.

So I wrote a paper on the topic, and presented it at a conference on Russian regional politics at the University of Dundee. The conference was organized by Cameron Ross, who kindly helped me to publish my paper in *Europe-Asia Studies*.[3] On the same panel at that conference were Domitilla Sagramoso and Richard Sakwa. The three of us met again on a panel that summer in Moscow, where we had a chance to discuss our views with several of our North Caucasian colleagues. Two years later, I organized a panel on the topic of Caucasian influence upon the evolution of Russia's federal politics at an annual meeting of the Political Studies Association. Richard Sakwa and Anna Matveeva presented papers on that panel.[4] Shortly after the panel, I met Marie-Claire Antonine of Bloomsbury Press, who expressed her interest in an edited volume on the topic.

In Bloomsbury's gracious offer, I recognized an opportunity to engage a group of experts in a conversation about a research question that seemed to be natural and yet surprisingly understudied. So I sent invitations to a number of experts on the Caucasus and Russia, scholars who represented a diversity of viewpoints. The essays in this volume are those of the colleagues who kindly accepted my invitation.

In the first part of this book, *Caucasian Causation*, the contributors consider how events in the Caucasus have fundamentally altered the development of Russia's society, religion, politics, and military from the earliest years of the Russian Federation.

Patrick Armstrong opens with the argument that Westerners have understood relations between Georgia and Russia within the context of "memes," or preconceptions that have structured the journalistic, scholarly, and policy debates about this region. Going back to the 1980s, Armstrong argues that regional problems stemmed from instabilities in Georgia that were partially due to Georgian chauvinism. These tensions led to conflict in South Ossetia (1991–2) and Abkhazia (1992–3). Armstrong further contends that these South Caucasian conflicts contributed to North Caucasian conflicts in North Ossetia and Ingushetia (1992) and in Chechnya (1994–6). In this way, Armstrong traces a chain of contributing causes that extends northward from Tbilisi. He argues that throughout the 1990s, Russia was reacting to problems that were partially Georgian in their origin.

In the next chapter, Domitilla Sagramoso and Akhmet Yarlykapov examine other influences that entered the Caucasus from the South as well as from the East. The authors survey the rise of Islamic influence in the Russian North Caucasus from 1990 to 2012, and go on to show how this predominantly Muslim region has affected developments further northward throughout Russia. Then, by analyzing the flow of causal influence southward from Moscow, they consider the impact of the Kremlin's religious and regional security policies on the North Caucasus. The authors argue that Moscow's repressive approach to "nontraditional" Islamic groups and violent *jihadist* fighters have contributed to the cycle of violence. Finally, they consider how the increasing Islamization of the North Caucasus has contributed to the region's growing alienation from the rest of Russia, as well as to anti-Caucasian sentiments in the heartland.

In the fourth chapter, Robert Schaefer and Andrei Doohovskoy comprehensively survey the many ways that the Russian military was fundamentally transformed by the wars in Chechnya. According to the authors, these wars entirely reconfigured Russian methods of "organizing, commanding, manning, equipping, and training their military formations." Russia's military overhaul was harshly mandated by its dramatic failure in the first Chechen war, was severely tested by the challenges of the second Chechen war, and was proven in Russia's brief war with Georgia in August 2008. The authors anticipate "the enduring influence of the Caucasus on the Russian military structure," with ramifications "throughout the social and political fabric of the Russian nation." This is because the military is among the most important socializing influences in Russia. As Schaefer and Doohovskoy point out, "the Russian military literally knocks at every young man's door."

In the second part of this volume, *Caucasian Consequences*, three contributors consider how these Caucasian instabilities have shaped Russia, especially in the years from 2000 to the time of this writing in 2012. This portion of the book looks at how a Russia, fundamentally transformed by the Caucasus, also acts in a reciprocal manner to alter the Caucasus in turn.

Andrew Foxall focuses the fifth chapter of this volume upon Stavropol'skii *krai*, surveying the out-migration of population from the North Caucasus republics, the widening of terrorism and insurgency, the rise of Russian nationalism and anti-Caucasian sentiments, the restructuring of the Russian federal system, the institutional separation of the North Caucasus from Russia "proper," and the shifting economic geography of southern Russia. In Foxall's words, the chapter suggests that "the economic, demographic, political, and social changes that have taken place in Stavropol'skii *krai* since 1991 reflect broader changes in Russia as a whole. In many respects, owing to its proximity to the North Caucasus republics, Stavropol'skii *krai* serves as a front-line barometer of Russian reaction to events in the North Caucasus." Foxall's analysis is particularly helpful in that it provides a clear and detailed understanding of various ways in which Caucasian instabilities are spreading northward in their influence upon the Federation.

In Chapter Six, Richard Sakwa provides a theoretical framework for the influences documented in the preceding chapters with his cogent argument that Russian politics is readily understood in terms of the Dual-state political Model. Sakwa's model focuses upon the divergence of arbitrary administrative decisions from constitutionally enshrined ideals. Sakwa contends that Russia really has become two states, one as it formally claims to be, and quite another as it operates in daily practice. He presents considerable evidence to show that the rise of this dualism has been connected with the exceptional autonomy that was extended by Vladimir Putin to Akhmed and Ramzan Kadyrov in Chechnya.

Walter Richmond provides a fascinating case study, in Chapter Seven, that bears on many of Sakwa's themes. His study focuses upon preparations for the 2014 Sochi Olympic Games, and particularly upon three areas of concern. First, Richmond presents Olympic preparations within a context of constitutional versus arbitrary decision making, much in the manner of Sakwa's Dual-state Model. Second, Richmond looks at the ecological issues raised by the Sochi development, and at responses from local populations, from Moscow, and from international organizations. Finally, Richmond surveys the pervasive corruption that he finds in Olympic construction projects, arguing that this maleficence is so extensive as to affect the Russian economy as a whole.

The third part of this volume, *Caucasian Crosscurrents*, looks at the ways that these multiple, influences, moving in complex patterns northward and southward, have begun to recombine and resonate in ways that are at once stunning, optimistic, and ominous.

Nicolai Petro offers a refreshing look at cooperation among Islamic, Orthodox Christian, and government officials in what he describes as the "Russian Model" of politico-religious partnership. Petro argues that the Russian Model incorporates tolerance of all religions, and is compatible with moderate secularism. He describes how Russian Islamic and Orthodox leaders have recognized that their faiths share core values that are challenged by the nihilism and commercialism that have accompanied the advancement of secularism in the modern world. In the aftermath of the Soviet Union, both traditional Islamic and Orthodox believers have found themselves facing new forms of spiritual competition from confessional variants arriving from the East as well as from the West. Thus they have found strong motives for cooperation in the North Caucasus and throughout the Federation.

More controversially, Petro argues for the benefits of cooperation between both of these faiths and the Russian state, an emerging moral partnership that has caught the attention of some critics. While there are important philosophical traditions—both Christian and Islamic—that support church-state partnership, some secularist proponents have been alarmed by the rise of the Russian Model. Critics found their fears to be realized in the case involving three members of a feminist protest band who were arrested and convicted during the months in which the essays of this volume were compiled. In the appendix, Nicolai Petro presents an analysis of this case, suggesting that its coverage may have illustrated some of the simplistic memes that Patrick Armstrong addresses.

Yet clearly there was an important democratic protest movement in the wake of irregularities during the December 2011 legislative elections in Russia, just as there was clear evidence that some of these protests were met with repression. Surely there is cause for legitimate concern about conflicts within Russia's political culture and emergent cleavages in Russian values. Are these indicative of the sort of problems that Sakwa explores in his Dual-state Model of Russian politics?

Anna Matveeva examines concerns of this nature as they coalesce in Russia's new "inner abroad," namely the republics of Ingushetia, Chechnya, and Dagestan. Drawing vividly upon her field work, Matveeva weaves an exotic tapestry of regional viewpoints that challenges conventional conceptions of Russian culture and citizenship. She argues that these republics diverge so sharply in their moral, religious, and legal practices as to seem only nominally Russian. Yet, as Matveeva shows, they still seek Russian leadership and solicit Moscow's ample subsidies. Ominously, she finds increasing antagonism and incoherence between perspectives looking, on the one hand, northward from this corner of the Caucasus, and on the other hand, looking southward from Moscow and the rest of the Russian Federation. Matveeva asks how far this trend can go, and how long this cultural incoherence will be tolerable either to North Caucasians or to other Russians?

Matveeva's account initially seems to support Sakwa's Dual-state Model. Yet Matveeva points out that the divergence between normative and arbitrary administrative styles applies in all three of these republics, and not in Chechnya alone. This is part of the reason that I argue, in the concluding chapter, for a modification of the Dual-state Model, which I describe initially as the "Chechenization Model" of Russian politics.

The Chechenization Model is derived from the argument that the Chechenization program, which Vladimir Putin inaugurated in Chechnya on June 12, 2000, subsequently became the template for the administration of the Russian Federation from September 2004 to July 2012. The template was exported next door to Ingushetia when Murat Zyazikov was installed as president in 2002. Then on September 13, in the immediate aftermath of the Beslan hostage tragedy in nearby North Ossetia—and a series of other terrorist attacks during the preceding summer—Putin announced an effective extension of the Chechenization template to all other subjects of the Federation. According to the Chechenization Model Russia's newly recentralized bureaucracy was extended outward and downward in a hierarchical manner to its terminal nodes in each of the Federation's administrative units. In many cases, these terminal nodes occurred at the administrative level of the republics, as in Chechnya, Ingushetia, North Ossetia, and Kabardino-Balkaria. In other cases, such as Dagestan, the terminal nodes extended deeper into the administrative substrata of the republic, to its *raions* and *djamaats*. Wherever a terminal node occurred, local administrators applied a more or less standard repertoire of sanctions and incentives in a manner that allowed them to maintain local control and to guarantee fealty to the federal center. After August 2008, this template was extended to allow for the quasi-incorporation of Abkhazia and South Ossetia into the administrative jurisdiction of the Russian Federation.

The Chechenization Model of Russian politics differs from a Dual-state Model primarily in that the Chechenization Model explicitly recognizes that from 2004 to 2012, Russian federal relations were formally modified along the lines of the Chechenization template. From 2004 to 2012 there was not simply a split between a formal–legal ideal and arbitrary local practices. Rather, a bureaucratic administrative structure that fundamentally incorporated arbitrary local practice was formally instituted. In short, the diversity and arbitrariness of local practices was built into the overarching formal–legal system adopted during those years.

This point may be overlooked if one focuses upon a duality between formal ideals and local deviations. A dualistic approach may also miss subtleties in the operation of terminal bureaucratic nodes throughout the Federation, and it may overlook the fact that from 2004 to 2012 the

Russian Federation formally switched from a democratic to an essentially bureaucratic administration. The Chechenization Model helps one to appreciate just how seminal Chechnya, along with Georgia, South Ossetia, Abkhazia, North Ossetia, Ingushetia, and Dagestan, has been in the evolution of the Russian Federation. Finally, the Chechenization Model views the Russia's democratic protest movement from 2011 onward not as a reformist attempt to reconcile institutionalized norms with political practice, but more significantly as a revolutionary movement aimed at subverting what had become a pervasively bureaucratic—that is, a fundamentally nondemocratic—political system.

Since its imposition at the end of 2004 and the beginning of 2005, the Chechenization Model has come with inherent weaknesses and frustrations for all concerned. Local administration is generally corrupt, frequently ham-fisted, and predictably brutal. Local laws and norms sometimes deviate from those in other parts of the Federation. Economic disparity and injustice prevail. No genuinely institutionalized and peaceful political opposition is countenanced. Therefore violent Islamist insurgency in the South, and massive or provocative democratic protests in the North, appear to some alienated Russian citizens to be their only viable alternatives.

These inherent tensions and difficulties led to changes in the Russian political system beginning in July 2012 when legislation was enacted, allowing cautiously restricted elections of local governors, along with a slightly relaxed latitude for local legislatures. These modifications suggest that problems in the Caucasus will continue to shape Russian politics and culture. Hence, the Chechenization Model must yield to a model of reciprocal causation (CRM) among these regions. There is an extensive literature documenting Russia's impact upon the Caucasus. The chapters of this volume explore some of the many ways that the Caucasus has shaped Russia, and the ways in which each is likely to impel the further transformation of the other.

I am deeply grateful to my ten colleagues who allowed me the benefit of conversations culminating in each of their contributions. As I conclude this introduction, I feel amazed that my one simple research query to each of these contributors evoked eight distinctive responses that, to my eye, cohere readily and helpfully to yield a satisfying answer to my question. I have learned a great deal, and I hope that readers also will find these essays provocative and informative. I believe that conversations of this sort—seasoned with a dash of collegial counterpoint—have an enduring place at the core of scholarship. So I am grateful to everyone at Bloomsbury Press who enabled me to convene this conversation; and I am particularly grateful to Marie-Claire Antoine, Nick Church, and Srikanth Srinivasan for their enthusiasm, support, flexibility, and steadiness through all of the ups and downs, twists and turns of a mountain ride.

Notes

1 Peter Reddaway, Gail Lapidus, Barry Ickes, Carol Saivetz, and George Breslauer "Russia in the Year 2003," *Post- Soviet Affairs*, 20(1) (2004): 1–45.
2 For example, see nearly any article in the popular Western media about Russia and the Caucasus. Scholarly examples include John Dunlop, *Russia Confronts Chechnya: Roots of a Separatist Conflict* (Cambridge: Cambridge University Press, 1998); Matthew Evangelista, *The Chechen Wars: Will Russia Go the Way of the Soviet Union* (Washington, DC: Brookings Institution Press, 2002); Carlotta Gall and Thomas de Waal, *Chechnya: Calamity in the Caucasus* (New York: NYU Press, 1999); James Hughes, *Chechnya: From Nationalism to Jihad* (Philadelphia: University of Pennsylvania Press, 2007); Anatol Levin, *Chechnya: Tombstone of Russian Power* (New Haven: Yale University Press, 1999); and Tony Wood, *Chechnya: The Case for Independence* (London: Verso, 2007).
3 Robert Ware, "Has the Russian Federation Been Chechenised?" *Europe-Asia Studies*, 63(3) (2011).
4 In particular, I am grateful to Anna Matveeva, Domitilla Sagramoso, and Richard Sakwa for their insights at our meetings, during the years in which I pondered this question, and to other contributors for their long, intellectual friendships. An occasional contrast in perspectives in no way diminishes respect.

PART ONE
Caucasian Causation

CHAPTER TWO

Enter the Memes

Patrick Armstrong

The Georgian tragedy is a story of a dominant nationality that made war on its minorities, only to have that war metastasize into a civil war of Georgians against Georgians.[1]

For 20 years many reporters and commentators have interpreted Russia through a series of preconceptions or "memes." These memes are considered to be so true as to need no evidence, and Georgia has figured among them. For example, one meme is that Russia "wants its empire back": Georgia was part of that empire. Another is that Russia wants to control energy routes: one passes through Georgia. Another is that Moscow "hates democracies," and that Georgia is democratic. The characteristics of memes are that they determine what the "facts" are and that they are very resistant to mere reality. Despite the reality that in August 2008 Moscow did not conquer Georgia, seize the pipeline route, or overthrow the Georgian government, the memes remain strong in many minds. This chapter attempts to illustrate this effect. In direct contradiction to the causal explanations created by these memes, it attempts to show how Russia has in fact been significantly and adversely affected by events that were fundamentally of Georgian origin. In short, Russia was not the actor, as the memes imply, it was the reactor.

Russians often complain that an "information war" is being waged against them.[2] Whether or not, as the term implies, there is some centrally directed policy in the service of some grand geopolitical game of controlling and directing Western media outlets so as to blacken Russia's name for their consumers, it is undeniable that the Western media is ever-ready to assume the worst, taking for granted assumptions about the malevolence of Russia's intentions. These I call "memes"[3] and this chapter will discuss several that adhere to common Western discussions and reporting of Russia–Georgia relations. But there are other memes as well: one is that Putin kills reporters and other opponents. A small but revealing case of this assumption at work—in the complete absence of any evidence—involved the Russo-French Lawyer Karinna Moskalenko who found mercury in her car in October 2008. Several media outlets[4] immediately jumped to the conclusion that this was another dastardly deed against one of Putin's enemies. But a few days later French police identified the cause: the car had been previously owned by an antiques dealer who had broken a mercury barometer inside it.

This rush to judgment, assuming the worst, is very common. One of the most demonstrable examples of this is found in the case of Georgia's accusations against Russia: they are almost always taken for granted, despite the number of times that Moscow's assertions have been proven true. Russians can be forgiven for believing that there is an "information war" against them.[5]

Inevitably Moscow's attitude to the outside world is affected. When every approach is rejected, every action condemned, every motive suspected, every utterance misquoted, it would be surprising indeed if Moscow were not more suspicious and hostile. Putin's famous speech at the Munich Security Conference in 2007 was branded as "inflammatory,"[6] "attacking the Western world," and so on. According to the BBC it was regarded either as threatening a new Cold War or just letting off steam.[7] Few made any attempt to try to understand what he was saying. In essence what he was saying was quite simple: Russia is not happy in a world in which its point of view is ignored; and it is not helpless. The second message was that a unipolar world is not a secure world; he even quoted Franklin Roosevelt: "When peace has been broken anywhere, the peace of all countries everywhere is in danger."[8] These are messages that he and other Russian spokesmen have endlessly and reasonably reiterated. Putin, back as President of Russia—a Russia that is on the way back up after the collapse of the 1990s—is visibly less patient than he was in 2000. The habit of so much reporting of Russia as if one were preparing a charge sheet for some indictment has contributed to this.

Georgia has been a prominent part of the charge sheet of Russia's crimes. This statement from the influential *Economist* in 1993 can stand as the prototype:

An independent state of Georgia existed for 2 ½ years, until Trotsky's Red Army snuffed it out in 1921. Mr Yeltsin has given its successor exactly the same amount of time. More or less secretly, Russian forces have backed rebellions by Muslims in the Abkhaz region and by Georgian followers of the former president, Zviad Gamsakhurdia. In this squeeze the current president, Eduard Shevardnadze . . . despairingly appealed to Moscow for help, and got it on terms that in effect mortgage his country's independence.[9]

This is a fine example of the "charge sheet" against Russia not just because it was one of the first to look at Georgia and see Russia: it has two characteristics that we will see again and again. There is the easy assumption of Russia's malevolence as the real explanation for Georgia's misery. And, almost every sentence in it is untrue; it is erected on an almost complete ignorance of reality. First, to call Abkhazia "Muslim" is incorrect—in fact a bishop from Pitsunda attended the Council of Nicea in 325 AD. It is true that with Ottoman influence many Abkhazians became Muslims but, after the Russian conquest in the late nineteenth century, many of the Muslim Abkhazians left and moved to the Ottoman Empire. Today's Abkhazia is in majority Christian. Second, the likelihood of Moscow supporting Gamsakhurdia, its implacable enemy and ally of another enemy, Dzhokhar Dudaev of Chechnya, is quite absurd. Third, the troubles between Sukhum[10] and Tbilisi began long before 1993—they were rooted in Stalin-Jughashvili's decision to subordinate Abkhazia to Tbilisi and subsequent events. The "rebellion" *The Economist* is talking about is not the first Abkhaz "rebellion" of the twentieth century against Tbilisi's dominance. Fourth, it was not *"Trotsky's* Red Army" that "snuffed out" the Georgian Democratic Republic in 1921; the invasion was engineered by the two most prominent Georgians on the Bolshevik high command—Stalin-Jughashvili and Ordzhonikidze;[11] but to say that—assuming the authors even knew it—would be to complicate the simple picture of Russian hostility that they want to sell. And finally, note the assumption that the Abkhaz viewpoint is irrelevant. In this construction, Georgia is a sort of canary in the coal mine of Russian imperialism. The assumption that Russia has imperialistic designs requires no proof beyond mere assertion:

> The Russian ruling elite has not reconciled itself to the separation of the fifteen dependent republics . . .[12]

So, in the earliest post-Soviet period, we find the memes that troubles in the former Union of Soviet Socialist Republics (USSR) are to be laid at Moscow's door and that Georgia, in particular, illustrates this pattern of Russian trouble-making.

The next development affecting Georgia's position in the "charge sheet" came with the discovery of large deposits of petro-carbons in the Caspian Sea. Georgia now became one of the fields of struggle in what was quickly called "the new Great Game," an imagined struggle between Russia and the West to control the deposits and their transportation routes. To many it was a zero-sum game: either Russia benefitted or "we" did. Ariel Cohen laid down the markers in 1996:

> Will a neo-imperialist Russia (aided and abetted by Iran) dominate the development of Eurasian oil and its exports, or will Russia be an equal and fair player in the region . . . the West has a paramount interest in assuring that the Caucasian and Central Asian states maintain their independence and remain open to the West. Otherwise, Moscow will capture almost monopolistic control over this vital energy resource, thus increasing Western dependence upon Russian-dominated oil reserves and export routes. . . . The wars in Chechnya, between Armenia and Azerbaijan, and in Georgia were started or exacerbated by the Russian military, and the outcome of these wars may determine who controls future pipeline routes . . .[13]

Others joined in the chorus

> Moscow's strategy of reasserting its economic and military-political influence in the region includes the goal of dominating the production and transportation of Caspian oil to world markets . . . Russia is suspected of being behind efforts to destabilize Azerbaijan and Georgia as part of its long-term strategy to control the Caucasus and its oil wealth.[14]

> Russia has also intervened decisively in the wars in Georgia, forcing Eduard Shevardnadze to take his country into the Commonwealth of Independent States . . .[15]

Geography made Georgia part of this "new Great Game" because any route that avoided Russia (Iran was not regarded as an option) must necessarily pass through it in order to get to the sea, and so Georgia became a key part of the strategy of denying Russia "almost monopolistic control." Evidence of Russia's enmity was simply asserted: "As is generally known, Russia has had great difficulty adjusting to the fact that its empire, built by conquest over centuries, disappeared in 1991, depriving it of rich borderlands and nearly half its population."[16] Caspar Weinberger warned "Russia has a truly ominous enlargement initiative of its own—'dominance of the energy resources in the Caspian Sea region.'"[17] A popular theory, often uttered in the same breath, was the assertion that Russia was busy destabilizing the countries of the Caucasus so as to gain monopoly over the routes:

> Georgia for a while resisted Russian demands for closer cooperation. To subdue it, Moscow initiated a "national liberation" movement among the 100,000 Abkhazians, a Muslim people occupying the western regions of Georgia. In the course of the rebellion, a quarter of a million Georgians

residing in Abkhazia were expelled. The rebellion stopped only after Georgia agreed to let in a force of some 8,000 Russian soldiers, forces they have been trying to get rid of ever since.[18]

And

> At the moment, Russian armies are in Moldova, Georgia, Azerbaijan, and Tajikistan and participate in some of the local civil wars with a strategy that seems designed to make the new republics, all of them members of the United Nations, rue their independence and return to the womb of imperial Russia . . .[19]
>
> [Russia] maintains bases on the territory of Georgia after fomenting a civil war there. . . .[20]

Therefore, from early times, the assumption was that Russia wanted its empire back partly because that is just what Russians were like and partly in order to gain a monopoly of the routes out of the Caspian to the West. In the pursuit of both aims it was fomenting wars in its southern neighbors. Georgia's independence had to be protected against Russia's "neo-imperialism." What never occurred to the zero-summers was that Moscow needs the money just as much as the customers need the oil and gas. Also absent from their consideration is that Moscow might want as much stability as possible in the turbulent Caucasus. But for them the assumption was that Russia was *nothing but* expansionist; no further thought was required.

The third element in the Georgian portion of the "charge sheet" against Russia, while never completely absent,[21] intensified with the arrival of Mikheil Saakashvili after the so-called Rose Revolution. To the "canary" and "new Great Game" memes was added Moscow's assumed hostility to a "democracy" on its borders. Until his mendacity in the 2008 war, most Western pundits believed everything Saakashvili said.

The Georgian catastrophe

The post-USSR history of Georgia has been a succession of disasters. Zviad Gamsakhurdia, elected President in May 1991, was overthrown in January 1992. South Ossetia and Abkhazia sought to preserve the rights they had had under the Soviet system against Tbilisi's refusals to countenance any such thing. The coup makers imported Eduard Shevardnadze in March 1992 and his position was regularized by election in 1995. Gamsakhurdia fled to his native Mingrelia to raise forces in the west; central Georgian forces invaded Abkhazia in August 1992 and a real war started there. North Caucasian volunteers, hoping to recreate the short-lived Mountaineer Republic of

1918, went to Abkhazia to fight.[22] Gradually fighting expanded in South Ossetia. Tbilisi's forces were driven out of South Ossetia and Abkhazia. In the years that followed, Zviadists,[23] sometimes allied with Chechens, attempted coups or assassination attempts against Shevardnadze. Chechen fighters and Arab mujahaddin took advantage of the vacuum and moved into the Pankisi Valley.

It is hardly surprising that Georgia did not flourish. Shevardnadze was pushed out in 2003 and Mikhail Saakashvili took power. At first the darling of the West, Georgia's experience under him has been a disastrous war, large protests, the defection of many of his associates to the opposition, little genuine economic improvement, and very high unemployment. Abkhazia and South Ossetia are lost to Tbilisi for the foreseeable future, Saakashvili's dream of North Atlantic Treaty Organization (NATO) membership is gone, and the recent overcoming of Tbilisi's "veto" on Russia's membership on the World Trade Organization (WTO) shows that the bloom is indeed off the rose.

For the most part, Western commentators naively repeated Tbilisi's side of the story, ignored the desires of the Abkhaz or Ossetians, and fitted events—when they noticed them at all—into the well-worn trope of Russian neo-imperialism and the "new Great Game." The 2008 war, however, may have forced some revision of these assumptions.

One of the most momentous errors of the standard Western coverage of events in Georgia is the lack of interest in Ossetians and Abkhazians.[24] This is implicit in the quotations above: there is no curiosity about how Moscow was supposedly able to foment trouble. Mingrelia, Svanetia, and Javakhetia have not historically been very happy with domination from Tbilisi and yet Moscow was unable to "initiate" troubles there. This blindness persisted in the European Union (EU) report on the 2008 war: there was no curiosity about why Ossetians would fight Georgians. There was no curiosity about why Abkhazia seized the opportunity to drive the last parts of Tbilisi's forces out of Kodori. Throughout the issue has been conventionally treated as if the only actors were Russia, Georgia, (and the West). But Georgia's modern troubles began with Abkhazia's and South Ossetia's attempts to hold what they had and Tbilisi's refusal to accommodate them.

Other successor states of the USSR had similar secessionist problems. Russians and Ukrainians living in Transdnestr did not want to suddenly find themselves in Romania that, at the time, was the aspiration of many in Moldova. Armenians living in Karabakh were not happy under Baku's rule. Chechens wanted out of Russia. These disputes led to fighting. But fighting was not the only option. Crimea, absorbed into the Russian Empire in 1783 and whimsically transferred to the Ukrainian Soviet Socialist Republic by Khrushchev in 1954, was an Autonomous Soviet Socialist Republic with certain privileges under the Soviet system and which the inhabitants wished to retain. This could have led to trouble, but in 1992 Kiev was wise enough

to listen and begin negotiations and Crimea is today an autonomous republic within Ukraine.[25] A similar wise arrangement was made in Moldova to
accommodate the language and cultural rights of the Gagauz, a Turkic people washed up by the tides of history in Central Europe. Reasonable compromise damped down the passions that elsewhere erupted into fighting.

The USSR, following Stalin's famous apothegm "nationalist in form,
socialist in content," had dealt with the multiethnic reality of the Russian
Empire by the construction of carefully graded national entities. Highest
were the 15 Soviet Socialist Republics (SSRs), in them were Autonomous
Soviet Socialist Republics (ASSRs), Autonomous Oblasts (AOs), and
Autonomous Okrugs[26] (AOs). There was a strong element of fakery in these
constructions because real power flowed through the Party structure but
there was also a not meaningless degree of local language and cultural
rights for the titular nationalities. The Center continually meddled with
the concept, changing borders and abolishing entities and changing the
very number of accepted ethonyms over time and for ideological requirements.[27] One change is very important in the Georgian context: Abkhazia's
status was changed from coequal with Georgia to subordinate to it (i.e.
from an SSR to an ASSR). But then Stalin, who ordered it—born Ioseb
Besarionis dze Jughashvili in Gori in 1878—was a Georgian as was his
then South Caucasus lieutenant and later political police chief, Lavrenti
Pavles dze Beria. Perhaps there was an element of Georgian chauvinism in
the decision.

The Georgian SSR had within it three autonomous regions: the
Abkhazian ASSR, the Ajarian ASSR, and the South Ossetian AO. Neither
Abkhazians nor Ossetians are Kartevelian[28] peoples. As Georgians agi-
tated for independence from the USSR, non-Kartevelians became nervous about their futures. And not surprisingly given that they were hearing
things like this:

Georgia stands on the brink of a real catastrophe—of extirpation.
What devil ruled our minds, when we yielded up our land, gained
inch by inch over the centuries, defended and soaked with our blood,
to every homeless beggar that has come down from the fringes of the
Caucasus, to tribes that have neither history nor culture? We must make
every effort to raise the percentage of Georgians in the population of
Georgia (currently 61%) to 95%. The remaining 5% must consist
of only those who know Georgian, who have a proper respect for
Georgia, who have been brought up under the influence of the Georgian
national phenomenon. We must persuade other nationalities, which are
multiplying suspiciously in the land of David the Builder, that ideal
conditions for the development of their personalities are to be found
only in their homelands.[29]

And this from a 1992 pamphlet devoted to countering claims that Ossetians and Abkhazians might have for independence or any retention of their Soviet-era privileges:

> The most important fact to be pointed out is that when Georgia was declared an independent state on the 26th of May 1918, its frontiers contained only a part of those territories which used to belong to it since the time of formation of the Georgian ethnos and statehood, i.e. for some millennia. Not an inch of this land which is now the country of Georgia, has ever been conquered by it, and the national minorities inhabiting its territory, except the Abkhaz, have lived together with the Georgians from time immemorial when they had come to Georgia in search of better life and shelter and safety, leaving their homelands.[30]

"Homeless beggars" who would be better off somewhere else were quite capable of taking the hint. An intimation of the future appeared in the Soviet referendum of March 17, 1991, on the question of support for the proposed new confederation. A number of jurisdictions—Georgia included—refused to hold the referendum at all on the grounds that they legally had never been part of the USSR.[31] However, the Abkhaz SSR voted anyway and a little over half opted to stay in the proposed new post-USSR union evidently believing that the future looked better under Moscow than under Tbilisi.[32]

The collapse of the USSR unleashed many national dreams and the dream of Georgian chauvinists was the Greater Georgia that existed about eight centuries ago reaching its apotheosis under the granddaughter of King David the Builder,[33] Queen Tamar (reg 1184–1213). During that time, one Georgian state ruled most of the South Caucasus. The eastern part of this Greater Georgian state was destroyed by the Mongol invasions. A remnant of a united Georgia survived in western Georgia until Alexander I (reg 1412–43). After his death, the kingdom was divided among his sons and, from then until the twentieth century, the territory of today's Georgia was divided into numerous kingdoms and principalities ever fearful of destructive invasions from the south. A terrible sack of Tbilisi in 1795 by Persians ended independence; Russian protection was sought and Georgian territories were absorbed into the Russian Empire.

The root of the chauvinist Georgian position today is the notion that this Greater Georgia of 800 years ago is the "true Georgia." It was precisely this sort of talk, very common in the Gamsakhurdia period—indeed the official version—that sparked off wars of independence by the Ossetians and the Abkhaz. "Georgia for Georgians" and "Nature has outlined the borders of Georgia and history has confirmed them"[34] are not calculated to make non-Kartvelians comfortable. The same thing had happened in the first independent Georgia of the twentieth century and, in its short existence, it had wars with the Ossetians and the Abkhaz as well as border scuffles with

Armenia.[35] It was this chauvinism, not Russian interference, that sparked the wars. Shevardnadze, who has said different things at different times to different audiences, after defeat in Abkhazia, had this to say:

> did we not create a terrible phenomenon of modern times, which is provincial fascism? . . . we were punished, we should have been punished and we were punished . . . we were robbing them [the Abkhazians] . . . let us also remember how we drove the Ossetians out of Tbilisi [and] how we tortured Ossetians.

As far as the so-called Russian responsibility, he said this:

> of course there was a betrayal from Russia's reactionary forces but, despite all this, Sukhumi would not have fallen under any circumstances, had it not been for the betrayal [of the Georgian forces at the last moment by the Zviadists].[36]

Thus Georgian chauvinist behavior,[37] informed and fed by the dream of a Greater Georgia into which all non-Georgians had come, by invitation—a conditional invitation—was the impetus for the Ossetians and Abkhazians to get out of a state that seemed to have no place for them.[38] This feeling was redoubled in Abkhazia because of attempts, probably engendered by Beria, to suppress Abkhazian culture in the 1940s.[39]

The election of Zviad Gamsakhurdia—who embodied this chauvinism—began a terrible period for the inhabitants of the former Georgian SSR. His overthrow led to a civil war between his supporters and the coup makers. This war merged into the struggles of Abkhazia and South Ossetia to preserve their Soviet-era status. As usual, atrocity bred atrocity and the demands ramped up to full independence. The following armed groups—each with its own lines of command and interests—struggled: Tengiz Kitovani and Tbilisi's official forces; Jaba Ioseliani's[40] paramilitary Mkhedrioni; Gamsakhurdia's forces; Abkhazian and South Ossetia militias; North Caucasians fighting on the side of the Abkhazians. "Russian"[41] troops were involved in this because they were stationed here and there in bases or at certain installations of importance to the Soviet defense system.[42] By the end of 1993, Abkhazia and South Ossetia had driven Tbilisi's forces out of their territories, the North Caucasians had gone back to Russia to start wars there and Gamsakhurdia was dead. An uncertain standoff was preserved by peacekeeping forces, dominated by Russians but with participation from the other two combatants, along the South Ossetia and Abkhazia borders. Under Shevardnadze things were comparatively quiet—even stagnant. There were assassination attempts[43] on him, continual skirmishing along the borders of Abkhazia and South Ossetia, and periodic bomb explosions and political murders, but at least nothing got dramatically worse.

The prevalent meme requires that Georgia's troubles be fitted into a story of "neoimperialistic" Russia versus Georgia. Very few Western commentators who subscribe to Georgia as "mine canary" or field of the "new Great Game" ever mention Abkhazians or Ossetians and when they do the assumption seems to be that they are simply tools of Moscow's troublemaking. But they are not: they are crucial actors too.

The *casus belli* in Abkhazia, as elsewhere in the Caucasus, has historical roots. The Abkhaz are autochthonous: in Classical days Abkhazia was known as Colchis. A thousand years ago, their leading family was united in marriage with King David's dynasty, but this association was broken by the Mongol destruction of Greater Georgia in the thirteenth century. Russia annexed Abkhazia in 1864 and a large part of the Muslim population emigrated, or was forced out, to the Ottoman Empire, leaving the Abkhaz a minority in their land.[44] After 1917, Abkhazia was part of the short-lived Mountain Republic but was invaded by independent Georgia, which claimed it. The issue had not yet been resolved when the Red Army extinguished Georgian independence. The Bolsheviks solved the problem of Abkhazia's status by proclaiming it a SSR in March 1921; in December, with a union treaty, it became associated with the Georgian SSR. But in 1931, it was taken into the Georgian SSR as an ASSR losing the coequal nature of the relationship.[45] When the musical chairs that the communists had been playing with the internal borders of the USSR stopped in 1991, the West and the United Nations recognized Stalin-Jughashvili's border.

The Gorbachev period awoke ambitions clamped shut in former years and the present troubles began in March 1989, when a gathering resolved that Abkhazia should regain the status of an SSR. Many of the Kartevelian residents opposed this and trouble began. Troops from the Soviet Ministry for Internal Affairs (MVD) gradually restored order. Then ensued a period of conflicting declarations: the Abkhaz parliament declaring "state sovereignty" and the Georgian parliament overruling it. But the real trouble began after Gamsakhurdia's overthrow. As a Mingrelian, his strength was in the west of Georgia and he fled there to set up his resistance to the coup makers. In March his supporters seized some towns in western Georgia and central troops and members of the Mkhedrioni[46] assembled to move there. In July, Abkhazia abolished the 1978 constitution and reverted to that of 1925 in direct response to Tbilisi's abolishing all Soviet legislation and declaring that the 1921 pre-Soviet constitution was reestablished, a constitutional arrangement in which Abkhazia had no special status. Up to that point, the Abkhazian-Georgian disagreement had been legalistic (apart from the violence of 1989) but fighting started in August after Gamsakhurdia's forces took the Georgian Interior Minister and other officials hostage in Zugdidi (the central city of Mingrelia). Shevardnadze authorized military/police action and, on August 14, 1992, Georgian forces entered Abkhazia and ran riot on Sukhum[47] despite the fact that Gamsakhurdia had nothing to do with Abkhazia. Now serious blood had been shed.[48]

Four days later, the Parliament of the Confederation of Mountain Peoples of the Caucasus, meeting in Groznyy, demanded Georgian withdrawal from Abkhazia and, a few days later, called for volunteers to fight in Abkhazia. In the end, several hundred volunteers from Circassia and Chechnya went to fight. Fighting, accompanied by much destruction, massacres, and atrocities, continued until the spring of 1993 when the Georgian forces, divided among themselves and harassed by the Zviadists, suffered serious reverses. A Russian-mediated ceasefire was achieved on July 22, 1993. Then the Zviadists struck—on September 7 they took the town of Gali (just inside Abkhazia), and gradually over the next few days extended their control through Mingrelia. The Abkhazians and their supporters grasped the opportunity and attacked the Georgian forces still in Sukhum. They pushed the Georgians out on September 27 and moved down the coast forcing the Georgians out of most of Abkhazia. The Zviadists then struck at the disorganized and retreating Georgian forces and took town after town in Western Georgia. Eventually a Russian-provided peacekeeping force together with UN monitors was established in the summer of 1994.

As now customary, Western commentators unaware of the background fitted these wars into the "new Great Game" and Russian imperialist templates. We have already seen *The Economist*'s take. Henry Kissinger opined in March 1997:

> Even post-Communist Russia is conducting some policies redolent of traditional Russian imperialism . . . it maintains bases on the territory of Georgia after fomenting a civil war there . . .[49]

Deep water harbors were what Moscow was after, we were told:

> The breakup of the Soviet Union deprived Russia of deep water harbors on the Black Sea coast. Such ports, however, existed in Georgia. In the summer of 1992, Abkhazia, the northwest corner of Georgia, was visited by Russian defense and intelligence officials. A short time later, the Abkhazians declared their independence. When Georgian troops tried to crush the revolt, they were defeated by an "Abkhazian" army which appeared out of nowhere and whose ranks were filled with mercenaries recruited by Russian intelligence.[50]

Georgian spokesmen were happy to avoid their own responsibility for this disaster and blame Moscow:

> The civil war in Georgia was inspired, plotted, and provoked by forces from outside Georgia, particularly in Russia. Russian civilian and military intelligence organizations perpetuated the civil war.[51]

But the question of Russian involvement was not as straightforward as claimed here. Abkhazian sources claimed that Moscow supported Tbilisi:

> "Experts" constantly disparage Abkhazian prowess by asserting it was Russians who inflicted the defeat on "hated Georgia," but such "experts" forget that Russia was supplying weapons to Georgia gratis, whereas Abkhazians had to pay dearly for everything not gained as booty, and that Russian planes actually bombed Abkhazian lines in the final push, as an outright Abkhazian victory in no way suited the Kremlin's purpose.[52]

Zviadists in their turn saw a plot by Shevardnadze, supported by Russia, to set Mingrelians against Abkhazians:

> It must be known that Abkhazian war was necessary for Shevardnadze for following reasons. He aimed first of all on creating ethnical conflict between Abkhazians and Megrelians [Mingrelians] and involving population of Megrelia into this war, thus two most fierce enemies of Shevardnadze: Megrelians and Abkhazians would be in permanent war and kill each other, what would give him better chances for establishing his dictatorship in Megrelia and Abkhazia, politically defeating President's [i.e. Gamsakhurdia—who was, after all, the lawfully elected President of Georgia[53]] supporters in both regions, turning great part of population to refugees and creating good situation for his marauding bands in that parts of Western Georgia. Reactionary forces of Russia also had interest in this, for strengthening their control over Abkhazia and Black Sea shore, which is very important from strategic point of view and as best resort zone and gave Russia good perspective in joining Abkhazia to Russia. By that reason units of Russian army, Cossacks and North Caucasians are involved in conflict, thus turning Caucasus into another Yugoslavia. [sic][54]

So the interesting thing is that all three sides agree on Russian involvement but *always on the other side*. For what it is worth—and to a devotee of Russian conspiracy theories, it is worth precisely nothing—official Russia many times called for a ceasefire and a restoration of the status quo ante bellum. The charge that Russia fomented the Abkhaz wars in presumably otherwise peaceful Georgia is important—David Satter, for example, uses it as one of the main buttresses to his argument that NATO expansion is necessary for protection against Russia.[55] No great Russian interference is necessary to explain the Georgian defeat in a war that it provoked by its policy of "Georgia for the Georgians," Kitovani's attack on Sukhum that was then carried out by three different and opposed groups: the National Guard, the Mkhedrioni, and the Zviadist forces, and led—and incompetently led—by men who were later to fall out with each other and with Shevardnadze.

Little surprise that a small force of Abkhazians, and determined and ruthless North Caucasians, defeated them.

The Ossetians were also nervous over the outburst of chauvinism in Georgia in the late Gorbachev period. Their lands are split between Russia and Georgia with about two-thirds living in North Ossetia-Alania in Russia. They also had reason to fear an independent Georgia—they remember what they call the "first genocide" in the time of the Georgian Democratic Republic when they say thousands of Ossetians were killed. As soon as Georgia started its move toward independence from the USSR, the Ossetians moved too. On September 20, 1990, the parliament proclaimed itself as the South Ossetia Soviet Democratic Republic and part of the USSR. The Georgian Supreme Soviet promptly overruled this and, a couple of months later, abolished the South Ossetian Autonomous Oblast altogether and ruled that the elections there had been illegal. Violence was already general and was gradually brought under control by central forces. Gamsakhurdia's election, with the concomitant increase in chauvinism, exacerbated the situation and South Ossetia called for union with North Ossetia. After the collapse of the USSR in December 1991 fighting intensified around Tskhinval. On January 19, 1992, a referendum was held and the voters overwhelmingly demanded to be incorporated into the Russian Federation. Ceasefires were announced and broken and the fighting did not stop until a Russian-Georgian-Ossetian peacekeeping force was established in the summer of 1992. Skirmishing was intermittent until the Georgian attack of August 2008 resulted in another Georgian defeat and the proclamation of full independence.

Had Tbilisi reacted to the first stirrings from Abkhazia and South Ossetia for retention of their autonomous status with the wisdom that Kiev showed in Crimea, perhaps none of this would have happened. As had happened in 1918, it was the behavior by actors in independent Georgia that provoked the wars of 1991. No Russian interference was needed to ignite the fire. The evidence for Russian interference is mostly assertion and a product of the two already established theories that Georgia was a "mine canary" for supposed Russian imperialism and the "new Great Game." No actual knowledge of the background—"hosts and guests," "homeless beggars," Abkhazia and South Ossetia's memories of the previous period of an independent Georgia—was thought worth gathering.[56] The truth is that these wars were caused as much by Stalin as by anyone (although Zviad Gamsakhurdia deserves special responsibility).

The fire spreads to Russia

Memes function as epistemological filters that determine what are seen to be facts and motives and where to look to find them. The memes made

their believers think that they understood what was really happening—the
principle of all Moscow's actions with respect to Georgia was an attempt
to reverse the collapse of the Soviet Empire. Interpretations of the 2008
war were cast in accord with this theory: Moscow was seizing its chance
to defeat and humiliate Georgia and secure a measure of control over its
behavior.[57] But the adherence to the memes, together with the general
ignorance of the context, Tbilisi's ambitions, the views of Ossetians and
Abkhazians, blinded their adherents to Moscow's preeminent concern. And
that was that Moscow feared that a fire set in Georgia would spread across
the mountains into the Russian Caucasus. Moscow feared this in 2008
because it had seen it happen before. Tbilisi's wars against the Ossetians
and Abkhazians in the early 1990s had been a direct cause of the first
Chechen war when the victorious North Caucasian fighters returned home
to complete the job; that war in turn attracted fighters from the international *jihad* who started the second war and the subsequent *jihadist* activities in the North Caucasus that continue today. One of Moscow's principal
motives in 2008 was to stop this from happening again.

The inhabitants of the North Caucasus—or "Mountaineers" as they
are often called—were conquered by Russia after long and brutal wars.
Thousands died and thousands more left their homelands for the Ottoman
Empire. When the Russian Empire collapsed in 1917 the Mountaineers
resumed their struggle for freedom. An assembly of North Caucasus peoples
proclaimed the Republic of the North Caucasus in May 1918. Germany,
Austria-Hungary, and Turkey recognized this new state but it was evanescent, falling to General Denikin's White army. In 1919 Sheikh Uzun
Haji declared the "Emirate of the North Caucasus" in southern Chechnya
and the Bolsheviks recognized and supported his Emirate against Denikin.
When Denikin was defeated in February 1920, the Bolsheviks entered the
North Caucasus, dissolved the Emirate and appointed Sheikh Uzun Haji
as Mufti.[58] The Bolsheviks, with their slogans of independence from the
"prison of nationalities" were at first welcomed by the Mountaineers but,
as they revealed their "war communism," the Mountaineers rose against
them and in August 1920 a new war began in Dagestan and Chechnya.
The Reds threw enormous forces into the efforts and by mid-1921 (assisted
by forces attacking from the newly absorbed Georgia) had crushed the
Mountaineers.

Meanwhile in January the Bolsheviks convened a congress of the
Mountaineers in Vladikavkaz that Stalin, then Commissar for Nationalities,
attended. He promised amnesty for all who gave in (although the Red offensive in Dagestan was in full swing) and declared that the Bolsheviks supported sovereignty and independence for the Mountaineers. He proposed
the creation of a Mountain Peoples' Autonomous Republic—comprising
the territories of the Chechens, Ingush, Ossetians, Kabardins, Balkars, and
Karachays together with Dagestan—to be an autonomous Soviet Republic.

The assembly accepted this proposal, which accorded well enough with their aspirations, along with the additional provision that their traditional law (*adat*) be continued. These promises were of course only temporary and wore away as the Bolsheviks consolidated their rule. There was another outbreak of fighting against Bolshevik power upon the introduction of forced collectivization but that was also crushed. Resistance never ended: the Chechens boast that the last abrek,[59] Khazaki Magomedov, died in combat against the communists in 1979.

The collapse of the USSR reignited the dream of a North Caucasian Federation and an organization of that name was founded in Groznyy the day after Dudaev was sworn in as President of Chechnya. In April 1991 a founding meeting of the Assembly of the Mountain People of the Caucasus had already been held in Sukhum, Abkhazia. That November, delegates from the North Caucasus and Abkhazia formed the Confederation of Caucasian Mountain Peoples. And next year, in October, the Congress of Mountain Peoples of the Caucasus met in Groznyy with delegates from Chechnya, Adygeya, Abkhazia, Ingushetia, Ossetia, Dagestan, Kabarda, and Circassia and delegations from the Karachay, Akin Chechens,[60] and Tatars. Dudaev was happy to host the meeting and believed that Chechens were the natural leaders:

> The union of all Caucasian nations on an equal basis is the only possible way for the future. As we hold a central geographic, strategic and economic position in the Caucasus and have the necessary human potential, we must be the initiators of this future union.[61]

At this point Chechnya was a powerful little entity in its local context. It had acquired quite a few weapons after the departure of Soviet forces,[62] had seen off Yeltsin's attempt to cow Dudaev in 1991, and had money to spend from oil sales. The military wing of these efforts was led by the Chechen Shamil Basaev who took fighters from the North Caucasus into Abkhazia to fight the Georgians. Western reporters, knowing little of this and wedded to the notion that Moscow was stage-managing the efforts, heard the Chechens and Circassians in Abkhazia speaking Russian and using Soviet weapons and assumed they were Russians sent from Moscow. But Russian was the only common language and every weapon was ex-Soviet.[63]

In the summer of 1993 Dudaev announced that Chechen armed formations had left Abkhazia. And they had been victorious: they had secured the western end of the putative Mountaineer Republic and they returned to Chechnya to complete the task there. Chechnya had in the meantime declared independence. Finally Moscow had had enough and instituted a disastrously ill-prepared and ludicrously over-optimistic "police action" to secure Groznyy and force Dudaev out. This first Russian-Chechen war of recent times ended in September 1996 with Russian defeat. The fighters had secured their second victory at the other end of the putative Mountaineer Republic.

Perhaps the Chechens would, once again, have fought Russia to secure the independence they had lost with the Imam Shamil's surrender in 1859 but the war that actually happened was a follow-on from the successful war in Abkhazia that in turn was in no small part a consequence of the chauvinism and brutality of Tbilisi against its minorities. Basaev's fighters, triumphant, blooded, returned to Chechnya to create the Eastern half of their Mountaineer Republic. After a terribly brutal war, they won de facto independence in 1996.

But there was more to come. The first war in Chechnya attracted foreign *jihadists*, in particular a carefully picked team led by the Arab Khattab,[64] to use Chechnya as the basis for an Islamic Emirate in the North Caucasus. Some time after 1996[65] Shamil Basev's objectives shifted from the reestablishment of the Mountaineer Republic to the creation of a *jihadist* emirate. Together Khattab and Basaev invaded Dagestan in August 1999, igniting the second Chechen war.

This war, however, was to have a significant difference: this time, many Chechens who had fought Moscow the first time around, most notably the Mufti (and his son after he was murdered), fought against the foreign *jihadists*. Chechnya is much quieter and ostensibly back in the Russian Federation, but a low-level *jihadist* insurgency has spread across the North Caucasus.

A wildfire, indeed. While it would be otiose to blame Gamsakhurdia in particular and Georgia in general solely for the Chechen horrors, the direct connection is plain to see—Kartevelian chauvinism about Abkhazia, the resistance of Abkhazians, the dream of a new independent "Mountaineer Republic," Basaev's and other North Caucasian militia activities, and the defeat of Georgian power in Abkhazia fed ambitions that encouraged Dudaev. The last thing Moscow needs is more Georgian adventures in Abkhazia. That is probably Moscow's main interest in Georgia being as quiet as possible.

The Pankisi Gorge controversy

The memes, now well imbedded, caused most Western commentators reflexively to take Georgia's side in any controversy with Russia. A small but revealing case was the issue over Georgia's wine exports. When Russia stopped the import of Georgian wines in 2006, many news outlets treated this as another example of Russian pressure on Georgia.[66] Far fewer reported the admission that the Georgian wine industry was rife with forgery and adulteration.[67] But more important was the earlier Pankisi Gorge issue in which, as events were to prove, what Moscow said was mostly true and what Tbilisi said was mostly false. This revelation was not, however, taken to heart.

The Pankisi Gorge lies in the northeastern part of Georgia, close to Chechnya on the Russian side of the border, and it is difficult to access from either the south or the north. For many years Chechens have lived there (locally they are known as Kists) and, fleeing the wars on the other side, many Chechens crossed the mountains as refugees. But with them came fighters—especially Ruslan Gelayev's force that appears to have moved there after the fall of Groznyy in 2000. Arab *jihadists* also set up operations there centering themselves on the villages of Tsinubani and Khalatsani. Moscow started complaining about this almost immediately and Tbilisi responded with continual denial.[68] *The Wall Street Journal* took up Tbilisi's line:

> Having faced exaggerated claims for years now that it is harboring terrorists (a Russian euphemism for any Chechen) . . . it seems clear that this latest crisis isn't about combating terrorism at all. Rather, as Vladimir Socor explains on the page opposite, it's part of Russia's longstanding desire to reassert control over its Westward-looking former satellite . . . It still dreams of former SSRs, such as Georgia and Moldova (another unwilling host to Russian military bases), as subordinates. . . .[69]

In 2002 Russia complained to the United Nations Security Council (UNSC) and the Organization for Security and Co-operation in Europe (OSCE):

> The successful progress of the counter-terror operation has forced the remaining bandits to flee to Georgia, where the Georgian authorities turn a blind eye to the fact that they are living a free and comfortable life there, and continue to receive military, financial and other assistance from abroad.[70]

But in 2002 Washington was listening to different things than it had before. Soon Tbilisi gave up the pretence that nothing was happening in the Pankisi Gorge. Paata Batiashvili, the head of the Kakhetia district division of Georgia's Ministry of State Security admitted in November 2002.

> If you look at the village of Tsinubani, three to four months ago it was mainly occupied by Chechen fighters and Arab terrorists.[71]

And next year a Georgian official finally admitted that everything Moscow had been saying was correct:

> The [film] footage publicized by the Security Ministry depicts movements of very well-equipped fighters in the gorge. According to the Ministry's information, there were around 700 Chechen and 100 Arab fighters in

the gorge, which is only 30 kilometers in length. The Ministry named all the field commanders that have ever found shelter in Pankisi. These are: Ruslan (Hamzat) Gelaev, who had 200–250 fighters in his group and who's arrest and extradition was repeatedly requested by Russia; someone called Batia ("Short") with 100–120 fighters, Doku Umarov (Hasanov) with 130–150 fighters, Husein Esebaev (Isibaev) with 130–140 fighters and Amjet (Abu Hapsi)—commander of 80 mojaheddins. Most of these commanders were more or less known to the public, however information about Amjet has been released for the first time. As the security official says, this person was very close to Osama Bin-Laden and is wanted by Interpol . . . Laliashvili stated that the Arab emissaries were very well organized. Along with the fighters, there also were Arab religious emissaries ("Spiritual Fathers of Wahhabism") in the Pankisi gorge, who were responsible for functioning of the Wahhabist schools in Pankisi. There were several such schools in the gorge, where children were taught Wahhabi ideology. "There are children in Pankisi, who speak Arab better than Georgian," Laliashvili told Civil Georgia. There also was an Internet center in Pankisi, with several notebook computers and a satellite communication system, used for propaganda and volunteer recruitment activities . . . Along with Wahhabist schools and the Internet center, the gorge also had several fighters' training centers as well. "We have recovered textbooks from these centers, which gives the detail explanation how to explode residential buildings, make explosive devices and so on," Laliashvili said. The Georgian State Security Ministry does not rule out the possible link between the London poison case and Pankisi. Laliashvili says the deadly poison ricin, which emerged most dramatically when traces of the poison and facilities for its production were discovered in north London on January 5, could be produced in Pankisi gorge. State Security Ministry reports that the militants in Pankisi had excellent financial support. They were receiving money directly from Al-Qaeda . . .[72]

What forced Tbilisi to confront reality was, of course, post-9/11 realities in Washington. 9/11 (temporarily as it happened) awoke it to what Putin had been trying to tell it for some time: namely that there really was a "terrorist international" and it was present in Chechnya and Georgia too. As Washington learned more, Pankisi began to appear in its viewfinder. On February 11, 2002 the American chargé d'affaires in Tbilisi said that some terrorists from Afghanistan were in the Pankisi Valley.[73]

The United States began an operation to "train and equip" Georgian security forces. Finally the Georgian authorities began an operation. There is quite a lot of evidence that it was a joint Georgian, Russian, and American operation. The Civil Georgia website admits this: "The Ministry's Spokesman told Civil Georgia that collection of this information and restoration of order in Pankisi was made possible with tight coopera-tion with the US and Russian special services."[74] Shevardnadze also alluded to Russian cooperation and his newly appointed National Security Council Secretary flat out said that Russians had been in the area for a long time.[75] Eventually, after several false starts, by the end of 2002 their efforts had had sufficient effect to push the Chechens and Arabs out. Gelaev's men entered Ingushetia and the Arabs dispersed out of Pankisi.[76]

Everything Moscow had charged was correct and everything Tbilisi had said up to the final admission was false and Tbilisi's friends were quite wrong to have uncritically added Moscow's allegations into the "charge sheet." The OSCE's failure during Gelaev's invasion of Abkhazia[77]—still an extremely murky event—did not contribute to Moscow's trust of that organization's impartiality and Moscow's support for it has visibly declined since.

The Pankisi Gorge episode ought to have taught some lessons: Russia is an ally in the war against *jihadism*; the power vacuum in Georgia can have longer and larger consequences than merely local ones but, most impor-tant, that Moscow can be telling the truth about Georgia. But, gradually, these lessons were forgotten and the long-familiar memes of Georgia came back to dominate the discourse.

Post-9/11 opportunities missed

When the United States was attacked by al-Qaeda, President Putin was one of the first foreign leaders to telephone President Bush and offer con-dolences and assistance. Condoleezza Rice tells us that on the morning of September 11 she phoned Putin to tell him that the heightening of the US security posture had nothing to do with Russia; Putin answered that he had already stood the Russian military down and offered his help.[78] Given that Russia itself had been under attack for years by international *jihadism* in Chechnya and elsewhere in the North Caucasus, it was perhaps Putin's hope that this first step would lead to some recognition of a common inter-est between Washington and Moscow. Moscow had earlier tried to tell the West about this threat—most notably at the Munich Security Conference in Spring 2001 when Sergey Ivanov had spoken of how Russia was in the front line defending against a common threat.[79] We have just learned from a BBC documentary that the Taliban approached the Russians and suggested an anti-American alliance. Moscow's answer was a rude "no!" We also learn that, at their first meeting, Putin had warned Bush that the United States would be targeted.[80]

At first there was meaningful cooperation—the Pankisi problem was tackled and Russia provided weapons to support the Northern Alliance in Afghanistan. But the cooperation faded away over time and, once again,

Georgia had a role in the change. Despite the confirmation that what Moscow had been saying about the Pankisi Gorge was true, President Bush appears to have been completely taken in by Saakashvili's version of reality. Medvedev relates that when he was Head of the Presidential Administration and visiting Condoleezza Rice, Bush walked into the room and the very first thing he said was: "You know, Misha Saakashvili is a great guy."[81] This admiration for Saakashvili was reiterated in Bush's memoirs where he described him as a "charismatic young democrat" and, during the South Ossetia war said "It was clear the Russians couldn't stand a democratic Georgia with a pro-Western president."[82] This was his response to Medvedev's trying to tell him that Saakashvili had actually fired first. Rice in the interview above, protested that cooperation with Russia had been good on several issues but the two problems were always democratization in Russia and its relations with its immediate neighbors, mentioning Georgia and Ukraine specifically.

Thus, what might have been, and what Moscow was certainly interested in—an alliance against a common enemy—was wrecked partly by Washington's perceptions about Tbilisi.

And many people suspect something even worse. There is nothing to suggest that Tbilisi encouraged the *jihadist* and Chechen fighter nest in the Pankisi Gorge before 2001: the most likely truth was that there was nothing that it could do about it. However, today there are those who suspect that Saakashvili's relationship with the *jihadists* is close. Julia Goren, for example, asserts that Tbilisi hosted a conference of Jamaats in 2009[83] and the assertion is repeated by a Georgian parliamentarian[84] and an American observer.[85] Nino Burjanadze (Saakashvili's partner in the "Rose Revolution" trio, now in opposition) has said Georgia is training Ingush fighters.[86] Whether this is true is not clear but it is not unbelievable.[87] If Saakashvili is indeed supporting *jihadists* today, this is more than merely a "lost opportunity."

Saakashvili and the 2008 war

The immediate cause of the overthrow of Shevardnadze was the parliamentary election of November 2, 2003. Bolstered by all the usual appurtenances of "colored revolutions," large-scale cheating was alleged; perhaps the precipitating event was the statement by a US foreign policy spokesman that Washington did not accept the results. Whether or not Shevardnadze intended to make a fight of it, it was evident that the security forces would not. Eventually the troika of Mikheil Saakashvili, Zurab Zhvania, and Nino Burjanadze took power. It is perhaps worth observing that today in 2012, Zvania is long-dead (murdered in Shevardnadze's opinion[88]) and Burjanadze is one of the leaders of Saakashvili's opposition.[89] The unity did not last long.

From the beginning, Saakashvili was determined to regain Abkhazia and South Ossetia and one of his first actions was to make a pilgrimage to the grave of King David and swear to do so.[90] He was also strongly opposed to Russia, which he believed to be the source of their defiance. And he was determined to get as close to Washington as possible and get Georgia into NATO.

The dangerous power vacuum in the Pankisi Gorge encouraged the United States to begin a training program for the Georgian security forces so that they would not again be unable to control their territory. But the training program had different effects from those originally planned. Saakashvili began to believe that the Georgian armed forces were the best in the area. Ludicrous propaganda films appeared[91] and he felt encouraged to dream of a military conquest of Abkhazia and South Ossetia.[92] His then Defense Minister Irakli Okruashvili (now in the opposition[93]) dreamed along with him, famously boasting "new year in Tskhinvali"[94] in 2006.

Georgia then engaged in an arms buying spree acquiring large numbers of tanks and self-propelled guns from Ukraine and the Czech Republic in particular.[95] Weapons that had nothing to do with the peacekeeping and internal security purposes for which the Americans were allegedly training them. The Georgian army was, as events were to prove, poorly disciplined, with poor-quality officers and no ability to hold in adversity. At its test in August 2008, it failed, broke, and ran in panic.

By the summer of 2008 the memes about Georgia were well-practiced reflexes: it was the very gauge of Russia's "neo-imperialism"; it was an essential energy route that Moscow "coveted" (the Baku-Çeyhan pipeline through Georgia was now operating); Saakashvili was acclaimed as a "democratic ruler" and Moscow could not abide a "democracy" on its border. Perhaps the only country that did not wholeheartedly subscribe was France where Salome Zurabishvili (Saakashvili's former Foreign Minister, now in opposition) had been a member of its Foreign Ministry and still maintained contacts there.[96]

We are told by Irakli Okruashvili that Saakashvili had always intended reconquest of South Ossetia and Abkhazia if he could not get them otherwise.[97] When Saakashvili's Ambassador to Russia (now in opposition), Erosi Kitsmarishvili, returned home in the summer of 2008, he heard that there was a plan to attack Abkhazia. For some reason that he did not know, that had been put off and he was told that Tbilisi had Washington's backing to attack. Kitsmarishvili was so concerned that he actually met with the US Ambassador to Georgia to ask if that was true.[98] He was assured that it was not and returned to his post in Moscow.

A review of events will show that on August 7, 2008, after Saakashvili announced a ceasefire and called on Moscow to broker a peace, Georgian forces attacked South Ossetia, in the process killing some of the Russian peacekeeping force that had been there since the 1990s. The Georgians were soon stopped in the center of Tskhinval by the Ossetian militia. Russian forces entered from the north, moving down the single road as refugees moved north, crossed the chokepoint at Didi Gupta,[99] and engaged the Georgian forces bogged down in the center of Tskhinval. Soon the Georgians broke and fled back to Tbilisi, abandoning Gori and a battle group's worth of armored vehicles and other weapons in one of the brand-new bases there. Georgian gunboats attacked a Russian ship, the Russians landed forces in the west and advanced in pursuit of the fleeing Georgians discovering another heap of abandoned weapons at another new military base in Senaki. Abkhaz forces, probably with some Russian assistance, reoccupied Kodori, the only part of the former Abkhazian ASSR under Tbilisi's control.

When the war finally ended, Georgian forces had been routed. Russian forces pulled back to Abkhazia and North Ossetia (taking the captured weapons—including some US vehicles) with them. Moscow then recognized Abkhazia and South Ossetia as independent countries. One reason being, Medvedev said, to prevent this from happening again.[100]

The Western media—*Der Spiegel* being the sole honorable exception[101]—fortified by two decades of the memes, passively retyped Tbilisi's story.[102] More to the point (and surprisingly given Kitsmarishvili's strong hint that Saakashvili was planning to attack) so did the US Embassy, passing on what it was told.[103]

Moscow's version of events never varied. It said that Georgia attacked on the night of August 7 and that Russian troops did not arrive in Tskhinval until the next day. Saakashvili's story, on the other hand, changed several times. On the seventh, a few hours before his forces opened fire, he made a speech, in which he said he had ordered a ceasefire adding "And I am offering the Russian Federation to be a guarantor of the South Ossetian autonomy within Georgia . . . I offer a very important role to Russia in resolving this conflict . . . Georgia is a natural ally for Russia . . . We need a real mediator."[104] The next day, when he believed victory was at hand: he claimed that Georgian forces now controlled "most of South Ossetia" and "A large part of Tskhinvali is now liberated and fighting is ongoing in the centre of Tskhinvali." In this speech he made two assertions to justify the attack: first that "South Ossetian militias responded to his peace initiative on August 7 by shelling Georgian villages" and second that "Georgia had come under aerial attack from Russian warplanes." There was no mention of Russian troops entering South Ossetia then.[105] Of course, his victory announcement was premature and a few days later, he needed a bigger justification for the advancing catastrophe. It was then that he started claiming that the Russians moved first.

"I am sickened by the speculation that Georgia started anything," Mr Saakashvili told reporters on 13 August. "We clearly responded to the Russians . . . The point here is that around eleven o'clock, Russian tanks started to move into Georgian territory, 150 at first. And that was a clear-cut invasion. That was the moment when we started to open fire with artillery, because otherwise they would have crossed the bridge and moved into Tskhinvali."

Saakashvili brought out all the memes: "I think they're not just trying to kill a country, but the ideal of free democracy and successful prosperity. They want to show the west who is boss. They've tried to cut off energy lines." "What we're seeing now on the ground is the long-standing effort to purify this area. No population, no problem—Stalin's slogan. No Georgia, no problem!" And even this: "They leveled Tskhinval, and they said the Georgians did it."[106] Then the story changed again: on September 23 in a piece he wrote in the *Washington Post*, Saakashvili claimed that "Russia then started its land invasion in the early hours of August 7, after days of heavy shelling that killed civilians and Georgian peacekeepers."[107] He expected his readership to believe that the Russians had had an 18-hour head start on a 60-kilometer race and that Georgia had invaded anyway.

Saakashvili's stories collapsed one after the other: the first story about a response to heavy Ossetian shelling was directly contradicted by two former British officers who were part of the OSCE team in the area: they reported "Georgian rockets and artillery were hitting civilian areas in the breakaway region of South Ossetia every 15 or 20 seconds" and denied that there was the shelling of Georgian villages that Saakashvili claimed on the eighth.[108] The second story of the Russians entering South Ossetia just before—"supported" with the laughable claim of an intercepted telephone call mysteriously "lost" for several weeks—collapsed in a BBC program in October.[109] Americans were finally introduced to the accurate version in the *New York Times* nearly three months after the war began.[110] As Saakashvili's stories crumbled, his supporters in the US State Department tried to change the subject: "I think we need to get away from looking at, you know, who did what first, because as I said, I don't think we'll ever really get to the bottom of that."[111]

Der Spiegel had been correct: lies. Finally, the long-overdue and exquisitely feeble EU report appeared over a year after the war had started. Yes, the Georgians had fired the first shot and the Ossetians and Russians had responded.[112]

Aftermath

The aftermath of the August 2008 war ought to have put to rest the Georgian memes. If they had been true, if Moscow had always wanted Georgia back in its empire, if Moscow wanted to get control of the "new Great Game" oil routes, if Moscow wanted to eliminate a hated democracy next door then the August war was its opportunity to do them all. There certainly was not much stopping the victorious Russian forces from moving south.

The (slow) revelation of Saakashvili's false claims has destroyed his credibility. Perhaps the final blow was the preposterous "War of the Worlds" broadcast of spring 2010.[113] More damage to his reputation will be done if he becomes Prime Minister in 2013 when his term ends: his compliant majority has changed Georgia's Constitution so that the "President will no longer direct and exercise domestic and foreign policy of the state—as the current constitution says. This authority will be delegated to PM and the government."[114] NATO membership is highly unlikely and the foreign aid that propped up Georgia's economy has fallen off. Saakashvili's attempt to capture South Ossetia by a coup de main relying on support from the West backfired. The war began eroding Saakashvili's reputation as reliable, truthful and democratic. Suddenly we are hearing that Georgia's mass media is under "strict censorship,"[115] that Georgia is fourth in the world in jailed citizens,[116] that Saakashvili's economic reforms were more appearance than reality,[117] the opposition—most of them former allies who know the man well—are finally finding an audience in Western media.

But Saakashvili still has his friends in the United States. Hillary Clinton has more than once demanded that Moscow end its "occupation of Georgian territory."[118] And the memes endure there, seemingly oblivious to reality: Mitt Romney, Republican candidate for President, managed to utter most of them at once.

> He is convinced that Putin dreams of "rebuilding the Russian empire." He says, "That includes annexing populations as they did in Georgia and using gas and oil resources" to throw their weight around in Europe.[119]

In the same foreign-policy speech, Romney asserted

> Vladimir Putin has called the breakup of the Soviet empire the great tragedy of the 20th Century.[120] Will he try to reverse that tragedy and bludgeon the countries of the former Soviet Union into submission, and intimidate Europe with the levers of its energy resources?[121]

Late in 2010 Senator Marco Rubio, attempted to push through an amendment calling on Washington to fast track Georgia's membership in NATO. It was blocked by another Republican Senator, Rand Paul.[122] However faded they may be in Europe, the memes will not soon die in the United States, bolstered by innumerable slanted news reports and lobbyists.

Conclusion

Cause and effect in a nation's behavior is never easy to determine and as Lord Palmerston observed, nations have no permanent *friends*, only permanent *interests*. Russia's interests, in the larger and more general sense have not changed much since the 1990s: Russia wants a quiet life in order to repair its internal deficiencies. As Stephen Cohen has argued[123] Washington has missed three important opportunities for a mutually beneficial relationship with Russia. The first when possibilities opened by the end of the USSR were met with NATO expansion; the second when Putin's overtures after 9/11 were ignored or forgotten; the third today. Three US administrations: three spoiled chances. In each of these missed opportunities, the effect of the Georgia memes can be seen. Russia's alleged hostility toward Georgia and other former Soviet or Warsaw Pact states was an argument for expanding NATO; Russia's alleged hostility toward Georgia (despite the validation of all that Moscow had said about Pankisi) and Saakashvili's image were significant contributors to the failure of the second chance; today we have the stubborn insistence that there is no validity to the point of view of Abkhazians or Ossetians; they are seen as modern-day serfs—when the territory changes ownership, so do they.

We have seen three principal memes assumed in most discussion of Russia–Georgia disputes: Russia wants to swallow Georgia, Russia wants the pipelines, and Russia hates democracies. And always, Russia is lying. If Moscow is less amenable in the future, the Georgia memes are part of the reason.

(Note: See the Appendix for a case study of memes—RBW.)

Notes

1   Ronald Grigor Suny, *Political Conflicts in the Caucasus; Russian, Ukraine The Caucasus and the US Response* (Queenstown, MD: Aspen Institute, 1994).
2   A quick search on Google turns up many cases; see, for example, "Global Media and Russia: Bias or The Information War?" (http://old.win.ru/en/win/7928.phtml), "Georgia wages information war against Russia" (www.moscowtopnews.com/?area=postView&id=1344), "Georgian TV fake invasion report "part of information war against Russia" (http://publicintelligence.net/georgian-tv-fake-invasion-report-part-of-information-war-against-russia/), "The Heritage Foundation's Information War Against Russia" (www.russiaotherpointsofview.com/2008/09/the-heritage-fo.html), "December 2011: Information War against Russia" (http://rt.com/politics/information-war-russia-panarin-009/). "Information war" is a long-held Soviet and Russian concept; see Timothy L. Thomas, "The Russian View of Information War, February 2000 (http://fmso.leavenworth.army.mil/documents/Russianvuiw.htm).

3 "Meme" is a word coined by Richard Dawkins and defined as "an idea,
   behavior or style that spreads from person to person within a culture." It was
   taken from the Greek word for imitation and was intended to suggest "gene." I
   use it here in the sense of an idea that quickly spreads and is assumed to be so
   true that it requires no further argument. Some memes in this context would
   be the assumptions that Moscow wants "its empire back"; that much of the
   trouble in the former USSR is instigated by Moscow in pursuit of this aim;
   that Saakashvili (and his predecessors in Georgia) is a truthteller and democrat
   (somewhat weakened since 2008). I contend that a great deal of comment on
   Russia in general, and Russian-Georgian relations in particular, are based on
   these memes. The essence of memes is that they appear very early in the story,
   usually from early reporting or comment. The appearance, years later, of more
   considered academic works, have little effect.
4 For example from the *Washington Post*: "Perhaps this was an unfortunate
   accident; the police in Strasbourg say they are still investigating. But history
   suggests otherwise. Numerous opponents of Mr. Putin have been killed or
   gravely sickened by poisoning." Note that this is almost a perfect illustration
   of a meme at work, particularly the sly implication: "Damn with faint praise,
   assent with civil leer, / And without sneering teach the rest to sneer" (www.
   washingtonpost.com/wp-dyn/content/article/2008/10/21/AR2008102102342.
   html). But other outlets covered the story along those lines. The *Washington
   Post*'s jumping to conclusions was savaged by Mark Ames at http://
   exiledonline.com/freddy-gets-fingered-how-i-busted-the-washington-posts-
   op-ed-page-editor/.
5 Perhaps an even more egregious example of reflexively blaming Russia was the
   Daily Telegraph's reaction to the sudden death at his English home of Badri
   Patarkatsishvili in 2008. In the now-inevitable style (note the sly implication
   again) it speculated "While the investigation into the death of Mr Patarkatsishvili—a
   sworn enemy of Russian President Vladimir Putin—remains at an early stage,
   even speculation that the Russia state could be involved will fan diplomatic
   flames." (www.telegraph.co.uk/news/uknews/1578568/Patarkatsishvili-death
   -threatens-UK-Russia-ties.html). The *Evening Standard* went even further in
   suggesting Putin did it. (Keith Dovkants, "The dead billionaire and the 'KGB
   poison killer,'" February 14, 2008, www.standard.co.uk/news/the-dead-billi
   onaire-and-the-kgb-poison-killer-6623008.html). When the writers learned
   what they should already have known, namely that Patarkatsishvili was "a
   sworn enemy" of *Georgian* President Mikheil Saakashvili, the story stopped
   suddenly and the official verdict of natural death was accepted with no
   speculation about "a number of compounds known to be used by the former
   KGB can induce heart failure, but leave virtually no trace." See Endnote 93
   for Okruashvili's (not necessarily reliable) accusation that Saakashvili had him
   killed.
6 Oliver Rolofs, "A Breeze of Cold War," www.securityconference.de/Putin-s-
   speech.381+M52087573ab0.0.html.
7 Rob Watson, "Putin's speech: Back to cold war?" BBC, February 10, 2007.
8 Some of Putin's remarks that sparked off this reaction: "This universal,
   indivisible character of security is expressed as the basic principle that 'security
   for one is security for all' . . . These words remain topical

today. Incidentally, the theme of our conference—global crises, global
responsibility—exemplifies this . . . However, what is a unipolar world?
However one might embellish this term, at the end of the day it refers
to one type of situation, namely one centre of authority, one centre of
force, one centre of decision-making . . . It is world in which there is one
master, one sovereign. And at the end of the day this is pernicious not only
for all those within this system, but also for the sovereign itself because
it destroys itself from within." Full text may be found on the Kremlin
website archive at http://archive.kremlin.ru/eng/speeches/2007/02/10/0138_
type82912type82914type82917type84779_118123.shtml. I wonder whether
people would consider this so "inflammatory" today?

9 *The Economist*, November 13, 1993: www.highbeam.com/
   doc/1G1–14556012.html.

10 Spelling is always a difficulty in disputed territories because choices
   have political impact. In this I will use the local spellings of "Sukhum"
   and "Tskhinval" rather than the Georgian variations of "Sukhumi" and
   "Tskhinvali."

11 Indeed it was this action that induced Lenin to start questioning Stalin's
   power in his famous "testament." Not that he made Stalin and Orjonikidze
   give it back.

12 Richard Pipes, "Russian Generals Plan for the Future," www.
   intellectualcapital.com, July 3, 1994.

13 Ariel Cohen, Senior Policy Analyst, "The New 'Great Game': Oil Politics in
   the Caucasus and Central Asia," The Heritage Foundation, January 25, 1996.

14 Rossen Vassilev, "The Politics of Caspian Oil," *Prism*, The Jamestown
   Foundation, January 12, 1996.

15 Tony Barber, "Back to the USSR," *The Independent on Sunday*, January 23,
   1994.

16 Richard Pipes: "Russia's Designs on Georgia," www.intellectualcapital.com,
   May 14, 1998. An ironic echo of the Soviet как известно . . . (As is well
   known . . .), which always prefaced some wild assertion.

17 Center for Security Policy, Washington, May 12, 1997.

18 Richard Pipes April 10, 1997, "The Caucasus: A New Middle Eastern
   Tinderbox?" Johnson Russia List, April 10, 1997.

19 Henry Kissinger, Senate Foreign Relations Committee, July 13, 1995.

20 Henry Kissinger "Helsinki Fiasco," *The Washington Post*, March 30, 1997.

21 The National Democratic Institute gave Shevardnadze its annual award for
   merits in democratic state-building in 1999. (www.jamestown.org/single/?no_
   cache=1&tx_ttnews[tt_news]=12107&tx_ttnews[backPid]=213). Suddenly
   this was forgotten and Vice President Cheney actually said to Saakashvili
   "After your nation won its freedom in the Rose Revolution." ("Cheney
   affirms ties with Georgia, assails Russia," *Los Angeles Times*, September 5,
   2008, http://articles.latimes.com/2008/sep/05/world/fg-georgia5). Freedom
   from whom one may wonder.

22 Some individuals and Russian news media outlets claim that Shamil Basaev,
   the leader of the Chechen forces who fought in Abkhazia, was recruited by
   the GRU (Soviet then Russian military intelligence) in order to make trouble
   for independent Georgia (see his Wikipedia entry for some references).

This charge, of course, supports the meme that Georgia would have been acceptably stable had Moscow not stirred up trouble. Several things need to be considered before this may be believed. First the Russian media in the 1990s was little more than the house organs of the oligarchs in their wars with each other: much content was subordinated to this purpose. Second, the period after the breakup of the USSR was one of extreme confusion: in particular the former "organs of state security" and the Armed Forces had little confidence in their future. As to Basaev the story is that he was noticed by the GRU at the White House siege in August 1991, trained, and inserted into Abkhazia (see Col. Stanislav Lunev: "Chechen Terrorists in Dagestan—Made in Russia," *Newsmax.com*, August 26, 1999 (http://archive.newsmax.com/articles/?a=1999/8/25/210119). The author claims to be a former GRU officer and was a source for, among other things, the "suitcase nuke" excitements of the 1990s. He defected to the United States in 1992: in short, about the time of the events he describes). Finally, there is a chronological problem. A month after the White House events, troubles began in Chechnya resulting in Dzhokhar Dudaev's presidency and his successful defiance of Moscow. Chechnya declared independence in March 1992 and resistance to Dudaev began to gather that summer. Surely Basaev was there: he is said to have been one of the hijackers of an Aeroflot aircraft to Turkey in November 1991. Some say that he fought in Karabakh in 1992. He seems to have appeared in Abkhazia around August 1992 and remained there until the end of the fighting. When the first Chechen war began in December 1994, he became one of the leading rebel commanders. Khattab arrived in Chechnya about summer 1995 and at some time Basaev joined forces with him. It is said that he received training in Afghanistan at one of Bin Laden's structures as he completed his transformation from fighter for an independent Chechnya to warrior in the international *jihad*. This schedule would not appear to leave much time for training from the GRU. I have never seen any real evidence to support the assertion that Basaev was trained by or was any sort of asset of the GRU and I do not take the assertion seriously: assertions are plentiful but evidence is not.

23 Zviad Gamsakhurdia's supporters; many of them Mingrelian.
24 In this respect Ronald Asmus, *A Little War that Shook the World: Georgia, Russia, and the Future of the West* (New York: Palgrave Macmillan, 2010) is interesting because there is no chapter on the Ossetian viewpoint. This leads us to what might be called the *grund* meme, which is that Moscow is the only actor: *Moscow* wants its empire; *Moscow* wants the pipelines; *Moscow* hates democracies. And so, *Moscow* initiates actions and others react. Under this assumption, the Ossetians, their history, their desires disappear: they are only puppets of Moscow and there is no need to include their point of view.
25 The process took some time and was not finally settled until 1995. The point is that Kiev and Sevastopol negotiated an acceptable settlement without fighting.
26 Formerly called National Okrugs but confusingly renamed Autonomous Okrugs in the 1977 USSR Constitution.
27 For example, in 1926 there were said to be 194 ethonyms, 99 in 1939, 109 in 1959, 104 in 1970 and 1979 and 128 in 1989 and 172 in the 1994

mini-census. The pattern is clear: the system began in the 1926 census, Stalin was successfully creating Homo *Sovieticus* in 1939, which implied the disappearance of groups as class consciousness displaced national consciousness. Khrushchev was freer, Brezhnev returned to building Soviet Man, and the pressures were reducing in 1989 and had vanished by 1994 (Emil Pain and Andrey Susarov quoted in *Rossiysikiye Vesti,* November 30, 1997).

28 The language group to which Georgians (as well as Mingrelians, Ajarians, Svans, and Laz) belong. Taken now to mean Georgians as in the Georgian name for the country Sakartvelo. Abkhazians are from the Adygey-Abkhazian Language Group and Ossetians from the Iranian Language Group.

29 Prof. Revaz Mishveladze, Georgian newspaper *Young Communist,* July 29, 1989.

30 Introduction, by Prof Levan Alexidze to Avtandil Menteshashvili, *Some National and Ethnic Problems in Georgia* (Tbilisi: Samshoblo Publishing House, 1992).

31 The Georgian argument was that the overthrow of the Georgian Democratic Republic by Soviet forces in 1921 had been neither legal nor ratified by the population.

32 Partial results at www.vremyababurin.narod.ru/Num5_2001/N5_2001.html.

33 It is said that Saakashvili believes himself to be a second David. See "David the Builder or Mikhail the Destroyer?" (www.georgiatimes.info/ en/articles/60614.html). Most recently in January 2012, *Civil Georgia,* "Saakashvili: 'We Live in the Epoch of Revival.'" "It took him 34 years to regain Tbilisi. Occupied territories are now the same as Tbilisi was at that time" (www.civil.ge/eng/article.php?id=24345).

34 Menteshashvili, *Some National and Ethnic Problems in Georgia*, 33.

35 "The free and independent Social-Democratic government of Georgia will ever remain in my memory as a classical example of an imperialistic minor nationality both in relation to its seizure of territory within its own borders and in relation to the bureaucratic tyranny inside the state. Its chauvinism exceeds the highest limits" (Carl Eric Bechhofer quoted in Denikin's *Russia and the Caucasus, 1919–1920* (London, W. Collins sons & co, Ltd., 1921)). Menteshashvili gives several reports of conversations in which British officers go to Georgian officials to complain about the way Abkhazians or Ossetians are being treated and are given a history lecture by the rather patronizing Georgian interlocutor.

36 Georgian TV, Tbilisi, in Georgian, 1731 GMT, January 5, 1994 (BBC Monitoring Service SWB SU/1980 F/1).

37 My first acquaintance of this point of view came at a conference at the University of New Brunswick in October 1990. A Georgian politician (intermittently active in the opposition to Saakashvili, who, according to him, is a Russian stooge) described Ossetians as being as foreign in Georgia as Cameroonians would be in England; Abkhazians as occupiers of Georgian land and Ajars as Georgians (temporarily) converted to Islam. The coming storm in Georgia was visible in his words.

38 And stranger things too. A Georgian friend showed me a book written in the Gamsakhurdia period that claimed 1) that Noah's Ark had been Georgian

and was still there, 2) that Georgia was the mystical center of the universe (the *omphalos*), and 3) that Georgian literature went back thousands of years. The Georgians are a very ancient people, but not that ancient.

39 In the 1940s Abkhaz schools were closed and their literature banned. Later that decade a self-taught Georgian, Pavle Ingorokva, claimed that Abkhazians only arrived in Georgia in the seventeeth century. But Lavrenti Beria (a Mingrelian) apparently decided against wholesale deportation of Abkhazians in favor of swamping them with Mingrelian immigrants. Ingorokva's theory made a comeback under Gamsakhurdia.

40 See their Wikipedia entries for more information.

41 The confusion and uncertainty of this period should be recalled. As of December 1, 1991, soldiers in Georgia were USSR troops legally stationed in a part of the USSR. At the end of that month, they became Commonwealth of Independent States (CIS) troops legally stationed in the CIS. This somewhat fictional arrangement dissipated over the next year. Some of the former Soviet republics "nationalized" the soldiers, and so, for example, former USSR/CIS troops in Ukraine became the Ukrainian Armed Forces legally stationed in Ukraine. But several of the new states, like the Baltics and Georgia, did not want to do this, regarding the troops as occupiers. At the same time former USSR forces were based in Eastern Europe. Moscow eventually took responsibility for all of these "orphan units" (The reader is invited to imagine what would have happened if Moscow had said that it would only take responsibility for *Russian* nationals and leave Lithuania and the others to look after their nationals in the multiethnic Soviet Armed Forces in Eastern Europe and the former USSR). Understandably the pressure from the West was to move the former USSR garrisons out of Eastern Europe and that is what was done first. As the former Soviet economy collapsed, conditions became harsh especially for the now-Russian Armed Forces garrisoned in places that did not want them. It would not be surprising if these forces, mostly unpaid, did what they had to do to survive by selling off what they had to the warring sides or kept themselves alive by crime and racketeering. But, some weapons were obtained by fighters by threatening the soldiers' families. At the same time some of these weapons were handed over to the new governments. It took years to sort all this out and, in the meantime, the dwindling garrisons remained there. And, when they were attacked by someone, as they occasionally were, they defended themselves. There is no reason to assume that official Moscow—which had innumerable problems of its own—had anything to do with this. On a personal note, I at the time was afraid that some unit in one of these places, with weapons and a degree of command and control, would go rogue and demand food and money from the locals along the lines of the marauding "White Companies" of the Hundred Years' War. It could have been much worse than it was.

42 Especially in Tkvarcheli. See http://en.wikipedia.org/wiki/Siege_of_Tkvarcheli.

43 An attempt in August 1995 wounded Shevardnadze. The former chiefs of the Georgian National Security Service and Ioseliani were arrested. The next attempt was made in February 1998; the culprits this time were Mingrelian Zviadists and Chechens, many of whom had been trained in Chechnya.

In March 1999, Georgian security officials arrested eight Mingrelians on suspicion of preparing an assassination attempt. It was of course, reflexive to blame Russia: "But when Georgian president Shevardnadze backed the Turkish proposal [the Çeyhan pipeline route], he was nearly killed in a bombing, in which Russian involvement was suspected." Rossen Vassilev, "The Politics of Caspian Oil," *Prism,* January 12, 1996.

44 A conscious effort was made to populate the now-empty (and very desirable) territory with Mingrelians. The Kartevelian/Mingrelian population climbed from about six percent in 1886 to 24 percent in ten years (Liana Kvarchelia, "Vision from Abkhazia," November 7, 1996 (www.abkhazia. org/vision2.html)).

45 A mysterious event, which I have never understood. The truth lies in the relationship between Stalin, Nestor Lakoba, and Beria. The reader is invited to view the movie *Baltazar's Feast* (www.amazon.com/Baltazars-Feasts-Stalin-Valtasara-Stalinym/dp/B000774E6M) and speculate.

46 A paramilitary organization of uncertain origins led by Jaba Ioseliani.

47 "The campaign of looting, rape, torture and murder mounted by the Mkhedrioni in the region did much to poison relations between Mingrelia and the rest of Georgia . . . Georgian forces behaved similarly upon their entry into Abkhazia in the summer of 1992." George Khutsishvili and Neil MacFarlane, "Ethnic Conflict in Georgia," paper presented at conference on Ethnic Conflict and European Security, Centre for International Relations, Queen's University, Kingston, September 23–4, 1994.

48 A report on the war from Human Rights Watch in March 1995 suffers from the weaknesses of the breed by attempting to accuse both sides evenly, the smoothing over of which was responsible for turning a legalistic dispute into a bitter war of atrocities. But even so, it is clear who started it: "Georgian combatants, loosely knit groups of soldiers and marauders, murdered and intimidated the local residents, who were taken by surprise and were almost entirely unarmed, and looted and pillaged homes extensively, targeting ethnic Abkhaz" (www.unhcr.org/refworld/country,,HRW,COUNTRYREP,GEO,,3ae6a 8274,0.html).

49 "Helsinki Fiasco," *The Washington Post*, March 30, 1997.

50 David Satter "The Danger of Russia's Great Power Illusions," *Prism*, March 6, 1998, The Jamestown Foundation.

51 Professor Zaza Gachechiladze, paper prepared with the assistance of Mr James Morrison, Visiting Fellow, Institute for National Strategic Studies, National Defense University, USA, March 1995, www.ndu. edu/ndu/inss/ strforum/forum21.html.

52 "The Caucasus: An Overview" by George Hewitt (Commissioned but never published by *The New Statesman*, date not given—www.channel1.com/ users/apsny/overview.htm#invasion). The post-USSR reality meant that some former USSR weaponry was passed to independent Georgia. But there is little information available about the details.

53 My insertion.

54 Information for the Secretary General of the UN, Mr Butros Butros Gali "International Alert" About Georgian-Abkhazian Conflict, Besarion Gugushvili—Prime Minister of Georgia in exile, Merab Kiknadze—

Temporary speaker of the Parliament of Georgia in exile, May 15, 1993 (www.clinet.fi /~bpg/abkhaz_1.html). Gugushvili was also the representative of Zelimkhan Yandarbiyev when he was Acting President of Chechnya after Dudaev's death, in Finland (see www.clinet.fi/~bpg/ichkeri1.html)—the Gamsakhurdia-Dudaev connection is one of the curious phenomena of the time.

55 "The record of Russia's actions in the former Soviet Union, however, strongly suggests that a threat to Eastern European stability does exist which could become a great deal more serious if Russia gains strength." *Prism*, op cit.

56 Admittedly, there were voices trying to say that it was more complicated than a story of "imperialist Russia versus innocent Georgia." And there have been reconsiderations since. But the whole point of a "meme" is that it is quickly and widely spread and, once it is, it takes an enormous effort to counter it. See Patrick Armstrong, "More Questions Than Can be Answered," *Russia Blog*, April 13, 2008 (www.russiablog.org/2008/04/more_questions_than_ can_be_ans.php) as a small example of how much effort it takes to counter a quickly written op-ed that simply strings the memes of the moment together.

57 "The main question today is whether Russia's leaders think they finished the job during the 2008 amputation, or whether they still hope to force out Georgian President Mikheil Saakashvili's democratically elected government." Svante Cornell, "Finishing the Job," *Foreign Policy*, July 2, 2009.

58 A Mufti is a judge of Muslim law. He is supposed to be a man of probity with sufficient knowledge to gain respect and have authority in his judgements.

59 "Bandit of honor."

60 Ethnic Chechens living in Dagestan.

61 Marie Bennigsen Broxup, "After the Putsch, 1991," in *The North Caucasus Barrier*, ed. Marie Bennigsen Broxup, 233 (London: Hurst & Co, 1992).

62 According to a tendentious Russian source, Dudaev's forces had 42 tanks, 34 BMP armored infantry vehicles, 139 artillery systems, 101 major anti-armor systems, 270 fixed wing aircraft (5 of them serious fighter planes and the rest jet trainers converted for military use), two helicopters, and 50,000 units of small arms (*Чеченская Трагедия: КтоВиноват* (*The Chechen Tragedy: Who is to blame*), Moscow, 1995). As usual in Russia there are two stories and no accepted facts. The first story is that the Russian Ministry of Defense sold the weapons to Dudaev or allowed him to have them. Proponents of this theory tie it into the supposed destabilization campaign Moscow ran against Georgia. Other stories (and those more common at the time) are that Dudaev obtained these weapons by a mixture of bribes and threats.

63 See Endnote 22 for discussion about Basaev's connections with Moscow.

64 Khattab's own account is that, when he returned to Afghanistan after the failed jihadist war in Tajikistan, he saw Chechen fighters on TV with the *Shahada* on their headscarves and decided that Chechnya was "a land of the jihad" that he should go to.

65 The precise dates are not clear. What we can say is that at the beginning Basaev's rhetoric was that of national liberation and by the time of his death it was that of the international jihad. The change was probably gradual.

66 C. J. Chivers, "A Russian 'Wine Blockade' Against Georgia and Moldova," *New York Times*, April 6, 2006. "It has also raised fresh questions about the

degree to which Russia is committed to free trade and willing to live within a market-based system, rather than using trade as a lever to reward or punish other countries for political reasons." Tom Parfitt, "Russian 'sour grapes' embargo leaves Georgian wine makers counting the cost," *The Guardian*, May 30, 2006. "The pro-western president, Mikhail Saakashvili, rubbished the Russian claims, saying: 'Georgian wine is being punished because of our freedom and democratic aspirations.'"

67 William M Dowd, "Conclusion is in: Too many Georgian wines are fakes," July 22, 2006 (http://winenotebook.blogspot.com/2006/07/decision-is-in-too-many-georgian-wines.html).

68 On September 15, 1999 the Georgian Foreign Ministry denied Russian allegations that arms, ammunition, and fighters transited Georgia to Chechnya and Dagestan; on December 29, 1999 the Deputy Security Minister denied Chechen fighters were using Pankisi as a base; on April 25, 2000 a State Security Ministry official denied it; on November 4, 2000 the Interior Ministry denied Gelaev was in Georgia; likewise on January 11, 2001.

69 "The Bush administration should use its friendlier lines of communication with the Kremlin to make it clear that the new Russia cannot simply paw and claw back an independent country." Editorial "Georgia on His Mind," *Wall Street Journal*, August 9, 2002.

70 Putin's letter to UNSC and OSCE, September 12, 2002 (RIA Novosti).

71 Robyn Dixon, "In the Caucasus, a Foreign Element Threatens," *Los Angeles Times* November 29, 2002.

72 Nika Laliashvili, Spokesman for the Georgian State Security Ministry quoted in Giorgi Sepashvili "Security Ministry Unveils Classified Details on Pankisi," *Civil Georgia*, www.civil.ge/cgi-bin/newspro/fullpnews. cgi?newsid1043058090,69020). All spellings and punctuation conform with the original.

73 "Islamic Radicals From Afghanistan Active in Georgia—US Diplomat," *Eurasianet.com*, February 14, 2002.

74 Civil Georgia.

75 On September 16, 2002 he said Russian special forces were "working" in Pankisi and that "US representatives are also present." Caucasus Press quoted National Security Council Secretary Tedo Japaridze as saying that the Russians had been in the district "for a long time" and were being regularly briefed on developments.

76 See Jaba Devdariani, "Georgia's Pankisi Dilemma," Institute for War and Peace Reporting, February 21, 2005, (http://iwpr.net/report-news/georgias-pankisi-dilemma).

77 See http://en.wikipedia.org/wiki/2001_Kodori_crisis. Or Thomas de Waal, *The Caucasus: An Introduction*, 2010, the chapter on Georgia. After Shevardnadze's protests the OSCE stationed an observer force in northern Georgia. It did not seem to notice this event.

78 Interview, February 2012, Uncommon Knowledge (www.powerlineblog.com/archives/2012/02/uncommon-knowledge-with-condoleezza-rice.php).

79 "Russia, a front-line warrior fighting international terrorism in Chechnya and Central Asia is saving the civilized world of the terrorist plague in the same way as it used to save Europe of Tatar-Mongol invasion in 13th century, paying with sufferings and privation." Ivanov, Speech at Munich Conference

on Security Policy, February 4, 2001 (www.worldsecuritynetwork.com/printArticle3.cfm?article_id=9103).

80 "The Taliban contacted our frontier guards on the Tajik-Afghan border," Ivanov said. "They said they had been sent by Taliban supreme leader Mullah Omar to propose that the Taliban and Russia unite against the United States. It was a proposal that we rejected with a well-known American hand signal: 'F . . . off.'" RIA NOVOSTI, January 20, 2012 (http://en.rian.ru/russia/20120120/170859831.html).

81 Medvedev interview, August 5, 2011 (http://eng.kremlin.ru/transcripts/2680).

82 George Bush, *Decision Points*.

83 www.jihadwatch.org/2010/04/more-details-on-the-georgia-hosted-jihadi-conference-emerge.html

84 http://nationalinterest.org/article/mishas-world-3309

85 James Jatras, "The Georgian Imbroglio—And a Choice for the United States," America-Russia Net, February 14, 2010 (www.america-russia.net/eng/face/236661338?user_session=4827e878c0267ddbdd6ee738f8212f1d). "But there is worse: Americans must be made aware of Saakashvili's extending refuge to *jihadists* responsible for countless acts of terror in southern Russia and his regime's extraordinary coordination efforts to permit them to step up attacks in the Caucasus region."

86 *Weekly Georgian Journal*, October 21, 2010, www.georgianjournal.ge/index.php?option=com_content&view=article&id=664:burjanadze-talks-about-danger-of-one-more-war-from-russia-&catid=9:news&Itemid=8.

87 See Gordon Hahn, "Irrationality and Rationality in the Caucasus: Connecting All the Dots," November 27, 2010 (www.russiaotherpointsofview.com/2010/11/irrationality-and-rationality-in-the-caucasus-connecting-all-the-dots.html) for more discussion of Tbilisi's possible connections with the jihadists in the North Caucasus.

88 "He dismissed the official government account that Zhvania was accidentally poisoned by a faulty gas heater. 'He was murdered,' he said, adding that he does not know by whom" (Paul Quinn-Judge, "Shevardnadze the Survivor," *Washington Post*, March 19, 2006). The rumor that Saakashvili had him killed persists (See www.georgiatimes.info/en/news/33463.html) and was given some impetus by Saakashvili's former Defense Minister Okruashvili in 2007 (www.civil.ge/eng/article.php?id=15869). *Honi soit qui mal y pense.*

89 She called Saakashvili "Europe's new dictator" in July 2011 ("'Stop the Dictatorship'—An Interview with Georgian Opposition Figure Nino Burjanadze," RFE/RL, July 7, 2011, www.rferl.org/content/georgia_nino_burjanadze_/24258110.html).

90 "Saakashvili's Vows Improvements with Drastic Measures," *Civil Georgia*, January 25, 2004 (www.civil.ge/eng/article.php?id=6090). "Georgia's territorial integrity is the goal of my life" and "I do not want to use troops in Abkhazia, but we should have strong economy and army to restore territorial integrity."

91 For example, see www.youtube.com/watch?v=fPWlcTZm9tw. What is especially preposterous about this are the medieval scenes: in those days

the Georgians would have welcomed Christian Russia's help against their Muslim Persian enemies.

92 For example, "In his televised address to the nation on May 25, President Saakashvili said that the event would aim to 'demonstrate Georgia's forces.' However, he also stated that Georgia would apply to only peaceful means to reunite Georgia. 'If you asked any Georgian soldier why he is serving in the armed forces, each of them would reply—"to restore Georgia's territorial integrity,"'" Saakashvili said adding that a peaceful resolution of the Abkhazia conflict is a primary goal of his government. He said Tbilisi was ready to grant the breakaway regions of Abkhazia and South Ossetia the largest possible autonomy within the Georgian state and vowed that Georgia would have the best army in the region in a couple of years. Maia Edilashvili, "Saakashvili Sends 'Love' Messages, Showcases 15,000 Soldiers at Independence Day Parade," *The Georgian Times*, May 28, 2007 (www. geotimes.ge/index.php?m=home&newsid=4705). Note the ambiguity "only peaceful means" but also the threat of force. Saakashvili's defenders quote the first and ignore the second; those likely to be on the receiving end notice the latter. His real meaning is "one way or the other."

93 And making all sorts of accusations about Saakashvili too, including the charge that Saakashvili intended to kill Badri Patarkatsishivili (who was actually found dead in the United Kingdom about five months after this interview. See Endnote 5). RFE/RL, "Former Georgian Minister Talks To RFE/RL Prior To Arrest," September 28, 2007.

94 "'My major goal, my purpose of being the Defense Minister, is restoration of Georgia's territorial integrity. I have no other goal more valuable than this and as soon as these two problems [the Abkhaz and South Ossetian conflicts] are solved, I will no longer stay in politics,' Okruashvili said while speaking on the political talk show 'Pirvelebi' (Leaders). Okruashvili reiterated his late December statement and said that Georgia will gain control over breakaway South Ossetia by January 1, 2007. 'If we fail to celebrate New Year in Tskhinvali on January, 2007 I will no longer be the Defense Minister of Georgia,' Okruashvili said." And, in connection with the issue of Georgian wine mentioned at the beginning of this chapter this: "Following Okruashvili's highly-controversial and harsh statements towards Russia including the statement that 'even feces can be sold on the Russian market' opponents have dubbed the Defense Minister a 'provoker.' This statement has also triggered discontent among some Georgian wine-producers, who are desperately trying to re-enter the Russian market, which was closed on March 27 after the Russian chief sanitary inspector said Georgian wines contained pesticides." "Okruashvili Speaks of Russia, Wine, Conflicts," *Civil Georgia*, May 2, 2006.

95 SIPRI Arms Transfers Database. Search on countries and dates for the details.

96 It is instructive that the war settlement was negotiated largely by France and that Foreign Minister Kouchner actually did what almost no one in the Western media or leadership ever thought to do: visit the Ossetian refugees in Vladikavkaz and listen to their side of the story (On his way

from Tbilisi to Moscow at the start of the negotiations; see www.lefigaro.
fr/flash-actu/
2008/08/11/01011–20080811FILWWW00496-kouchner-rencontre-des-
refugies.php).

97   "But Okruashvili, a close Saakashvili ally who served as defense minister
from 2004 to 2006, said he and the president worked together on military
plans to invade South Ossetia and a second breakaway region on the Black
Sea coast, Abkhazia." "Saakashvili 'planned S. Ossetia invasion': ex-minister,"
Reuters, September 14, 2008 (www.reuters.com/article/2008/09/14/
us-georgia-russia-
opposition-idUSLD12378020080914?sp=true).

98   "In the second half of April, 2008, I have learnt from the President's inner circle
that they have received a green light from the western partner to carry out a
military operation. When asked to specify 'the western partner' Kitsmarishvili
said: after a meeting with the U.S. President George W. Bush [the meeting
between Bush and Saakashvili took place in Washington on March 19], our
leadership was saying that they had the US support to carry out the military
operation. In order to double-check this information, I have met with John
Tefft, the US ambassador in Tbilisi and asked him whether it was true or not;
he categorically denied that." Kitsmarishvili also refers to an earlier planned
attack on South Ossetia after a failed "special operation" in 2004. Testimony
before Georgian parliamentary commission studying the August war, *Civil
Georgia*, November 25, 2008 (www.civil.ge/eng/article.php?id=20026).

99   A long bridge over a valley. A perfect chokepoint for the Georgians to have
held up the Russian column. But they never managed, despite their head
start, to get the 20-odd kilometers to it. See Patrick Armstrong, "Could
the Georgians have Done Better?" *Russia Blog*, August 14, 2008 (www.
russiablog.org/2008/08/could_the_georgians_have_done.php).

100   "We restored peace, but we could not extinguish fears and hopes of the peoples of South Ossetia and Abkhazia in a situation when Saakashvili continued (with participation of and encouraged by the US and a number of other
NATO members) to speak of re-arming his military and re-establishing control over 'the Georgian territory' . . . Russia was left no choice." "Medvedev
on recognition of independence of Sukhum and Tskhinval," *Regnum News*,
August 28, 2008 (www.regnum.ru/english/1047550.html).

101   "One source who is personally familiar with the reports summarized the findings as follows: 'Saakashvili lied 100 percent to all of us, the Europeans and
the Americans.'" "The Cold Peace," *Der Spiegel*, September 1, 2008 (www.
spiegel.de/international/world/0,1518,575581,00.html).

102   Perhaps the stand-out in this lamentable performance was CNN's showing footage of Tskhinval and passing it off as Gori (see www.youtube.com/
watch?v=NVNblG9PJMk). I have heard reports, however, that it was not
alone in doing so and indeed the reports alleging great destruction in Gori
turned out to be untrue. Then there was the US TV interviewer who had a
refugee on his program and was visibly surprised to hear her thank Russia
for saving the Ossetians from the Georgian attackers (See www.youtube.com/
watch?v=gWLu04m2d1E).

103 Patrick Armstrong, "Wiki Leaks and the South Ossetia War," November 30, 2010 (www.russiaotherpointsofview.com/2010/11/wiki-leaks-and-the-south-ossetia-war.html).

104 "Saakashvili Appeals for Peace in Televised Address," *Civil Georgia*, August 7, 2008 (www.civil.ge/eng/article.php?id=18931). The timing makes it obvious that the order to attack had already been given when he made this speech.

105 "'Most of S. Ossetia Under Tbilisi's Control'—Saakashvili," *Civil Georgia*, August 8, 2008 (www.civil.ge/eng/article.php?id=18955&search=control%20ossetia).

106 Press conference with Western reporters, August 13, 2008 (http://noconsensus.wordpress.com/2008/08/16/georgia-president-discussing-russian-motives-worth-reading/).

107 Mikheil Saakashvili, "Answering Russian Aggression," *Washington Post*, September 23, 2008 (www.washingtonpost.com/wp-dyn/content/article/2008/09/22/AR2008092202581.html).

108 Reported in *The Times*, November 9, 2008, but direct reference no longer available on the internet (see http://newsuc.com/newsfun/index.php/funny-not-funny-news/2008/11/10/georgia_fired_first_shot_say_uk_monitors).

109 Part 1 (www.youtube.com/watch?v=3QfotxKFdtQ), go to 7:20. For once the BBC interviewer, rather than passively swallowing the meme, cross-examines on how something this important could have been "lost."

110 "Georgia Claims on Russia War Called Into Question," *New York Times*, November 6, 2008 (www.nytimes.com/2008/11/07/world/europe/07georgia.html?_r=2&pagewanted=1&ref=europe&oref=slogin).

111 Robert Wood, a deputy spokesman for the State Department, *Civil Georgia*, November 8, 2008 (www.civil.ge/eng/article.php?id=19910).

112 A poor report, saying nothing that had not been known at the time by observers not wedded to the memes about Georgia and Russia. See Patrick Armstrong, "The EU Report: Little and Late," October 8, 2009 (www.russiaotherpointsofview.com/2009/10/the-eu-report-little-and-late.html). See also "EU Investigators Debunk Saakashvili's Lies," *Der Spiegel*, October 1, 2009 (www.spiegel.de/international/world/0,1518,652512,00.html).

113 "Russian invasion scare sweeps Georgia after TV hoax," *The Guardian*, March 14, 2010 (www.guardian.co.uk/world/2010/mar/14/russia-georgia-fake-invasion-report).

114 "Key Points of Newly Adopted Constitution," *Civil Georgia*, October 15, 2010. Nino Burjanadze, "Unparliamentary Language in Tbilisi," *The National Interest*, November 11, 2010 (http://nationalinterest.org/commentary/unparliamentary-language-tbilisi-4399). "Such 'details' show that the new constitution is simply a façade behind which Saakashvili and his team are planning to remain in power."

115 The Assembly of Delegates of International PEN, meeting at its seventy-fifth Congress in Linz, Austria, October 19–25, 2009.

116 International Centre for Prison Studies (www.prisonstudies.org/info/world-brief/wpb_stats.php?area=all&category=wb_poprate).

117 Irakli Rukhadze and Mark Hauf, "The Georgian Economy under Saakashvili," finchannel.com, April 21, 2009. "Georgian president, Mikhail Saakashvili,

has presented the Georgian people and his world audience with a view that his presidency brought democracy and economic rehabilitation to the country. Unfortunately for Georgia, this has been more a well-crafted PR myth that an actual reality."

118   "We continue to call on Russia to end its occupation of Georgian territory, withdraw its forces and abide by its other commitments under the 2008 cease-fire agreements." Voice of America, October 6, 2010 (www.voanews. com/english/news/usa/Clinton-Renews-Call-for-Russian-Withdrawal-From-Georgia-104427328.html).

119   Mitt Romney interview, *Washington Post*, October 7, 2011, www. washingtonpost.com/blogs/right-turn/post/exclusive-mitt-romney-interview/2011/03/29/gIQADp6OTL_blog.html

120   He did not say "the greatest": the Russian is very clear (www.russiaotherpointsofview.com/2010/11/the-third-turn.html), but this has now become a firm prop of the meme that Moscow wants its empire back.

121   Mitt Romney, Speech at the Citadel, October 7, 2011 (www.huffingtonpost.com/2011/10/07/mitt-romney-speech-foreign-policy_n_1000158.html; www.mittromney.com/blogs/mitts-view/2011/10/mitt-romney-delivers-remarks-us-foreign-policy).

122   Patrick Buchanan, "Marco Rubio vs Rand Paul," *The American Conservative*, December 8, 2011 (www.theamericanconservative.com/blog/2011/12/08/marco-rubio-vs-rand-paul/). Buchanan points out the effects of Georgia's lobby in the United States: especially Randy Scheunemann's influence on John McCain ("We are all Georgians now"). As he concludes: "The resolution was pulled. But these people will be back."

123   Stephen F. Cohen, "America's Failed (Bi-Partisan) Russia Policy," *Huffington Post*, February 28, 2012 (www.huffingtonpost.com/stephen-f-cohen/us-russia-policy_b_1307727.html). "In short, every opportunity for a U.S.-Russian partnership during the past twenty years was lost, or is being lost, in Washington, not in Moscow."

Bibliography

Author's note

The principal characteristic of memes is that they exist prior to the event; the event is then interpreted through these memes and facts become "facts" only when they fit the memes. Therefore the useful sources in discussing memes are the immediate ones. Books written years later will have only a slight effect on the now deeply embedded memes. What follows, therefore, is less of a bibliography than suggestions for further reading.

Blanch, Leslie, *The Sabres of Paradise*, New York, Carroll & Graf Publishers, 1960 (about the Imam Shamil and the Great Caucasus War; useful to give some background on the latent passions).

Broxup, Marie Bennigsen (ed.), *The North Caucasus Barrier*, London, Hurst & Co, 1992.

de Waal, Thomas, *The Caucasus: An Introduction*, Oxford, Oxford University Press, 2010.

Griffin, Nicholas, *Caucasus*, New York, St Martin's Press, 2001.

King, Charles, *The Ghost of Freedom: A History of the Caucasus*, Oxford, Oxford University Press, 2008.

CHAPTER THREE

Caucasian Crescent: Russia's Islamic Policies and its Responses to Radicalization

*Domitilla Sagramoso and
Akhmet Yarlykapov*

This chapter examines in detail Islamic developments in the Russian North Caucasus since the end of the Soviet Union up until the early 2010s. It shows how this predominantly Muslim region has affected in a very significant way views and perceptions of Islam throughout Russia over the past decade. In particular, it analyzes the impact of Russia's religious policies toward Islam in the region and the Kremlin's handling of the jihadist violence that has engulfed the North Caucasus since the late 1990s. It shows how Moscow's repressive policies against "non-traditional" Islamic groups and violent jihadist fighters in the North Caucasus have exacerbated the cycle of violence in the area . In turn, it explains how the outbreak of Islamic violence in Chechnya and the North Caucasus has affected Russia's national feelings, and has led to the rise of xenophobic attitudes against North Caucasians among many segments of the Russian population. It argues that as a result of the upsurge in Islamic-inspired violence in Chechnya, and the spread of terrorist attacks to other Muslim regions of

*Russia, strong anti-Caucasian feelings and intolerant views
towards non-Russians have emerged in many areas of Russia. In
addition, it describes how as a result of the increased Islamization
of the North Caucasus, the region has become increasingly
alienated and distanced from the rest of Russia. In essence,
the chapter shows how the relation of Russia with its Muslim
communities in the North Caucasus has been one of mutual
interaction and reciprocal influence.*

Introduction: A new threat

When the Soviet Union collapsed, Russia lost control over a large portion of Muslims communities inhabiting the former Soviet space, in particular, those living in the newly independent states of Central Asia, in
Azerbaijan, and the Crimean peninsula. However, a significant number of
Muslim groups remained inside the newly formed Russian state, primarily
inhabiting the vast steppes of the Volga-Ural region and the mountainous
areas of the North Caucasus. This forced the Kremlin to develop effective
policies of engagement with its Muslims citizens to ensure their loyalty and
allegiance—a real challenge given the strength of national and religious
sentiments in most Muslim areas. But whereas accommodation was soon
reached with Muslims in the Volga regions, the Russian North Caucasus
remained a restive area, where national sentiments often prevailed over
allegiance to the Russian state. The determination of the Chechen republic
to press ahead with its claims of independence, and the subsequent outbreak of war in Chechnya in December 1994 created a serious challenge
to the integrity of the Russian state. In the late 1990s, however, a new and
in many ways much more serious threat emerged from Chechnya and the
North Caucasus—the spread of radical Islamic movements, which challenged Russia's authority in the region, along religious, rather than ethnic
lines. More specifically, Chechnya became the source of radical Wahhabi
ideas calling for military *jihad* against the local authorities and for the
establishment of an Islamic state in the entire North Caucasus.

However, the Kremlin's highly repressive policies in response to the
growth of terrorist violence served only to exacerbate the existing violence.
In the mid-2000s many young Muslims in the North Caucasus started to
engage in a violent struggle or *jihad* against the existing secular regimes in
all Muslim republics of the region, to avenge their own sufferings and the
loss of their loved ones. Moreover, a series of structural factors, which were
present, to varying degrees, in all republics of the North Caucasus, also
induced many young individuals to take up arms. These included, among
others, the perpetuation of corrupt ruling elites, the absence of political

pluralism, severe economic hardship, youth unemployment, and high levels of income inequality. All of these factors combined to create a deep sense of frustration and disillusionment among the local Muslim youth and therefore enhanced the appeal of violent *jihadist* ideas among young Muslims. These elements were supported by the very effective mobilizing efforts conducted by Chechen rebel fighters, to galvanize young Muslims in the region in support of the Chechen cause.

In the late 2000s, as this chapter shows, these fighting *jamaats* radicalized even further, and became closer in their aims and strategies to the global Islamic *jihadist* movement. Moreover, this period also witnessed a growing trend among the various *jihadist* North Caucasian movements to be less ethnically based and more pan-Caucasian in terms of their objectives and organization. This was clearly demonstrated by the declaration of the Caucasian Emirate, by Chechen leader Doku Umarov in November 2007, and by the appointment of non-Chechen fighters to key positions in the resistance movement. In turn, governments in the region, especially in Chechnya and Dagestan, adopted an increasingly Islamic agenda in the early 2010s, in response to the growing Islamization of the local population. These developments contributed to the further alienation of the region from Russia—an estrangement that has been exacerbated by the growth of anti-Caucasian sentiments among various sections of the Russian population. Despite the more inclusive and enlightened efforts conducted by the Kremlin in the past years to address the Islamic challenges posed by the region, the violence continues unabated and the schism between the North Caucaus and Russia seems only to increase.

Islamic revival in the North Caucasus

During various periods of the Soviet era, especially in the late 1920s and during the mid-1950s and 1960s, major efforts were conducted to eradicate the Islamic faith in all Muslim regions of the Soviet Union, including the North Caucasus. Almost all mosques, *madrasahs*, *maktabs*, and other Islamic institutions were closed or destroyed; Muslim clerics were persecuted, killed, or forced to flee abroad; the publication of Islamic literature and periodicals was stopped and religious education was banned.[1] In turn, rapid industrialization and atheist education severely weakened the previous attachments to Islam, especially among urban dwellers. Nevertheless, the more popular or traditional forms of Islam survived, and these Islamic traditions remained an important regulator of Muslim lives in the North Caucasus. At the time of the collapse of the Soviet Union, the knowledge of Islam among the Muslim inhabitants of the North Caucasus was thus rather limited, with the exception of Dagestan, where a religious and scholarly tradition had been preserved. Although the Islamic faith remained a relevant source of identity for Muslims in the Caucasus, knowledge of its main tenets and theological principles remained very superficial, even among religious figures. The absence of a proper system of Islamic education and the isolation of Muslims from their co-religionists abroad had undermined the development of Islam. Instead, a local form of Islam developed, often described as "traditional Islam," which was characterized by an abundance of rites of non-Islamic origin.

The advent of *perestroika* and *glasnost* represented a watershed in relations between the Soviet authorities and the Islamic faith. For the first time since Soviet rule was fully established in Russia, freedom of religion and freedom of conscience were guaranteed in a series of laws that were adopted by the Union of Soviet Socialist Republics (USSR) and in the Russian Republic (RSFSR) Supreme Soviets (or parliaments) in October 1990. The USSR's law "On Freedom of Conscience and on Religious Organizations" (October 9, 1990) guaranteed the right of individuals to profess any kind of religion "individually or in conjunction with others," and to "express and disseminate convictions associated with his/her relationship to religion."[2] Persecution on religious grounds was banned, and the rights of religious organizations were significantly extended and protected by law. Private religious education was allowed, particularly in specialized educational institutions.[3] The RSFSR law "On Freedom of Religion" (October 25, 1990), reiterated many of the principles upheld in the USSR law, and went even further in protecting individual religious rights, by declaring freedom of religion an "inalienable right of the citizens of the RSFSR."[4]

These new laws were not specifically designed to promote Islam in the Soviet Union. They were primarily intended to ensure freedom of worship for the Russian Orthodox Church and its followers. However, they contributed significantly to the thriving of the Islamic faith in the USSR, as pressure on religious activities became relaxed and contacts were established with the rest of the Islamic world. Starting in the late 1980s, all Muslim republics of the North Caucasus, to varying degrees, witnessed the construction of new mosques, the development of Islamic education, and the publication and widespread distribution of Islamic literature. Various Islamic institutions were set up in the North Caucasus in order to teach the Islamic faith to the young—Sunday schools, schools attached to mosques (*primechetskie shkoly*), *maktabs*, *madrasahs*, and Islamic institutes of higher learning. Also, private organizations teaching the Arabic language were established, and foreign Islamic missionaries acquired permission to preach and distribute Islamic literature in the region. Such developments both reflected and contributed to an increased level of religiosity among the population, especially among the young, as a growing number of Muslims started regularly to attend mosques, observe fasting, and perform daily prayers. In the early 1990s, the region experienced a mushrooming of Islamic communities involved in the practice of the Islamic religion. In Dagestan, the most religious of all North Caucasus republics, the number of registered mosques and Muslim communities increased from 27 in 1989 to over 600 by the end of 1991.[5] In Checheno-Ingushetia, over 200 mosques were built under the Chechen Communist Party leader Doku Zavgaev during the last two years of the Soviet rule.[6] By 1999, the number of mosques in Chechnya had doubled to over 400.[7] In Kabardino-Balkaria, Islamic communities emerged in almost every republican settlement during the 1990s.[8] Every community had either a mosque or a house of prayer near the cemetery around which it gathered.[9] In Karachaevo-Cherkessia, the number of officially registered communities more than quadrupled during the 1990s, from 26 in 1989, to 117 in 1999.[10] By the early 2000s, almost all villages and towns inhabited by Muslims had set up a religious Islamic community.[11]

The revival was also accompanied by increased contacts with the broader Muslim world. Through the *hajj*—the religious pilgrimage to the holy places of Mecca and Medina in Saudi Arabia—young Muslims from the Caucasus came in contact with Muslims from the entire world and joined the broader Islamic *umma* (community). Moreover, many young Muslims from the North Caucasus, eager to enhance their knowledge of the Islamic faith, studied Islam in institutes and universities in several Middle Eastern countries. Through these contacts and experiences, they significantly increased their knowledge and understanding of Islam. More importantly, they also became acquainted with nontraditional forms of Islam such as Salafism—an Islamic trend that calls for a return to the Islamic practices of the first generations of Muslims and the purging of foreign influences and doctrinal innovations.[12] The spread of Islam and Salafism in the North Caucasus was also fostered by the various Islamic funds and organizations that opened offices in the North Caucasus, many of which had a clear Salafi or *Wahhabi* leaning, such as *Islamic Relief*, the *International Islamic Salvation Organization*, *Al Haramein*, and the *Islamic Benevolence Foundation*.[13] They contributed to the spread of Salafi Islam, by distributing Islamic literature, financing the construction of mosques and sponsoring Arab Islamic teachers at local Islamic institutions.[14]

It should be noted, however, that Islamic communities, or *jamaats*, adhering to strict Islamic Salafi principles were not new to the region. The first underground Salafi communities appeared in several mountainous villages of Dagestan as early as the 1970s. But in the 1990s, Salafi ideas received further impetus with the various contacts and exchanges that developed with Middle Eastern scholars.

Salafi ideas proved to be particularly appealing to young individuals in the Caucasus, many of whom found themselves at a loss as a result of the collapse of communism and the failure of Western liberal democracy. Salafism was seen as providing an answer to the moral and social crisis that engulfed the region. With its strict moral codes, its egalitarian attitude and its concern for social justice, as well as its ability to transcend

ethnic divides and local cleavages, Salafism was seen as capable of effectively addressing the very many social ills affecting the region.[15] Salafi ideas
also proved attractive to young individuals in the North Caucasus because
they provided an alternative to the more discredited "traditional" forms
of Islam, which were preached by the old Islamic clergy. The older imams
lacked any kind of proper Islamic education, and were therefore incapable
of engaging in any sort of theological debate with the new generation of
young imams emerging in the region. The young imams were much better trained, spoke fluent Arabic, and had often learnt Islam in the Middle
East. They were thus much better able to provide answers to the queries
and concerns of young individuals in the Caucasus, who felt disoriented
after the fall of communism and dismayed at the corruption and crime that
engulfed the region. During the early 1990s, thus, Salafi communities led
by young and well-trained imams emerged in all Muslim republics of the
North Caucasus. They generally embraced a peaceful form of Salafism and
proved eager to operate according to the law, by officially registering their
Islamic communities and conducting their activities in the open. Their leaders focused most of their efforts on educational and proselytizing activities. Their main confrontation was generally not with the government, but
with the official Islamic structures and the old clergy, and in the case of
Dagestan and Chechnya, with Sufi brotherhoods or *tariqats*.

The early 1990s also saw a revival of "traditional" or "folk" Islam in the
North Caucasus, especially among the older generations. Traditional Islam
represented an amalgam of Islamic principles, local customs (*adat*), and
Sufi practices, which had developed over time in the Caucasus ever since
Islam first arrived in the area in the seventh century. It resembled the form
of Islam that predominated, with a few exceptions, in the Caucasus before
the tsarist and Soviet attacks on Islamic culture.[16] Traditional Islam, however, was not a homogenous trend, and instead was characterized by great
diversity. Whereas in the western end of the North Caucasus, the practice
of Islam was heavily influenced by local customs and traditions, mystical Sufism and Sufi rituals predominated toward the eastern end. With the
advent of *perestroika*, Sufi practices were strongly revived in Ingushetia,
Chechnya, and Dagestan, as Sufi *tariqats* or brotherhoods reemerged from
the underground, and succeeded in gaining strong influence among various local Islamic communities.[17] More significantly, Sufis in Dagestan succeeded in co-opting the official Islamic structures, the Spiritual Board of
Muslims, which had been set up by Soviet authorities in the 1940s to manage and control the Islamic faith. In the late 1980s, prominent Dagestani
Sufis were able to evict the older leadership of the Spiritual Board of
Muslims of the Caucasus (DUMSK) headed by Mufti Mahmud Gekkiev,
and had him replaced with a series of younger imams, with close ties to the
Naqshbandiya tariqat. Also, in the early 1990s, Avar *tariqatists* succeeded
in ensuring that the Avar *Naqshbandi* Sheikh Sayid-Afandi Chirkeisky be

named "Supreme Sheikh of Dagestan," a position that gave him significant influence and weight in the political and religious life of the republic. Similar developments also occurred in neighboring Chechnya, where Sufi leaders succeeded in heading the official Islamic structures and exert significant influence over the newly-elected Chechen leadership. The Chechen Spiritual Board of Muslims was headed first by Mahmud Garkaev, a member of the *Naqshbandiya tariqat*, and a supporter of the full respect of Islamic law in the republic, then, in 1995 by Akhmed Kadyrov, a member of the *Qadiriya tariqat*, and a strong opponent of Salafi and Wahhabi Islam in Chechnya.

Despite the increasing relevance of Islam, the Islamic revival in the North Caucasus took place outside the control and monitoring of the secular authorities, with the exception of Chechnya and Ingushetia, whose leaders proved more willing to embrace Islamic practices. In most North Caucasian republics instead, regional leaders and the local *nomemklatura* treated Islam with great suspicion, although in Dagestan, the newly emerging leaders of national movements often utilized Islamic symbols and rhetoric for their own interests. Of particular relevance in this respect, was the figure of Magomed Khachilaev, the leader of the Lak national movement *Kazi-Kumukh*, who established close ties with the Union of Muslims of Russia, an all-Russian religious organization headed by his brother Nadirshakh in the mid- and late 1990s.[18] In addition, some genuine Islamic political parties and movements did emerge in the North Caucasus during the early 1990s, the most influential being the Dagestani branch of *Islamic Renaissance Party* (IRP), which was headed by Akhmed-hadji Akhtaev, and which adopted a moderate Salafi ideology.[19] Akhtaev and his followers were eager to ensure a return to the pure forms of Islam in Dagestan and rid local Islamic practices from *bid'a*, or sinful innovations.[20] They were particularly critical of the veneration of saints and sheikhs as intercessors between believers and *Allah*—a practice that they saw as a deviation from monotheism. They emphasized, however, their adherence to peaceful means of Islamic proselytizing, and recognized the authority of secular organs of power in Dagestan. Akhtaev advocated the gradual re-Islamization of Dagestani society as a precondition for the subsequent re-Islamization of the state, rather than the violent overthrow of the existing secular regime. To this end, he set up the cultural and educational organization "Al-Islamiyya" and helped revive the system of Islamic education in Dagestan, which had been destroyed in the 1920s–1930s.

A more radical Salafi group led by the brothers Bagautdin and Abbas Kebedov, and known as the *Jamaat ul-Islamiiun ad-Dagestaniia*, also emerged in Dagestan in the early 1990s. Bagautdin Kebedov and his followers embraced a more radical form of Salafism, which interpreted the principle of monotheism or *tawhid* in its strictest sense. They were therefore very critical of Sufi practices, which were considered to be a form of polytheism, and therefore incompatible with Islam. In the mid-1990s, they conducted an active ideological struggle against Sufi Sheikhs in Dagestan, which was generally characterised by a verbal propaganda war, but which occasionally also took a violent form. More importantly, Kebedov and his followers deemed the secular government of Dagestan to be *kafir* (god-less) and, therefore illegitimate. Rather than supporting the gradual intro-duction of the *shariah* at state level, they concentrated their efforts on the immediate implementation of *shariah* law at local level. They looked to the Islamic regimes of Sudan and Afghanistan, as models of statehood, as in their view, these systems totally fulfilled the Islamic principles of *tawhid*.

In neighboring Chechnya (Checheno-Ingushetia at the time), a local branch of the more moderate IRP also emerged. Led by Islam Khalimov and Akhmad Mataev, the Chechen IRP was very critical of many Sufi rituals practiced in Chechnya, such as the veneration of Sufi Sheiks and ancestors, and the visiting of their places of worship.[21] However, the influence of the IRP on Chechen Muslims remained rather limited at the time as the party lacked well-trained and charismatic leaders capable of attracting a large number of followers. Moreover, in 1992–3, Salafis had to compete with existing traditional Islamic structures, the *Qadiriya* and *Naqshbandiya* Sufi *tariqats*, which had become very influential in Dzhokhar Dudaev's semi-independent Chechnya. To counteract the growing opposition to his government in 1992–3, Dudaev relied increasingly upon the fealty of tradi-tional Islamic structures to sustain his power—the *Qadiriya* Sufi brother-hoods, the lower clergy and the revived Council of Elders (Mekhk-Kkhel or Mexk-Kxel), all of which called, in varying degrees, for the introduc-tion of Islamic rule in Chechnya. However, Dudaev rejected such calls and instead remained supportive of a secular form of government. Moreover, he embraced a traditional interpretation of Islam, which involved components of *adat* or Chechen customary law, and Islamic principles, as opposed to a Salafi version of Islam.

In neighboring Kabardino-Balkaria, a new generation of young imams with much deeper theological knowledge of Islam than their predecessors emerged in the early 1990s. They were led by Musa Mukozhev, Anzor Astemirov, and Rasul Kudaev. These young imams proved eager to purify the Islamic faith from the traditional Islamic practices observed in the region and were very critical of the older imams because of their lack of religious knowledge and their unconditional support for the authorities.[22] However, Mukozhev and Astemirov were vehemently opposed to the use of force for the sake of spreading the Islamic faith. Instead they supported the peaceful indoctrination of younger generations through education and prayer.[23] They believed that the situation in Kabardino-Balkaria was not yet ripe for the establishment of an Islamic state ruled by the *shariah* law, given the low level of religiosity of the local population.[24] Thus, Mukozhev and Astemirov supported a cooperative relationship with the authorities of

Kabardino-Balkaria and conducted their proselytizing work in the open and in accordance with the law. Because of their appealing message and their peaceful ways, Musa Mukozhev and his comrades gained quite a large following during the mid- and late 1990s, especially among young people in rural areas.

The western North Caucasian republic of Karachaevo-Cherkessia also saw the emergence of Salafi communities during the early 1990s. In this particular case, however, local Salafis were very closely linked to the Karachay national movement, which had emerged in the republic at the time of the collapse of the Soviet Union. Salafis were led by Muhammad Bidzhiev, a Karachay religious scholar who supported the establishment of an Islamic state in the Karachay areas of the republic.[25] In November 1991, as the Soviet Union began to unravel, Bidzhiev set up a new independent Muslim spiritual center in the Karachay-inhabited town of Karachaevsk, and named it the "Karachay Imamate." Although Bidzhiev became very popular among young Karachay Muslims, he never succeeded in creating a well-organized and influential *jamaat* as Mukozhev and Astermirov had done in Kabardino-Balkaria. His actions were instead focused on achieving power in the Karachay areas, rather than on converting a high number of Muslims to "pure" Islam. Unsurprisingly, his projects faced strong opposition from the local authorities and from the traditional Islamic structures in the republic, which saw him as a fierce competitor. Thus, in 1993 the Imamate and Bidzhiev's religious organization *Al-Islamiya* had to be disbanded and he was forced to flee the republic.[26]

The Chechen war and its impact on Islam in the North Caucasus

A major turning point in the development of Islam in the region occurred in 1995, with the outbreak of war in Chechnya. The first Chechen war created a sense of solidarity among Muslims in the Caucasus, and contributed toward the further ideological radicalization of many Salafi *jamaats* in the region. As the republic of Chechnya became increasingly Islamicized, and as the influence of Salafis and Wahhabis grew, the ideas of violent *jihad* began to take hold among many Islamic groups throughout the North Caucasus. The arrival in Chechnya of Wahhabi religious figures, such as Sheikh Ali Fathi al-Shishani, and Arab fighters, such as Ibn al-Khattab, significantly contributed to such developments. A veteran of the Afghan civil war, Fathi set up the first Wahhabi *jamaats* in the republic and became very popular among young fighters. He possessed very good theological knowledge of Islam and proved inspirational to many young Chechens, to whom he spoke in their native language. He talked about the need to live according to *shariah* law and called for the gradual introduction of Islamic principles through education and proselytizing activities. Bagautdin Kebedov, the renowned Dagestani Salafi scholar who escaped to Chechnya in December 1997, also proved to be very influential among the Chechen youth. Kebedov preached a very strict form of Salafi Islam, and called for violent *jihad* in neighbouring Dagestan to overthrow the "infidel" Dagestani government.[27] Arab Mujahaddin fighters, such as al-Khattab, in turn, provided valuable financial, logistic, and military support to the Chechen war effort. Al-Khattab and his Arab companions set up training camps in the mountainous regions of Chechnya, where they taught Wahhabi Islam, and trained Islamic fighters from all over the North Caucasian region.[28] These training camps in Chechnya provided a valuable network of assistance and support, which eventually facilitated the emergence of radical *jamaats* in other North Caucasian republics during the late 1990s.

More significantly, Chechnya became the source of radical Wahhabi ideas calling for military *jihad* in order to establish an Islamic state in the entire North Caucasus.[29] In 1998, Movladi Udugov, a radical Chechen Wahhabi, created the "Islamic Nation" movement with the aim of uniting Chechnya and Dagestan under a single Islamic state. With the support of al-Khattab, he set up the "Congress of Peoples of Ichkeria and Dagestan," under the leadership of Shamil Basaev, to fulfill this aim. The Congress was soon transformed into a military-political organization, whose military wing—the Islamic Peace-making Battalion—was intended to unify Chechnya and Dagestan under Islamic rule through violent means.[30] In order to realize this objective, Khattab and Basaev led an invasion force of approximately 2,000 Chechen and Dagestani Wahhabis into the Botlikh region of Dagestan in August 1999. As noted by Basaev himself, "What is going on in Dagestan is a mighty '*jihad*', a holy war to expel the infidels from an Islamic land, which has been in the Islamic fold for thirteen centuries . . . We are fighting for the proclamation of an Islamic republic and the establishment of a greater Chechen empire in Chechnya, Dagestan and later also Ingushetia."[31] More radical Wahhabis such as Udugov saw the attack as part of a global *jihad* aimed at liberating all Muslim lands. After the invasion, Udugov declared that Dagestanis and Chechens were not only fighting Russians but also world Zionism. The final aim of the war, in his view was the "liberation of Jerusalem."[32] Later on in the war, he expressed his support for the introduction of *shariah* law in Chechnya, and in 2005, he also called for the establishment of an Islamic state in Chechnya, which should function as a territorial basis for the spread of global *jihad* worldwide.[33]

It should be noted however, that at the time, such views did not have widespread support among Muslims in Chechnya, let alone in the rest of the North Caucasus. Chechen President Aslan Maskhadov strongly opposed Khattab's Salafi projects. In 1998, he managed to outlaw Wahhabi practices, with the strong backing of Chechen Sufi *tariqats* and traditional Islamic structures, although his successes proved to be only temporary.[34] In Ingushetia, President Ruslan Aushev succeeded in discouraging most young Muslims from participating in the Chechen *jihadist* fight. Similarly, in Kabardino-Balkaria, Musa Mukozhev and Anzor Astemirov worked arduously to dissuade young Muslims from joining the *jihad* in neighboring Chechnya. Despite these efforts, radical ideas still gained ground among some young Muslims in the region. In the late 1990s, several young men from Kabardino-Balkaria, Karachaevo-Cherkessia, Ingushetia, and Dagestan set off for Chechnya to receive military and ideological training in the camps set up by Wahhabis in the districts of Serzhen-Yurt, Achkhoi-Martan, and Urus-Martan.[35] Moreover, in four mountainous villages of the Dagestani Buinaksky district (Karamakhi, Chabanmakhi, Durangi, and Kadar), local Wahhabis led by Djarulla Radjbaddinov, proclaimed an "Islamic state," and introduced *shariah* law in August 1998. However, these were isolated cases, as Wahhabis in the North Caucasus remained a minority. During 1995–9 the vast majority of Salafi *jamaats* in the North Caucasus, with the exception of Chechnya and some Salafi communities in Dagestan, did not espouse violence.

The Russian government, at federal level, remained passive and reactive in the face of such developments. Although some efforts were conducted to address the growing challenges posed by radical Islamic groups, they proved to be insufficient and ineffective. In October 1997, under pressure from the Orthodox Church and the nationalist majority in the Russian Duma, President Yeltsin approved a bill on "Freedom of Conscience and of Religious Association," which undermined the equality of religions and restricted the freedoms of some religious groups present in Russia.[36] Although the law was primarily aimed at limiting the influence of Western Christian religions, it was also intended to curtail the operation of religious sects and other proselytizing groups, which had arrived in Russia during the 1990s, including those led by Wahhabi and Salafi preachers. However, the law was not properly enforced in the North Caucasus by the Federal Authorities, and thus, it failed effectively to curb the activities of Wahhabi and Salafi groups in the region. After the withdrawal of Russian troops from Chechnya in 1996, the Kremlin's response to the spread of Wahhabi groups in the North Caucasus was characterized by accommodation and compromise. This was best exemplified by the Kremlin's efforts aimed at diffusing the tensions that had developed in the Buinaksky district of Dagestan after the proclamation of an "Islamic state" by local Wahhabis. During his visit to the region in September 1998, Russia's Minister of Internal Affairs Sergei Stepashin allowed local Wahhabis to continue operating as long as their laws did not violate the Russian constitution, and also assured them that no forcible actions would be taken against them, and against any person professing nontraditional forms of Islam in Dagestan.[37] Thus, the Russian government, at federal level, proved unable effectively to address the spread of Wahhabism until large-scale violence broke out once again in Chechnya in the summer of 1999.

Local authorities instead, began a more active campaign of repressions against Salafi *jamaats*, well before the Botlikh invasion of 1999. In Dagestan, the first strong actions by local government against radical Salafis took place in late December 1997, after the attack by al-Khattab and a group of Dagestani Wahhabis on a Russian military detachment deployed in the Dagestani town of Buinaksk. Thereafter, the Center *Kavkaz* belonging to the radical Salafi *Jamaat ul-Islamiuun ad-Dagestaniya* was closed down by the police, and its Chairman, Muhammad-Shafi Dzhangishiev, was arrested. Many members of the *Jamaat* were detained and subjected to beatings and forced interrogations, and the leader of the *Jamaat*, Bagautdin Kebedov, was forced to flee to Chechnya.[38] On December 25, 1997, the Dagestani parliament passed a new law on the "Freedom of Conscience and Religion," which significantly curtailed the activities of Salafi communities, emulating the same law adopted at national level.[39] The law empowered the Spiritual Board of Muslims of Dagestan (DUMD) and the Committee on Religious Affairs to monitor all religious literature in the republic, supervise all religious associations, and determine whether or not they enjoyed the right to the practice their religion.[40]

In Kabardino-Balkaria, the first wave of violent repressions against young Muslims began in the summer of 1998, in response to an attack on the premises of the Ministry of Internal Affairs in the capital city of Nalchik. Thereafter, Interior Ministry troops conducted an extensive search operation, which was characterized by severe brutality and widespread abuses.[41] The cruelty of such operations served only to radicalize local Salafis even further.

Repressions and radicalization of Salafi *Jamaats*

The second Russian military campaign against Chechnya in the autumn of 1999 put a serious brake on Salafi–*jihadist* dreams of creating an Islamic state in the eastern republics of the North Caucasus. Russia crushed the advances of Basaev and Khattab into Dagestan's Botlikh district, bombed the Wahhabi enclaves in the Kadar zone of Dagestan, and used massive force to bring Chechnya back into Russia's fold.[42] Moreover, in all republics of the North Caucasus, a ban on the practice of "Wahhabism" was introduced, which was followed by a campaign of severe repressions against suspected fighters and genuine Salafi followers. As a result, most members of Salafi *jamaats* in the North Caucasus were pushed underground, and many moderate Salafis became increasingly radicalized.[43]

In Dagestan, the authorities began a widespread campaign in August 1999 against all Wahhabi activity in the republic. Wahhabi organizations were outlawed, their offices and property were confiscated, and many Wahhabis were arrested. On December 16, 1999, a law prohibiting Wahhabism and other extremist activities in Dagestan was adopted by the Dagestani parliament. The law proved to be highly flawed, and lent itself to very broad interpretation, since it did not provide any kind of legal content to the concept of Wahhabism, nor did it specify any criteria for the identification of someone as a Wahhabi.[44] This allowed the DUMD, which had been given the authority to define Wahhabism and identify Wahhabis, to open fire at its ideological opponents.[45] Along with the militia, the DUMD took part in searches and expert assessments of religious writings, and thus contributed to the arrest of many Salafi followers. Law enforcement bodies also plunged into persecutions of suspected Wahhabis. The militia was allowed to identify potential extremists by their ideological convictions, their attitudes to Sufism, and their affiliation to different Islamic schools or *madhhabs*. Policemen often planted weapons, ammunition, and drugs on individuals, in order to arrest suspected Wahhabis.[46] Detainees were usually tortured, beaten up, and subjected to other forms of violence in order to obtain confessions.[47] These fabricated confessions, obtained under torture, often formed the basis of accusations and subsequent convictions. The cruelty and arbitrariness of the police and law enforcement structures drew many young men into the hands of the extremists, as those who had been subjected to torture tried to avenge their sufferings. As a result, during 2004–7, the republic was shaken by a significantly high number of terrorist attacks, and targeted killings of police and law enforcement personnel.[48]

Violence and repressions against Islamic Salafi communities also became particularly intense in Kabardino-Balkaria, immediately after the invasion of Dagestan by Chechen and Dagestani Wahhabis. The independent *Islamic Center*, which had been set up by the young Imam Musa Mukhozhev, was closed down, along with all the Islamic schools attached to it.[49] The activities of foreign Islamic funds and organizations were also discontinued, and most foreign missionaries were sent back to their countries of origin.[50] Moreover, a campaign of anti-Wahhabi propaganda was launched in the media and efforts were conducted by the local administrations to distribute information about radical Islamic groups in the republic.[51] Between 2001 and 2002, several *madrasahs* were closed down, including the largest one in the republic, which was named after Adam Dymov, an outstanding Adyg educator of the early twentieth century, and which had been established in 1991 in the city of Baksan.[52]

In the summer of 2003, after a failed attempt to detain Shamil Basaev in the town of Baksan, the authorities in Kabardino-Balkaria began a widespread campaign of repressions against suspected Islamic militants.

Anyone looking somehow religious—a young man with a beard, a young woman wearing a head scarf, regular mosque attendants—fell under suspicion. Those arrested were held in detention for several days, where they were beaten and humiliated.[53] Moreover, several mosques in the capital, Nalchik, and in various rural districts were closed down.[54] In December 2004, after a series of attacks took place against law-enforcement structures, repressions became even more severe. Dozens of young people were arrested arbitrarily at mosques after evening prayers on suspicion of being radical Islamist. The police behaved brutally, punishing innocent people, and thus alienating the population at large. Also, a series of targeted operations against insurgents were conducted by law-enforcement agencies, which often involved substantial material destruction and the killing of innocent civilians caught in the line of fire.[55]

After the attack of October 13, 2005 by a group of about 150 rebel fighters against law enforcement structures and military sites in the capital city of Nalchik, the authorities launched a general crackdown on anyone suspected of Islamic militancy.[56] Many innocent Muslims as well as the families of rebel fighters were targeted, as well as those included in the Federal Security Service (FSB) "Wahhabi" lists. Detainees were severely tortured, and in some instances beaten to death, until they confessed to their crimes or pointed to other suspects.[57] Police brutality and arbitrariness reached astounding proportions, and led to increased tensions between the authorities and religious communities, and encouraged many young Muslims to turn to violence in pursuit of vengeance.[58] Following the Nalchik raid, the new President of Kabardino-Balkaria, Arsen Kanokov, indicated his willingness to put an end to the heavy-handed tactics of his predecessor, indirectly blaming him and his repressive policies for the upsurge of the violence in the republic.[59] However the ability of Kanokov to influence the situation remained quite limited as the counterterrorist policies in the republic were conducted primarily by federal law-enforcement and intelligence agencies. Despite a change at the head of the local Interior Ministry, arbitrary arrests of suspected militants continued unabated.

The Karachay *jamaat* in neighboring Karachaevo-Cherkessia also suffered significant losses in late 1999 when, under the pretext of looking for culprits responsible for the apartment bombings that had taken place in Moscow and Volgodonsk in September 1999, several dozen Salafi *jamaat* members were rounded up and arrested.[60] Moreover, many Salafis were forced underground in the republic after a series of quite effective counterterrorism operations were conducted between 2000 and 2002 against suspected Wahhabis and Islamic militants in the republic.

Much of the violence in the North Caucasus was a legacy of the brutality that epitomized the last two Chechen wars. Military operations during both campaigns were characterized by an excessive and nonselective use of force by the Russian military, as well as by the adoption of guerrilla tactics and indiscriminate terrorist attacks by Chechen rebel fighters. During the first stages of the second war, Federal troops resorted to massive aerial bombardment and shell attacks that caused the deaths of thousands of unprotected civilians. When conducting counterinsurgency operations, the Russian armed forces showed little regard for the loss of the lives of innocent civilians trapped in the line of fire. Russian special forces also resorted to large-scale mop-up operations—usually referred to as "*zachistkas*," which were characterized by significant abuses and massive human rights violations.[61] During these operations, young men were detained arbitrarily and taken to temporary filtration camps, where they were brutally tortured and badly beaten.[62]

At the same time, Chechen rebels, resorted to guerrilla tactics that often involved the killing of a high number of innocent civilians as well as unarmed officials working in the republic's administration. The most notorious attack involved the seizure of a children's school in Beslan, North Ossetia, in September 2004, as a result of which a high number of individuals, including many children, were killed. To counter such attacks, Russian forces started relying increasingly on pro-Russian Chechen forces, led by Ramzan Kadyrov, son of the then President of Chechnya, Akhmed Kadyrov. Kadyrov's troops conducted smaller and clearly-targeted mop-up operations, which although effective, were characterized by substantial brutality. Usually, masked armed men in camouflage broke into people's houses, dragged out suspected individuals and took them to temporary detention centers, where they were subjected to violent tortures, threats, and beatings.[63] In many instances, those detained died as a result of the injuries inflicted upon them when being tortured. In other occasions, they were simply subjected to summary executions. In a lot of cases, though, those detained simply "disappeared," with no record or trace left of their whereabouts.[64] Such atrocities contributed to the emergence of an atmosphere of lawlessness and intimidation in Chechnya, which, in turn, helped to perpetrate the cycle of violence.

Ingushetia proved particularly vulnerable to the spread of violence from neighboring Chechnya because of the high number of Chechen refugees who arrived in the republic right after the outbreak of the war in 1999—estimated at over 300,000 in the autumn of that year.[65] When FSB General Murat Zyazikov became President of Ingushetia in 2002, he ordered tough mop-up operations against presumed rebels hiding in refugee camps and private homes in Ingushetia. Many of these operations followed the same pattern as the sweeps carried out in neighboring Chechnya. They were usually characterized by severe human rights violations—arbitrary arrests, ill-treatment of prisoners, and "disappearances" of suspected militants became the norm.[66] These abuses, and the lack of accountability of the perpetrators, led to an upsurge of violence in the republic. The situation became even more violent when Ingush civilians increasingly became the target of indiscriminate operations. By 2005–6, Ingushetia had turned into one of the most unstable republics in the North Caucasus, with attacks against law enforcement officials, Russian troops, and members of the local administration occurring almost on a daily basis. Although hardly reported in the media, repressions were also conducted against anyone with religious appearances, speaking Arabic, or having studied abroad in Middle Eastern countries.[67]

Such brutal measures and abuses significantly contributed to the further radicalization of Islamic groups in the region, and led to calls for the toppling of local regimes in the Caucasus . In Ingushetia, the radical Islamic "Shura of Ingushetia" appealed in the summer of 2004, "for the liberation of all territories seized by the 'occupiers', including the foothill districts [Prigorodny *raion*], and for the establishment of an Islamic state."[68] Likewise, in Dagestan, the *jamaat* "Shariat" called for violent *jihad* to establish an Islamic state in November 2005:

> For our *Jamaats*, military *jihad* is not an end in itself. *Jihad* is today the only correct way to defend the honor and dignity of Muslims . . . Our purpose— is the establishment of a valid society on the basis of the laws of *Allah*.[69]

The influential Dagestani Islamic scholar Yasin Rasulov, who joined the Islamic rebels in 2006 and became one of leading ideologues, furnished an elaborate justification for the war against law-enforcement structures carried out by young Muslims in Dagestan, in a series of articles printed in the local Dagestani press in the spring of 2004.[70] In his later work *Jihad in the North Caucasus*, published on the internet in 2006, he glorified the resistance movement of Imam Shamil, the religious figure who united Dagestan and Chechnya in their struggle against Russian rule during the nineteenth century Caucasian wars, and called on Islamic movements to emulate his deeds.[71] He built a historical link between current *jihadists* and the resistance movement of Imam Shamil in the nineteenth century, and stressed the proximity of the religious-political ideology of the first Dagestani Imams and the current radical Islamists.[72]

In Kabardino-Balkaria, the fighting *jamaat* "Yarmuk," called in 2005 for armed *jihad* against the "Russian invaders and their puppets," until "*Shariah* law is restored as the law and guidance of life."[73] Moreover, in 2006, Mukozhev and Astemirov, the spiritual leaders of the Kabardino-Balkarian *jamaat*, joined the fight and called on all Muslims in the republic to fight violent *jihad* against the Russian infidels. In Mukozhev's own words:

> What is the position of Muslims who live today in a *kafir* state? There is only one answer, to engage in war against the infidel, leave and wage *jihad*—to fight against the *kafirs* and *munafiqs*. . . . [He who does not wage *jihad*] is a sinner . . .[74]

These views provided an inspiration for many young Muslims ready to turn to violence in the North Caucasus. The indiscriminate attacks and repressive measures perpetrated by the local authorities against suspected terrorist and pious Muslims encouraged many young individuals to utilize violence in order to avenge their own sufferings and the loss of their loved ones. In addition, the perpetuation of corrupt ruling elites, the absence of political pluralism, severe economic hardship, youth unemployment, and high levels of income inequality combined to create a deep sense of frustration and disillusionment among the local Muslim youth, and enhanced the appeal of violent Salafi–*jihadist* ideas.[75] As a result, many young Muslims, including previously peaceful Salafis, started to engage in violent *jihad* against the existing secular regimes. By the mid-2000s, a network of fighting *jamaats* ready to fight for the withdrawal of Russian troops and for the establishment of an Islamic state, ruled by *shariah* law had emerged in all Muslim republics of the North Caucasus—Ingushetia, Chechnya, Dagestan, Kabardino-Balkaria, and Karachaevo-Cherkessia – and in some regions of southern Russia such as in the Neftekumskii raion of Stavropol *krai*.[76]

Continued violence and further radicalization of Salafi *Jamaats*

In the late 2000s, as violence and repressions escalated, fighting *jamaats* in the North Caucasus radicalized even further. They became engaged in a relentless campaign of violence against the local authorities, especially in Ingushetia, Dagestan, but also in Chechnya, Kabardino-Balkaria and Karachaevo-Cherkessia, with the combined aims of toppling the local regimes, forcing the withdrawal of Russian troops from the North Caucasus, and establishing an Islamic state. More significantly, in the late 2000s fighters came closer in their aims and strategies to the global Islamic *jihadist* movement. Most Islamic fighters in the North Caucasus started increasingly to view themselves as members of the broader Islamic global *jihadist* movement and to adhere strictly to the main Salafi principles of *tawhid* (monotheism) and *takfir* (apostasy). As stated by Astemirov himself in 2008, "*Tawhid* (monotheism) is the purpose of our life, we fight for it and are ready to die for it . . . *Allah* sent down the Laws and ordered us how to live accordingly."[77]

A new generation of younger fighters emerged, whose national aspirations slowly gave way to transnational Islamic dreams of participating in the ongoing "global *jihad*." Moreover, the various *jihadist* North Caucasian movements partly lost their ethnic allegiance, and instead, became more pan-Caucasian in terms of their objectives and overall organization. This was amply demonstrated by the declaration of the Caucasian Emirate, by Chechen leader Doku Umarov in November 2007, and by the appointment of non-Chechen fighters to key positions in the resistance movement. In July 2007, Emir Magas (Akhmad Yevloev), an ethnic Ingush, and the leader of the Ingush *jamaat* was appointed by Umarov as top military commander, or military Amir, of the Armed Forces of the Chechen Republic of Ichkeria, a position previously held by Shamil Basaev. In September of that same year, Anzor Astemirov was appointed Chairman of the *Shariah* Court, thus making a Kabardian, the third-ranking official in the resistance movement. When Astemirov was killed by the security forces in March 2010, he was replaced by a Dagestani, Magomed Vagapov (Seifullah Gubdenskii), who at the time was the Amir of the Dagestani *vilayet* of the Caucasian Emirate.[78]

Furthermore, the *jihadists'* websites, such as Kavkazcenter, started making constant references to other *jihads* taking place in the Muslim world—in Afghanistan, Iraq, and Palestine—and regularly reported the views of famous Islamic *jihadist* preachers, such as Sheikh Anvar Al-Awlaki and Sheikh Abu Muhammad Asem al-Maqdisi.[79] More significantly, Islamic preachers were consulted for advice and guidance on issues related to Islam and the development of the Caucasian Emirate.[80] North Caucasian *jihadist* also started to adopt a more explicit anti-Western and anti-Jewish discourse, as shown in several of their speeches and publications, placed on their various websites.[81] Also, *jihadist* fighters began once again in 2010 to conduct indiscriminate terrorist acts against civilians, causing a high number of casualties and replicating a practice usually conducted by *jihadist* closely associated with Al Qaeda.[82] This followed the revival in April 2009 of the *Riyadus-Salikheen Brigade of Martyrs* in Chechnya —a battalion of suicide bombers who became engaged in suicide attacks against government officials and military targets in the republic. More significantly, *jihadist* fighters also started to actively target members of the "traditional" Islamic clergy, Sufi imams, as well as representatives of the official Islamic structures, clearly indicating their determination to fight a religious war against what they considered be religious *apostates,* and allies of the Russian authorities.[83] For example, in September 2011, Zainudin Daiziev, the Imam of a mosque in the village of Kadar was killed by radical *jihadist*, and a month later, in October 2011, Sirazhutdin Khuriksky (Israfilov), the Imam of the large mosque in the city of Derbent was also shot dead by members of radical *jihadist* groups. In addition, highly relevant religious figures and representatives of official Islamic structures were also killed in the late 2000s to early 2010s, such as the Mufti of Kabardino-Balkaria, Anas Pshikhachev, in December 2010, the deputy Mufti of the Spiritual Board of Karachaevo-Cherkessia, Ismail Bostanov, in September 2009, and Sheikh Sayid-Afandi Chirkeisky, the spiritual leader of Dagestani Sufis, in August 2012. Individuals who openly condemned violence and supported the development of Sufi Islam also suffered from fatal attacks, such as Maksud Sadikov, the rector of the Islamic University of Makhachkala, who was shot dead in June 2011.[84] All this clearly indicated that the fight had a strong ideological Salafi-*jihadist* component.

The Russian government responded to this upsurge in violence by continuing with its forceful and often quite brutal counterinsurgency campaign against *jihadist* fighters, with varying degrees of success. On the one hand, several well-known Islamic leaders belonging to the Salafi-*jihadist* movement were killed during the late 2000s to early 2010s, including the well-versed Kabardian Islamic scholar Anzor Astemirov, his Salafi companion Musa Mukozhev, the renowned Buryat Islamic preacher, Sheikh Sayeed Buryatsky, and the young Dagestani Islamic scholar Yasin Rasulov. Also, during this period, several military leaders of the various North Caucasus fighting *jamaats* were either killed—for example, Asker Dzhappuev, the leader of the Kabardino-Balkarian *jamaat*, as well as Magomedali Vagabov and Israpil Validzhanov, both leaders of the Dagestani *Jamaat Shariat*—or captured—such as Emir Magas, the head of the Ingush *jamaat*.[85] However, at the time of writing, many relevant figures continued in their fight, such as Doku Umarov, the leader of the entire Caucasian resistance movement and several Chechen field-commanders such as Hussein Gakaev, Aslambek Vadalov, and Tarkhan Gaziev. Moreover, the *jihadist* movement was able during the late 2000s to early 2010s, to replace quite rapidly those killed with fighters from a younger pool of recruits. Thus, in the early 2010s, *jihadist* violence in the North Caucasus continued unabated, with attacks against high-ranking government officials, military servicemen, local policemen, and religious figures taking place on an almost daily basis.

Official policies of engagement

Aware of the serious challenges posed by the *jihadist* insurgency, and conscious of the need to win the support of the local populations of the North Caucasus, the Russian government decided in 2011 to reinforce its socioeconomic assistance to the region. With the aim of driving unemployment down and restarting economic growth, Prime Minister Vladimir Putin devised in January 2011 a development project for the North Caucasus whereby the Russian government and Russian private companies would together provide USD13 billion worth of investment to the region during the period 2011–25. The specific objective of the program was to provide funding for the development of a series of major projects in the energy, construction, and tourism sectors of the North Caucasus, in order to boost the local economies and create over 400,000 new jobs.[86] The project was received skeptically by the Ministry of Finance and the Ministry of Economic Development and Trade at the time, because of concerns over the country's growing budget deficit, and, as a result, the money has not been forthcoming.

In addition, in order to win the "hearts" of rebel fighters, renewed efforts were conducted in the early 2010s, to demobilize and reintegrate into civilian life those former combatants willing to cease any kind of military activity. To this end, special commissions on demobilization were set up in almost all North Caucasian republics—Dagestan, Ingushetia, Kabardino-Balkaria, Karachaevo-Cherkessia.[87] These initiatives slightly differed from the previous disarmament and demobilization efforts that had been carried out in Chechnya, as early as 2000–3. The Chechen scheme involved a series of amnesties that were awarded to those rebel fighters who proved willing to live peacefully and cooperate with the authorities. Within this framework, hundreds of combatants were brought back from the mountains during the 2000s, and allowed to operate legally in Chechnya. But the process was characterized by serious abuses and missteps. Many of those giving themselves up, instead of being amnestied, were often detained, beaten, and tortured by the authorities in order to obtain further information on the rebel movement.[88] Moreover, little assistance was ever granted to help former fighters readapt to civilian life. Instead, many former rebels were integrated into the official Chechen security structures and thus encouraged to reengage in military activities against the remaining rebel forces.[89]

The new initiatives, which were started in November 2010 in Dagestan, focused instead on reintegrating former fighters into civilian life, by helping them to find jobs, enroll as students, and socially readapt to their new lives. More importantly, the commissions on reintegration were also responsible for assessing whether or not the demobilized fighters were entitled to clemency and reduced sentences.[90] The aim was to reduce the chances of abuse by the judicial or police authorities and to entice rebels to abandon their fight. However, by the time of writing, the results were not very impressive. In 2012, only the Dagestani commission had been able to conduct a genuine rehabilitation program that allowed a number of militants to return to civilian life. But even in the Dagestani case, the figures were not very significant—only a few dozen cases had been considered by the Commission since it had been set up in 2010.[91]

Renewed approach toward Islam

More interestingly, the early 2010s also witnessed a significant change in the government's approaches toward Islam in the Caucasus. On the one hand, efforts were conducted by the Kremlin and the regional authorities to improve Islamic education in the Caucasus, in order to attract young local Muslim students, and dissuade them from travelling abroad to study the Islamic religion. On the other hand, the federal and regional authorities in the Caucasus began to change their uncompromising attitude toward nontraditional forms of Islam, by encouraging a dialogue with moderate, nonviolent Salafi groups, and in this way including them into the official and legal Islamic space.

Embracing moderate Salafi Islam

One of the most significant changes in government policy toward Islam in the early 2010s, was the decision by the authorities to gradually drop the rhetorical division of Islam into two mutually exclusive categories—"traditional" (the loyal Islam as practiced in Russia) and "non-traditional" (Salafi and Wahhabi Islam of a foreign nature). This approach, which dominated official discourse and government policy throughout the 1990s and 2000s, considered the Islamic positions upheld by the Spiritual Boards of Muslims as the only true and acceptable forms of Islam. All other forms were seen as nonadmissible and therefore forbidden. However, the division of Islam in Russia into these two categories proved to be totally inadequate, as Russia's North Caucasus Islamic community was, and still is, extremely numerous and diverse. At the time of writing, it was characterized by a variety of tendencies, directions, and schools of jurisprudence, which could not simply be divided into either "traditional" or "non-traditional" forms. Moreover, clear differences existed within the interpretations of "traditional" Islam itself—for example, in Dagestan, "traditional" Islam was generally equated with Sufism, whereas in Kabardino-Balkaria "traditional Islam" referred to the Hanafi *madhhab* of Islam, and had no relation at all to Sufism. Moreover, such an approach also had negative policy implications as it excluded a significant number of Islamic groups from any kind of religious-state dialogue, and in many instances, it placed Islamic communities outside the law. "Non-traditional" Islamic groups were often denied official registration and were subjected to persecution and repressions, simply on the basis of being considered "non-traditional," as was described above.

The first signs of change were seen in 2008, when Vladimir Putin for the first time made a positive assessment of Wahhabi Islam in the public domain. In an interview with French newspaper *Le Monde*, which was reproduced in the Russian press, he stated that, "Wahhabism in its original form is a normal tendency within Islam and there is nothing terrible in it. But there are extremist tendencies within the framework of Wahhabism [which should be condemned]."[92] These statements opened the door for a change of attitude toward moderate forms of Salafism, and allowed for a distinction between *jihadist* fighters and peaceful Salafis.

In 2010, a significant modification in government policy toward
"non-traditional" forms of Islam was observed. For the first time, the
republican authorities in Dagestan, with the support of the Kremlin,
started gradually to adopt a more inclusive and comprehensive approach
toward Salafi Islam, and to devise ways in which they could bring moderate "non-traditional" Islamic groups back into the legal fold.[93] A
year later, in 2011 a new and open dialogue was initiated in Dagestan
between "traditional" Sufis and "non-traditional" moderate Salafis. The
latter were led by the prominent Salafi scholar Abbas Kebedov, and were
grouped around the organization, Association of Islamic Scholars *Ahl al-
Sunna wa-l-Jamaa*. *Ahl al-Sunna*, represented the views and opinions
of most moderate Salafi groups in Dagestan, and therefore carried significant political weight. Sufis, in turn, headed the DUMD and had the
backing of the republican authorities. The dialogue was also facilitated
by the introduction of a radical change in the Dagestani government's
suppressive policies toward moderate Salafi groups. In 2011, the authorities ordered all repressive actions against peaceful Salafis to cease, and
as a result many Salafis religious groups were able once again to operate
in the open.[94]

All these changes facilitated a major rapprochement among the Sufis and
Salafis, and paved the way for the historical agreement that was reached,
on April 29, 2012, between representatives of the DUMD and members
of *Ahl al-Sunna*. At the meeting, both sides managed to reduce their differences and bring their positions closer together. Salafis and Sufis recognized that they both upheld genuine, albeit distinct, Islamic positions, and
that they both belonged to a single Islamic *umma*, or world community.[95]
They agreed to stop vilifying each other, and to set up a joint body for the
debate of Islamic issues. This new agreement represented a watershed in the
history of Sufis-Salafi relations in Dagestan, and helped to sharply reduce
the level of tension and confrontation between the two groups. However,
the hope that such a dialogue would put an end to violence turned out to
be short-lived. Soon after the agreement was signed, on May 3, 2012, a
major terrorist suicide attack was carried out by Dagestani *jihadists* against
a police station in the capital city of Dagestan, in which 12 people were
killed and over 100 injured. Moreover, on June 28, 2012, the Sufi imam
of the local mosque in the village of Karamakhi, who was known for his
uncompromising opposition to any kind of violence, was shot.[96] More significantly, on August 28, 2012, Sheikh Sayid-Afandi Chirkeisky, the very
influential 74-years-old spiritual leader of Dagestani Sufis was killed in a
suicide bomb attack—an event that shattered the large Sufi community in
Dagestan. These attacks clearly indicated that the *jihadist* wing of Salafis in
Dagestan remained determined to continue its violent struggle against local
Sufis and the Dagestani secular authorities, and persisted in its rejection of
any kind dialogue with its Sufi opponents.

Supporting Islamic education

With the advent of religious freedom in the early 1990s, Islamic religious education was again revived in the North Caucasus, as was described above. But by the early 2010s, the system still suffered from severe shortcomings. First, the North Caucasian republics, with the exception of Dagestan, and to a lesser extent, Chechnya and Ingushetia, had failed to establish a proper system of *lower* Islamic education. Although several Islamic schools, *maktabs* and *madrasahs* emerged in the Muslim republics of the western North Caucasus during the 1990s, many were closed down by the local authorities in the early 2000s in an attempt to curtail the spread of Salafi Islam. Moreover, the local authorities and the Spiritual Boards of Muslims in the western North Caucasus failed to develop a clear and coherent policy on Islamic education and to provide the necessary funding for its advancement.[97] Even within those schools that survived the closures, the standards of education remained quite low, due to the lack of fully-qualified teachers, adequate funding, and relevant textbooks.

Secondly, in those republics where educational systems at the lowest levels (*maktabs* and *madrasahs*) were developed more fully—Dagestan, Chechnya, Ingushetia—the standards still remained quite low in the early 2010s. Teaching was conducted on the basis of outdated material—the text books and specialized publications that were utilized dated from the nineteenth and early twentieth centuries. Moreover, the curricula of Islamic institutions lacked thorough elaboration, teachers were poorly trained, and funding was often lacking. More importantly, independent Islamic education had been severely restricted during the repressions against Salafi groups in the early 2000s, and, by the time of writing, had not been able to recover. Most Islamic education institutions in Dagestan remained under the control and supervision of the DUMD in the late 2000s to early 2010s, and anyone having received an Islamic education in the Arab Middle East, however qualified, found it hard to get a teaching job or a position of imam in a mosque.[98] In addition, the Islamic educational system in the eastern North Caucasus was characterized by a strong Sufi dimension, making it hard for the system to be reproduced in those regions of the North Caucasus where Sufi Islam had not yet flourished.[99] Thus, all those wanting to study Islam thoroughly, but not wishing to receive a Sufi-type of education could not study in Dagestan, Ingushetia, or Chechnya, and instead preferred to go abroad.

Aware that education played such a prominent role in shaping young Muslims' consciousness and religious beliefs, the federal government tried to improve and influence the system of Islamic learning in the North Caucasus. To this end, in 2010 the Federal Authorities decided to create, in collaboration with the various Spiritual Boards of Muslims of the Caucasus, two religious educational centers, reflecting the two *madhhabs* that exist in the North Caucasus—one for the adherents of the Hanafi *madhhab*, at the Islamic University in Nalchik, in the western North Caucasus, and another one for the followers of the Shafii *madhhab*, at the Islamic University in Makhachkala, in the eastern North Caucasus. The main goal of these two institutions was to create a unified system of Islamic education for the training of Islamic scholars, imams, and Islamic teachers, and also to provide high-level Islamic education for young individuals inside Russia, and in this way reduce the number of students wishing go to abroad to study Islam.[100] In the long-run, the overall objective was to turn these two religious centers into the engines of renovation of the Islamic higher education system in the region. Once established, these centers developed partnerships with leading secular Institutions in the North Caucasus, specializing in Oriental and Islamic studies—respectively the Kuban State University in the city of Krasnodar and the Pyatigorsk State Linguistic University in Stavropol *krai*—so as to improve their academic standards.[101] In May 2012, this project was superseded by a decision of Alexander Khloponin, the Kremlin's representative to the North Caucasus, to establish an Islamic University at the secular Stavropol North Caucasus University, which would teach students a variety of aspects of Islam, ranging from Islamic theology, to Islamic jurisprudence, Islamic history, and Islamic literature.[102]

Doubts remained at the time of writing, however, as to whether or not these institutions would be able to develop adequately, and whether or not they would be able to attract local students and reduce the numbers of North Caucasian Muslims studying abroad. Lack of well-trained specialists, and absence of proper state funding remained key problems in 2012, despite government pledges to support Islamic education.[103] Moreover, it remained unclear to what extent secular institutions were better placed than religious ones, to train and teach students to the highest standards in the field of religious Islam. At the time of writing, it was too early to tell whether or not these institutions had succeeded in their objectives, despite the positive intentions of the Federal government.

Growing Islamization of public life in the North Caucasus

Another interesting new trend that could be observed in the sphere of Islam in the North Caucasus in the early 2010s was that of an increase in Islamic rhetoric in the discourse of local politicians and in the speeches of government officials, as well as growing reference to Islamic topics and Islamic debates in the local media. These new trends reflected a concerted effort by politicians and public officials alike to show their allegiance to Islam, in order to gain local people's support, and pull young individuals away from radical Islamic trends. The eastern North Caucasian republics—Dagestan, Chechnya, and Ingushetia—were particularly relevant in this respect, as these republics were characterized by a high level of Islamization and a profound degree of religiosity among their local populations. Within them, Islamic themes became one of most significant components of public discourse and of the republics' socio-political life.

The Chechen Republic led the way in this respect. In the late 2000s to early 2010s, Ramzan Kadyrov, the head of the republic presented himself as a pious Muslim believer, and strongly pushed for the Islamization of the republic's public life and for the promotion of Islamic morals. Prayer rooms were made obligatory in all government buildings and private business offices, and prayers became almost compulsory at work. During the month of Ramadan, a special work schedule was introduced in the republic.[104] Wearing headscarves became mandatory for girls when attending school or work, while men were encouraged to dress in the traditional Chechen manner.[105] Buying alcohol was severely restricted at regular times, and was totally outlawed during the months of Ramadan.[106] A Center for morality and spirituality was created to promote and enforce Islamic moral values, and in particular, to ensure that women dressed and behaved according to very strict Islamic principles—a practice that lead to severe abuses.[107]

On a more spiritual level, Kadyrov showed his strong devotion for Sufi Islam and thus, conducted major efforts aimed at its revival. In particular, he promoted the cult of the nineteenth-century Chechen Sufi preacher Kunta-hadji Kishiyev, one of the most venerated representatives of the *Qadariya tariqat*. To this end, he allowed the grave of Kunta-hadji Kishiyev's mother, located in the mountainous village of Ertan, to become a shrine and a place of worship once again.[108] Kadyrov also personally supported the transfer of two sacred Islamic relics to Chechnya—a chalice allegedly owned by the Prophet Muhammed and two rugs that temporarily covered his grave—and ensured their public display.[109] Hundreds of new mosques were built in Chechnya at Kadyrov's initiative in the second half of the 2000s, including a huge mosque in the center of Grozny, named after Kadyrov's father Akhmed-hadji Kadyrov, and capable of hosting 10,000 worshipers.[110] Kadyrov also strongly promoted the development of "traditional" Islamic education in Chechnya. Besides the 19 *madrasahs* that operated in Chechnya, three schools that prepared young Muslim pupils for the *hafiz* (the memorization of the *Qur'an*) were opened in 2011–12 in the village of Tsentoroi, in the city of Gudermes and in Grozny. In addition, a dedicated Islamic TV channel, *The Way*, regularly transmitted the sermons of well-known Chechen theologians, thus helping to promote local Sufi Islam. Ramzan Kadyrov also backed the opening of a Theology Department within the Kunta-Khadji Kishiev Islamic University, with the aim of teaching students the principles of "traditional" Islam.[111] The main objective of Kadyrov's policies was to discredit the Salafi ideology as a legitimate option in the minds of Chechen young people. But as a result of these practices, the Chechen republic increasingly became a distinct territory in which the principles of the Russian secular state were, in essence, no longer observed.

Dagestan also witnessed the rapid Islamization of the republic's political life and of its social space. In the late 2000s and early 2010s, a growing display of Islamic religiosity could be observed among the republican leadership, starting with the head of the republic, Magomedsalam Magomedov, who decided to regularly attend Friday prayers at the central mosque in the city of Makhachkala. Also, government officials stepped up their references to Islam in public discourses and official engagements. For example, Bekmurza Bekmurzaev, the Minister for Nationalities, presented himself as a devout Muslim, and more specifically as a follower of Dagestani Sufism.

His ministry also regularly sent out congratulations on Muslim holidays and, in particular, wished Muslims in the republic a successful month of Ramadan. Adilgerei Magomedtagirov, the Dagestani Minister of the Interior who was shot dead by a sniper in July 2009, also openly positioned himself as a supporter of Sufism and encouraged the opening of prayer rooms at the Department of Internal Affairs. Moreover, almost every newspaper in Dagestan contained a section devoted to the discussion of Islamic topics—Islamic theology, jurisprudence, and Muslim world affairs. Similarly, regional radio stations and television channels also provided ample air-time to programs of an Islamic nature. These changes clearly indicated a gradual drift of the republics of the eastern North Caucasus away from the officially sanctioned separation of state and religion, and toward a growing Islamization of the region's sociopolitical life—a trend that seriously challenged the unity of the legal space of the Russian Federation.

The impact of Islamic developments in the North Caucasus on Russia: Ultra-nationalism and xenophobia

The upsurge in Salafi-*jihadist* violence in the Russian North Caucasus, the growing Islamization of the region's political life and the increased religiosity of the local Muslim population, all created a significant cultural and political cleavage between the North Caucasus and the rest of Russia. In the late 2000s to early 2010s, the Russian population to a greater extent perceived individuals from the Caucasus as not being truly Russian citizens, but instead as foreigners in terms of the country's national identity. As a result, the membership of North Caucasians to the Russian state and their contribution to the country's identity became increasingly questioned. Although opinion polls for 2011 showed that just 18 percent of Russians favored a separation of the North Caucasus from Russia, only 26 percent supported the use of any means, including military force, to keep the region inside Russia.[112] Resentment over the vast amount of subsidies that had been transferred over the years to Chechnya and the rest of the North Caucasus republics to secure their loyalty led to increased calls for the separation of the region from Russia. In 2011, the nationalist groups *Russian Public Movement* and the *Russian Civic Union* launched a campaign aimed at cutting the region off financially from Russia.[113] Under the slogan "Stop Feeding the Caucasus," they demanded that the Kremlin cease supporting the economies of the region and instead provide help to other deprived regions of Russia also in need of assistance, thus attracting broad support and significant sympathies among many sectors of the Russian population. The anger of many Russians was forged not only by the continued *jihadist* violence in the North Caucasus—and the ensuing bloody terrorist attacks in Moscow—but also by the regional elites' brazenly public displays of wealth.[114]

These trends were reinforced by the growth of ultranationalist and xenophobic sentiments among the Russian population. Whereas during the 1990s ultranationalist sympathies and chauvinistic discourse were predominant only among marginal groups in Russia, they became mainstream during the 2000s. By the mid-2000s, nationalism of an ethnic kind grew in popularity and became legitimized in public politics, official speech, and mass political discourse. Nationalist politicians like Vladimir Zhirinovsky, who was named deputy Chairman of the Russian Duma in December 2003, talked openly about the need to recognize Russians' special place within the Russian Federation, and expressed strongly anti-Caucasian, and especially anti-Chechen sentiments. Nationalist and xenophobic attitudes were primarily caused by a sense of insecurity and national humiliation among the Russian population, which resulted from the traumatic political and economic experiences they endured in early 1990s, when the Soviet Union collapsed.

However, the growth in nationalist and above all xenophobic sentiments against Caucasians can also be attributed to the outbreak of war in Chechnya, first in 1994 and then again in 1999 – a war that was characterized by severe brutality and massive killings also among members of the Russian Armed Forces. Anti-Chechen xenophobia was exacerbated in the late 1990s and early 2000s by a series of hostage-taking incidents, which led to the death of several hundred Russians at the hands of Chechen rebel fighters—Budenovsk in 1995, Kizlyar-Pervomaiskoe in 1996, Moscow in 2002, and the Beslan hostage crisis in 2004. This was compounded by a series of bomb explosions in apartment buildings that took place in Moscow and Volgodonsk in September 1999, and in the Dagestani city of

Kaspiysk in 2002, and which resulted in a high number of civilian casu-alties. Thereafter, negative sentiments against Chechens increased signif-icantly, as these attacks were regularly attributed to Chechen rebels. As a result, Chechens were often assimilated to terrorists and international *jihadists*. Xenophobic feelings against Chechens, however, also resulted from the negative perceptions that organized criminal groups of Chechen origin, which were active in Moscow in the 1990s, had left in the minds of many ordinary Russians.

In the 2000s, these anti-Chechen sentiments were superseded by a growth of negative attitudes toward all individuals of Caucasian origin. Although anti-Caucasian sentiments had been in display since the late Soviet days, they increased in intensity in the late 1990s to early 2000s, in response to violent developments in Chechnya and in reaction to the wave of migra-tions by North Caucasian citizens to other regions of Russia, especially to the southern provinces of Stavropol, Krasondar, and Rostov. Natural attrition among locals coupled with high birth rates among Caucasian individuals changed the demographic picture of these regions. Tensions developed among these communities as once predominantly monoethnic regions became increasingly multiethnic, and no adequate mechanisms to adapt locals and newcomers to the new realities were ever put in place.[115] Caucasians were seen as alien migrants in Russian cities and were blamed, together with immigrants from Central Asia, for the spread of organized crime, the outbreak of terrorist attacks, the resurgence of petty-crime and rape, and the fall in living standards.[116] These negative sentiments were accompanied by the emergence of groups calling for an end to immigra-tion from the Caucasus, the most prominent of which was the *Movement Against Illegal Immigration* headed by the ultranationalist Alexander Belov.

More worryingly, the 2000s witnessed an upsurge of violent attacks by Russian skinheads against individuals of Caucasian and Central Asian nationality—a total of 632 in 2007 and as much as 515 in 2008.[117] Particularly fierce was the racist violence that took place in the town of Kondopoga, in the northwestern republic of Karelia, in September 2006. Following a fight outside a restaurant between a group of Russians and Caucasians that led to the death of two ethnic Russians, riots against Caucasians (primarily Chechens) broke out in town. Chechens were attacked at random, and many of their stores looted and burned. As a result, most Caucasian natives left the town.[118] The police took quite a while to intervene, whereas the local authorities seemed pleased about the "cleansing of their town."[119]

In the early 2010s, "Caucasiophobia," or negative sentiments against all ethnic Caucasians, developed even further, partly due to the fact that many North Caucasians had also been involved in bloody terrorist attacks in sev-eral Russian cities, including the Moscow metro bombing in March 2010.

However, concerns over the high number of migrants from the Caucasus to Russian cities, and more importantly, resentment over the vast amount of financial subsidies to the North Caucasus also played a part in developing negative feelings against Caucasians among right-wing Russian nationalists. These anti-Caucasian sentiments were brought to the fore during the anti-Caucasian pogrom staged by Russian nationalists and football fans in the heart of Moscow on December 11, 2010. The Manezh square pogrom began when a group of several hundred fans of the Spartak soccer club responded violently to the release of all but one of the suspects of the death of a Russian soccer fan, Yegor Sviridov, at the hands of an ethnic Kabardian, Aslan Cherkesov.[120] Chanting slogans like "Russia for Russians" the mob attacked anyone who resembled North Caucasians. Beating, stabbings, and shootings of darker-skinned people who appeared to come from North Caucasus took place.[121] More worryingly, the police were slow to intervene, and failed to put an immediate stop to the violence.[122]

The December 2010 violence proved to be particularly acute. It brought to the fore the growing sense of alienation of Russians from the North Caucasus and the increased sense of insecurity felt by individuals of North Caucasian origin in Russian cities. More importantly, the reaction of several Russian politicians, including that of Vladimir Zhirinovsky, who stated at a Russian TV program in January 2011, that North Caucasians did not want to work and honestly earn their own living, but instead preferred to live at the expense of the ethnic Russians, and that they abused Russian laws and the ethnic Russian people, caused a major uproar among individuals and governments in the North Caucasus.[123] It was perceived as a direct act of hostility against North Caucasian peoples and reinforced the sense of separation from Russia felt by individuals in the region.[124]

Conclusion

This chapter has shown how Islam and Islamic radicalism have evolved over the past 20 years in the Russian North Caucasus, and how the upsurge in Islamic-*jihadist* violence has resulted, to a great extent, from the Kremlin's and the local governments' repressive policies against all forms of "non-traditional"—in particular Salafi—Islam in the region. In turn, the chapter has revealed how terrorist violence in the region, and the ongoing military engagement by Federal troops against the *jihadist* insurgency, have affected nationalist feelings in Russia, resulting in a rise in extremism and anti-Caucasian xenophobia among right-wing sectors of the Russian population. In this way, this chapter has underscored the mutual interaction and reciprocal influence of Islamic violence in the North Caucasus and developments in Russia as a whole.

Although in the early 2010s, the Russian government undertook a series of bold initiatives to address the existing Islamic challenges—it recognized the legitimacy of peaceful forms of Salafi Islam and opened a dialogue with moderate Salafi groups—the results so far have not been very satisfactory. This can partly be explained by the fact that the underlying drivers of violence in the North Caucasus have remained unchanged. The perpetration of corrupt and discredited ruling elites in the region, the persistence of severe economic hardship, youth unemployment, and high income inequality, coupled with the absence of effective mechanism of political expression, all continue to create a strong sense of frustration and dissatisfaction among the local population. As a result, many young individuals are constantly being pushed to join radical Islamic-*jihadist* groups, calling for the toppling of the existing regimes, the withdrawal of Russian troops from the region, and the introduction of Islamic rule. In the absence of any legal, peaceful alternative, violence is seen by some young Muslims as the only option left available in order to modify the existing sociopolitical circumstances.

In the late 2000s to early 2010s, Islamic fighters radicalized even further, and came closer in their aims and tactics to the global *jihadist* movement, thus reducing the chances of a peaceful outcome to the fight. This further radicalization has been not only a consequence of the brutal repressive policies carried out by the local and federal authorities but also a result of the influence of Arab preachers such as Seif Islam, and local Salafi-*jihadist* ideologues, such as Yasin Rasulov and Anzor Astemirov, on North Caucasian Muslims. Both Rasulov and Astemirov advocated peaceful forms of Salafi Islam in the early 2000s, but in the mid-2000s they became increasingly supportive of violent *jihad*, appalled by the harsh repressions conducted by the security structures against peaceful Salafis. Horrified by the authorities' abuses, they joined the rebel *jihadist* movement and provided fighters with strong religious arguments that justified their violent acts. As noted by Astermirov himself, "Every Mujahideen must know what he is fighting for . . . [he is fighting] for the sake of *Allah*, in order to elevate His word above everything else . . . saving the Faith is more important than saving one's own life, and the lives of one's loved ones."[125]

The process of Islamization of the entire North Caucasus rebel movement, however, began already in the late 1990s with the outbreak of the second war in Chechnya and the emergence of fighting *jamaats* in the other Muslim republics of the region. It received special impetus in 2005, when Sheikh Abdul-Khalim Sadulaev became leader of the Chechen rebel movement. Under his leadership, the rebel's "Ichkerian" constitution was brought further into line with Islamic law, Islamic institutions were established to run the "Chechen Republic of Ichkeria," and, more significantly, all Islamic fighting *jamaats* in the North Caucasus were organized into Caucasian Fronts, which swore allegiance to Sadulaev. As a result, the rebel movement took an increasingly Islamic and North Caucasian dimension.

The unification of the North Caucasian rebel movement around the Islamic Salafi ideology proved to be particularly appealing to rebel fighters. With its egalitarian and universalist approach, Salafi-*jihadism* allowed North Caucasian *jamaats* to overcome existing ethnic divisions and unite under a single banner—Islam—a religion with a strong tradition in the region. Moreover, through Islam, a connection could be established with the previous North Caucasian wars of the eighteenth and nineteenth centuries against the Russian Empire, which had been portrayed by local fighters as "holy wars" or *gazawat*. Many contemporary *jihadists*, such as Yasin Rasulov, tried to establish a direct line of continuity between the current *jihad* taking place in the North Caucasus and the Caucasian wars of the nineteenth century, arguing they were all inspired by the same Salafi-*jihadist* ideology. Although Salafi trends existed in the North Caucasus well before the end of the Soviet Union their impact on current fighters remains harder to discern. While there is little doubt that the nineteenth century *gazawat* plays a key inspirational role among North Caucasian fighters, its Salafi component is more difficult to ascertain. On the other hand, the influence of foreign Salafi-*jihadist* ideologies on young fighters and Islamic preachers is hard to dispute. Through the works of radical Islamic ideologues, the presence of Arab fighters, travels to Muslim countries, and contacts with Salafi figures in the Arab world, radical Salafi ideologies have reached this seemingly remote, but turbulent, Muslim region, inspiring many individuals to fight.

More recently, electronic sources, such as radical Islamic internet sites, *jihadist* videotapes, and mobile phone messages, have also become important conveyers of radical Salafi views and ideas to the region. Significantly, a new generation of younger fighters, with no memories or ties to the old Soviet regime, has joined the fight in the North Caucasus. These young Muslims are not well-versed in "traditional" forms of Islam. For them, Salafi Islam represents a new and very appealing ideology. Not only does it emphasize social justice and equality, it also allows young Muslims to break with existing traditions, domineering clan structures, and deeply ingrained social hierarchies. Although the North Caucasian *jamaats* are neither closely connected to Al Qaeda, nor financially or logistically dependent on Osama Bin Laden's network, they share a similar radical Salafi-*jihadist* ideology, making it hard for them to reach any sort of compromise to bring the violence to an end.

In addition, the North Caucasus leaderships and the North Caucasus populations as a whole are becoming increasingly Islamicized. Not only do people in the Muslim republics of the North Caucasus feel strongly attached to the Islamic religion (polls in Dagestan show that about 80 percent of the population consider themselves religious),[126] Islam is increasingly penetrating many relevant sectors of public life in the North Caucasus—from education to legislation, the media and public discourse—, and this is especially so in Dagestan and Chechnya. As a result, the North region is becoming increasingly distinct from Russia, a phenomena that is compounded by the growth of anti-Caucasian feelings among ethnic Russian populations in other parts of Russia. Paradoxically, recent efforts by the Kremlin to accommodate Islamic developments in the North Caucasus, while they may be helping to reduce the violence, are actually increasing the cleavages between the North Caucasus region and the rest of Russia.

Notes

1 Galina Yemelianova, *Russia and Islam: A Historical Survey* (New York: Palgrave, 2002), 114.
2 "O svobode sovesti i religioznykh organizatsiyakh," *Pravda*, October 9, 1990, 2.
3 Ibid.
4 "O svobode veroispovedaniya," Vedomosti RSFSR, issue no.21, in Harold Berman, "Religious Rights in Russia at a time of tumultuous Transition: A Historical Theory," in *Religious Human Rights in Global Perspective: Legal Perspective*, vol. 2, eds. Johan D. Van der Vyver and John Witte, Jr., (The Hague, Boston, London: Martinus Nijhoff Publishers, 1996), 296.
5 Vladimir Bobrovnikov, Amir Navruzov, Shamil Shikhliev, "Islamic Education in Soviet and post-Soviet Daghestan," in *Islamic Education in the Soviet Union and its Successor States*, eds. Michael Kemper, Raoul Motika, Stefan Reichmuth, Kemper 140, 143 (London: Routledge, 2010).
6 Igor Dobaev, *Islam v sovremennykh respublikakh Severnogo Kavkaza*, (Rostov na-Donu: Tsentr Sistemnykh regionalnkykh issledovanii i prognozirovaniya, RAN, 2002), 81.
7 Mairbek Vatchagaev, "The Kremlin's War on Islamic Education in the North Caucasus," *North Caucasus Analysis*, 7(34) (September 8, 2006), available at www.jamestown.org/single/?no_cache=1&tx_ttnews%5Btt_news%5D=3334
8 Irina Babich, "Sovremennoe islamskoe dvizhenie v Kabardino-Balkarii," in *Islamskoe vozrozhdenie v sovremennoi Kabardino-Balkarii: perspektivy i posledstviya*, ed. Irina Babich and Akhmet Yarlykapov (Moscow: RUDN, 2003), 68.
9 Domitilla Sagramoso and Galina Yemelianova, "Islam and Ethno-Nationalism in the North Western Caucasus," in *Islamic Radicalisation in the Post-Soviet Space*, ed. Galina Yemelianova (London & New York: Routledge, 2010), 122.
10 Evgeny Kratov and Natalya Kratova, *Islam v Karachaevo-Cherkesskoi Respublike* (Moscow: Logos, 2008), 41.
11 Sagramoso and Yemelianova, "Islam and Ethno-Nationalism," 131
12 Salafis view the first three generations of Muslims, Prophet Muhammed's companions, and the two succeeding generations after them, as examples of how Islam should be practiced. They idealize an uncorrupted, pure religious community, and believe that Islam's decline after the early generations is a result of foreign innovations (*bid'ah*). They call for the purification of the Islamic religion by strictly following the principles of the *Qur'an* and the *Sunnah* (the traditions of the Prophet Muhammed).

13 Brian Glyn Williams "Al Qaeda, Transnational Jihadis, and the Chechen Resistance: Assessing the Role of Chechnya in the War on Terror" (Paper Presented at the CESS Conference, Harvard: Harvard University, October 2003), 12. Salafism has often been used interchangeably with "Wahhabism," also in a derogatory way, especially in Russia. Wahhabism, named after its leader Muhammad Ibn 'Abd al-Wahhab is a form of fundamentalist Salafi Islam, which also calls for a return to the pure, unadulterated Islam of the period of the Prophet. It is based on the most strict and rigid Hanbali *madhhab* (school) of Sunni Islam, and was the religious ideology of the political unification of Saudi Arabia. In this essay, the term Wahhabism and Salafism will be used interchangeably.

14 Dmitry Makarov, *Ofitsial'nyi i neofitsial'niyi Islam v Dagestane* (Moscow: Tsentr strategicheskikh i politicheskikh issledovanii, 2000), 48.

15 Ibid., 38.

16 Ruslan Kurbanov, "'Urban' and 'Rural' Islam in the Caucasus: Modernisation versus Conservation," *Religion, State and Society*, 39(2/3) (June/September 2011): 349. Traditional Islam, however, is not a homogenous trend, and instead is characterized by great diversity. Whereas the practice of Islam is heavily influenced by local customs toward the western end of the North Caucasus, Sufism predominates toward the eastern end.

17 In Chechnya and Ingushetia, most individuals belong to the *wird* of the Qadiri sheikh Khunta-hadji Kishiev, whereas in Dagestan, the majority adhere either to the *Khalidiyya-Mahmudiyya* branch of the *Naqshbandiya tariqat* or to the *Naqshbandiya-Khalidiya* branch of the *Naqshbandiya tariqat*.

18 Galina Yemelianova, *Russia and Islam: A Historical Survey* (New York: Palgrave, 2002), 140.

19 The all-Union IRP, which was formed in June 1990 in Astrakhan, emphasized its peaceful character and advocated the gradual re-Islamicization of historically Muslim regions of the USSR.

20 Makarov, *Ofitsial'nyi i neofitsial'niyi Islam*, 25.

21 Vahit Akaev, "Religiozno-prosvetitel'skaya rol' gazety 'Zori Islama,' Yuzhnorossiiskoe obozrenie," available at http://ippk.edu.mhost.ru/elibrary/elibrary/uro/v1/a1_17.htm. Accessed July 23, 2009.

22 Irina Babich, "Sovremennoe islamskoe dvizhenie," 84.

23 Sagramoso and Yemelianova, "Islam and Ethno-Nationalism," 124

24 Akhmet Yarlykapov, "Novoe islamskoe dvizhenie na Severnom Kavkaze: vzglyad etnografa," in *Rasy i narody: sovremennye etnicheskie i rasovye problemy* (Moscow: Nauka, 2006), 210.

25 R. Temirbulatov, "Vashe vremya proshlo," *Islam-Niuriu*, July 2004, 4.

26 Kratov and Kratova, *Islam v Karachaevo-Cherkesskoi Respublike*, 30.

27 Makarov, *Ofitsial'nyi i neofitsial'niyi Islam*, 25.

28 Galina Yemeliyanova, "Kinship, Ethnicity and Religion in Post-communist Societies: Russia's Autonomous Republic of Kabardino-Balkariya," *Ethnicities*, 5(1) (March 2005): 68.

29 Brian Glyn Williams, "Jihad and Ethnicity in Post-communist Eurasia: On the Trail of Transnational Islamic Holy Warriors in Kashmir, Afghanistan, Central Asia, Chechnya and Kosovo," *The Global Review of Ethnopolitics*, 2(3–4) (March–June 2003): 20.

30 Makarov, *Ofitsial'nyi i neofitsial'niyi Islam*, 49.
31 *Al-Aman*, September 17, 1999.
32 Video cassette Jihad-3, quoted by Igor Rotar, "Under the Green Banner: Islamic Radicals in Russia and the Former Soviet Union," *Religion, State and Society*, 30(2) (2002): 110.
33 "Razmyshleniya modzhakheda," KavkazCenter, August 11, 2005, www. kavkazcenter.com/russ/analitik/reflections_of_mujahid/. Accessed August 30, 2012.
34 Vahit Akaev, *Sufizm i Wakhkhabizm na Severnom Kavkaze*, Issledovaniya po prikladnoi i neotlozhnoi etnologii (Moscow: Rossiiskaya Akademiya Nauk, 1999), 12–15.
35 Yemelianova, *Russia and Islam*, 68.
36 Rossiiskaya Federatsiya, "Federal'nyi Zakon o Svobode Sovesti i o Religioznykh ob'edineniyakh," September 26, 1997, available at http://base. consultant.ru/cons/cgi/online.cgi?req=doc;base=LAW;n=61456; see also Alexander Verkhovsky, "Russian Approaches to Radicalism and 'Extremism' as Applied to Nationalism and Religion," in *Russia and Islam: State, Society and Radicalism*, ed. Roland Dannreuther and Luke March (New York: Routledge, 2010), 33.
37 Ilya Maksakov, "Moskva nedootsenivaet ugrozhaiushchee razvitie sobytii v Dagestane,. *Nezavisimoe voennoe obozrenie,*, September 4, 1998, 2.
38 Makarov, "Ofitsial'nyi i neofitsial'niyi Islam," 42.
39 Vladimir Bobrovnikov and Akhmet Yarlykapov, "Wakhkhabity" Severnogo Kavkaza, in *Islam na territorii byvshey Rossiiskoyu imperii* (Moscow: Vostochnaya Literatura, 1999), 22.
40 Moshe Gammer, "Walking the Tightrope between Nationalism(s) and Islam(s): The Case of Daghestan," *Central Asian Survey*, 21(2) (2002): 139.
41 Police intruded into several mosques, detained and beat parishioners, and spit and swore inside the premises. It caused an uproar among Islamic communities, but did not lead to outright violence.
42 "Gornye voiny, Epizod II," *Kommersant*, August 31, 1999, 1, 3.
43 Domitilla Sagramoso, "Violence and Conflict in the Russian North Caucasus," *International Affairs*, 83(4) (July 2007): 681–705.
44 Akhmet Yarlykapov, *Problema vakhkhabisma na Severnom Kavkaze* (Moscow: Rossiiskaya Akademiya Nauk, Institut Etnologii i Antropologii, 2000), 5.
45 Ruslan Kurbanov, "Interaction between Power and Religion in Daghestan: Experience, Errors and Lessons," *Central Asia and the Caucasus*, 33(3) (2005): 79–80.
46 Nabi Abdullaev, "A Murderous Cycle of Revenge in Dagestan," *Moscow Times*, March 15, 2005, 1.
47 Nabi Abdullaev, "Bad Investigators Will Surely Find Us All Guilty," *Moscow Times*, July 4, 2001, 11.
48 Abdullaev, "A Murderous Cycle of Revenge," 1.
49 Yarlykapov, "Novoe islamskoe dvizhenie," 218.
50 Yemelianova, "Kinship, Ethnicity and Religion," 68.
51 Milrad Fatullayev, *Nezavisimaya gazeta*, February 2, 2005, 2; Babich, "Sovremennoe islamskoe dvizhenie," 109–10.
52 Babich, "Sovremennoe islamskoe dvizhenie," 98.

53 Memorial, "Conflict Spill-Over Outside the Chechen Republic in 2004–2005, Ingushetia and Kabardino-Balkariya," March 2, 2006, available at www.memo.ru/hr/hotpoints/caucas1/msg/2006/03/m53212.htm
54 Milrad Fatullayev, *Nezavisimaya gazeta*, October 14, 2003, 3.
55 Nikolai Critchin and Yuri Spirin, *Izvestia*, January 28, 2005, 1.
56 Tatyana Gritsneko, *Vremya Novostei*, October 14, 2005, 1. For claims of responsibility see Kavkaz Center, "Units of the Caucasus Front Enter Nalchik," October 13, 2005, available at http://old.kavkazcenter.com/eng/content/2005/10/13/4146.shtml
57 "V Nal'chike 'zachistili' deputata 'Edinoi Rossii,'" *Gazeta*, October 26, 2005, 1.
58 Jean-Christophe Peuch, "Nalchik Raids Trigger new Wave of Harassment Against Muslims," *RFE/RL News and Analysis*, November 4, 2005, available at www.rferl.org/featuresarticle/2005/11/b35c88ff-8aa8–499c-b210–610dedc50c0f.html
59 "Peregib byl sovershen pravookhrannitel'nymi organami," *Kommersant*, October 17, 2005, 2.
60 Mairbek Vatchagaev, "Karachay jamaat: Counter-measures, Connections and Composition, Part 2," *North Caucasus Weekly*, June 7, 2007, available at www.jamestown.org/single/?no_cache=1&tx_ttnews%5Btt_news%5D=4218
61 For details see *Human Rights Watch, Swept Under: Torture, Forced Disappearances, and Extra-judicial Killings during Sweep Operations in Chechnya*, 14(2) (February 2002): 13–18 and 26–41.
62 Memorial and Demos, *Counter-terrorism Operations by the Russian Federation in the Northern Caucasus throughout 1999–2006* (MoscowMemorial Human Rights Center,: 2006), 12, available at www.memo.ru/hr/hotpoints/N-Caucas/dkeng.htm
63 For details of cases see Memorial and Demos, *In a Climate of Fear: "Political Process" and Parliamentary Elections in Chechnya* (Moscow: Zven'ya, November 2006), 57–65; Human rights Watch, *Widespread Torture in the Chechen Republic*, November 13, 2006; Memorial and FDIH, *Pytki v Chechne: "stabilisatsiya" koshmar*a (Moscow Memorial Human Rights Center: November 2006).
64 For details of individual cases see *Worse Than a War: "Dissapearences" in Chechnya—A Crime Against Humanity*, Human Rights Briefing Paper, March 2005; Memorial and Demos, *In a Climate of Fear*, 73–81.
65 Itar-tass world service, June 17, 2003, citing Ingush Prime Minister Timur Mogushkov, June 17, 2003. Not all of the refugees stayed in Ingushetia permanently. After a few months, some returned to Chechnya and many moved elsewhere inside Russia.
66 Memorial, *A Conveyer of Violence: Human Rights Violations During Anti-terrorist Operations in the Republic of Ingushetia* (Moscow: Zven'ya, 2006), 9.
67 Personal interviews of the authors with local NGOs, Nazran, Ingushetia, June 2007.
68 "Boeviki Ingushetii ob'yavili dzhikhad po vsei respublike," July 8, 2004, available at www.newsru.com/arch/russia/08jul2004/djihad.html

69   "Jamaats 'Shariat': Our Purpose—Establishment of the Validity," KavkazCenter, November 7, 2005, available at www.kavkazcenter.com/eng/content/2005/11/07/4201.shtml

70   Yasin Rasulov, "Pochemu ubivaiut militsionerov v Dagestane?" *Chernovik*, April 16, 2004, available at www.chernovik.net/news/44/POLITICS/2005/01/04/3586

71   Yasin Rasulov, "Dzhikhad na Severnom Kavkaze," KavkazCenter, 2006, available at www.kavkazcenter.com/russ/islam/jihad_in_ncaucasus/PDF_version.pdf

72   Ibid.

73   "The Doors of Jihad are Open," KavkazCenter, January 21, 2005, available at www.kavkazcenter.com/eng/content/2005/01/21/3461.shtml. Accessed June 12, 2012. See also "Kabardino-Balkarian Jamaat declares jihad," KavkazCenter, August 24, 2004, available at www.kavkazcenter.com/eng/content/2004/08/24/3136.shtml. Yarmuk was a splinter group of the Kabardino-Balkarian jamaat, and was led by Muslim Atayev.

74   "Musa Mukozhev," KavkazCenter, November 8, 2006, available at http://old.kavkazcenter.com/eng/content/2006/11/08/6318.shtml

75   For details see, Sagramoso, "Violence and Conflict," 681–705.

76   Domitilla Sagramoso, "The Radicalization of Salafi *Jamaats* in the North Caucasus: Moving closer to the Global *Jihadist* Movement?," *Europe-Asia Studies*, 64(3) (2012): 561–95.

77   "Amir Seifulla: o protsesse podgotovki k provozglasheniu Kavkazkogo Emirata," KavkazCenter, November 20, 2007, available at www.kavkazcenter.com/russ/content/2007/11/20/54479.shtml

78   When Seifullah Gudbesnkii was killed in August 2010, he was again replaced by a Dagestani, Ali Abu Muhammad al-Dagestani.

79   See http://kavkazcenter.com/eng/content/2009/11/13/11180.shtml. Accessed February 10, 2012.

80   For example, Sheikh al-Maqdisi was asked for his legal opinion regarding the dispute over the leadership of the Caucasian Emirate that erupted in the summer of 2010. See "Fatwa of Sheikh Abu Muhammad al-Maqdisi about discord in Caucasus Emirate," September 2010, available at http://al-qimmah.net/showthread.php?t=20209&langid=1

81   See, for example, the work by the Caucasian Emirate Qadi, Ali Abu Muhammad, Кадий ИК Абу Мухаммад: Оправдание по невежеству, и крайности, в которые попали две группы, September 19, 2011, available at http://vdagestan.com/kadij-ik-abu-muxammad-opravdanie-po-ne.htm. In the text, there are several negative references to Jews and Christinas as *kafirs*.

82   A suicide attack took place in the Moscow metro station in March 2010, which left 40 people dead and over 100 injured. In January 2011, an explosion occurred at the Moscow Domodedovo airport, which killed 37 people and injured about 170. Terrorist attacks also occurred in the North Caucasus.

83   "V Dagestane ubit Said Chirkeisky, lider dagestanskikh sektantov," KavkazCenter, August 28, 2012, available at www.kavkazcenter.com/russ/content/2012/08/28/92739.shtml. Accessed August 31, 2012.

84   Andrew Kramer, "Rector at Muslim University in Russia Is Shot to Death," *New York Times*, June 7, 2011, 3.

85 For example, Emir Magas, the head of the Ingush *jamaat*, Asker Dzhappuev, the leader of the Kabardino-Balkarian jamaat, Magomedali Vagabov (Emir Seiffulah) and Israpil Validzhanov (Emir Hassan), both leaders of the Dagestani Jamaat Shariat, were killed.

86 Tai Adelaja, "A prisoner of the Caucasus," *Russia Profile*, January 26, 2012, available at http://russiaprofile.org/business/53317/print_edition/

87 The first "Commission Responsible for Dealing with those Individuals who have Decided to Cease all Kinds of Terrorist and Extremist Activities and are ready to return to a Civilian Life" was set up in Dagestan on November 2, 2010, under the leadership of the Dagestani President, Magomedsalam Magomedov. Demobilization and reintegration committees were also established in several municipalities of Dagestan. Similar commissions were also established in Ingushetia (September 2011), in Kabardino-Balkaria (January 24, 2012), and in Karachaevo-Cherkessia (March 2012).

88 Natalya Estemirova, "Chechnya: Amnesty Fails to Inspire," IWPR, February 21, 2005, available at http://iwpr.net/report-news/chechnya-amnesty-fails-inspire

89 Many of these former fighters were not trusted by the Chechen authorities as many continued to provide information to the rebels and often refused to fight their former comrades-in-arms (Octavian Manea and Robert W. Schaefer, "The Russian COIN campaign in the North Caucasus," *Small Wars Journal* website, June 28, 2012, available at http://smallwarsjournal.com/jrnl/art/the-russian-coin-campaign-in-north-caucasus).

90 Tom Parfitt, "Jihadist Rehabilitation in the North Caucasus," May 25, 2011, available at http://pulitzercenter.org/articles/makhachkala-dagestan-muslim-boyeviki-insurgency-jihad

91 "Vice Premier Dagestan oversaw the adaptation of former fighters to civilian life, goes to the State Duma," December 12, 2011, available at www.bakutoday.net/vice-premier-dagestan-oversaw-the-adaptation-of-former-fighters-to-civilian-life-goes-to-the-state-duma.html

92 "Kadyrov ne soglasen s Putinym," Islamnews.ru, available at www.islamnews.ru/news-14133.html

93 Konstantin Kazenin, "'Islamskoe primirenie' i budushcheie Dagestana," *Regnum*, July 6, 2012. www.regnum.ru/news/polit/1548709.html

94 Salafi mosques opened in several Dagestani towns (Shamkhal, Gubden, and Bynaksk), Salafi businessmen were able to operate legally, and Salafi prayer groups started to worship freely (Akhmet Yarlykapov, "Respublika Dagestan: stabil'naya nestabil'nost," in *Severnyi Kavkaz: vzglyad iznutri: Vyzovy i problem sotsial'no-politicheskogo razvitiya*, ed. Anna Matveeva, (Moscow: Saferworld and Institut Vostokovedeniya RAN, March 2012), 146).

95 "Rezolutsiya sovmestnoi vstrechi Assotsiatsii uchenykh Akhliu-Sunna v Dagestane i Dukhovnogo Upravleniya Musulman Dagestana," www.mirislama.com, May 1, 2012, available at www.mirislama.com/news/435-rezolyuciya-sovmestnoy-vstrechi-associacii-uchenyh-ahlyu-sunna-v-dagestane-i-duhovnogo-upravleniya-musulman-dagestana.html

96 "Imam, killed in Dagestan, was known for negating militants' ideas," *Kavkazskii uzel*, June 29, 2012, available at www.eng.kavkaz-uzel.ru/articles/21437/?print=true

97 Babich, "Sovremennoe islamskoe dvizhenie," 91.
98 Geraldine Fagan, "Russia: Dagestan's Controls on Islamic Education," *Forum 18 News Service*. June 2, 2010, available at www.forum18.org/Archive. php?article_id=1453
99 Curricula and teaching methods reflected the Sufi current of Islam, and were based on the works of prominent Sufi scholars of the North Caucasus. See Andrew Kramer, "Rector at Muslim University in Russia Is Shot to Death," *New York Times*, June 7, 2011, 3.
100 Anna Nemtsova, "Kremlin in the Caucasus: Pushing for a moderate Islam," *Russia Beyond the Headlines*, August 25, 2010, available at http://rbth.ru/ articles/2010/08/25/kremlin_in_the_caucasus_pushing_for_a_moderate_is-lam04898.html
101 The secular institutions were expected to help the Islamic centers review their teaching curricula, modernize their textbooks and manuals, and introduce secular topics. These ties were also expected to provide the necessary funding for the modernization of Islamic education, given that religious education in Russia was not entitled to receive direct state funding.
102 "Nam neobkhodim svetskii islamskii universitet—A. Khloponin," *Islam v Evrazii*, May 30, 2012, available at http://islamvevrazii.ru/newsru541.php
103 "Medvedev o bor'be s terrorismom: vazhen dialog s islamskim dukhov-enstvom," Vesti.ru, July 18, 2011, available at www.vesti.ru/doc. html?id=512328
104 Mairbek Vatchagaev, "Moscow Is Trying to Outsmart the Salafis in Chech-nya," North Caucasus Analysis, May 10, 2012, available at www.jamestown. org/single/?no_cache=1&tx_ttnews%5Btt_news%5D=39356
105 Tanya Lokshina, "Chechnya: Choked by Headscarves," *Open Democ-racy*, September 27, 2010, available at www.hrw.org/news/2010/09/27/ chechnya-choked-headscarves
106 "V Chechne vvoditsya ogranichenie na prodazhu 'energetikov,'" Grozny Inform, July 1, 2011, available at http://grozny-inform.ru/main.mhtml? Part=12&PubID=26718
107 Lokshina, "Chechnya: Choked by Headscarves."
108 C. J. Chivers, "A Whirling Sufi Revival With Unclear Implications," *New York Times*, May 24, 2006, 5.
109 Maria Bondarenko, "V Groznyi dostavlena islamskaya svyashchennaya relikviya—volos Proroka Mukhammeda," *Nezavisimaya gazeta*, January 27, 2012, 10.
110 "V Chechne proshel nabor v shkolu khafizov," July 28, 2011, available at www.islamrf.ru/news/russia/rusnews/17047
111 "V Rossiiskom islamskom universitete im. Kunta-Khadzhi Kishieva otkroetsya fakultet 'Teologii,'" May 5, 2012, available at http://regions.ru/ news/2406477/
112 Levada Analytical Center, *Obshchestvennoe Mnenie:2011* (Moscow: Analyti-cal Center Yuri Levada, 2012), 190.
113 Alexsander Chernykh and Dmitry Burtin, "Khuzhe gor mogut byt' tol'ko gorki," *Kommersant*, April 25, 2011, available at www.kommersant.ru/doc/1628411; "Nationalists demand Moscow 'stop feeding the Caucasus,'" *RT*, September 29, 2011, available at http://rt.com/politics/moscow-stop-feeding-caucasus-651/

114 For his thirty-fifth birthday on October 5, 2011, Chechen leader, Ramzan Kadyrov, put on a glittering celebration complete with a troupe of foreign acrobats and a performance by the British celebrity violinist Vanessa-Mae, Michael Schwirtz, "Russian Anger Grows over Chechnya Subsidies," *New York Times*, October 8, 2011, 4.

115 Andrew C. Kuchins, Mathew Malarkey, and Alexei Malashenko, *The North Caucasus: Russia's Volatile Frontier* (Washington, DC, Center for Strategic and International Studies, March 2011).

116 Marlene Laruelle, *In the name of the Nation: Nationalism and Politics in Contemporary Russia* (New York: Palgrave Macmillan, 2009), 75.

117 Nataliya Iudina, Vera Al'perovich, Aleksandr Verkhovsky, "Mezhdu Manezhnoi i Bolotnoi: Ksenofobiya i radikal'nyi natsionalizm i protivodeistvie im v 2011 gody v Rossii," SOVA center, February 24, 2012, available at www.sova-center.ru/racism-xenophobia/publications/2012/02/d23739/. The numbers for victims of xenophobic attacks in 2010 were 42 dead and 401 injured (ibid.)

118 Simon Saradzhyan and Evgenia Ivanova, "Violent Mobs Attack Immigrants in Karelia," *The St. Petersburg Times*, September 5, 2006, available at www.sptimes.ru/index.php?action_id=2&story_id=18713

119 Marlene Laruelle, *In the name of the Nation*, 37.

120 Anna Arutunyan and Lidia Okorokova, "Race riot on Manezhnaya," *The Moscow News*, December 13, 2010, available at www.themoscownews.com/politics/20101213/188276816.html

121 Will Englund, "Riots in Russia rooted in nationalism, hatred of immigrants," *The Washington Post*, December 14, 2010, 3.

122 Anna Arutunyan and Lidia Okorokova, "Race riot on Manezhnaya," *The Moscow News*, December 13, 2010, available at www.themoscownews.com/politics/20101213/188276816.html

123 "Dagestani authorities condemn Zhirinovsky's utterances on North-Caucasian nations," *Caucasian Knot*, January 22, 2011, available at www.eng.kavkaz-uzel.ru/articles/15904/

124 Akhmet Yarlykapov, "Respublika Dagestan: stabil'naya nestabil'nost," 142.

125 "Amir Seifulla: o protsesse podgotovki k provozglasheniu Kavkazkogo Emirata," KavkazCenter, November 20, 2007, available at www.kavkazcenter.com/russ/content/2007/11/20/54479.shtml

126 Zaid M. Abdulagatov, *Islam v massovom soznanii dagestantsev* (Makhachkala: IIAE DNTS RAN, 2008), 68–71.

Bibliography

Abdulagatov, Zaid M., *Islam v massovom soznanii dagestantsev*. Makhachkala: IIAE DNTS RAN, 2008.

Abdullaev, Nabi, "Bad Investigators Will Surely Find Us All Guilty," *Moscow Times*, July 4, 2001, 11.

— "A Murderous Cycle of Revenge in Dagestan," *Moscow Times*, March 15, 2005, 1.

Adelaja, Tai, "A Prisoner of the Caucasus," *Russia Profile*, January 26, 2012. http://
russiaprofile.org/business/53317/print_Edition/ (accessed September 5, 2012).
Al-qimmah.net, "Fatwa of Sheikh Abu Muhammad al-Maqdisi about Discord
in Caucasus Emirate," September 2010. http://al-qimmah.net/showthread.
php?t=20209&langid=1 (accessed July 18, 2012).
Akaev, Vahit, "Religiozno-prosvetitel'skaya rol' gazety 'Zori Islama,'
Yuzhnorossiiskoe obozrenie." http://ippk.edu.mhost.ru/elibrary/elibrary/uro/
v1/a1_17.htm (accessed July 23, 2012).
— *Sufizm i Wakhkhabizm na Severnom Kavkaze*, Issledovaniya po prikladnoi i
neotlozhnoi etnologii. Moscow: Rossiiskaya Akademiya Nauk, 1999.
Analytical Center Yuri Levada, *Obshchestvennoe Mnenie:2011*. Moscow:
Analytical Center Yuri Levada, 2012.
Arutunyan, Anna and Lidia Okorokova, "Race Riot on Manezhnaya," *The
Moscow News*, December 13, 2010. www.themoscownews.com/politics/
20101213/188276816.html (accessed August 29, 2012).
Babich, Irina, "Sovremennoe islamskoe dvizhenie v Kabardino-Balkarii," in
*Islamskoe vozrozhdenie v sovremennoi Kabardino-Balkarii: perspektivy i pos-
ledstviya*, edited by Irina Babich and Akhmet Yarlykapov, 53–82. Moscow:
RUDN, 2003.
BakuToday.net, "Vice Premier Dagestan Oversaw the Adaptation of Former
Fighters to Civilian Life, goes to the State Duma," December 12, 2011.
www.bakutoday.net/vice-premier-dagestan-oversaw-the-adaptation-of-former-
fighters-to-civilian-life-goes-to-the-state-duma.html (accessed July 20, 2012).
Berman, Harold, "Religious Rights in Russia at a time of tumultuous Transition:
A Historical Theory," in *Religious Human Rights in Global Perspective: Legal
Perspective*, vol. 2, edited by J. D. Van der Vyver, 1996.
Bobrovnikov, Vladimir, Amir Navruzov, and Shamil Shikhliev, "Islamic
Education in Soviet and Post-Soviet Daghestan," in *Islamic Education in
the Soviet Union and its Successor States*, edited by Michael Kemper, Raoul
Motika, Stefan Reichmuth, 107–67. London: Routledge, 2010.
Bobrovnikov, Vladimir and Akhmet Yarlykapov, "'Wahhabity' Severnogo
Kavkaza," in *Islam naterritorii byvshey Rossiiskoyu imperii*, 20–2. Moscow:
Vostochnaya Literatura, 1999.
Bondarenko, Maria, "V Groznyi dostavlena islamskaya svyashchennaya relikviya—
volos Proroka Mukhammeda," *Nezavisimaya gazeta*, January 27, 2012, 10.
Caucasian Knot, "Dagestani authorities condemn Zhirinovsky's utterances on
North-Caucasian nations," *Caucasian Knot*, January 22, 2011. www.eng.
kavkaz-uzel.ru/articles/15904/ (accessed July 22, 2012).
Chernykh, Aleksandr and Dmitry Burtin, "Khuzhe gor mogut byt' tol'ko gorki,"
Kommersant, April 25, 2011, available at www.kommersant.ru/doc/1628411
Chivers, C. J., "A Whirling Sufi Revival With Unclear Implications," *New York
Times*, May 24, 2006, 5.
Dobaev, Igor, *Islam v sovremennykh respublikakh Severnogo Kavkaza*. Rostov
na-Danu: Tsentr Sistemnykh regionalnkykh issledovanii i prognozirovaniya.
RAN, 2002.
Englund, Will, "Riots in Russia rooted in nationalism, hatred of immigrants,"
The Washington Post, December 14, 2010, 3.
Estemirova, Natalya, "Chechnya: Amnesty Fails to Inspire," IWPR, February 21,

2005. http://iwpr.net/report-news/chechnya-amnesty-fails-inspire (accessed July 10, 2012).

Fagan, Geraldine, "Russia: Dagestan's Controls on Islamic Education," *Forum 18 News Service*. www.forum18.org (accessed August 10, 2012).

Fatullayev, Milrad, " Mecheti budut otkryvats' tol'ko po pyatnitsam," *Nezavisimaya gazeta*, October 14, 2003, 3.

Gammer, Moshe, "Walking the Tightrope between nationalism(s) and Islam(s): The Case of Daghestan," *Central Asian Survey*, 21(2) (2002): 133–42.

Gazeta, "V Nal'chike 'zachistili' deputata 'Edinoi Rossii,'" *Gazeta*, October 26, 2005, 1.

Gritsneko, Tatyana, "Goryachee mnogotochie," *Vremya Novostei*, October 14, 2005, p.1.

Grozny-inform.ru, "V Chechne vvoditsya ogranichenie na prodazhu 'energetikov,'" July 1, 2011. http://grozny-inform.ru/main.mhtml?Part=12& PubID=26718 (accessed July 11, 2012).

Human Rights Watch, *Swept Under: Torture, Forced Disappearances, and Extra-judicial Killings during Sweep Operations in Chechnya*, Human Rights Watch, February 2002. www.unhcr.org/refworld/country,,HRW,COUNTRY REP,RUS,,3cb179fa6,0.html (accessed September 2, 2012).

— *Worse Than a War: "Disappearances" in Chechnya—A Crime Against Humanity*, Human Rights Briefing Paper, March 2005.

Islam v Evrazii, "Nam neobkhodim svetskii islamskii universitet—A. Khloponin," *Islam v Evrazii*, May 30, 2012. http://islamvevrazii.ru/newsru541.php (accessed July 30, 2012).

Islamnews.ru, "Kadyrov ne soglasen s Putinym," www.islamnews.ru/news-14133. html (accessed August 30, 2012).

Islamrf.ru, "V Chechne proshel nabor v shkolu khafizov," July 28, 2011. www.islamrf.ru/news/russia/rusnews/17047 (accessed July 20, 2012).

Iudina, Nataliya, Vera Al'perovich, and Aleksandr Verkhovsky, "Mezhdu Manezhnoi i Bolotnoi: Ksenofobiya i radikal'nyi natsionalizm i protivode- istvie im v 2011 gody v Rossii," SOVA center, February 24, 2012. www. sova-center.ru/racism-xenophobia/publications/2012/02/d23739/ (accessed August 28, 2012).

KavkazCenter. "Amir Seifulla: o protsesse podgotovki k provozglasheniu Kavkazkogo Emirata," November 20, 2007. www.kavkazcenter.com/russ/ content/2007/11/20/54479.shtml (accessed July 20, 2012).

— "Amir Seifulla: o protsesse podgotovki k provozglasheniu Kavkazkogo Emirata," KavkazCenter, November 20, 2007. www.kavkazcenter.com/russ/ content/2007/11/20/54479.shtml (accessed July 30, 2012).

— "V Dagestane ubit Said Chirkeisky, lider dagestanskikh sektantov," Kavkazcenter, August 28, 2012. www.kavkazcenter.com/russ/content/ 2012/08/28/92739.shtml. Accessed August 31, 2012).

— "The Doors of Jihad are Open," KavkazCenter, January 21, 2005. www. kavkazcenter.com/eng/content/2005/01/21/3461.shtml A (accessed June 12, 2012).

— "Musa Mukozhev," KavkazCenter, November 8, 2006. http://old. kavkazcenter.com/eng/content/2006/11/08/6318.shtml (accessed June 30, 2011).

— "Jamaats 'Shariat': Our Purpose—Establishment of the Validity," KavkazCenter, November 7, 2005. www.kavkazcenter.com/eng/content/ 2005/11/07/4201.shtml (accessed June 30, 2012).

— "Kabardino-Balkarian Jamaat declares jihad," KavkazCenter, August 24, 2004. www.kavkazcenter.com/eng/content/2004/08/24/3136.shtml (accessed June 30, 2011).

— "Razmyshleniya modzhakheda," KavkazCenter, August 11, 2005. www. kavkazcenter.com/russ/analitik/reflections_of_mujahid/ (accessed August 30, 2012).

Kavkazskii uzel, "Imam, killed in Dagestan, was known for negating militants' ideas," Kavkazskii uzel, June 29, 2012. www.eng.kavkaz-uzel.ru/ articles/21437/?print=true (accessed July 20, 2012).

Kazenin, Konstantin, "Islamskoe primirenie" i budushcheie Dagestana," *Regnum*, July 6, 2012. www.regnum.ru/news/polit/1548709.html (accessed July 20, 2012).

Kommersant, "Peregib byl sovreshen pravookhrannitel'nym organam," *Kommersant*, October 17, 2005, 2.

— "Gornye voiny, Epizod II," *Kommersant*, August 31, 1999, 1, 3.

Kramer, Andrew, "Rector at Muslim University in Russia Is Shot to Death," *New York Times*, June 7, 2011, 3.

Kratov, Evgeny and Natalya Kratova, *Islam v Karachaevo-Cherkesskoi Respublike*. Moscow, Logos, 2008.

Kritchin Nikolai and Yuri Spirin, "Besieged Militants Pelted with Grenades," *Izvestia*, January 28, 2005, 1, in The Current Digest of the Post Soviet Press, 57(4) (February 23, 2005): 13.

Kuchins, Andrew C., Mathew Malarkey, and Alexei Malashenko, *The North Caucasus: Russia's Volatile Frontier*, Center for Strategic and International Studies, March 2011.

Kurbanov, Ruslan, "Interaction Between Power and Religion in Daghestan: Experience, Errors and Lessons," *Central Asia and the Caucasus*, 33(3) (2005): 76–82.

— "'Urban' and 'Rural' Islam in the Caucasus: Modernisation versus Conservation," *Religion, State and Society*, 39(2/3) (June/September 2011): 347–65.

Laruelle, Marlene, *In the name of the Nation: Nationalism and Politics in Contemporary Russia*. New York: Palgrave Macmillan, 2009.

Lokshina, Tanya, "Chechnya: Choked by Headscarves," *Open Democracy*, September 27, 2010. www.hrw.org/news/2010/09/27/chechnya-choked-headscarves (accessed July 17, 2012).

Makarov, Dmitri, *Ofitsial'nyi i neofitsial'niyi Islam v Dagestane*. Moscow: Tsentr strategicheskikh i politicheskikh issledovanii, 2000.

Maksakov, Ilya, "Moskva nedootsenivaet ugrozhaiushchee razvitie sobytii v Dagestane, *Nezavisimoe voennoe obozrenie*, September 4, 1998, 2.

Manea, Octavian and Robert W. Schaefer, "The Russian COIN campaign in the North Caucasus," *Small Wars Journal* website, June 28 2012. http://smallwarsjournal.com/jrnl/art/the-russian-coin-campaign-in-north-caucasus (accessed September 1, 2012).

Memorial, *A Conveyer of Violence: Human Rights Violations During Anti-terrorist Operations in the Republic of Ingushetia*. Moscow: Zven'ya, 2006.

— "Conflict Spill-Over Outside the Chechen Republic in 2004–2005, Ingushetia and Kabardino-Balkariya," March 2, 2006. www.memo.ru/hr/hotpoints/caucas1/msg/2006/03/m53212.htm (accessed June 4, 2011).

Memorial and Demos, *Counter-terrorism Operations by the Russian Federation in the Northern Caucasus throughout 1999–2006*, Moscow, 2006. www.memo.ru/hr/hotpoints/N-Caucas/dkeng.htm (accessed June 10, 2012).

— *In a Climate of Fear: "Political Process" and Parliamentary Elections in Chechnya*, Moscow: Zven'ya, November 2006.

Memorial and FDIH, *Pytki v Chechne: "stabilisatsiya" koshmara*, Moscow: Memorial, November 2006.

Nemtsova, Anna, "Kremlin in the Caucasus: Pushing for a moderate Islam," Russia Beyond the Headlines, August 25, 2010. http://rbth.ru/articles/2010/08/25/kremlin_in_the_caucasus_pushing_for_a_moderate_islam04898.html (accessed July 30, 2012).

Newsru.com, "Boeviki Ingushetii ob'yavili dzhikhad po vsei respublike," July 8, 2004. www.newsru.com/arch/russia/08jul2004/djihad.html (accessed September 8, 2011).

Parfitt, Tom, "Jihadist Rehabilitation in the North Caucasus," May 25, 2011. http://pulitzercenter.org/articles/makhachkala-dagestan-muslim-boyeviki-insurgency-jihad (accessed July 22, 2012).

Peuch, Jean-Christophe, "Nalchik Raids Trigger new Wave of Harassment Against Muslims," *RFE/RL News and Analysis*, November 4, 2005. www.rferl.org/featuresarticle/2005/11/b35c88ff-8aa8–499c-b210–610dedc50c0f.html (accessed July 4, 2012).

Pravda, "O svobodi sovesti i religioznikh organisatsiyakh," *Pravda*, October 9, 1990, 2.

Rasulov, Yasin, "Dzhikhad na Severnom Kavkaze," KavkazCenter, 2006. www.kavkazcenter.com/russ/islam/jihad_in_ncaucasus/PDF_version.pdf (accessed June 9, 2011).

— "Pochemu ubivaiut militsionerov v Dagestane?" *Chernovik*, April 16, 2004. www.chernovik.net/news/44/POLITICS/2005/01/04/3586 (accessed September 2, 2012).

Regions.ru, "V Rossiiskom islamskom universitete im. Kunta-Khadzhi Kishieva otkroetsya fakultet 'Teologii,'" May 5, 2012. http://regions.ru/news/2406477/ (accessed August 10, 2012).

Rossiiskaya Federatsiya, "Federal'nyi Zakon o Svobode Sovesti i o Religioznykh ob'edineniyakh," September 26, 1997. http://base.consultant.ru/cons/cgi/online.cgi?req=doc;base=LAW;n=61456 (accessed June 3, 2012).

Rotar, Igor "Under the Green Banner: Islamic Radicals in Russia and the Former Soviet Union," *Religion, State and Society*, 30(2) (2002): 89–153.

Sagramoso, Domitilla, "The Radicalization of Salafi *Jamaats* in the North Caucasus: Moving Closer to the Global *Jihad*ist Movement?," *Europe-Asia Studies*, 64(3) (2012): 561–95.

— "Violence and conflict in the Russian North Caucasus," *International Affairs*, 83 (July 4, 2007): 681–705.

Sagramoso, Domitilla and Galina Yemelianova, "Islam and Ethno-Nationalism in the North Western Caucasus" in *Islamic Radicalisation in the Post-Soviet Space*, edited by Galina Yemelianova, 112–45. London & New York: Routledge, 2010.

Saradzhyan, Simon and Evgenia Ivanova, "Violent Mobs Attack Immigrants in Karelia," *The St. Petersburg Times*, September 5, 2006. www.sptimes.ru/index.php?action_id=2&story_id=18713 (accessed September 2, 2012).

Schwirtz, Michael, "Russian Anger Grows Over Chechnya Subsidies," *New York Times*, October 8, 2011, 4.

Temirbulatov, R., "Vashe vremya proshlo," *Islam-Niuriu*, July 2004, 4.

Vatchagaev, Mairbek, "Karachay jamaat: Counter-measures, Connections and Composition, Part.2," *North Caucasus Weekly*, June 7, 2007. www.jamestown.org/single/?no_cache=1&tx_ttnews%5Btt_news%5D=4218 (accessed June 4, 2011).

— "The Kremlin's War on Islamic Education in the North Caucasus," *North Caucasus Analysis*, 7(34) (September 8, 2006). www.jamestown.org/single/?no_cache=1&tx_ttnews%5Btt_news%5D=3334 (accessed July 30, 2012).

— "Moscow Is Trying to Outsmart the Salafis in Chechnya," North Caucasus Analysis May 10, 2012. www.jamestown.org/single/?no_cache=1&tx_ttnews%5Btt_news%5D=39356 (accessed August 30, 2012).

VDagestan.com, "Kadii IK Abu Mukhammad: Opravdanie po nevezhestvu, i krainosti, v kotorye pooali dve gruppy," September 19, 2011. http://vdagestan.com/kadij-ik-abu-muxammad-opravdanie-po-ne.htm (accessed July 25, 2012).

Verkhovsky, Alexander, "Russian approaches to radicalism and "extremism" as applied to nationalism and religion," in *Russia and Islam: State, Society and Radicalism*, edited by Roland Dannreuther and Luke March. New York: Routledge, 2010, pp.26–43.

Vesti.ru, "Medvedev o bor'be s terrorismom: vazhen dialog s islamskim dukhovenstvom," *Vesti.ru*, July 18, 2011. www.vesti.ru/doc.html?id=512328 (accessed July 27, 2012).

Williams, Brian Glyn, "Al Qaeda, Transnational Jihadis, and the Chechen Resistance: Assessing the Role of Chechnya in the War on Terror," Paper Presented at the CESS Conference. Harvard: Harvard University, October 2003.

— "Jihad and Ethnicity in Post-Communist Eurasia: On the Trail of Transnational Islamic Holy Warriors in Kashmir, Afghanistan, Central Asia, Chechnya and Kosovo," *The Global Review of Ethnopolitics*, 2(3–4) (March–June 2003): 3–24.

Yarlykapov, Akhmet, *Problema vakhkhabisma na Severnom Kavkaze*. Moscow: Rossiiskaya Akademiya Nauk, Institut Etnologii i Antropologii, 2000.

— "Novoe islamskoe dvizhenie na Severnom Kavkaze: vzglyad etnografa," in *Rasy i narody: sovremennye etnicheskie i rasovye problemy*, Arutyunov, S. (ed.) 210–24. Moscow: Nauka, 2006.

— "Respublika Dagestan: stabil'naya nestabil'nost'," in *Severnyi Kavkaz: vzglyad iznutri: Vyzovy i problemy sotsial'no-politicheskogo razvitiya*, edited by Anna Matveeva, 137–53. Moscow: Saferworld and Institut Vostokovedeniya RAN, March 2012.

Yemelianova, Galina, "Kinship, Ethnicity and Religion in Post-communist Societies: Russia's Autonomous Republic of Kabardino-Balkariya," *Ethnicities*, 5(1) (March 2005): 51–82.

— *Russia and Islam: A Historical Survey*. New York: Palgrave, 2002.

CHAPTER FOUR

War in the Caucasus: Moving the Russian Military into the Twenty-first Century

Lt. Col. Robert W. Schaefer and 1LT Andrei Doohovskoy

The modern Chechen wars (beginning in 1994)—Russia's first significant military conflict since the fall of the Soviet Union— taught military and political leaders painful but important lessons that triggered and continue to drive Russian military transformations. Failures in Chechnya exposed the need for a better-equipped, better-trained, better-led, and more responsive force capable of reacting quickly to a broad spectrum of conventional and unconventional threats. Lessons from the 2008 conflict with Georgia largely confirm conclusions already formulated on the basis of Chechen combat experience. Failures in Chechnya also stimulated a closer review of likely current and future threats—and the military's capacity to address them—a process that shaped the opinions of Russian leaders regarding the optimal methods for organizing, commanding, manning, equipping, and training their military formations. Analysis of current Russian military reforms reveals ties to the recent Chechen conflict and underscores the extent to which the lessons of Chechnya are a powerful and enduring factor in shaping the modern Russian military.

This chapter has been reviewed by the Department of Defense's (DOD) Office of Security Review and has been cleared for open publication. The statements of fact, opinion, or analysis expressed in this chapter are those of the authors and do not reflect the official policy or position of the DOD or the US Government. Review of the material does not imply DOD or US Government endorsement of factual accuracy or opinion.

Introduction

In September 2008 President Medvedev presented a plan for a *"noviy oblik"* (new look) for the Russian military. He discussed changes to the Russian military establishment that mark some of the most radical military reforms in Russia since World War II and the reforms of 1860–70.[1] The past three decades have wrought exceptional transformation, instability, and conflict through which the Russian military has played a role both in military action and in representing compelling social and political issues. The wars and the ongoing insurgency have not just changed how the military operates; they have also had a profound effect on society because the Russian military literally knocks at every young man's door—thus projecting the influences and consequences of military service throughout the social and political fabric of the Russian nation, with significant consequences both domestically and internationally. Wars have always been crucibles for military organizations, and the hotter the conflict, the greater the transformations. It is significant to note that Russia's last groundbreaking military transformation in the late 1800's was conducted following a 40-year campaign against the forces of Imam Shamil in the North Caucasus and poor performance in the Crimean War (notwithstanding the changes wrought by the Soviet buildup in World War II). The nuances of nineteenth-century Russian reforms are outside the scope of this analysis, but the coincidence of two conflicts in Chechnya preceding groundbreaking military reform point to the larger theme of the enduring influence of the Caucasus on the Russian military structure. The recent acceleration of military transformation within Russia and current geopolitical developments call for further examination of the role of the First (1994–6) and Second (1999–2002)[2] Chechen wars, as well as the ongoing insurgency in the North Caucasus in these processes.

Context

Although there are those who would argue that Russian military reform would have evolved naturally, even the highest authorities in Russia have acknowledged the need for reforms in order to make up for shortfalls observed over the last 30 years.[3] Because the campaigns in Chechnya represent the first significant military conflicts that the nation faced after the fall of the Soviet Union, they fundamentally influenced the evolution of the military; because the conflict continues to drag on, it cannot help but continue to shape that evolution. The following analysis will examine the Russian military experience in the first and second Chechen wars as representing visceral and undeniable indicators to Russian officials that key aspects of warfare have evolved and must be addressed,[4] and significant changes in the military are necessary to accomplish these objectives. Additionally, this analysis will show that the experience in the first and second Chechen wars was a central factor in conceptualizing and motivating many of the ongoing changes in the Russian military.[5]

The Russian army that entered Chechnya in 1994 was woefully unprepared for the asymmetric and irregular nature of the conflict that awaited them. The institutional mindset of the Russian military was still focused on the Soviet experience of World War II and the anticipated battles of the Cold War. Nonetheless, the Soviet Army had been a proficient one, so the challenges of achieving victory in Chechnya should have been apparent to the new Russian military establishment based on the extensive military history in the region and the lessons learned from Soviet counterinsurgency campaigns over the past 70 years. But the lessons of the past were forgotten or ignored, and the Kremlin underestimated the task of preserving unity between Russia and Chechnya through force.

Instead of fighting large enemy formations on the tank-friendly undulating terrain of Eastern Europe, the Russians found themselves battling small groups of highly motivated fighters in rugged mountain environments. Instead of bypassing heavily defended cities in order to achieve "mass" and "surprise" as their manuals had taught them, Russian soldiers were drawn into brutal urban combat in a city still populated by many civilians. Instead of conducting total war then presiding over relative calm, the Russian army endured bloody battles separated by periods of inactivity that would lull them into complacency, making them vulnerable targets for the next round of attacks. Instead of fighting with their country fully mobilized behind them, Russian officers and conscripts experienced a conflict marked by domestic and international criticism.

Ultimately, there was a wide chasm between what the situation required and the situational assessments, institutional mindset, and training that the

Russians brought to the conflict. These contrasts resulted in painful and bloody lessons learned—many of which were incorporated between the wars, and led to greater success in 1999 and the current counterinsurgency (COIN) campaign.

Many of these lessons were originally learned in Afghanistan, but then forgotten or ignored in the transition from Soviet Union to Russian Federation.[6] The Afghan War had largely been a failure and most Russians simply wanted to forget about it. Soviet (later Russian) political and military leaders did not anticipate or desire to fight a similar conflict in the future, and therefore did not make any changes to prepare for it. Just as the US military did not fundamentally change its structure following the Vietnam War, the Soviets did not institutionalize and integrate the lessons of the Afghan War into their army prior to Chechnya. The Chechen conflict, unexpected and (to a degree) thrust upon the new government, convinced the Russians that they had ignored the lessons of Afghanistan to their detriment. Over time, the Russians recognized that the Chechen wars represented the "future threat," and it was this realization that led to major reforms. And though recently cited as the impetus for greater military reforms, the 2008 war with Georgia was simply a confirmation of the need for many of initiatives previously begun as a result of the Chechen conflicts—and a sign to the Kremlin that these initiatives must be pursued with greater urgency and persistence.

Key elements of the Russian military reforms (the "New Look"— originally announced in 2008) include reducing the armed forces to a strength of one million by 2012; reducing the number of officers; professionalization of the noncommissioned officers corps (NCOs or sergeants); increasing the number of civilian logistics and auxiliary staff; elimination of cadre-only units; reorganizing the army into a brigade system;[7] refitting the units with updated equipment; improving training throughout the force; and reorganizing air forces into an air base system instead of regiments. In this chapter we will explore the effects of the Caucasus experience (primarily the Chechen campaigns) on the most important aspects of the "New Look" reforms.

Personnel

The first Chechen campaign (1994–6)

Manning during the first Chechen war was abysmal. In 1994 the army was short 12,000 platoon leaders, and military academies graduated their cadets early to fill positions.[8] Officers did not remain in the service long enough to fill higher level positions and shortages in the numbers of qualified NCOs and conscript soldiers contributed to the overall catastrophe of unpreparedness.[9]

The conscripts were often the least educated (and least healthy) of their peers, and the poor training they received did not prepare them at all for combat in Chechnya. Moreover, unlike other conflicts where "green" soldiers can still add value to the effort while learning on the job, the difficult urban and mountainous terrain—combined with the challenge of fighting highly motivated and skilled combatants defending their home turf—made them virtually nothing more than cannon fodder.

The trouble with conscription is embodied by "*dedovschina*," an endemic system of brutal hazing, which results in hundreds of deaths every year, and which makes every Russian family uneasy about sending its sons to the army. During the war, the military further exacerbated this unease by underreporting casualties and purposely misleading the families of soldiers about their ultimate fates—all of which led to increased scrutiny and criticism of the conflict and ultimately weakened Russia's ability to continue the war. The systemic problems of the conscription system were too difficult to address during the first Chechen war—indeed, many of them are too difficult to address even today—although changing the conscript system had been discussed at the time. As a result, many conscripts were not thinking about contributing to the mission during combat; rather, they were focused on surviving their conscription period. Although in some instances, more seasoned soldiers might lead from the front and conduct the more difficult parts of an operation, the author's (Schaefer) own observations were that even elite forces like the airborne considered the newest soldiers to be the most expendable, and unit Standard Operating Procedures (SOP) dictated they walk 20–50 meters ahead of the main squad in order to draw hostile fire and thereby identify enemy positions. Once discovered, the more experienced (and reliable) soldiers could then use fire and maneuver to defeat the enemy or (as was more often the case) call mortars or artillery on the position.[10]

However, the linchpin of successful small unit operations is the small-unit leader—lieutenants and sergeants—and in an unconventional environment such as Chechnya, the demands on junior leaders are even more considerable and require even greater levels of competency.[11] The Chechen conflict starkly exposed the problems of the Russian enlisted system and demonstrated that the lack of a strong NCO corps significantly limited the capability and capacity of the Russian army, since NCOs provide the vital link between individual action on the ground and the intent of officers and policy makers.

Between the Wars (1996–9)

The Russian populace had reacted poorly to sending large numbers of conscripts to Chechnya to endure significant hardship and risk. To mollify his electorate, President Yeltsin delivered a speech to the Armed Forces and promised that service in combat would be henceforth conducted on a voluntary basis alone.[12] Although this ruling was later reversed, it indicates the trend of leaders seeking to minimize reliance on conscription after the experience in Chechnya.[13] To make up for the lack of conscripts, the Russians attempted to put more soldiers on a "contract" basis—which in theory should have increased the number of professional soldiers available to the military. Because the "*kontraktniki*" were paid higher wages and were given a greater degree of authority (and respect at the platoon and company level), it was hoped that ever-increasing numbers of soldiers would choose to extend their service contract voluntarily, like Western-style professional armies.

Additionally, Russian defense officials made increasing permanent readiness units a priority immediately following the war. As Yeltsin stated in an address in 1996, "Is it normal that poorly trained greenhorns were used against professional, experienced mercenaries? This must not happen. Instead of several hundred divisions, most of which exist only on paper, we should have several dozen divisions, but they should be manned with professionals."[14] In 1998, Minister of Defense Sergeyev outlined reforms dictating that the Armed Forces would have ten permanent-readiness units, capable of conducting combat operations without personnel and armament reinforcements, by January 1, 1999.[15]

President Yeltsin also ordered reductions in the overall size of the Army and the number of cadre-strength units (paper tigers) in an effort to produce a more mobile and well-equipped force.[16] This is significant because it is generally assumed that major reforms of this nature were not initiated until 2008 (and therefore not related to the Chechen campaigns). Yet it is apparent that the genesis of the later reforms can be directly linked to the 1994–6 campaign, which illustrated the evolution of conflicts the Russian Federation would likely face in the future.

The second Chechen campaign (1999–2002)

Having learned from their mistake in the first war, Russian leaders committed a significantly larger number of troops to the second conflict.[17] Yet despite the overall higher number of troops, there were efforts to limit the number of conscripts sent into combat, an initiative that encountered varied success. However, the hoped-for advantages of the *kontraktniki* never materialized on a scale that significantly affected the outcome, and many of the same problems that plagued the conscripts manifested themselves in the contract system, preventing any significant professionalization of the enlisted corps. Commanders soon began taking the higher pay of the *kontraktniki* for themselves, the military often reneged on its contractual obligations, and additional problems of recruiting, retention, and funding considerably slowed the shift toward the dream of a contract army.[18] Yet these efforts, despite their failures, indicated a realization among Russian leaders that a conscript army was not the optimal force for future conflicts, nor could such an army be wielded with the same flexibility as a professional one—politically or tactically.[19]

After the wars (2002–present)[20]

Current attempts to improve the conscript system are largely tied to the Chechen experience. The Russian populace did not support exposing large numbers of conscripts to the difficult conditions in Chechnya, and their protests became an issue politicians could not ignore. It is important to remember that the decision to end the first war with Chechnya and grant them de facto independence was entirely a political decision, based in part on the extreme unpopularity of the war and concern about the high casualty rate. To this end, Russian leaders endeavored to reduce the number of conscripts sent to Chechnya by increasing the number of contract soldiers deployed there, and by pushing for increased numbers of contract personnel in the military overall.[21]

The NCO corps also received a lot of attention and the Committee on Foreign Defense and Politics (*Sovet po Vneshnei Oborone i Politike*) announced that development of a professional NCO corps should be *the* top priority in the Russian military.[22] This sentiment has generally been embraced by policy makers and resulted in the establishment of an NCO academy in Ryazan to begin to address the crisis.[23] However, the effort has been fraught with problems and setbacks; since 2010 there have been nine separate programs to create a professional NCO corps and all have been scrapped. Although still a struggling and nascent effort, building a modern NCO corps represents a potentially significant transformation.[24]

Building the NCO corps will be accompanied by reductions in the officer corps, as part of the effort to make the force less "top-heavy." According to Defense Minister Serdyukov's reform plan, officer posts will be reduced from 355,000 to 150,000 (although, positions for junior officers will increase from 50,000 to 60,000).[25]

Chechnya revealed stark inadequacies in the Russian officer corps—from complacency at the highest levels to lack of combat skills in junior officers. Yet unlike the problems with the nonexistent professional NCO corps, the problems with the officer corps were rooted in insufficient training and development. The problem has been recognized and is a high-visibility topic in the Defense Ministry, which enumerates officer training and development as a priority. Chairman of the General Staff Makarov stated that the Russian officer must be "a specialist in military affairs, and above all else educated, cultured and intelligent."[26] Multiple official documents including statements from the Russian President note that officer educational reform is necessary, and that the professional military officer corps must be supported by the government in order to attract and maintain quality personnel.[27]

Overall, the Chechen campaigns demonstrated that the Russian manning and mobilization system was wholly unsuited for twenty-first-century conflicts, which Russian analysts project to be unconventional, sudden, and comparably small.[28] The Soviet-legacy system of "paper tiger" units manned by skeleton crews of officers awaiting an influx of mobilized reservists was not useful in reacting quickly to such conflicts. This point was vividly illustrated in 1994 when Russian leaders had difficulty fielding combat-ready units to Grozny.[29]

Increasing the numbers of permanent readiness units, therefore, continues to be a priority task for the Russian Ministry of Defense.[30] As noted above, progress was made in this area in preparation for the second invasion into Chechnya—and although Chechnya is not the sole reason for this vector in military development, it was certainly the catalyst for it in recent years.[31]

Equipment development

The first Chechen campaign (1994–6)

In 1994, the Russian army was poorly equipped for operations in Chechnya. By some accounts, the army was receiving only 30–40 percent of what it needed for funding and supplies during this time.[32] In 1994, equipment had not been updated since the war in Afghanistan, and was increasingly obsolete.[33] Poor maintenance was endemic and resulted in almost universal equipment failures across the spectrum of vehicles and weapon systems.[34] Shortages and flaws in night vision optics significantly impeded both ground forces and aviation. Aging and discontinued satellite coverage over Chechnya hindered the ability of commanders to use Global Navigation Satellite System (GLONASS; the Russian version of the Global Positioning System (GPS)) to see the battlefield and move decisively.[35]

As all soldiers do, Russian troops modified their equipment to overcome its inherent limitations, and thereby improve their units' capabilities and effectiveness. For example, as in Afghanistan, Russian soldiers rigged mesh cages about their armored vehicles to protect against shaped charges,[36] and anti-aircraft machine guns were included on armored columns because of their ability to incline and decline to the sharp angles required in urban and mountain combat.[37]

Overall, there were not any significant transformations in equipment development during the first war because there simply was not enough time to make the necessary changes. As in many other areas, the conflict revealed striking inadequacies in many of the systems and equipment upon which the Russian military relied. Implementing solutions was extremely difficult, but leaders were unable to ignore the pressing need for changes in order to equip their army for success.

Between the wars (1996–9)

It is important to remember that the Russian defense industry was in shambles after the fall of the Soviet Union, and, in some cases, still has not fully recovered to this day. By comparison, even with its new streamlined system, the United States is hard-pressed to issue complete sets of new equipment or develop significant weapon upgrades over the span of five or six years—so an immediate overhaul of military equipment was simply not realistic in Russia during the late 1990s. As a result, there were few significant changes in equipment during the brief time between the wars. Alternatively, there were perfectly good options that were available to the Russians on the open market, and, given the state of the Russian military industrial complex, the Kremlin would have done its soldiers a great service if they had purchased some of this equipment for its troops prior to the second invasion. Politics, pride, and price, however, precluded that policy.

However, improving logistical support to get the equipment to the troops, as well as improving training to facilitate the proper employment of equipment was possible—and far more relevant and effective. During this time President Yeltsin promised to increase spending for military equipment and proposed a program designed to put the best equipment with units in actual combat.[38] A plan was also put forth to create an integrated system for manufacturing military equipment in an effort to consolidate resources and maximize efficiency and output.[39]

The second Chechen campaign (1999–2002)

The anemic pace of the Russian armament industry in developing new equipment continued during the second Chechen war but logistical coordination and resupply operations were somewhat improved, which meant that, unlike the first war, Russian units were fed and got ammunition and supplies on a more regular basis.[40] However, fundamental and systemic problems continued to permeate the system of equipping Russian forces.

Aircraft continued to be a problem as machinery aged or was destroyed, and few new aircraft were added to aviation units.[41] Ground vehicles had little cross-country capability and there was minimal equipment for crossing water obstacles.[42] Night vision capabilities remained extremely limited, both in the ground forces and in aviation, despite plans for increased supply.[43]

Combat in Chechnya dictated the need for general upgrades in weaponry, such as more grenade launchers mounted on rifles.[44] Limited reconnaissance equipment did make its way to Russian troops and in September 1999, Russian forces received the Stroy II unmanned aerial vehicle/complex (UAV or drone) in very limited numbers—which suggested a level of technological potential, but also underscored the problems of production and distribution in the Russian system.[45] Additional weapon systems introduced during the second Chechen war included improved flamethrowers capable of firing thermo-baric rounds at long ranges.[46]

After the wars (2002–present)

Overall, the second war in Chechnya confirmed an urgent need for equipment and weaponry—a need that could not be supplied by Russia's poor logistical system[47]—which was characterized by insufficient funds to produce anything more than prototypes of improved versions of existing materiel and an inefficient system for utilizing existing resources.[48] Experience in Chechnya revealed the extent to which these issues affected the army's ability to conduct effective operations and, most importantly, win battles.

To overcome these deficiencies, Russian officials are pursuing improvements as part of the current reforms. In 2009, President Medvedev stated that it is a "crucial task to field the services with advanced materiel. There is no need to deliberate . . . as far as this task is concerned."[49] Many of the problems encountered in Chechnya resurfaced during the Georgian War, which has further galvanized resolve to address the issue.[50] Following the President's call, Russian leaders are attempting to stimulate and modernize the system of procurement and supply through increased funding and better oversight.[51]

Helicopter development and production is one example of such initiatives. There are large upgrades and additions to the helicopter fleet planned for 2012.[52] As a result of experience in the Caucasus, some forms of equipment may be less emphasized or redesigned. For example, General Shamanov notes that tanks are vulnerable in many conditions in which the army must fight.[53] While this is surely a hotly debated topic, the underlying point is that experience in Chechnya has also affected the perception of requirements for military equipment. This represents a significant transformation in the Russian military.[54]

The Russian army's problem with equipment is complex and closely tied to economic factors. General Shamanov cut to the heart of the matter, stating that the gap between those procuring equipment and the requirements of troops for combat must be removed. This gap became clear in 1994 in Chechnya when Shamanov publicly remarked, "we were armed worse than the rebels."[55] As noted by leaders and analysts, a solution in this area must incorporate integrating and optimizing the structure of equipment production and development in order to create a competent workforce, stimulate both civilian and government applications of high-tech equipment, and create a system of legislation that will support the industry internationally and domestically.[56]

Doctrine, tactics, and training

The first Chechen campaign (1994–6)

Any tactical course of action is fundamentally shaped by one's own troops, the enemy, and the terrain. In Chechnya, all of these factors posed problems for the Russian military because the Chechens were able to attack and then simply fade into the civilian populace—which frustrated and angered untrained Russian soldiers, whose formations, experience, and expectations were not structured or prepared to combat this sort of enemy behavior. Furthermore, the majority of the battles were fought in urban and mountainous terrain, which presented even greater difficulties for Russian forces, which were not adequately trained or equipped to fight in such environments.[57]

This is a critical point to understand because, in effect, these factors "shrunk" the battlefield, and stripped the Russian Army of its natural advantages and forced small units to function independently—something the Russian military has never been good at—because it is entirely reliant upon initiative from junior leaders. In 1994, Russia did not have (nor has it subsequently developed) a professional cadre of NCOs; moreover, the Soviet system discouraged and punished independent thinking at the lower levels, breeding indecisiveness, inaction, and lethargy.[58] The Chechen campaigns, therefore, represented a step toward an era that would be dominated by asymmetric conflicts occurring on domestic (or formerly domestic) territory. For this reason, the Chechen campaigns were a central factor in the evolution of Russian tactics and training.

Russia fought its first major battles in Chechnya in urban terrain—with disastrous consequences. Poor planning, untrained soldiers, and deficient equipment produced some of the worst tactical defeats in modern Russian military history because the Russian units that attacked Grozny in 1994 still operated along the tenets of the Soviet Army—which directed commanders to avoid urban battles whenever possible, and only operate in urban settings that had been cleared of civilians and subdued by extensive artillery fires.[59]

What unfolded on New Year's Eve 1994 was a bloody and difficult lesson in urban combat. Armored columns drove down narrow streets into the heart of Grozny, unaware of the stiff resistance that awaited them.[60] Employing shoulder-fired anti-tank missiles, the Chechens pinned down these armored columns by means of the time-honored technique of immobilizing the first and last vehicles to halt movement and prevent escape.[61] Then, firing down from the upper levels of the apartment buildings at angles that exceeded the maximum elevation of Russian heavy machine guns and tank turrets, the Chechens unleashed an onslaught of deadly fire. Russian soldiers, not trained to fight independently of their vehicles, remained inside of them and failed to counteract the enemy through fire and maneuver.[62] It was a slaughter—in just a few hours the Chechens destroyed more than 400 tanks and armored personnel carriers; the official number of dead and missing Russian soldiers from this single day of combat was at least 1,800 (with some estimates as high as 4,000).[63]

As further combat operations took place, Russian forces were able to make adjustments to achieve some success. Units—out of dire necessity—began to develop an ad hoc institutional knowledge for the tasks of urban combat. Russian leaders developed "storm troop" detachments, previously seen in World War II, that combined various elements into one specially equipped unit that now had the assets and specialties needed to conduct urban combat. Additionally, the crucible of brutal combat effected further changes: tactical units were reduced to a more manageable and effective size; Russian soldiers learned to prepare urban defenses through booby traps and by mining potential enemy approaches;[64] and soldiers began wrapping armored vehicles with wire mesh cages to make shoulder fired rockets explode prematurely.[65] Furthermore, FSB (the successor to the KGB) and Ministry of Internal Affairs (MVD) troops began to augment forces with snipers, which played a key role in controlling the battle space.[66]

Although the Russian military-industrial complex was unable to provide improved equipment, out of necessity, Russian soldiers quickly learned to adapt their tactics to best utilize the equipment they did have. As mentioned previously, anti-aircraft machine guns (ZSU 23–4 Shilka and 2S6) were integrated into armored attacks because they are able to elevate and traverse at the sharp angles required in urban and mountain combat—while better artillery planning and reconnaissance asset integration improved success and lowered casualties. Additionally, Russian soldiers began to carry portable ladders and grappling hooks to enter buildings without using doors, clear rooms with grenades, and integrate flamethrowers into urban combat.[67] Although these tactical improvements were not enough to change the outcome of the first Chechen war, such adjustments under fire helped the Russians begin to win more battles and decrease the number of casualties.[68]

Yet these improvements were not incorporated into doctrine, so despite some additional training centers hastily built in the Mozdok area, the average Russian soldier was still unprepared for combat in Chechnya; additional training to improve fighting skills and survivability was too little too late, and the soldiers who survived generally did so by learning from experience.[69]

Between the wars (1996–9)

The crushing defeats suffered at the First and Second Battles of Grozny[70] required that urban warfare tactics, training, and doctrine be reviewed, debated, and analyzed—and leaders constantly discussed many of the lessons Russian soldiers had learned "on the job." Military analysts stressed the need in future operations for adequately isolating an urban area (a key weakness in the first assault on Grozny), applying psychological measures to the enemy inside, and equipping ground troops with the necessary tools such as grenade launchers, flamethrowers, radios, and sniper rifles. Experts also identified "fire and maneuver" at the lowest levels (squads and buddy teams) as another key area in need of improvement, as well as coordination with armor and artillery assets.[71] Leaders also discussed reducing fratricide by improving the methods for marking the locations of friendly units operating in urban terrain, as well as better integrating air assets with ground operations.[72] Additionally, there were attempts to increase training for convoys on winding roads to prepare soldiers to react to mines and ambushes.[73]

Despite the signing of the Khasavyurt Agreement in 1996 (granting de facto independence to Chechnya), and the 1997 Peace Treaty signed by Russian President Yeltsin and the democratically elected President of Chechnya, Aslan Maskhadov, in which both sides pledged to solve all their future disputes peacefully, further conflict between the two sides was generally understood to be inevitable. By July of 1998 the Russian military was conducting exercises that spanned large territories in the Caucasus, obviously preparing for future operations in Chechnya.[74] Training exercises included many government agencies—law enforcement, intelligence, emergency services, and border guards—and touched on weaknesses identified during the first war: hostage rescue; urban operations; anti-terrorist actions; etc.[75] Extra funds for equipment and training were allocated to those units designated to return to Chechnya,[76] increased emphasis was placed on mountain training, and in the summer of 1999, a sniper school was formed to further develop this capability as it had proven to be critical during urban combat.[77]

Even "old school" Soviet-era Generals increasingly began to accept the concept of the "reinforced battalion"—pushing critical assets to lower levels and equipping battalions to conduct operations with greater independence. For example, in preparation for the second Chechen war, each maneuver company had an artillery or mortar battery assigned to it—which meant that they could get fire support within minutes instead of hours.[78] This general shift is reflected in the much broader changes that are currently taking place within the military as part of its transformation.

The second Chechen campaign (1999–2002)

The second campaign in Chechnya was conducted in a more deliberate and methodical manner, although the Russian army itself was not much different than it had been in 1994. Tactics were still evolving—both in theory and in implementation—but had not yet resulted in drastic changes on the ground. The most fundamental differences were in planning, command, and attitude—primarily at the strategic, rather than tactical level. Russian leaders took the campaign seriously and were able to achieve better results with much the same resources they had had the first time in Chechnya, even as more substantial transformations continued to take shape.[79]

The Russian army returned to the traditional, simple but effective tactics of utilizing overwhelming artillery and air power to support ground forces.[80] Russian forces avoided the cauldron of urban warfare, choosing to surround resistant urban settlements and use other measures—ultimatums, psychological operations, and artillery before committing ground troops.[81] The Russians employed local militias as guides, and there were some improvements in coordination between interagency security forces.[82] Unlike the first campaign, armored vehicles were positioned on nearby key terrain in overwatch positions to provide covering fire, and generally kept out of cities and villages.[83] Emphasis was placed on encircling the enemy—often through the use of air insertion to cut off escape routes—a tactic used with great success during the Russian siege of Grozny in 2000 and inflicted heavy losses on Basaev's forces as they attempted to retreat from the city.[84]

Overall, Russian troops relied heavily on artillery, which was less affected by weather and maintenance issues than combat aviation. One study concluded that artillery units required 60–75 percent less time than aviation units to react to calls for support.[85]

Paradoxically, this "return" to basic tactics should be considered part of the ongoing trajectory toward reforms because this shift was not a return to Soviet "large war" doctrine inasmuch as it was a step forward in accepting and conceptualizing the conflict as a counterinsurgency/counterterrorism operation. And despite the fact that Soviet/Russian counterinsurgency doctrine differs greatly from Western doctrine, the methods used by the Russians in the second Chechen war (like carpet bombing) were consistent with their traditional unconventional warfare doctrine—and thus represent a conscious move toward methods that they considered necessary to fight emerging and future threats.[86]

However, Russian officers employed more than just traditional techniques from the "old days." During this campaign, the Russians aggressively attacked Chechen command and control nodes by employing electronic warfare teams to monitor and disrupt enemy communications while equipping their own troops with more and better radios and training the operators to use encryption capabilities to improve operational security.[87]

Overall, the troops were better prepared as well—regular troops had slightly more training, and elite units were sent to the region in larger numbers. Training in critical specialty skills identified during the interwar years continued to increase,[88] and in 2000 it was reported that 1,500 snipers had been trained in the North Caucasus military district to offset the devastating casualties that Chechen snipers were inflicting on Russian troops.[89] By this time, the Russian carpet bombing campaign had reduced Grozny to a pile of rubble—what the European Union would call the "most destroyed city on Earth." Within this maze of broken buildings, Chechen and Russian snipers conducted their own war, with hundreds of them scattered throughout the city—often occupying different floors of the same building. Russian outposts had been easy targets for the Chechens, but that changed with the influx of Russian snipers—who deployed with larger teams than their Chechen foes.

These lessons underscored the importance of the small unit in the outcome of a mission, a shift from the "mass army" mindset typical in the Soviet and Russian armies. Commanders found that increased focus on platoon, squad, and team training was necessary to meet the challenges in the Chechen conflict.[90]

Russian generals and academics have examined this development at length, noting the efficacy of small teams of diverse occupational specialties;[91] in particular, integrating snipers into these teams significantly increased snipers' capability by providing cover and enhanced target acquisition and spotting—which was a change from how snipers had been employed during the first conflict.[92]

Overall, throughout the second Chechen campaign there were noteworthy developments in training and tactics based on combat experience in engaging unconventional fighters, conducting operations with integrated units, and operating in urban and mountain terrain. And while there was a dearth of official manuals and codified doctrine, there was an abundance of combat training instructions and recommendations based on experience in Chechnya that was available to Russian leaders—and these documents marked the first perceptible step in the transformation of Russian tactics and doctrine.[93]

However, despite these tactical changes and the greater success they enabled, improvements in tactical operations alone were not sufficient to win the second war. Rather, it was the changes made at the strategic level (discussed later) that made the difference in the second war and brought Chechnya back into the Russian Federation.

After the wars (2002–present)

After the Chechen wars, training the force has become a priority—both at the individual and collective (unit) level—and numerous sources indicate that Chechnya served as the impetus for the increased emphasis. The list of changes include: increased training intensity and reality; more live fires;[94] increased night training; training for reaction to Improvised Explosive Devices (IEDs) and ambushes; mountain operations; convoy training; checkpoint training; increasing training focused on the small unit; and drilling coordination with artillery and aviation.[95] The General Staff has emphasized the need for realism in training, and, to this end, has discussed revising shooting ranges and marksmanship tables, as well as plans to train units in unfamiliar terrain in order to add more realism to training.[96] Even the Deputy Minister of Defense felt the need to write an article on the topic, noting that new targeting systems will allow for increased flexibility and reality on ranges.[97]

In terms of collective training, Russian officials have incorporated lessons from the Chechen conflict into training at multiple levels. Overall, the combat experience in Chechnya has stimulated a renewed commitment to training—both in financial and in practical terms.[98] As former Defense Minister Ivanov noted in 2003, "we are paying for years wasted without combat training. . . . Hence the dramatic catastrophes of the past years provoked by the human factor."[99] From basic to brigade level training, combat experience in the North Caucasus has made a mark on Russian military training. Newly developed training doctrine for permanent readiness standardizes unit training cycles and increases the frequency of individual specialty training for soldiers in order to adjust to compressed service requirements for conscripts.[100]

The Caucasus experience is also reflected in the Russian military's large operational exercises of the past few years. For example, Vostok-2010 (and 2005) included counterguerilla/counterterrorist scenarios with an integrated, interservice force, incorporating rapid transport of forces to theater.[101] Other large military exercises including Kavkaz 2008 and 2009, Zapad-2009, Lodoga-2009, and Tsentr-2011 have displayed similar shifts in mentality and focus that can be traced to recent experience in Chechnya and Georgia.[102] As this book goes to print, the Russians are conducting Kavkaz-2012 in the Southern Military District in order to test aspects of the ongoing reforms, including the new command structure (brigades), integrated operations, and digitized command and control (C2) systems. It will involve over 8,000 military personnel including airborne, ground, naval, and missile forces. Although these exercises have preceded major combat operations in the past (1999, 2008), they are generally conducted in order to test the success of the ongoing Russian reforms inspired by their Caucasus experiences.

As for tactics, analysis of the Chechen campaigns continues, and tactical doctrine is being reviewed and updated both at the practical and theoretical levels—yet another indicator of the transformation taking place within the Russian military. As previously discussed, the local, asymmetric character of the Chechen campaign necessitated a change in tactics, mentality, and training in the Russian army starting at the soldier level. Small changes in troop organization and procedures improved survivability for some units, but the improved tactics, techniques, and procedures (TTPs) were not institutionalized and therefore not transferred to incoming personnel and units. However, as the campaign continued, and in the interim between the wars, these ground level TTPs were disseminated throughout army combat units on an informal basis while senior leaders and analysts discussed the concepts of "local wars" and the need for mobility, versatility, and flexibility. Changes in government policy reflected the new thinking and were implemented through the creation of battalion tactical groups and a greater focus on platoons and companies in combat and training. These changes were also reflected in the shift to the brigade system, and increased focus on preparing for unconventional threats.

Combat organization

The first Chechen campaign (1994–6)

The Russian military in 1994 continued to operate on the mobilization concept—a large officer corps served as headquarters staff officers in skeleton units designed to be filled by mobilized reservists in the event of war.[103] Although this structure had proven its efficacy to muster a mass army, it was wholly unsuitable for rapid deployment to resolve local, unconventional, or unexpected conflicts—which became abundantly clear during the first Chechen war. The major flaw of this system is that it sends raw conscripts to combat in hastily produced formations with soldiers they barely know and with whom they have never trained.[104]

Moreover, in 1994 these "skeleton units" proved extremely slow to mobilize, many of them were barely manned, and most of them had little combat capability.[105] This forced Russian leaders to combine units in order to produce formations "theoretically" able to conduct the mission.[106] However, units patched together in this way were ineffective: they lacked collective training; any sense of esprit de corps; trust among their fellow soldiers; or any type of general familiarity that could forge capable fighting units.[107] During the war there was little the military could do to change this reality or to produce organic units ready to deploy. The most viable solution was to send ever greater numbers of elite units—such as airborne or Special Forces—which had remained at higher states of readiness, were always close to fully manned, consistently trained together, and were therefore more capable of performing combat operations.

As units were cobbled together and deployed both to Grozny and the surrounding areas, it was not long before the Russians realized the utility of the "reinforced battalion" concept. Conducting irregular warfare in the challenging Chechen terrain, the largest unit that could consistently be employed tactically was a battalion. For this reason, "reinforcing" a battalion with assets and attachments traditionally held at higher levels allowed for independence and sustainability at the level where it was most needed.[108] Subsequently, the most successful battalions continued to push assets down to the squad and team levels, which could then effectively operate in urban terrain with the specific mix of equipment and personnel needed to accomplish the mission.

Nonetheless, it was the rare commander who was willing to pass his most powerful assets to young lieutenants and sergeants—where they often fell into the hands of the Chechens. And although the trend at the end of the first war was toward greater reinforcement at lower levels, overall, the experience in the first war revealed that the Russian military structure was top-heavy, both administratively and tactically. Structural changes in ensuing years are evidence of this lesson learned.[109]

Between the wars (1996–9)

Following the first war, the Commander of the North Caucasus Military District, General Viktor Kazantsev stated that "the experience of hostilities in overgrown mountains showed that the bulk of responsibility in battles is shouldered by small combat groups, mostly motorized and reconnaissance platoons and companies. They are better suited for acting in the mountains."[110] Indeed, their own experiences during the first war led Russian officers at all levels to discuss the necessity of organizing diverse assets at the battalion-level and below to facilitate the execution of complex and multifaceted missions. As a result, interservice formations were more frequently trained, while analysts examined the changing nature of conflicts worldwide—and what implications they had for adjusting military formations and doctrine in Russia.[111]

However, there was not sufficient time to affect any significant improvements to military formations, doctrinal increases to force integration, or smaller tactical formations during the short period between the wars. Although these issues would continue to attract attention and be revisited with great emphasis in the ensuing years, during the interwar period there was merely time to analyze the experiences of the first Chechen campaign. Nonetheless, that analysis represents the first stage of the major transformations that would later manifest themselves fully in the present reforms.

The second Chechen campaign (1999–2002)

Despite the need evinced during the first war—and the analysis during the inter-bellum years—there were only moderate changes to the organization of combat units during the second Chechen war. More permanent readiness units meant that fewer units were patched together at the last minute, and the newly reinforced battalions and tactical combat groups were able to employ artillery assets and combine engineer and infantry competencies at lower levels for increased flexibility and capability.[112] The creation of "Storm Detachments" was the most successful example of this effort.

After the wars (2002–present)

The Chechen conflict led to momentous changes in the employment and organization of Russian troop formations. This combat experience, when taken together with international experience in small to midsized irregular conflicts, led to the decision to transform the Russian army into a brigade system.[113] Additionally, initiatives such as creating various types of brigades—heavy, medium, light—are measures aimed at improving reaction time to an evolving spectrum of threats.[114] And although some observers might argue that the primary motivation for these fundamental changes stems from the lessons of the Georgian War, studying NATO deployments, or merely the need to keep up with the times, discounting the significant influence of the Chechen experience is simply counterproductive. The Chechen wars served as the first and most prominent modern catalyst for closer examination of future threats and of the corresponding need for mobility and versatility within Russian military formations.

A major step in that direction—and one of the most significant aspects to the "New Look"—was the reorganization of the Russian military into four joint strategic commands, and from a four to a three-tiered command structure—an adjustment aimed at increasing efficiency and responsiveness by eliminating intermediate levels of command.[115] In effect, the Ministry of Defense eliminated regiments and divisions—making the new reinforced brigades the principal combat organization of the Russian Armed Forces. Assets that previously belonged at the division level (artillery, mortars, air defense, etc.) have now been pushed to the reinforced brigades, which in turn pushed assets down to battalions and companies.

For example, companies now have their own mortars, battalions have artillery companies, and brigades have their own artillery battalions. In the past, each of those assets resided at one higher echelon. It is now much easier for commanders to get immediate indirect fire support because they need not ask for it—a vast improvement on the old model. Multiple factors contributed to this shift, but the experience of recent conflicts—notably those in the Caucasus—played a significant part in the reform's development. As Chief of the General Staff Makarov noted, "the regimental structure was created for those forces that . . . faced NATO. . . . But the experience of Afghanistan and two Chechen wars . . . has shown that this system is outdated."[116]

The reorganization has resulted in 85 newly formed brigades: 36 motorized infantry; 12 artillery; nine tank; and nine rocket. Designed to be permanent readiness brigades, they are, however, still undermanned and rely on large numbers of conscripts—called up twice a year for 12 month periods—so at any given moment half of them have been serving for less than six months.[117]

Precursors to this official change toward a streamlined and joint command structure first appeared in Chechnya with the creation of the Obyedinennaya Gruppirovka Federal'nykh Voisk (OGV, Joint Group of Federal Forces).[118] With the growing consensus that future conflicts would increasingly share characteristics of the Chechen wars, the concept of joint command naturally gained momentum and the committee on foreign and defense politics institutionalized this trend in 2004 when it made special note of the need for integrated commands in facing future threats.[119] Deputy Defense Minister Kolmakov's comments illustrate this need as well: "The experience of local wars . . . of the last decade shows the increasing role of . . . inter-service . . . troops. [The] outcome of the armed struggle mainly depends on the coordination . . . of the different services."[120]

Overall, the Chechen experience led to greater emphasis on the small unit, and increasing its assets and autonomy. The situation on the ground required Russian officers to fashion specialized tactical groupings in order to complete the tasks at hand. Each battalion became a "battalion-plus," and tactical groups at the lowest levels were provided with assets and diverse specialties required for the missions. A direct consequence of this wartime expedient is that Russian officials have incorporated this concept into training and the new structure of the peacetime army.[121] Defense Minister Sergei Ivanov emphasized this point in 2003, noting that the Chechen wars had demonstrated that units at the battalion-level and below are the most useful in unconventional conflicts.[122] In 2009, Chief of the General Staff Makarov echoed this point, stating that "it's necessary to form battalion tactical groups during peacetime, and not later and in a hurry . . . as it happened in the Chechen campaign."[123]

Command and Control

The first Chechen Campaign (1994–6)

Command and control (C2) and force coordination were among the most glaring weaknesses revealed in the first Chechen war and often led to undeniable, costly, and wholly preventable losses including tragic instances of fratricide and civilian casualties.[124] The Russians quickly relearned that effective C2 is absolutely vital to achieving success, and that lacking it can outweigh almost any other advantage on the battlefield.[125]

Especially at the outset of the first Chechen war, C2 was a problem not only among disparate units operating in a common area, but within organic units as well.[126] In Unconventional Warfare (UW) environments there is generally little distinction between enemy and friendly lines, which can lead to a chaotic mix of military, government, and civilian organizations working in a single area—often conducting seemingly unrelated tasks that can restrain or endanger friendly personnel. Chechnya was not an exception, and challenging terrain added to the difficulties of force coordination. Multiple units and subunits—ground, air, police, etc.—were working in one space, but communicating ineffectively, or not at all.[127]

Russian units—minimally trained to begin with—struggled to establish and maintain C2 as their soldiers negotiated urban and mountain terrain that naturally segmented the battlefield. Furthermore, commanders struggled to coordinate with outside units to arrange for much needed artillery and air support. As if things were already not bad enough, the already faulty and antiquated radios were put in the hands of undertrained soldiers and made communications all but impossible.[128] Russian commanders also lacked the benefit of a fully operational satellite system in the region, which further limited their operational vision.[129] Finally, inappropriate and excessive levels of command—Military District, Army, Division, and Regiment—increased bureaucracy (especially in approving combat orders), and resulted in an unresponsive and inefficient chain of command.[130]

Aslan Maskhadov's son is fond of retelling the story about his father (then Chief of Staff of Chechen Forces) moving at a maddeningly slow pace to relocate his headquarters after being surrounded by Russian forces during the first war. Despite his son's frantic requests to move, Maskhadov quietly worked at his field desk for a few more hours before calmly packing up and moving out—still well before the village started taking artillery rounds. Maskhadov later told his son that the Russians had to get permission for everything—so once the soldiers surrounding the village had dug into their positions, the request for fire would have to go through multiple echelons of command before the order to begin the assault would be given—and each level would take several hours.

During the first Chechen campaign there were no significant command and control solutions implemented. Small improvements in C2 were simply the military's attempts to "make it work" despite unwieldy command structures, shoddy equipment, poor planning, and untrained soldiers. Although units improved their level of coordination on the battlefield out of sheer necessity, these adjustments should not be viewed as genuine organizational development—they were, however, the precursors to it.

Between the wars (1996–9)

There were improvements in C2 during the interim between the Chechen campaigns—as evidenced by changes in training.[131] Significantly, the Russian Minister of Defense felt improving C2 was important enough to write an article about it and senior generals attempted to synchronize and improve communications by updating equipment and developing a more efficient logistical support system.[132]

With regard to force coordination, new training and doctrine began to authorize overriding authority to a single commander, who would manage the disparate forces in a given area—basic military principles referred to as "unity of command" and "unity of effort."[133] The causal link between the first Chechen war and the effort to improve C2 was unmistakable; numerous exercises were conducted to improve coordination and C2, while professional articles with names like "The Caucasus Will Teach Us" proliferated and described attempts by the police, military, border guards, and intelligence forces to improve interoperability.[134]

The second Chechen campaign (1999–2002)

By the time the second Chechen campaign had commenced, it was obvious that the mindset of the Russian military had shifted vis-à-vis command and control. The Russians began planning the reinvasion of Chechnya by March of 1999, and by that point, politicians and military commanders were already working in closer cooperation, which resulted in clearer objectives.[135] This improved military outcomes, in contrast to the very poorly planned campaign of 1994.[136]

Moreover, a great deal of attention had been paid to the legal justification for reinvasion through careful reframing of the conflict as a counterterrorism fight against international terrorists. This was critical to command and control because, if the Russian military was to lead the invasion and do the bulk of the fighting, then it would be granting de facto legal recognition of Chechen sovereignty. After all, if, as the Russians claimed, Chechnya was still a part of Russia, then it should be a matter solely for the police and interior ministry troops. If, however, the planned Russian invasion was designed to root out international terrorists who sought to undermine the foundation of the state, then a counterterrorism mission involving military forces (and their associated heavy weaponry, air assets, and firepower) was well within the mandates of the Russian constitution and specifically addressed by new Russian counterterrorism laws passed in 1998.[137]

So army commanders were placed in leadership positions within the MVD to facilitate coordination between military and other security forces,[138] and integrated training continued to address coordination and C2 issues right up to the October invasion.[139] The challenge of coordinating disparate forces still resulted in mistakes, but there was improvement from the first campaign.[140]

Unfortunately many of the same C2 troubles still plagued Russian units at lower levels. Junior officers struggled to coordinate troops or request artillery and air support on the battlefield.[141] Small combat units (6–12 man squads) generally lacked any communication equipment and were forced to rely on hand and arm signals between squads, or sound and light signals for coordination between platoons and company commanders.[142] Communication equipment had not been substantially improved, although there were some basic semi-reliable encryption capabilities that could prevent the Chechens from intercepting messages.[143] The GLONASS satellite system continued to function poorly.[144]

After the wars (2002–present)

Following the second Chechen campaign and the 2008 war with Georgia, the Russians initiated significant evolutionary changes in C2. However, the transition has been slow, and the need for additional improvements in this area has not diminished. Moreover, concerns over potential new threats and changes in equipment and force structure continue to place heightened demands on this function of the armed forces. It is therefore not surprising that command and control has been identified as one of the most significant areas for improvement in Russian military reforms of the past few years.

Removing intermediate levels of command dramatically improves combat power, and it also significantly improves C2. The Chechen experience, in particular, demonstrated the need to increase autonomy at the lower levels because the terrain and enemy required swift decisions from small unit leaders.[145] The adjustments that have since been incorporated into the enhanced brigades and battalion tactical groups indicate an acknowledgment of the necessity for responsive military units unencumbered by intermediary command levels, as well as efficient tactical formations that are mobile and independent enough to operate in complex environments.[146]

In Chechnya and in Georgia, incompatible systems made interservice communication all but impossible, a fact that had prompted the Russian defense ministry to intensify ongoing efforts at developing and implementing improved command and control systems.[147] President Medvedev has noted this issue specifically, stressing the urgent need for updating obsolete analog communications systems to digital platforms.[148] However, the process is slow and only the Russian Airborne forces are expected to be fully fielded with the new Polet-K (a highly touted automated C2 system that has been under development for over 10 years) by the end of 2012—although the system is expected to be widely tested during Kavkaz-2012.

Concluding thoughts

Military organizations—especially large ones—only make radical changes in formations, tactics, training, manning, and equipment when their governments determine that their current system of defense is inadequate to meet future and emerging threats. This is primarily because reforms of this nature are extremely expensive and difficult to implement. The transformation of the Russian military during the first two Chechen wars was evolutionary and iterative as lessons learned and improvements to standard operating procedures were slowly disseminated throughout the force and integrated into Russian doctrine. However, the fact that there is still an ongoing insurgency in the North Caucasus, and the realization that the Russian army was (and still is) unsuited for the threats that are likely to confront Russia in the foreseeable future has caused the evolutionary nature of change to become revolutionary—as the lessons of the Caucasus campaigns are now being institutionalized and implemented across the force.[149]

Russia's leading military theorists and strategists believe the reforms will need to go even deeper and that officers must develop entirely new methods of analyzing and conceptualizing tactical operations in order "to shake off the positional forms of confrontation . . . [and understand that] the classical principles of combined arms tactics will be somewhat altered, with new principles emerging . . . [and that] Network-centric . . . tactics means that troops and forces act . . . simultaneously over the entire fighting space of the enemy disposition."[150] In the security policy realm, the relatively new "Net-centric" concept is becoming increasingly more relevant (especially when describing nonstate adversaries) because it highlights the evolving nature of warfare as a continuously evolving, complex community of people, devices, information, and services interconnected by a communications network to achieve optimal benefit of resources and better synchronization of events and their consequences. These emerging principles reflect the growing relevance of unconventional conflict—relevance demonstrated in the Chechen wars where the Russian army was challenged with large scale asymmetric warfare.

The Chechen campaigns occupy a unique place in the development of the Russian Federation. Challenging, complex, and bloody, they were the first serious conflicts that the new Russian government encountered. These campaigns involved aspects of warfare that, although not new, were nonetheless unexpected, and reflected the fast-evolving and fundamentally different world that had formed since the fall of the Soviet Union and its last comparable combat experience in Afghanistan. Furthermore, these campaigns revealed the weaknesses of a country that had yet to reorganize after significant social and political transition.

As demonstrated throughout this chapter, the Caucasus campaigns highlighted lessons that cannot be ignored by Russian military and political leaders. Consequently, they initiated transformations within a military that had been reactionary, bureaucratic, and reliant on nuclear weapons and unskilled masses of conscripts for its projection of power. The transformation currently taking place is marked by a mental shift within the Russian security establishment, and by the ambitious (but largely unrealized) reforms that have been undertaken. These changes span the broad range of concerns that every large military organization must consider: social welfare, force structure, future threats, leader development, combat training, tactics, and equipment.

Ultimately, the experience in Chechnya has formed a resolve within Russian leadership to develop its military into an effective, modern force that is capable of fulfilling its function in today's world and meeting emerging and existent threats. While the full extent of these reforms remains to be seen, the effects of the North Caucasus conflicts in these processes are undeniable and enduring.

Notes

*Many sources below have been obtained through the East View database, which provides access to a variety of Russian newspapers, academic and professional journals, and other materials in electronic form both in English and in Russian. Use of this database is noted below and links to sources have been provided whenever possible. Access to the East View database is gained through subscription or institutional affiliation.

1 Roger N. McDermott, *The Reform of Russia's Conventional Armed Forces* (Washington, DC: The Jamestown Foundation, 2011), 49.
2 Because there is an ongoing guerrilla war in the Caucasus, the end date for the 1999 War is completely arbitrary. 2002 was chosen because it represents

the end of major ChRI operations and the beginning of Basayev's "Terrorism Phase." We have broken down the present guerrilla campaign into four periods: Bez Predel (a savage Guerrilla War, February 2000–May 2002), Basayev's War (the Terrorism Phase, May 2002–October 2005), the latent and incipient phase (October 2006–December 2007), and the Caucasus Emirate Phase (December 2007 to the present). See Robert W. Schaefer, *The Insurgency in Chechnya and the North Caucasus: From Gazavat to Jihad* (Santa Barbara: Praeger Security International, 2011), 192 for a full explanation of these phases.

3 See, *Current Digest of the Russian Press.* "Medvedev Gives His First State of the Nation Address," November 25, 2008: 1–7; as accessed in translation in East View database (www.ebiblioteka.ru/browse/doc/19428551) . For additional reference to these issues, see also, *Current Digest of the Russian Press.* "Defense Minister Launches Radical Military Reform," November 18, 2008: 1–6; as accessed in translation in East View database (www.ebiblioteka.ru/browse/doc/19397163). Comments by Deputy minister of Defense Aleksandr Kolmakov also demonstrate this point, "We must assemble a new army: professional, mobile, and which corresponds to all contemporary requirements," Aleksandr Kolmakov, "New System of Combat Training," *Russian Military Review,* 7 (July 2008), pp. 8–13; as accessed in translation in East View database (www.ebiblioteka.ru/browse/doc/19425271).

4 Robert Cassidy's analysis of the Russian military in regard to counterinsurgency is extremely useful. He notes that most militaries tend to focus on their "last good war," and that the Russian military's "last good war" was World War II—a high-intensity, conventional war, demanding a mentality that often proves counterproductive in irregular warfare. See: Robert M. Cassidy, *Counterinsurgency and the Global War on Terror* (London: Praeger Security International, 2006). See also, Robert M. Cassidy, "Strategic Studies Institute." *Russia in Afghanistan and Chechnya: Military Strategic Culture and the Paradoxes of Asymmetric Conflict.* February 2003. www.strategicstudiesinstitute.army/mil/pubs/display/.cfm?pubID=125. Accessed December 2, 2011.

5 It is undeniable that the 2008 Georgia conflict produced unique lessons learned and shaped current reforms and changes in the Russian military. The fact still remains, however, that many lessons discussed in the context of the Georgia conflict are simply confirmations of earlier learning points identified in Chechnya, and that many reforms and changes were already planned or underway, with the Georgia conflict serving to build support for and accelerate the process.

6 For analysis of the Soviet Counterinsurgency in Afghanistan, see: Andrei A. Doohovskoy, *Soviet Counterinsurgency in the Soviet Afghan War Revisited: Analyzing the Effective Aspects of the Counterinsurgency Effort* (Masters Thesis, Cambridge: Harvard University, 2009).

7 A brigade is a subcomponent of a division, commanded by a colonel and typically comprising 3,000–4,500 soldiers (in the US Army). The brigade system has come to replace the regimental system both in the US Army and in the Russian army. The "brigade concept" or brigade combat team is seen as a flexible unit, complete with built-in support elements that allow it to function independently. Brigades are considered more effective for responding quickly

to regional or asymmetric conflicts that do not require the full mass and power of larger formations.

8 Jane's Information Group. "Special Report, The Chechen Conflict: No End of a Lesson?" *Jane's Intelligence Review*, September 1, 1996.

9 One source puts the shortage of privates and sergeants at 384,000 in 1995; see, Report by the Directorate of Information of the Defence Ministry of the Russian Federation. "Russian Army Concerns." *Military News Bulletin*, October 1, 1995; as accessed in translation in East View database (www. ebiblioteka.ru/browse/doc/137181).

10 Robert W. Schaefer, *The Insurgency in Chechnya and the North Caucasus: From Gazavat to Jihad* (Santa Barbara: Praeger Security International, 2011), 190.

11 Deputy Defense Minister Kolmakov has commented on this point, discussing the changing nature of conflicts and the resulting demands such conflicts place on the Armed Forces; see, Aleksandr Kolmakov, "New System of Combat Training," *Russian Military Review*, 7 (July 2008), pp. 8–13; as accessed in translation in East View database (www.ebiblioteka.ru/browse/doc/19425271).

12 "Letter of President of the Russian Federation Boris Yeltsin to the Personnel of the Russian Armed Forces of May 23, 1996 (under article heading: Military Reform and Military Upgrading as a Task of National Importance)," *Military News Bulletin*, June 1996; as accessed in translation in East View database (www.ebiblioteka.ru/browse/doc/137232).

13 Vladimir Yermolin, "Six Months' Service and Into the Regular Army," *Current Digest of the Russian Press*, November 17, 1999: 16; as accessed in translation in East View database (www.ebiblioteka.ru/browse/doc/19928457).

14 "Letter of President of the Russian Federation Boris Yeltsin to the Personnel of the Russian Armed Forces of May 23, 1996 (under article heading: Military Reform and Military Upgrading as a Task of National Importance)," *Military News Bulletin*, June 1996; as accessed in translation in East View database (www.ebiblioteka.ru/browse/doc/137232).

15 Another account cites plans for three all-arms divisions, three airborne divisions, and four all-arms brigades, which would have 80 percent of personnel by wartime standards; see, RIA Novosti. "The Reform. A New Stage of Military Development," *Military News Bulletin*, no. 009 (September 1998); as accessed in translation in East View database (www.ebiblioteka.ru/browse/doc/137491).

16 "Letter of President of the Russian Federation Boris Yeltsin to the Personnel of the Russian Armed Forces of May 23, 1996 (under article heading: Military Reform and Military Upgrading as a Task of National Importance)," *Military News Bulletin*, June 1996; as accessed in translation in East View database (www.ebiblioteka.ru/browse/doc/137232).

17 Troop levels reached 100,000; see, Timothy, L. Thomas, "A Tale of Two Theaters: Russian Actions in Chechnya in 1994 and 1999," *Analysis of Current Events*, 12(5–6) (September 2000); http://fmso.leavenworth.army. mil/documents/chechtale.htm.

18 Alexander Golts, "FSB Dictates as Chechnya Rages On," *The Russia Journal*, May 25, 2001; also available at: (http://russiajournal.com/archive/ The_Russia_Journal/2001/May/25.05.2001/Defense/May.25–01.pdf) and (http://russiajournal.com/node/4882) . See also: Alexander Baranov, "Filth of the War," *Versty*, July 20, 2000: 1; as accessed in translation in East View database, Defense and Security, No 86, July 26, 2000 (www.ebiblioteka.ru/ browse/doc/2723323).

19 For discussion of resistance from civilian groups, such as the Committee of Soldiers' Mothers, see: Irina Belasheva, and Kirill Vasilenko, "Slow Change is Better Than No Change At All," *Vremya Novostei*, November 24, 2000: 3; as accessed in translation in East View database, Defense and Security, No 138, November 27, 2000 (www.ebiblioteka.ru/browse/doc/2724550). The US Army encountered a similar phenomenon with reserve component forces in Iraq and Afghanistan that brought the issues of the war to American communities and the political arena in a direct and powerful way.

20 Again, a completely arbitrary date, we refer to 2002–present as "After the Wars" for simplicity; see endnote 2 above.

21 Igor Kostyshin, "New Tasks of the Armed Forces of Russia," *Voennyi Diplomat*, December 31, 2004: 5–7; as accessed in translation in East View database (www.ebiblioteka.ru/browse/doc/7331105). It should be noted that a shift to more contract soldiers was resisted by many within the army establishment. Arguments for maintaining an army based on the mobilization concept often pointed to Russia's long borders, proximity to China, and overall unique geographic and geopolitical position. Also, many career officers simply felt threatened by potential changes to the system in which they thrived.

22 Sovet po Vneshnei i Oboronnoi Politike. "Voennoe Stroitel'stvo i Modernizatsia Vooruzhennikh Sil Rossii," *Doklad SVOR*, April 2004. http:// svop.ru/documents/74. Accessed January 10, 2012.

23 "Russian President's Address and Russia's Armed Forces," *Voennyi' Diplomat*, 3 (2009): 3–4; as accessed in translation in East View database (www.ebiblioteka.ru/browse/doc/21063523). See also: Rossiyskaya Gazeta. "Ryazan Will Turn Into Big Base for Training of Professional Junior Commanders for the Ground Forces," *Defense and Security*, June 15, 2009; as accessed in translation in East View database (www.ebiblioteka.ru/browse/ doc/20211615).

24 For discussion of professionalizing the NCO corps, see: Roger McDermott, "Russia's 'New Look' Contract NCOs," *Eurasia Daily Monitor,* April 17, 2012; also available at (www.jamestown.org/single/?no_cache=1&tx_ ttnews%5Btt_news%5D=39276). See also: Inna Matveyeva, "Military Sociology: Commander, Instructor, Tutor," *Russian Military Review*, March 31, 2006: 28–31; as accessed in translation in East Vew database (www.ebiblioteka.ru/browse/doc/9651740). See also: Aleksey Oborsky, "Social Portrait of the Junior Commander of the Armed Forces of the Russian Federation," *Russian Military Review*, February 2007: 44–9; as accessed in translation in East Vew database (www.ebiblioteka.ru/browse/ doc/11831264).

25 Yury Gavrilov, "Defense Minister Launches Radical Military Reform," *Rossiskaya Gazeta,* October 15, 2008: 1; as accessed in translation in East View database, Current Digest of the Russian Russian Press, No 43, Vol. 60, November 18, 2008, pp. 1–6 (www.ebiblioteka.ru/browse/doc/19397163).

26 McDermott, The Reform of Russia's Conventional Armed Forces, 48.

27 Sovet po Vneshnei i Oboronnoi Politike. "Voennoe Stroitel'stvo i Modernizatsia Vooruzhennikh Sil Rossii," *Doklad SVOR,* April 2004. http://svop.ru/documents/74. Accessed January 10, 2012. See also: Aleksandr Kolmakov, "New System of Combat Training," *Russian Military Review,* 7 (July 2008), lpp. 8–13; as accessed in translation in East View database (www.ebiblioteka.ru/browse/doc/19425271). For discussion of officer development and its effect on training, see: Colonel General Alexei Maslov, "Military Development: Field Training and Teamwork," *Russian Military Review,* March 31, 2006: 12–17; as accessed in translation in East View database (www.ebiblioteka.ru/browse/doc/9651737). In 2009 President Medvedev announced plans for founding new military institutions for training officers in the Moscow and St. Petersburg regions as part of an overall effort to raise the prestige of Russian military service, which President Medvedev named as a priority in 2011. Efforts to provide housing for military families and increases in pay also represent efforts to "increase the social status" of military service and attract quality personnel to the ranks. According to one source, starting January 1, 2012, Russian Platoon Leaders will receive 50,000 rubles and most senior officers will receive 150,000 rubles—a significant increase. However, as of this writing, the housing situation for officers still remains dismal; see, *Military Parade,* "Modernization of the Army—A Priority Objective," 2011: 4–7; as accessed in translation in East View database (www.ebiblioteka.ru/browse/doc/24802618). For outline of the RF's plan for improving social conditions for military service members, see: *Russian Military Review,* "The Strategy of the Social Development of the Armed Forces of the Russian Federation for the Period Until 2020," May 2008: 40–9; as accessed in translation in East View database (www.ebiblioteka.ru/browse/doc/18693084). For comments by CGS Makarov on increasing pay and benefits for service members, see: Voennyi' Diplomat, "Russian President's Address and Russia's Armed Forces," *Voennyi' Diplomat,* 3 (2009): 3–4; as accessed in translation in East View database (www.ebiblioteka.ru/browse/doc/21063523). Russian officials also seek to develop a culture of health and fitness as part of the make-over of Russian military life. For comments on this topic, see: Aleksandr Kolmakov, "New System of Combat Training," *Russian Military Review,* 7 (July 2008), pp. 8–13; as accessed in translation in East View database (www.ebiblioteka.ru/browse/doc/19425271).

28 "Military Doctrine of the Russian Federation (2000)," Military News Bulletin, May 1, 2000; as accessed in translation on East Vew database (www.ebiblioteka.ru/browse/doc/136494). For an interesting discussion of the reasons and history behind evolving requirements for size and makeup of armies, see: V. G. Naryshkin, "The Makeup of the Russian Federation's

Armed Forces in Regard to Their Purposes and the Country's Status,"
Military Thought, 4 (2009), p. 11; as accessed in translation in East View
database (www.ebiblioteka.ru/browse/doc/21297450). It should be noted that
reduction in the overall size of the Russian Armed Forces is a controversial
issue, and that many Russian analysts and leaders maintain that some form
of mobilization should be retained (similar to the US reserve components)
and caution against allowing the force to grow too small.

29 M. A. Gareyev, "Forces, Lessons and Conclusions Drawn from the Experience
of the Great Patriotic War as Applied to the Building Up and Training of the
Armed Forces," *Military Thought*, 2 (2010): 28; as accessed in translation in
East View database (www.ebiblioteka.ru/browse/doc/22878525).

30 See, *Voenno-promyshlennyi Kur'er*, "Army of the 21st Century: What
will be the 'new look' of the Russian Armed Forces?" June 24, 2009: 7, as
accessed in East View database with author cited within text as Nikolai E.
Makarov (www.ebiblioteka.ru/browse/doc/20260986). See also, Dmitry
Litovkin, "Army General Vladimir Boldyrev, Commander of the Ground
Forces: 'Ground Forces Should Become Compact and Mobile,'" *Defense and
Security*, June 26, 2009; as drawn from the newspaper: Izvestia (Moscow
issue), June 23, 2009, p. 3, and accessed in translation in East View database
(www.ebiblioteka.ru/browse/doc/20274581). This has been the case for some
time—for earlier discussion of this topic by former Defense Minister Ivanov,
see: Conference of leading staff of the RF Armed Forces, "New Quality of
the Russian Armed Forces," *Military News Bulletin*, October 31, 2003: 9; as
accessed in translation in East View database (www.ebiblioteka.ru/browse/
doc/5879575).

31 The sudden nature of the conflict with Georgia in 2008 serves as another
confirmation of the need for units of permanent readiness.

32 Olga Oliker, Russia's Chechen Wars 1994–2000: Lessons from Urban
Combat (Santa Monica: RAND, 2001), 14.

33 For analysis of the Soviet war in Afghanistan, as well as equipment issues in
this conflict, see: Andrei A. Doohovskoy, *Soviet Counterinsurgency in the Soviet
Afghan War Revisited: Analyzing the Effective Aspects of the Counterinsurgency
Effort* (Masters Thesis, Cambridge: Harvard University, 2009).

34 Alexander Frolov, "Soldaty Na Peredovoi i Polkovodtsy v Mozdoke,"
Izvestia, January 11, 1995; available in East View database (www.ebiblioteka.
ru/browse/doc/3180633).

35 Simon Saradzhyan, "Arms Industry to Get $960M Boon," *Moscow Times*,
January 28, 2000; available in East View database (www.ebiblioteka.ru/
browse/doc/224795).

36 Oliker, Russia's Chechen Wars 1994–2000, 25.

37 Ibid., 24.

38 "Letter of President of the Russian Federation Boris Yeltsin to the Personnel
of the Russian Armed Forces of May 23, 1996 (under article heading:
Military Reform and Military Upgrading as a Task of National Importance),"
Military News Bulletin, June 1996; as accessed in translation in East View
database (www.ebiblioteka.ru/browse/doc/137232).

39 RIA Novosti, "The Reform. A New Stage of Military Development," *Military
News Bulletin*, 009 (September 1998); as accessed in translation in East View
database (www.ebiblioteka.ru/browse/doc/137491).

40 It should be noted, however, that OMON and SOBR troops did not have any rear logistic services at their disposal, see: Col. Gen. L. S. Zolotov, "Counter-Terrorist Operation in Dagestan and Chechnya: Main Lessons and Conclusions," *Military Thought*, May 2000; as accessed in East View database (www.ebiblioteka.ru/browse/doc/2449342).

41 A handful of Mi-8 helicopters did arrive in Chechnya equipped with night vision capabilities, but the small number was not enough to make a broad impact on operations; see, Ilya Kedrov and Alexander Shaburkin, "Russian Flag Raised Over Komsomolskoe," *Defense and Security*, March 24, 2000; as drawn from the newspaper: Nezavisimaya Gazeta, March 22, 2000, p. 2, and accessed in translation in East View database (www.ebiblioteka.ru/browse/doc/2722137). Also, for superb analysis of this and other tactical issues in Chechnya, see, Mark Kramer, "Guerilla Warfare, Counterinsurgency and Terrorism in the North Caucasus: The Military Dimension of the Russian-Chechen Conflict," *Europe-Asia Studies*, March 2005: 209–90.

42 Zolotov, "Counter-Terrorist Operation in Dagestan and Chechnya," 2000.

43 One account notes that at the start of the second Chechen campaign Russian forces had no helicopters capable of functioning at night; see, *Military Parade*, "What Federal Troops are Lacking in Chechnya," January 1, 2000; as accessed in translation in East View database (www.ebiblioteka. ru/browse/doc/167889). See also: Pavel Koryashkin, "Russia-Chechnya Armament," *Itar-Tass Weekly News*, September 28, 1999; as accessed in translation in East View database (www.ebiblioteka.ru/browse/ doc/3006239). There were plans for increased delivery of night vision equipment to troops in Chechnya, but little follow-through as demonstrated in multiple reports.

44 Zolotov, "Counter-Terrorist Operation in Dagestan and Chechnya," 2000.

45 *Military Parade*, "What Federal Troops are Lacking in Chechnya," January 1, 2000; as accessed in translation in East View database (www.ebiblioteka.ru/browse/doc/167889).

46 Lester W.Grau and Timothy L. Thomas. "Russian Lessons Learned From the Battles For Grozny," *Marine Corps Gazette*, April 2000; available at (http://fmso.leavenworth.army.mil/documents/Rusn_leslrn.htm).

47 Col Gen M. I. Karatuyev, "Counter-Terrorist Operation in Northern Caucasus: Main Lessons and Conclusions," *Military Thought*, May 2000; notes from a round-table discussion with input from Col Gen Y.D. Bukreyev, Col Gen M.I. Karatuyev and Col Gen L.S. Zolotov, as accessed in translation in East View database (www.ebiblioteka.ru/browse/doc/400033).

48 *Military Parade*, "What Federal Troops are Lacking in Chechnya," January 1, 2000; as accessed in translation in East View database (www. ebiblioteka.ru/browse/doc/167889). For comments on this topic by Defense Minister Ivanov, see: From a speech by Sergei Ivanov, "Reequipment of the Armed Forces," *Russian Military Review*, 3 (March 2007): 68–70; as accessed in translation in East View database (www.ebiblioteka.ru/browse/doc/12212713).

49 Voennyi' Diplomat, "Russian President's Address and Russia's Armed Forces," *Voennyi' Diplomat*, 3 (2009), pp. 3–4; as accessed in translation in East View database (www.ebiblioteka.ru/browse/doc/21063523). President Medvedev has noted equipment development as a priority in 2011 as well;

see, *Military Parade*, "Modernization of the Army—A Priority Objective," 4–7; as accessed in translation in East View database (www.ebiblioteka.ru/browse/doc/24802618).

50 Weaknesses in communications equipment during the conflict with Georgia caused Russian officials to reassess the program for improving these systems. It was found that improvements, mandated in the aftermath of Chechen campaigns, had not been adequately achieved; see, Oleg Vladykin, "Technology Behind the Point of Backwardness," *Defense and Security*, June 2, 2010; as drawn from the journal: Nezavisimoe Voennoe Obozrenie, No. 19, May 28 – June 03, 2010, p. 1, and accessed in translation in East View database (www.ebiblioteka.ru/browse/doc/21929136). President Medvedev has stated that it is necessary to replace all analog systems with digital systems, and also to improve real-time capabilities of the GLONASS satellite system; see, RIA Novosti, "President Medvedev: About 85% of Communications Equipment in the Army is Outmoded.," *Defense and Security*, No 54, May 24, 2010; as drawn from: RIA Novosti, May 21, 2000, and accessed in translation in EastView Database (www.ebiblioteka.ru/browse/doc/21889835).

51 Note President Medvedev's comments on this theme, "An efficient military hardware procurement system must be established, as well as a balance between national defense deliveries and exports," Voennyi' Diplomat, "Russian President's Address and Russia's Armed Forces," *Voennyi' Diplomat*, 3 (2009): 3–4; as accessed in translation in East View database (www.ebiblioteka.ru/browse/doc/21063523). For discussion of increased funding, see also: From a speech by Sergei Ivanov, "Reequipment of the Armed Forces," *Russian Military Review*, 3 (March 2007): 68; as accessed in translation in East View database (www.ebiblioteka.ru/browse/doc/12212713). For comments by Defense Minister Serdyukov on management of military production, see: Yuri Mukhin, "On the Way to the Creation of the Contemporary and Effective Armed Forces," *Russian Military Review*, February 2008: 11; as accessed in translation in East View database (www.ebiblioteka.ru/browse/doc/17619003).

52 See, Yury Kuznetsov, "Priorities in Procurement of Aviation Equipment for the Armed Forces of the Russian Federation," *Military Parade*, 2011: 34–5; as accessed in translation in East View database (www.ebiblioteka.ru/browse/doc/26226420).

53 Konstantin Rashchepkin and Andrei Lunev, "Lieutenant General Vladimir Shamanov: Training and Look of the Army Will Change," *Defense and Security*, June 27, 2008; as drawn from the periodical: Krasnaya Zvezda, June 24, 2008, pp. 1, 2, and accessed in translation in East View database (www.ebiblioteka.ru/browse/doc/18533498).

54 It should be noted that Lieutenant General Shamanov is likely to be biased against armor, since his career developed primarily in Airborne (light infantry) units. The important point, however, is that equipment such as the tank—so long a fixture in the Soviet army—is being reassessed, at least in part due to experience in the North Caucasus.

55 Rashchepkin, Konstantin, and Lunev, "General Shamanov: Training and Look of the Army Will Change." *Defense and Security*, 2008; as drawn

from the periodical: Krasnaya Zvezda, June 24, 2008, pp. 1, 2, and accessed in translation in East View database (www.ebiblioteka.ru/browse/doc/18533498).

56 For more detailed discussion of this topic, see: Col. P.A. Kokhno, "Priority Development of the Military-Industrial Complex in Russia," *Military Thought*, 1 (2010): 20–7; as accessed in translation in East View database (www.ebiblioteka.ru/browse/doc/21945805).

57 See: Aleksandr Zhilin, "Boris Gromov: 'The Operation was Prepared in Deep Secrecy.'" *Current Digest of the Russian Press*, February 2, 1995: 6; as accessed in translation in East View database (www.ebiblioteka.ru/browse/doc/13582022).

58 Though not always the case, it is often observed that systems in the Russian military stifle initiative, and dissuade junior leaders from making decisions, such that high-ranking officers complete an inordinately large share of decision-making. This tendency can be traced to training that does not require soldiers to take initiative; see, V. G. Kiknadze, "Operational Training: Views of the Second Half of the 20th Century and Contemporary Development of the Military," *Military Thought*, 4 (2011): 142–51; as accessed in translation in East View database (www.ebiblioteka.ru/browse/doc/26459727).

59 See: David R. Stone, "Stalingrad and the Evolution of Soviet Urban Warfare," *The Journal of Slavic Military Studies*, 22(2) (2009): 196. Also: Oliker, *Russia's Chechen Wars 1994–2000: Lessons from Urban Combat*, 23. It is also worth noting that the Russian army that entered Chechnya had not conducted a divisional exercise since 1992; see, . See also: Pavel Felgengauer, "Military Reform After Chechnya: Generals should not be Berated but Retrained," *Current Digest of the Russian Press*, 48(52) (January 1997): 6–7; as accessed in translation in East View database (www.ebiblioteka.ru/browse/doc/13564161).

60 See, Felgengauer, "Military Reform After Chechnya," 6–7.

61 See, Frolov, "Soldaty Na Peredovoi i Polkovodtsy v Mozdoke." For an analysis of Russian vehicle vulnerabilities, see: Lester W. Grau, "Russian-Manufactured Armored Vehicle Vulnerability in Urban Combat: The Chechnya Experience," *Foreign Military Studies Offices*, January 1997. www.fas.org/man/dod-101/sys/land/row/rusav.htm. Accessed February 5, 2012.

62 See, Frolov, "Soldaty Na Peredovoi i Polkovodtsy v Mozdoke." This lesson had already been learned in Afghanistan, where Soviet conscripts were also loath to leave their vehicles. Failures to incorporate the lessons of the previous conflict were paid for in the Chechen conflicts. It is interesting to note, that Colonel General Boris Gromov, who had extensive experience in Afghanistan, was relieved of his duties as Defense minister in December 1994 for criticism of the planning of the Chechen war, see: Zhilin, "Boris Gromov: 'The Operation was Prepared in Deep Secrecy.'" Also see: Lester W. Grau and Timothy L. Thomas, "Russian Lessons Learned From the Battles For Grozny," *Marine Corps Gazette*, 2000; http://fmso.leavenworth.army.mil/documents/Rusn_leslrn.htm.

63   Ib Faurby and Marta-Lisa Magnusson, "The Battles of Grozny," *Baltic Defense Review*, 2(1999): 86.

64   Oliker, *Russia's Chechen Wars 1994–2000*, 25–7.

65   Lester W. Grau, "Russian-Manufactured Armored Vehicle Vulnerability in Urban Combat." *Foreign Military Studies Offices*, 1997; http://fmso. leavenworth.army.mil/documents/rusav/rusav.htmhttp://fmso.leavenworth. army.mil/authors.html.

66   For an interesting perspective on snipers in Chechnya, see: Aleksandr Petrenko and Lester W. Grau, Translation/Commentary by Lester W. Grau. *Night Sniper*. January 2000. http://fmso.leavenworth.army.mil/documents/ Night-sniper.pdf. Accessed December 29, 2011.

67   Oliker, *Russia's Chechen Wars 1994–2000*, 23, 25, 54.

68   Pavel Felgengauer, "Gudermes is Retaken: Chechens Lose Again in a Battle of Attrition," *Current Digest of the Russian Press*, January 24, 1996: 13; as accessed in translation in East View database (www.ebiblioteka.ru/browse/ doc/13555581).

69   See: Jane's Information Group, "Chechen Conflict: No End of a Lesson?" for discussion of a training center stood up in Mozdok during the first Chechen war.

70   The Second Battle of Grozny was a masterstroke in planning and execution— and perhaps one of the greatest operations of the twentieth century. In a brilliant coup de main, the Chechens were able to completely turn the tide of the war and gain independence. See Schaefer, *The Insurgency in Chechnya and the North Caucasus*, 134, 139–42.

71   Col. Gen. Viktor Kazantsev, "North Caucasian Military District: Reforming on the Go," *Military News Bulletin*, 12(December 1998); as accessed in translation in East View database (www.ebiblioteka.ru/browse/ doc/137517).

72   For discussion of this topic, see: Col. V. V. Kilunin, "New Views on Urban Warfare," *Military Thought*, 003(May 1998); as accessed in translation in East View database (www.ebiblioteka.ru/browse/doc/401110). Markings become extremely important in urban operations, since clearly identifying units' locations on the battlefield is difficult in urban conditions, and essential for integrating indirect fire or air support. Also, tracking which areas have been cleared is vital for security and coordination of ground units.

73   Col. Gen. Viktor Kazantsev, "Reforming on the Go," *Military News Bulletin*, 12 (1998); as accessed in translation in East View database (www.ebiblioteka. ru/browse/doc/137517).

74   See, Yekaterina Glebova, Nikolai Gritchin, and Viktor Litovkin, "Caucasus Will Teach Us—Army, Police, Rescue Workers, Border Troops and Intelligence Officers Hold Large Scale Exercises," *Current Digest of the Russian Press*, 50(30) (August 1998): 11; as accessed in translation in East View database (www.ebiblioteka.ru/browse/doc/13566917). This article demonstrates that the failures in the first Chechen war stimulated more earnest training (or creating the appearance of it), as this exercise was carried out with full troops, air assets, and artillery.

75   Valery Shanayev, "Russia Police Exercises," *Itar-Tass Weekly News*, December 1997; as accessed in translation in East View database (www.

ebiblioteka.ru/browse/doc/2940358). See also, Oliker, *Russia's Chechen Wars 1994–2000*, 37. See also: Valentina Lezvina, "Exercises in the Caucasus," *Kommersant Daily*. July 31, 1998. www.kommersant.ru/doc/202679. Accessed January 11, 2012.

76 Ilya Kedrov, "'New Type' of Division Created in the Army," *Current Digest of the Russian Press*, 50(15) (May 1998): 17; as accessed in translation in East View database (www.ebiblioteka.ru/browse/doc/13565621).

77 For an excellent discussion of Russian snipers see: Lester W. Grau, and Charles Q Cutshaw, "Russian snipers: In the mountains and cities of Chechnya," *Infantry* (July 2002) pp. 7–11; also available at (www.globalsecurity.org/military/library/report/2002/snipers.pdf). Grau and Cutshaw note that Soviet sniper training was cut back significantly in 1952, and that the first class of 12 students in 1999—a response to combat in Chechnya—signified renewed focus on the art of sniping. The course culminated with a month-long live fire exercise conducted in Chechnya in the mountains near Bamut, and resulted in increased numbers of snipers employed in Chechnya both as a part of line units and as "pure" snipers working independently. Overall, the Chechen war has increased attention on the training and employment of snipers—a key factor on the the unconventional battlefiled. Snipers have received more and more attention in the US army as well in recent and current conflicts. See also, Oliker, *Russia's Chechen Wars 1994–2000*, 37 and Krasnaya Zvezda, "Joint Command Exercises in North Ossetia," *Defense and Security*, 113 (September 19, 1998), 1; as accessed in translation in East View database (www.ebiblioteka.ru/browse/doc/2729300). Also see: Col. Gen. Viktor Kazantsev, "North Caucasian Military District: Reforming on the Go," *Military News Bulletin*, 12 (December 1998); as accessed in translation in East View database (www.ebiblioteka.ru/browse/doc/137517). Also: Valery Shanayev, "Russian 58th Army to Mark Third Anniversary," *Itar-Tass Weekly News*, May 1998; as accessed in translation in East View database (www. ebiblioteka.ru/browse/doc/2959687).

78 Oliker, *Russia's Chechen Wars 1994–2000*, 58. It is also noteworthy that junior officers were given much more leeway to call for indirect fire than in the first Chechen conflict. This is standard practice in the US Army, where each company has a mortar and artillery section and platoon leaders routinely call for indirect fire.

79 Thomas, "A Tale of Two Theaters."

80 Karatuyev, "Counter-Terrorist Operation in Northern Caucasus." Also see, Robert Garwood, "The second Russo-Chechen Conflict (1999 to date): 'A modern military operation'?" *The Journal of Slavic Military Studies*, 15(3) (September 2002), pp. 60–103. For a discussion of these and other concepts as they were applied by Soviet forces in World War II, see: M. A. Gareyev, "Forces, Lessons and Conclusions Drawn from the Experience of the Great Patriotic War as Applied to the Building Up and Training of the Armed Forces," 23–41; as accessed in translation in East View database (www. ebiblioteka.ru/browse/doc/22878525).

81 Col. Gen. Y. D. Bukreyev, "Counter-Terrorist Operation in Northern Caucasus: Main Lessons and Conclusions," *Military Thought*, 003 (May 2000); notes from a round-table discussion with input from Col Gen Y.D.

Bukreyev, Col Gen M.I. Karatuyev and Col Gen L.S. Zolotov, as accessed in translation in East View database (www.ebiblioteka.ru/browse/doc/400033) This, of course, reduced casualty rates and yielded success, but continuing collateral damage likely caused more difficulties—and casualties—in the long term.

82 Bislan Gantemirov was a prominent figure in this effort. For description of Bislan Gantemirov announcing the creation of a staff of Chechen armed forces in Achkoi-Martan, see: "Situation in North Caucasus," *Military News Bulletin*, December 1, 1999; as accessed in translation in East View database (www.ebiblioteka.ru/browse/doc/137665). Also see: "Situation in the North Caucasus," *Military News Bulletin*, January 1, 2000; as accessed in translation in East View database (www.ebiblioteka.ru/browse/doc/136446), for reference of Gantemirov acting as a guide. For description of the use of Bislan Gantemirov's militia as scouts, see: Grau and Thomas, "Russian Lessons Learned From the Battles For Grozny." See also: Oliker, *Russia's Chechen Wars 1994–2000*, 43, 44, 51, 52.

83 See: LTC Andrei Shevtsov, "Lt Gen Vladimir Popov: Modern Battle Techniques Should Emphasize Manueverability," *Soldat Otechestva*, June 10, 2000: 1; as accessed in translation in East View database, Defense and Security, No 73, June 26, 2000, (www.ebiblioteka.ru/browse/doc/2723007). Also see: Grau and Thomas, "Russian Lessons Learned From the Battles For Grozny."

84 See: Alexander Balakin, "Combat Training: Purges in the Urals.," Podrobnosti Defense and Security, No 43, March 1620, 2001; as accessed in translation in East View database (www.ebiblioteka.ru/browse/doc/2726000): 2. This is an example of a training event focused on establishing a cordon, and integrating air and artillery assets. This was a tactic that had been employed in Afghanistan with great frequency. Learning it again points to failures in the Russian military organization to transfer knowledge. See also: Bukreyev, "Counter-Terrorist Operation in Northern Caucasus."

85 Karatuyev, "Counter-Terrorist Operation in Northern Caucasus." As a result, some analysts therefore argued for expanding the numbers of soldiers serving in these units. Also see: Anatoly Yurkin, "Artillery Learning New Tactics in Chechnya," *Itar-Tass Weekly News*, November 1999; as accessed in translation in East View database (www.ebiblioteka.ru/browse/doc/3013283). The technique "see, destroy" was used to facilitate rapid strikes on mobile targets.

86 See, Schaefer, The Insurgency in Chechnya and the North Caucasus, chapters 3–4. See also, Doohovskoy, Soviet Counterinsurgency in the Soviet Afghan War Revisited.

87 Oliker, *Russia's Chechen Wars 1994–2000*, 52. See also: Grau and Thomas, "Russian Lessons Learned From the Battles For Grozny."

88 Major O. Finaev, "We Took Combat Experience Into Account When Working Out Our Plans," *Voennyi Vestnik Yuga Rossii*, 23 (May–June 2000): 3; as drawn from Defense and Security, No 76, July 3, 2000, and accessed in translation in East View database (www.ebiblioteka.ru/browse/doc/2723086). See also, Maj. Gen. I. N. Vorobyov, "Battle Team Tactics," *Military Thought*,

January 2001: 30–4 (as accessed in translation in East View database at www.ebiblioteka.ru/browse/doc/400102), in which General Vorobyov also notes the importance of training for mountain operations, citing the 3–4 month train up in the Turkestan for troops going to Afghanistan, which was lacking in the case of Chechnya.

89 Zolotov, "Counter-Terrorist Operation in Dagestan and Chechnya." It is also noted that initially these snipers had little impact on combat as most commanders did not understand how to employ them. Furthermore, Russian sniper rifles reportedly had less than half the range of the foreign-made rifles used by Chechens. As discussed below, Russian officers began to train on the proper employment of snipers. For discussion of increased sniper and counter-sniper training, see: LTC V. Tsymbalyuk, "Considering the Lessons of the Caucasus Conflict," *Na Strazhe Rodiny*, June 1, 2000: 1–2; as drawn from Defense and Security, No 80, July 12, 2000, and accessed in translation in East View database (www.ebiblioteka.ru/browse/doc/2723172).

90 See: Tsymbalyuk, "Considering the Lessons of the Caucasus Conflict." Leaders also found that it was important to conduct increased training in individual and team skills and maneuvers at times of limited visibility.

91 See: Bukreyev, "Counter-Terrorist Operation in Northern Caucasus." Lt. Gen Popov discusses the point that small, diverse task forces are a necessity in urban battles, see: Shevtsov, "Gen Popov: Modern Battle Techniques Should Emphasize Manueverability," *Soldat Otechestva*, 2000.

92 Vorobyov, "Battle Team Tactics." These teams included engineer, RPG, flamethrower, and various machine gun specialists.

93 Maj Gen I. N. Vorobyov, "New Plane in the Development of Tactics," *Military Thought*, March 1, 2001: 18–26; as accessed in translation in East View database (www.ebiblioteka.ru/browse/doc/400121). This transformation was generally characterized by a shift from the "mass army" mentality to one valuing joint and mobile capabilities. For example, a conference in Chita was dedicated to teaching officers small unit tactics based on lessons in Chechnya: *Krasnaya Zvezda*. "Siberian Military District Unit Commanders Study Small Group Combat Tactics," November 28, 2000: 1; as drawn from Defense and Security, No 140, December 1, 2000, and accessed in translation in East View database (www.ebiblioteka.ru/browse/doc/2724610).

94 "Live fires" refer to maneuver training in which units use live ammunition. This training requires significant focus in order to prevent one moving element from firing upon another. This training is extremely valuable, however, because it instills the precision and confidence needed in combat.

95 Sergei Bogdanov, "Combat Training: Learning to Win," *Krasnaya Zvezda*, June 1, 2005: 1; as drawn from Defense and Security, No 60, June 3, 2005, and accessed in translation in East View database (www.ebiblioteka.ru/browse/doc/7789046). Former Defense Minister Ivanov notes that training is increasing in the military, with the first battalion-level live fire exercise in post-Soviet history conducted in 2005, see: From a speech by Sergei Ivanov. "Reequipment of the Armed Forces," *Russian Military Review*, 3 (March 2007): 68–70; as accessed in translation in East View database (www.ebiblioteka.ru/browse/doc/12212713). For discussion of mountain training and plans for a mountain

training center building on the experience of the Daryal mountaineering
testing ground of the Southern Military District, see: Lt. Gen. V. G. Yevnevich,
"Features of Combat Training for the Changing Armed Forces," *Military
Thought*, 4 (2010): 144–8; as accessed in translation in East View database
(www.ebiblioteka.ru/browse/doc/24406314). In 2007 a mountain unit
from the Caucasus Military District conducted training on Mt. Elbrus to
incorporate climbing skills in a combat scenario, see: Defense and Security.
"For the First Time in Russia's History an Army Unit Climbed," *Defense and
Security*, August 15, 2007; as drawn from RIA Novosti, August 13, 2007, and
accessed in translation in East View database (www.ebiblioteka.ru/browse/
doc/12447586). Additionally, a military occupation specialty "mountaineering"
was added to the Russian military in 2009, and a mountain training center
is slated to open in 2012 at the tourist base Terskol in Kabardino-Balkaria,
see: Vzglyad. "A Mountain Training Center of the Armed Forces Will Appear
in Kabardino-Balkaria." *Defense and Security*, November 7, 2011; as drawn
from Vzglyad, November 02, 2011, and accessed in translation in East View
database (www.ebiblioteka.ru/browse/doc/26203483).

96 Rashchepkin and Lunev, "General Shamanov: Training and Look of the Army
Will Change."

97 Kolmakov also discusses the inclination for excessive repetition on
set-piece training scenarios where soldiers could anticipate exactly where
and when targets would appear. He maintains that new equipment and a
more combat-focused mentality (which is a result of recent experience in
Chechnya) will help change this tendency in training. See, Kolmakov, "New
System of Combat Training," 12; as accessed in translation in East View
database (www.ebiblioteka.ru/browse/doc/19425271). General Boldyrev
oversaw training in 2009 that incorporated new elements of targetry and
a mentality of realism, and in which units were required to function as if
the situation were real, see: "A Tactical Research Exercise Will Take Place
in Kemerovo Region Between March 16 and 23," *Defense and Security*,
March 13, 2009; as drawn from RIA Novosti, March 11, 2009, and
accessed in translation in East View database (www.ebiblioteka.ru/browse/
doc/19729258).

98 For example, in 2010 combat training was increased by 30 percent, see:
Military Parade. "Modernization of the Army—A Priority Objective," 4–7; as
accessed in translation in East View database (www.ebiblioteka.ru/browse/
doc/24802618). See also: Rashchepkin and Lunev, "General Shamanov:
Training and Look of the Army Will Change."

99 Conference of leading staff of the RF Armed Forces. "New Quality of the
Russian Armed Forces," *Military News Bulletin*, October 31, 2003: 11; as
accessed in translation in East View database (www.ebiblioteka.ru/browse/
doc/5879575).

100 Yevnevich, "Features of Combat Training for the Changing Armed Forces,"
145–6.

101 Gen. Yuri Baluyevsky, "Vostok-2005: A Theory Put to Test," *Russian Military
Review*, August 31, 2005: 54–7; as accessed in translation in East View
database (www.ebiblioteka.ru/browse/doc/8438480). Also: Anton Bondarenko and Vladimir Galaiko, "Hero of Russia LT GEN Vladimir Shamanov,

Director of the Main Department of Combat Training and Service of Troops of the Armed Forces: The War Confirmed the Need for Reforms," *Defense and Security*, 14 (February 13, 2009); as accessed in translation in East View database (www.ebiblioteka.ru/browse/doc/19599343).

102 Center-2008 involved a partial call-up of reservists, joint interservice training, and an unconventional threat: the enemy "southern" attempted to seize key fuel and energy infrastructure, see: Vladimir Mukhin, "Caucasus Experience for Troops in Urals," *Defense and Security*, 97(September 3, 2008); as drawn from the newspaper: Nezavisimaya Gazeta, September 2, 2008, p. 7, and accessed in translation (www.ebiblioteka.ru/browse/doc/18843939). Also: Leonid Yakutin, "Center 2008 Exercise," *Military Parade*, 2008: 50–1; as accessed in translation in East View database (www.ebiblioteka.ru/browse/doc/19127316). Ladoga-2009 and West-2009 involved quick deployment to Belarus, which trained mobility and responsiveness—a shift that can be linked to the Chechen experience, see: Dmitry Litovkin, "Network Exercise," *Defense and Security*, 107(September 30, 2009); as drawn from the newspaper: Izvestia (Moscow issue), September 28, 2009, pp. 1, 5, and accessed in translation in East Vew database (www.ebiblioteka.ru/browse/doc/20682696).

103 Officers of these units theoretically maintained equipment and administrative functions for this possibility. These units are also referred to as cadre-strength units or paper units.

104 See: Tatyana Scorobogatko, "Blood is Flowing in the Streets," *Moscow News*, 1995. See also, M. A. Gareyev, "Forces, Lessons and Conclusions Drawn from the Experience of the Great Patriotic War as Applied to the Building Up and Training of the Armed Forces." 28; as accessed in translation in East View database (www.ebiblioteka.ru/browse/doc/22878525).

105 The result: units with vehicles and crews, but no infantry soldiers, see: Lester W. Grau, "Changing Russian Urban Tactics: The Aftermath of Grozny." *INSS Strategic Forum*, 38 (July 1995), available at: http://fmso.leavenworth.army.mil/documents/grozny.htm.

106 See, Gareyev, M. A. "Forces, Lessons and Conclusions Drawn from the Experience of the Great Patriotic War as Applied to the Building Up and Training of the Armed Forces," 28; as accessed in translation in East View database (www.ebiblioteka.ru/browse/doc/22878525).

107 Many accounts describe Russian soldiers going into combat as barely knowing one another, and having little understanding of the mission. See, Tatyana Scorobogatko, "Blood is Flowing in the Streets."

108 Rod Thornton, " Organizational Change in the Russian Airborne Forces: The Lessons of the Georgian Conflict," *Strategic Studies Institute*, December 23, 2011, 26, 27, 32. www.strategicstudiesinstitute.army.mil/pubs/display.cfm?pubID=1096. Accessed December 28, 2011.

109 As discussed further, we now see the Russian military shifted to the Brigade structure, with a reduced officer corps. Chechnya, of course, was not the sole factor in this transformation, but played a central role in making the case for these changes.

110 Kazantsev, "Reforming on the Go."

111 For a discussion of integrated force groupings in this period, see: Col. Yu. N. Tuchkov, "Integrated Forces and Their Employment in Armed Conflicts and

Local Wars," *Military Thought*, 002 (March 1997); as accessed in translation in East View database (www.ebiblioteka.ru/browse/doc/401014).

112 Vorobyov, "Battle Team Tactics."

113 See, Dmitry Litovkin, "Army General Vladimir Boldyrev, Commander of the Ground Forces." General Boldyrev discusses how the Brigade system addresses requirements for the army.

114 Maj. Gen. I. N. Vorobyov, "Improvement on the Structure and Organization of Combined-Arms Units," *Military Thought*, 001 (March 31, 2004): 163–71; as accessed in translation in East View database (www.ebiblioteka.ru/browse/doc/6225186).

115 See, *Military Parade*. "Modernization of the Army—A Priority Objective," 2011: 4–7; as accessed in translation in East View database (www.ebiblioteka.ru/browse/doc/24802618). President Medvedev announced these structural changes to the Russian military that addressed the issue of command and control on September 20, 2008. McDermott, *The Reform of Russia's Conventional Armed Forces*, 48.

116 See, *Voenno-promyshlennyi Kur'er*. "Army of the 21st Century: What will be the 'new look' of the Russian armed Forces?" 7; as accessed in East View database with author cited within text as Nikolai E. Makarov (www.ebiblioteka.ru/browse/doc/20260986). It should be noted that CGS Marshal N. V. Ogarkov had proposed a brigade System for the Soviet army. Thus, the idea was not entirely new, but one that gained support and was shaped by the Chechen conflict, see: Gregory Lannon, "Russia's New Look Army Reforms and Russian Foreign Policy," *Journal of Slavic Military Studies*, 24(January 2011): 26–54. For detailed discussion and background of this topic, see P. N. Kryazhev, "Development of the Military Administrative Territorial Structure of the Armed Forces of the Russian Federation," *Military Thought*, no. 4 (2011): 47–60; as accessed in translation in East View database (www.ebiblioteka.ru/browse/doc/26459719). For a discussion of the shift to strategic commands as well as other initiatives, see: Irina Isakova, "Russian Defense Reform: Current Trends," *Strategic Studies Institute*, November 2006, 10. www.strategicstudiesinstitute.army.mil/pubs/display.cfm?PubID=740. Accessed December 3, 2011.

117 Pavel Felgenhauer, "The Failure of Military Reform in Russia," *Eurasia Daily Monitor*, 9(123) (June 28, 2012). www.jamestown.org/programs/edm/single/?tx_ttnews%5Btt_news%5D=39554&cHash=4e903614dc162b52d6e862c413348301

118 While the concept of the OGV was probably the only way to address the problem of coordination, Mark Kramer points out that this specific organization continued to experience problems of coordination, see: Mark Kramer, "Guerilla Warfare, Counterinsurgency and Terrorism in the North Caucasus: The Military Dimension of the Russian-Chechen Conflict," *Europe-Asia Studies*, March 2005: 209–90.

119 Sovet po Vneshnei i Oboronnoi Politike. "Voennoe Stroitel'stvo i Modernizatsia Vooruzhennikh Sil Rossii," *Doklad SVOR*, April 2004. http://svop.ru/documents/74. Accessed January 10, 2012. Also see: "Military Doctrine of the Russian Federation (2000)," *Military News Bulletin*, May 1, 2000; as accessed in translation on East Vew database (www.ebiblioteka.ru/browse/doc/136494).

120   Kolmakov,"New System of Combat Training."
121   Maslov, "Military Development: Field Training and Teamwork," 12–17.
122   Sergey Ivanov comments on the need for focusing on battalion size units and smaller, and also notes that the probability of a classical-type war in the future is less likely; see, Andrei Naryshkin, "Chechen Campaigns Force RF Armed Forces to Change Tactics," *Itar-Tass Weekly News*, July 25, 2003; as accessed in translation in East View database (www.ebiblioteka.ru/browse/doc/5133286). See also, Yevnevich, "Features of Combat Training for the Changing Armed Forces," *Military Thought*, (2010): 146. The battalion is now the focus of training, to be developed for joint and independent operations.
123   *Voenno-promyshlennyi Kur'er.* "Army of the 21rst Century: What will be the 'new look' of the Russian Armed Forces?" 7; as accessed in East View database with author cited within text as Nikolai E. Makarov (www.ebiblioteka.ru/browse/doc/20260986).
124   President Yeltsin admitted this in a speech to the armed forces in 1996, stating that "mistakes have been made by the authorities, politicians and military leaders. The failure to coordinate their actions, and sometimes lack of professionalism, resulted in considerable losses among both servicemen and peaceful civilians." See: "Address of President of the Russian Federation Boris Yeltsin to the Leaders of the Russian Armed Forces on May 29, 1996 (under article heading: Military Reform and Military Upgrading as a Task of National Importance)," *Military News Bulletin*, June 1996; as accessed in translation in East View database (www.ebiblioteka.ru/browse/doc/137232).
125   For instance, in January of 1996 Russian Special Forces surrounded a Dagestani village containing Salman Raduyev's troops, but were unable to capitalize on the situation due to poor C2 and coordination with air and artillery assets, see: Pavel Felgengauer, "Military Reform After Chechnya: Generals should not be Berated but Retrained," *Current Digest of the Russian Press*, 48(52) (January 1997): 6–7; as accessed in translation in East View database (www.ebiblioteka.ru/browse/doc/13564161).
126   For example, one account describes a commander and staff of artillery having only one outdated communications channel, which had to be shared with the air defense commander: Lt. Gen. M. I. Karatuyev, "Missile Forces and Artillery in Local Wars and Armed Conflicts." *Military Thought*, February 1998; as accessed in translation in East View database (www.ebiblioteka.ru/browse/doc/401080).
127   This led to instances of fratricide between ground units and also from artillery and air support. Law enforcement and military entities had notoriously poor connections, and the former had little experience or training in coordinating indirect fire or air support. See, Pavel Felgengauer, "Gudermes is Retaken," 13. Also see, Oliker, *Russia's Chechen Wars 1994–2000*, 33.
128   This reality should not have come as a surprise to an army that had returned from Afghanistan only five years earlier. For discussion of command and control issues, as well as analysis of other weaknesses in Russian army during the first Chechen war see, Aleksandr Zhilin, "Russian Army: Lost and Lonely," *Moscow News*, September 12, 1996. For additional discussion of C2 issues and lack of proper coordination of intelligence support, see, Oleg Blotsky, "Initiative is in

Rebels' Hands: The Course and Pace of Fighting are being Set by
Dudayev's Staff," *Current Digest of the Russian Press*, April 10, 1996: 1
6–17; as accessed in translation in East View database (www.ebiblioteka.ru/
browse/doc/13547655). For discussion of a break in Russian C2 at the end of
1994 that resulted in coordinated artillery and air support restored only on
January 3, 1995. See also: Pavel Felgengauer, "Russia on the Brink of Catastrophe, Apocalypse Now: The Russian Units that Entered Grozny are Routed,"
Current Digest of the Russian Press, February 1, 1995: 5–6; as accessed in translation in East View database (www.ebiblioteka.ru/browse/doc/13581898).

129　See, Saradzhyan, "Arms Industry to Get $960M Boon," 2000. There were
also insufficient maps for officers to plan and execute operations in Chechnya, one eye-witness noted that officers were using 1:100,000 maps, where a
much closer view of the city, such as 1:25,000, would have been far better for
conducting combat operations, see Frolov, "Soldaty Na Peredovoi i Polkovodtsy v Mozdoke."

130　This system also resulted in an oversized officer corps that was maintained to
preside over an influx of reservists in the event of mobilization. Subsequent
efforts to change this system were naturally resisted by many officers seeking
to maintain this beneficial status quo.

131　During this time, Colonel Kolibaba refers to the interaction between forces
as "a task of major theoretical and practical urgency," Col. V. G. Kolibaba,
"Interaction Between Armed Forces and Other Troops of the RF and Allied
Armed Forces," *Military Thought*, 003 (January 1997); as accessed in translation in East View database (www.ebiblioteka.ru/browse/doc/401026).

132　See: RIA Novosti. "The Reform. A New Stage of Military Development,"
where the defense minister Marshal Igor Sergeyev enumerates command
and control as a priority reform objective. Also, see: Col A. A. Dremkov,
"Unconventional Warfare: Essence, Problems, Prospects," *Military Thought*,
January 1998; as accessed in translation in East View database (www.ebib-
lioteka.ru/browse/doc/401102), for an assessment that unconventional war
calls for increased attention to centralizing command and control and developing coordination for mixed force groupings. See also: Maj. Gen. V. E.
Shulgin, "Development of Weapons and Military Equipment in New Economic Conditions," *Military Thought*, January 1998; as accessed in translation in East View database (www.ebiblioteka.ru/browse/doc/401098), for
discussion of developing communications, logistics and weapon systems for
local conflicts.

133　As noted in an article in Military Thought, this territorial command and control principle required aviators to adjust to the integrated ground command,
see: A. B. Krasnov and Col. Yu N. Shemuranov. "Role of Aviation in Armed
Conflicts." (as accessed in translation in East View database (www.ebibli-
oteka.ru/browse/doc/401079).

134　For example, the stated objective of one particular exercise in 1998 was "to
work out the details of command and control," see: Glebova, Gritchin, and
Litovkin. "Caucasus Will Teach Us," 11.

135　Former Russian Prime Minister Sergei Stepashin, as quoted by Sergei Pavosu-
dov, "Bloka OVR voobsche moglo i ne bit'," *Nezavisimaya Gazeta*,

January 14, 2000; available in East View database (www.ebiblioteka.ru/browse/doc/267285).

136 For a discussion of poor planning in the first campaign, see: Zhilin, "Boris Gromov: 'The Operation was Prepared in Deep Secrecy.'" See also: Thomas, "A Tale of Two Theaters."

137 Schaefer, *The Insurgency in Chechnya and the North Caucasus*, 203–4. For further reading on related topics see also: Matthew Evangelista, *The Chechen Wars: Will Russia go the Way of the Soviet Union?* (Washington, DC: Brookings Institution Press, 2002); James Hughes, *Chechnya: From Nationalism to Jihad* (Philadelphia, PA: University of Pennsylvania Press, 2007); Richard Sakwa, *Chechnya: From Past to Future* (London: Anthem Press, 2005) (specifically articles by Pavel Baev and John Russel); Tony Wood, *Chechnya: The Case for Independence* (New York, NY: Verso, 2007).

138 For example, General Shevtsov, a career Army officer, was appointed as MVD commander of the North Caucasus region, see: Grau and Thomas, "Russian Lessons Learned From the Battles For Grozny." See also, Thomas, "A Tale of Two Theaters."

139 For an example of training aimed at building coordination between army and MVD units, see, Balakin, "Combat Training: Purges in the Urals."

140 Thomas, "A Tale of Two Theaters."

141 This was attributed to weaknesses in military training and education, see Zolotov, "Counter-Terrorist Operation in Dagestan and Chechnya."

142 Vorobyov, "Battle Team Tactics." Vorobyov notes that this necessitated reliance on the independence and initiative within the small team itself— a typical example of how unconventional conflict demands considerable self-sufficiency at the small unit level.

143 There was some use of Akveduk radios that were capable of encryption, which reduced the Chechens' ability to intercept communications, see: Grau and Thomas, "Russian Lessons Learned From the Battles For Grozny."

144 See: Moscow Times. "Cabinet Approves Funds for GLONASS," *The Moscow Times*, August 3, 2001: 3; available in East View database (www.ebiblioteka.ru/browse/doc/232634). Plans were made to increase funding for the GLONASS system during this time, see: Saradzhyan, "Arms Industry to Get $960M Boon." For discussion of improving military satellite and navigation capabilities, see: Maj. Gen V. G. Elyushkin, Col. E. I. Dolgov, and Col. V. S. Vdovin, "Reforming the Topographic, Geodetic and Navigation Support System," *Military Thought*, July 1, 2000: 54–62; as accessed in translation in East View database (www.ebiblioteka.ru/browse/doc/400067).

145 General Gareyev makes this point in commenting that that command and control must be fundamentally adjusted due to changing tempos and requirements in modern conflicts, which necessitate greater flexibility and independence at lower levels, M. A. Gareyev, "Forces, Lessons and Conclusions Drawn from the Experience of the Great Patriotic War as Applied to the Building Up and Training of the Armed Forces," *Military Thought*, 2 (2010): 40; as accessed in translation in East View database (www.ebiblioteka.ru/browse/doc/22878525).

146   Andrei Naryshkin,. "Chechen Campaigns Force RF Armed Forces to Change
       Tactics," *Itar-Tass Weekly News*, July 25, 2003; as accessed in translation in
       East View database (www.ebiblioteka.ru/browse/doc/5133286).
147   *Voenno-promyshlennyi Kur'er.* "Army of the 21rst Century: What will be the
       'new look' of the Russian Armed Forces?" 7; as accessed in East View data-
       base with author cited within text as Nikolai E. Makarov (www.ebiblioteka.
       ru/browse/doc/20260986).
148   See: Voennyi' Diplomat. "Russian President's Address and Russia's Armed
       Forces." *Voennyi' Diplomat*, 3 (2009): 3–4; as accessed in translation in East
       View database (www.ebiblioteka.ru/browse/doc/21063523). The need for
       modern communications platforms and equipment is acknowledged across
       the board. For reference to the need for improved communications equipment
       to improve command and control at the tactical level, see: Litovkin, "Army
       General Vladimir Boldyrev, Commander of the Ground Forces."
149   Potential threats facing Russia include: terrorist and insurgent activities in
       Chechnya, Dagestan, and surrounding areas; terrorist/criminal organizations
       gaining influence and threatening energy infrastructure/interests in Central
       Asian republics; and the destabilizing spread of violent extremist organiza-
       tions (VEOs) and narco-trafficking emanating from an unstable Afghanistan.
150   Maj. Gen. I. N. Vorobyov and Col V. A. Kiselyov, "From Present-Day Tactics
       to Network-Centric Action," *Military Thought*, July 2011: 70–9; as ac-
       cessed in translation in East View database (www.ebiblioteka.ru/browse/
       doc/26095939).

Bibliography

*Many sources below have been obtained through the East View database, which
provides access to a variety of Russian newspapers, academic and professional
journals, and other materials in electronic form both in English and in Russian.
Use of this database is noted below and links to sources have been provided
whenever possible. Access to the East View database is gained through subscription or institutional affiliation.

"Address of President of the Russian Federation Boris Yeltsin to the Leaders of
    the Russian Armed Forces on May 29, 1996 ,(under article heading: Military
    Reform and Military Upgrading as a Task of National Importance)," *Military
    News Bulletin*, June 1996; as accessed in translation in East View database
    (www.ebiblioteka.ru/browse/doc/137232).
Alexander Balakin, "Combat Training: Purges in the Urals," *Defense and
    Security*, No 43, March 16, 2001; as accessed in translation in East View data-
    base (www.ebiblioteka.ru/browse/doc/2726000).
Arbatov, Alexei, G. "Transformation of Russian Military Doctrine: Lessons
    Learned from Kosovo and Chechnya," *The Marshall Center Papers*, No. 2,
    July 2000.
Baluyevsky, Gen. Yuri, "Vostok-2005: A Theory Put to Test," *Russian Military
    Review*, August 31, 2005: 54–7; as accessed in translation in East View data-
    base (www.ebiblioteka.ru/browse/doc/8438480).

Baranov, Alexander, "Filth of the War," *Versty*, July 20, 2000: 1; as accessed in translation in East View database, Defense and Security, No 86, July 26, 2000 (www.ebiblioteka.ru/browse/doc/2723323).

Belasheva, Irina and Kirill Vasilenko, "Slow Change is Better Than No Change At All," *Vremya Novostei*, November 24, 2000: 3; as accessed in translation in East View database, Defense and Security, No 138, November 27, 2000 (www.ebiblioteka.ru/browse/doc/2724550).

Blank, Dr Stephen, *Studying Soviet Low-Intensity Conflicts*. Soviet Studies, Air Power Research Institute. Maxwell Air Force Base: Air University Press, 1989.

Blank, Stephen J., Marcel de Haas, Jacob W Kipp, and Alexander G Savelyev, Russian Military Politics and Russia's 2010 Defense Doctrine Carlisle, PA: Strategic Studies Institute, 2011.; *www.StrategicStudiesInstitute.army.mil*

Blotsky, Oleg, "Initiative is in Rebels' Hands: The Course and Pace of Fighting are being Set by Dudayev's Staff," *Current Digest of the Russian Press*, April 10, 1996: 16–17; as accessed in translation in East View database (www. ebiblioteka.ru/browse/doc/13547655).

Bogdanov, Sergei, "Combat Training: Learning to Win," *Krasnaya Zvezda*, June 1, 2005: 1; as drawn from Defense and Security, No 60, June 3, 2005, and accessed in translation in East View database (www.ebiblioteka.ru/browse/doc/7789046).

Bondarenko, Anton and Vladimir Galaiko, "Hero of Russia LT GEN Vladimir Shamanov, Director of the Main Department of Combat Training and Service of Troops of the Armed Forces: The War Confirmed the Need for Reforms," *Defense and Security*, February 13, 2009; as accessed in translation in East View database (www.ebiblioteka.ru/browse/doc/19599343).

Borisova, Yevgenia, "In Chechnya, A War Against the Press," *The Moscow Times*, January 5, 2000; available in East View database (www. ebiblioteka. ru/browse/doc/224508).

Bukreyev, Col. Gen. Y. D., "Counter-Terrorist Operation in Northern Caucasus: Main Lessons and Conclusions," *Military Thought*, May 2000; notes from a round-table discussion with input from Col Gen Y.D. Bukreyev, Col Gen M.I. Karatuyev and Col Gen L.S. Zolotov, as accessed in translation in East View database (www.ebiblioteka.ru/browse/doc/400033).

Cassidy, Robert M., *Counterinsurgency and the Global War on Terror*. London: Praeger Security International, 2006.

— "Strategic Studies Institute," *Russia in Afghanistan and Chechnya: Military Strategic Culture and the Paradoxes of Asymmetric Conflict*, February 2003. www.strategicstudiesinstitute.army/mil/pubs/display/.cfm?pubID=125 (accessed December 2, 2011).

"CDI: Russia Weekly (Rossiskaya Gazeta)," *Sergey Ivanov Eyes Army Priorities, Reform, Contract Manning*, January 14, 2003. www.cdi.org/russia/240–13. cfm (accessed February 2, 2012).

Cohen, Ariel and Robert E. Hamilton, "Strategic Studies Institute," *The Russian Military and the Georgia War: Lessons and Implications*. June 2011. www. StrategicStudiesInstitute.army.mil/ (accessed December 29, 2011).

Conference of leading staff of the RF Armed Forces, "New Quality of the Russian Armed Forces," *Military News Bulletin*, October 31, 2003: 3–12; as accessed in translation in East View database (www.ebiblioteka.ru/browse/doc/5879575).

Current Digest of the Russian Press, "Defense Minister Launches Radical Military Reform," November 18, 2008: 1–6; as accessed in translation in East View database (www.ebiblioteka.ru/browse/doc/19397163).

— "Medvedev Gives His First State of the Nation Address," November 25, 2008: 1–7.

Defence and Security, "A Command-Staff Exercise in the North Caucasus," September 23, 2005; as accessed in translation in East View database (www.ebiblioteka.ru/browse/doc/8290361).

— "For the First Time in Russia's History an Army Unit Climbed," August 15, 2007; as drawn from RIA Novosti, August 13, 2007, and accessed in translation in East View database (www.ebiblioteka.ru/browse/doc/12447586).

— "Interview with Colonel General Alexander Postnikov: The Army Reform Helps Combat Training," December 13, 2010; as accessed in translation in East View database (www.ebiblioteka.ru/browse/doc/23065309).

— "A Tactical Research Exercise Will Take Place in Kemerovo Region Between March 16 and 23," March 13, 2009; as drawn from RIA Novosti, March 11, 2009, and accessed in translation in East View database (www. ebiblioteka.ru/browse/doc/19729258).

Doohovskoy, Andrei A. Soviet Counterinsurgency in the Soviet Afghan War Revisited: Analyzing the Effective Aspects of the Counterinsurgency Effort. Masters Thesis, Cambridge: Harvard University, 2009.

Dremkov, Col. A. A., "Unconventional Warfare: Essence, Problems, Prospects," *Military Thought*, January 1998; as accessed in translation in East View database (www.ebiblioteka.ru/browse/doc/401102).

Elyushkin, Maj. Gen. V. G., Col. E. I. Dolgov, and Col. V. S. Vdovin, "Reforming the Topographic, Geodetic and Navigation Support System," *Military Thought*, July 1, 2000: 54–62; as accessed in translation in East View database (www.ebiblioteka.ru/browse/doc/400067).

Evangelista, Matthew, *The Chechen Wars: Will Russia go the Way of the Soviet Union?* Washington, DC: Brookings Institution Press, 2002.

Felgengauer, Pavel, "Gudermes is Retaken: Chechens Lose Again in a Battle of Attrition," *Current Digest of the Russian Press*, January 24, 1996: 13; as accessed in translation in East View database (www.ebiblioteka.ru/browse/doc/13555581).

—. "Military Reform After Chechnya: Generals should not be Berated but Retrained," *Current Digest of the Russian Press*, 48(52) (January 1997): 6–7; as accessed in translation in East View database (www.ebiblioteka.ru/browse/doc/13564161).

— "Russia on the Brink of Catastrophe, Apocalypse Now: The Russian Units that Entered Grozny are Routed," *Current Digest of the Russian Press*, February 1, 1995: 5–6; as accessed in translation in East View database (www. ebiblioteka.ru/browse/doc/13581898).

Finaev, Maj. O., "We Took Combat Experience Into Account When Working Out Our Plans," *Voennyi Vestnik Yuga Rossii*, 23 (May–June 2000): 3; as drawn from Defense and Security, No 76, July 3, 2000, and accessed in translation in East View database (www.ebiblioteka.ru/browse/doc/2723086).

Frolov, Alexander, "Soldaty Na Peredovoi i Polkovodtsy v Mozdoke," *Izvestia*, January 11, 1995: 4; available in East View database (www.ebiblioteka.ru/ browse/doc/3180633).

From a speech by Sergei Ivanov, "Reequipment of the Armed Forces," *Russian Military Review*, 3 (March 2007): 68–70; as accessed in translation in East View database (www.ebiblioteka.ru/browse/doc/12212713).

Gareyev, M. A., "Forces, Lessons and Conclusions Drawn from the Experience of the Great Patriotic War as Applied to the Building Up and Training of the Armed Forces," *Military Thought*, 2 (2010): 23–41; as accessed in translation in East View database (www.ebiblioteka.ru/browse/doc/22878525).

Garwood, Robert, "The second Russo-Chechen Conflict (1999 to date): 'A modern military operation'?" *The Journal of Slavic Military Studies*, September 2002: 60–103.

Gavrilov, Yury, "Defense Minister Launches Radical Military Reform," October 15, 2008: 1; as accessed in translation in East View database, Current Digest of the Russian Russian Press, No 43, Vol. 60, November 18, 2008, pp. 1–6 (www.ebiblioteka.ru/browse/doc/19397163).

Glebova, Yekaterina, Nikolai Gritchin, and Viktor Litovkin. "Caucasus Will Teach Us—Army, Police, Rescue Workers, Border Troops and Intelligence Officers Hold Large Scale Exercises," *Current Digest of the Russian Press*, 50(30) (August 1998): 11; as accessed in translation in East View database (www.ebiblioteka.ru/browse/doc/13566917).

Golotyuk, Yury, "Chechnya: Heavy Fighting Resumes in Grozny—Moratorium on Military Operations Leads to a New Round of Tension," *Current Digest of the Russian Press*, May 31, 1995: 12; as accessed in translation in East View database (www.ebiblioteka.ru/browse/doc/13582191).

Golts, Alexander, "FSB Dictates as Chechnya Rages On," *The Russia Journal*, 4(20) (May 25, 2001), pp 1 and 4; also available at: (http://russiajournal.com/ archive/The_Russia_Journal/2001/May/25.05.2001/Defense/May.25–01.pdf) and (http://russiajournal.com/node/4882).

Grau, Lester W., "Bashing the Laser Range Finder With a Rock," *Military Review*, 77(3) (May/June 1997): 43; available at (http://fmso.leavenworth. army.mil/documents/techy.htm).

— "Changing Russian Urban Tactics: The Aftermath of Grozny," *INSS Strategic Forum*, 38 (July 1995), available at http://fmso.leavenworth.army.mil/documents/grozny.htm

— "Russian-Manufactured Armored Vehicle Vulnerability in Urban Combat: The Chechnya Experience," *Foreign Military Studies Offices*, January 1997. www. fas.org/man/dod-101/sys/land/row/rusav.htm (accessed February 5, 2012).

— "Something Old, Something New: Guerillas, Terrorists, and Intelligence Analyis," *Military Review*, July–August 2004: 42–49; available at: (http:// fmso.leavenworth.army.mil/documents/old-new.pdf)

Grau, Lester W. and Charles Q. Cutshaw. "Russian snipers: In the mountains and cities of Chechnya." *Infantry*, (July 2002): 7–11; also available at (www. globalsecurity.org/military/library/report/2002/snipers.pdf).

Grau, Lester W. and Timothy L. Thomas, "Russian Lessons Learned From the Battles For Grozny," *Marine Corps Gazette*, April 2000.; available at (http:// fmso.leavenworth.army.mil/documents/Rusn_leslrn.htm).

— "'Soft Log' and Concrete Canyons: Russian Urban Combat Logistics in Grozny," *Marine Corps Gazette*, October 1999, available at (http://fmso. leavenworth.army.mil/documents/softlog/softlog.htm).

Isakova, Irina, "Russian Defense Reform: Current Trends," *Strategic Studies Institute*, November 2006. www.strategicstudiesinstitute.army.mil/pubs/display. cfm?PubID=740 (accessed December 3, 2011).

Karatuyev, Col. Gen. M. I., "Counter-Terrorist Operation in Northern Caucasus: Main Lessons and Conclusions," *Military Thought*, May 2000; notes from a round-table discussion with input from Col Gen Y.D. Bukreyev, Col Gen M.I. Karatuyev and Col Gen L.S. Zolotov, as accessed in translation in East View database (www.ebiblioteka.ru/browse/doc/400033).

— "Missile Forces and Artillery in Local Wars and Armed Conflicts," *Military Thought*, February 1998; as accessed in translation in East View database (www.ebiblioteka.ru/browse/doc/401080).

Kazantsev, Col. Gen. Viktor, "North Caucasian Military District: Reforming on the Go," *Military News Bulletin*, 12 (December 1998); as accessed in translation in East View database (www.ebiblioteka.ru/browse/doc/137517).

Kedrov, Ilya, "'New Type' of Division Created in the Army," *Current Digest of the Russian Press*, 50(15) (May 1998): 17; as accessed in translation in East View database (www.ebiblioteka.ru/browse/doc/13565621).

Kedrov, Ilya and Alexander Shaburkin, "Russian Flag Raised Over Komsomolskoe," *Defense and Security*, March 24, 2000; as drawn from the newspaper: Nezavisimaya Gazeta, March 22, 2000, p. 2, and accessed in translation in East View database (www.ebiblioteka.ru/browse/ doc/2722137).

Kiknadze, V. G., "Operational Training: Views of the Second Half of the 20th Century and Contemporary Development of the Military." *Military Thought*, no. 4 (2011): 142–51; as accessed in translation in East View database (www. ebiblioteka.ru/browse/doc/26459727).

Kilcullen, David, The Accidental Guerilla: Fighting Small Wars in the Midst of a Big One. New York: Oxford University Press, 2009.

Kilunin, Col. V. V., "New Views on Urban Warfare," *Military Thought*, 003 (May 1998); as accessed in translation in East View database (www.ebiblioteka.ru/browse/doc/401110).

Kokhno, Col. P. A., "Priority Development of the Military-Industrial Complex in Russia," *Military Thought*, 1 (2010): 20–7; as accessed in translation in East View database (www.ebiblioteka.ru/browse/doc/21945805).

Kolibaba, Col. V. G., "Interaction Between Armed Forces and Other Troops of the RF and Allied Armed Forces," *Military Thought*, January 1997; as accessed in translation in East View database (www.ebiblioteka.ru/browse/ doc/401026).

Kolmakov, Aleksandr, "New System of Combat Training," *Russian Military Review*, No. 7, July 2008, pp. 8–13; as accessed in translation in East View database (www.ebiblioteka.ru/browse/doc/19425271).

Koryashkin, Pavel, "Russia-Chechnya Armament," *Itar-Tass Weekly News*, September 28, 1999; as accessed in translation in East View database (www. ebiblioteka.ru/browse/doc/3006239.

Kostyshin, Igor, "New Tasks of the Armed Forces of Russia," *Voennyi Diplomat*, December 31, 2004: 5–7; www.ebiblioteka.ru/browse/doc/7331105.

Kramer, Mark, "Guerilla Warfare, Counterinsurgency and Terrorism in the North Caucasus: The Military Dimension of the Russian-Chechen Conflict," *Europe-Asia Studies*, 57(2) (March 2005): 209–90.

Krasnaya Zvesda, "Joint Command Exercises in North Ossetia," *Defense and Security*, 113 (September 19, 1998): 1; as accessed in translation in East View database (www.ebiblioteka.ru/browse/doc/2729300).

— "Perspectives of Military Development," *Military News Bulletin*, 008 (August 5, 1998); as accessed in translation in East View database (www.ebiblioteka.ru/browse/doc/137482).

— "Siberian Military District Unit Commanders Study Small Group Combat Tactics," November 28, 2000: 1; as drawn from Defense and Security, No 140, December 1, 2000, and accessed in translation in East View database (www.ebiblioteka.ru/browse/doc/2724610).

Krasnov, A. B. and Col. Yu N. Shemuranov, "Role of Aviation in Armed Conflicts," *Military Thought*, February 1998; as accessed in translation in East View database (www.ebiblioteka.ru/browse/doc/401079).

Kryazhev, P. N., "Development of the Military Administrative Territorial Structure of the Armed Forces of the Russian Federation," *Military Thought*, 4 (2011): 47–60; as accessed in translation in East View database (www.ebiblioteka.ru/browse/doc/26459719).

Kuznetsov, Yury, "Priorities in Procurement of Aviation Equipment for the Armed Forces of the Russian Federation," *Military Parade*, 2011: 34–5; as accessed in translation in East View database (www.ebiblioteka.ru/browse/doc/26226420).

Lannon, Gregory, "Russia's New Look Army Reforms and Russian Foreign Policy," *Journal of Slavic Military Studies*, January 2011: 26–54.

"Letter of President of the Russian Federation Boris Yeltsin to the Personnel of the Russian Armed Forces of May 23, 1996 (under article heading: Military Reform and Military Upgrading as a Task of National Importance)," *Military News Bulletin*, June 1996; as accessed in translation in East View database (www.ebiblioteka.ru/browse/doc/137232).

Lezvina, Valentina, "Exercises in the Caucasus," *Kommersant Daily*, July 31, 1998. www.kommersant.ru/doc/202679 (accessed January 11, 2012).

Litovkin, Dmitry, "Army General Vladimir Boldyrev, Commander of the Ground Forces: 'Ground Forces Should Become Compact and Mobile,'" *Defense and Security*, 66 (June 26, 2009); as drawn from the newspaper: Izvestia (Moscow issue), June 23, 2009, p. 3, and accessed in translation in East View database (www.ebiblioteka.ru/browse/doc/20274581).

— "Network Exercise," *Defense and Security*, 107 (September 30, 2009); as drawn from the newspaper: Izvestia (Moscow issue), September 28, 2009, pp. 1, 5, and accessed in translation in East Vew database (www.ebiblioteka.ru/browse/doc/20682696).

Maslov, Col. Gen. Alexei, "Military Development: Field Training and Teamwork," *Russian Military Review*, March 31, 2006: 12–17; as accessed in translation in East View database (www.ebiblioteka.ru/browse/doc/9651737).

Matveyeva, Inna, "Military Sociology: Commander, Instructor, Tutor," *Russian Military Review*, March 31 (2006): 28–31; as accessed in translation in East Vew database (www.ebiblioteka.ru/browse/doc/9651740).

McDermott, Roger, "Russian Combat Training: Quantity Vs. Quality," *Eurasia Daily Monitor*, 8(108) (June 2011); available at (www.jamestown.org/single/?no_cache=1&tx_ttnews%5Btt_news%5D=38018).

— "Russian Military Manpower: Recurring Zugzwang," *Eurasia Daily Monitor*, 7 (December 7, 2010); www.jamestown.org/single/?no_cache=1&tx_ttnews%5Btt_news%5D=37254

— *The Reform of Russia's Conventional Armed Forces.* Washington, DC: The Jamestown Foundation, 2011.

"Military Doctrine of the Russian Federation (2000)," *Military News Bulletin*, May 1, 2000; as accessed in translation on East Vew database (www.ebiblioteka.ru/browse/doc/136494).

"Military News Bulletin," *National Security Concept of the Russian Federation*, January 2, 2000. www.ebiblioteka.ru/browse/doc/136450.

— "Situation in North Caucasus," December 1, 1999; as accessed in translation in East View database (www.ebiblioteka.ru/browse/doc/137665).

— "Situation in the North Caucasus," January 1, 2000; as accessed in translation in East View database (www.ebiblioteka.ru/browse/doc/136446).

Military Parade, "Modernization of the Army—A Priority Objective," 2011: 4–7; as accessed in translation in East View database (www.ebiblioteka.ru/browse/doc/24802618).

— "What Federal Troops are Lacking in Chechnya," January 1, 2000; as accessed in translation in East View database (www.ebiblioteka.ru/browse/doc/167889).

Moscow Times, "Cabinet Approves Funds for GLONASS," *The Moscow Times*, August 3, 2001: 3; available in East View database (www.ebiblioteka.ru/browse/doc/232634).

Mukhin, Vladimir, "Caucasus Experience for Troops in Urals," *Defense and Security*, September 3, 2008; as drawn from the newspaper: Nezavisimaya Gazeta, September 2, 2008, p. 7, and accessed in translation (www.ebiblioteka.ru/browse/doc/18843939).

Mukhin, Yuri, "On the Way to the Creation of the Contemporary and Effective Armed Forces," *Russian Military Review*, February 2008: 8–11; as accessed in translation in East View database (www.ebiblioteka.ru/browse/doc/17619003).

Naryshkin, Andrei, "Chechen Campaigns Force RF Armed Forces to Change Tactics," *Itar-Tass Weekly News*, July 25, 2003; as accessed in translation in East View database (www.ebiblioteka.ru/browse/doc/5133286).

Naryshkin, V. G., "The Makeup of the Russian Federation's Armed Forces in Regard to Their Purposes and the Country's Status," *Military Thought*, 4 (2009): 10–23; as accessed in translation in East View database (www.ebiblioteka.ru/browse/doc/21297450).

Oborsky, Aleksey, "Social Portrait of the Junior Commander of the Armed Forces of the Russian Federation," *Russian Military Review*, February 2007: 44–9; as accessed in translation in East View database (www.ebiblioteka.ru/browse/doc/11831264).

Oliker, Olga, Russia's Chechen Wars 1994–2000: Lessons from Urban Combat. Santa Monica: RAND, 2001.

Panchenkov, Vasily, "Priority of Mountain Training," *Krasnaya Zvezda*, August 24, 2005: 1; as drawn from Defense and Security, No 96, August 26, 2005, and accessed in translation in East View database (www. ebiblioteka.ru/ browse/doc/8149607).

Petrenko, Aleksandr and Lester W. Grau, *Night Sniper.* Translation/Commentary by Grau. January 2000. http://fmso.leavenworth.army.mil/documents/Night-sniper. pdf (accessed December 29, 2011).

Purtova, Natalya, "The Army has put a Barbed-Wire Fence Between Itself and Journalists," *Current Digest of the Russian Press*, September 22, 1999: 1–3; as accessed in translation in East View database (www.ebiblioteka.ru/browse/ doc/19928217).

Rashchepkin, Konstantin and Andrei Lunev, "Lieutenant General Vladimir Shamanov: Training and Look of the Army Will Change," *Defense and Security*, June 27, 2008; as drawn from the periodical: Krasnaya Zvezda, June 24, 2008, pp. 1, 2, and accessed in translation in East View database (www. ebiblioteka.ru/ browse/doc/18533498).

Report by the Directorate of Information of the Defence Ministry of the Russian Federation, "Russian Army Concerns," *Military News Bulletin*, October 1, 1995; as accessed in translation in East View database (www.ebiblioteka.ru/ browse/doc/137181).

RIA Novosti, "President Medvedev: About 85% of Communications Equipment in the Army is Outmoded," *Defense and Security*, 54(May 24, 2010); as drawn from: RIA Novosti, May 21, 2000, and accessed in translation in EastView Database (www.ebiblioteka.ru/browse/doc/21889835).

— "The Reform. A New Stage of Military Development," *Military News Bulletin*, 009 (September 1998); as accessed in translation in East View database (www. ebiblioteka.ru/browse/doc/137491).

Rossiyskaya Gazeta, "Ryazan Will Turn Into Big Base for Training of Professional Junior Commanders for the Ground Forces," *Defense and Security*, 61 (June 15, 2009); as accessed in translation in East View database (www.ebiblioteka.ru/browse/doc/20211615).

Russian Military Review, "Handbook for Junior Commanders," *Russian Military Review*, June 2007: 54; as accessed in translation in East View database (www.ebiblioteka.ru/browse/doc/13179283).

— "The Strategy of the Social Development of the Armed Forces of the Russian Federation for the Period Until 2020," May 2008: 40–9; as accessed in translation in East View database (www.ebiblioteka.ru/browse/ doc/18693084).

Sakwa, Richard, *Chechnya: From Past to Future.* London: Anthem Press, 2005.

Saradzhyan, Simon, "Arms Industry to Get $960M Boon," *Moscow Times*, January 28, 2000; available in East View database (www.ebiblioteka.ru/ browse/doc/224795).

— "Army Learned Few Lessons From Chechnya," *The Moscow Times*, December 15, 2004; available in East View database (www.ebiblioteka.ru/ browse/doc/7162253).

Schaefer, Robert W., The Insurgency in Chechnya and the North Caucasus: From Gazavat to Jihad. Santa Barbara: Praeger Security International, 2011.

Shanayev, Valery, "Russia Police Exercises," *Itar-Tass Weekly News*, December 1997; as accessed in translation in East View database (www. ebiblioteka.ru/browse/doc/2940358).

— "Russian 58th Army to Mark Third Anniversary," *Itar-Tass Weekly News*, May 1998; as accessed in translation in East View database (www.ebiblioteka.ru/browse/doc/2959687).

Shevtsov, LTC Andrei, "Lt Gen Vladimir Popov: Modern Battle Techniques Should Emphasize Manueverability," *Soldat Otechestva*, June 10, 2000: 1; as accessed in translation in East View database, Defense and Security, No 73, June 26, 2000 (www.ebiblioteka.ru/browse/doc/2723007).

Shlykov, Vitaly, "Global Security," *The War in Chechna: Implications for Military Reform*, 1995. www.globalsecurity.org/military/library/report/1995/shl.htm (accessed December 3, 2011).

Shulgin, Maj. Gen. V. E. "Development of Weapons and Military Equipment in New Economic Conditions." *Military Thought*, January 1998; as accessed in translation in East View database (http://www.ebiblioteka.ru/browse/doc/401098).

Sovet po Vneshnei i Oboronnoi Politike, "Voennoe Stroitel'stvo i Modernizatsia Vooruzhennikh Sil Rossii," *Doklad SVOR*. April 2004. http://svop.ru/documents/74 (accessed January 10, 2012).

Stone, David R., "Stalingrad and the Evolution of Soviet Urban Warfared," *The Journal of Slavic Military Studies*, 22(2) (2009): 195–202.

Thomas, Timothy L., "Russian Tactical Lessons Learned Fighting Chechen Separatists," *The Journal of Slavic Military Studies*, 18(4) (n.d.): 731–66; available at (http://fmso.leavenworth.army.mil/documents/CHECHENTACTICS.pdf).

— "A Tale of Two Theaters: Russian Actions in Chechnya in 1994 and 1999," *Analysis of Current Events*, 12(5–6) (September 2000); (http://fmso.leavenworth.army.mil/documents/chechtale.htm).

Thornton, Rod, " Organizational Change in the Russian Airborne Forces: The Lessons of the Georgian Conflict," *Strategic Studies Institute*. December 23, 2011. www.strategicstudiesinstitute.army.mil/pubs/display.cfm?pubID=1096 (accessed December 28, 2011).

Tsymbalyuk, LTC V., "Considering the Lessons of the Caucasus Conflict," *Na Strazhe Rodiny*, June 1, 2000: 1–2; as drawn from Defense and Security, No 80, July 12, 2000, and accessed in translation in East View database (www.ebiblioteka.ru/browse/doc/2723172).

Tuchkov, Col Yu. N., "Integrated Forces and Their Employment in Armed Conflicts and Local Wars," *Military Thought*, 002 (March 1997); as accessed in translation in East View database (www.ebiblioteka.ru/browse/doc/401014).

Vladykin, Oleg, "Technology Behind the Point of Backwardness," *Defense and Security*, June 2, 2010; as drawn from the journal: Nezavisimoe Voennoe Obozrenie, No. 19, May 28 – June 03, 2010, p. 1, and accessed in translation in East View database (www.ebiblioteka.ru/browse/doc/21929136).

Voenno-promyshlennyi Kur'er, "Army of the 21rst Century: What will be the 'new look' of the Russian Armed Forces?" June 24, 2009: 7; as accessed in

East View database with author cited within text as Nikolai E. Makarov (www.ebiblioteka.ru/browse/doc/20260986).

Voennyi' Diplomat, "Russian President's Address and Russia's Armed Forces," *Voennyi' Diplomat*, 3 (2009): 3–4; as accessed in translation in East View database (www.ebiblioteka.ru/browse/doc/21063523).

Vorobyov, Maj. Gen. I. N., "Battle Team Tactics," *Military Thought*, January 2001: 30–4; as accessed in translation in East View database at (www.ebiblioteka.ru/browse/doc/400102).

— "Improvement on the Structure and Organization of Combined-Arms Units," *Military Thought*, March 31, 2004: 163–71; as accessed in translation in East View database (www.ebiblioteka.ru/browse/doc/6225186).

— "New Plane in the Development of Tactics," *Military Thought*, March 1, 2001: 18–26; as accessed in translation in East View database (www.ebiblioteka.ru/browse/doc/400121).

Vorobyov, Maj. Gen. I. N. and Col. V. A. Kiselyov, "From Present-Day Tactics to Network-Centric Action," *Military Thought*, 2011: 70–9; as accessed in translation in East View database (www.ebiblioteka.ru/browse/doc/26095939).

Vzglyad, "A Mountain Training Center of the Armed Forces Will Appear in Kabardino-Balkaria," *Defense and Security*, 269 (November 7, 2011); as drawn from Vzglyad, November 02, 2011, and accessed in translation in East View database (www.ebiblioteka.ru/browse/doc/26203483).

Wood, Tony, *Chechnya: The Case for Independence*. New York, NY: Verso, 2007.

Yakutin, Leonid, "Center 2008 Exercise," *Military Parade*, 2008: 50–1; as accessed in translation in East View database (www.ebiblioteka.ru/browse/doc/19127316).

Yermolin, Vladimir, "Six Months' Service and Into the Regular Army," *Current Digest of the Russian Press*, November 17, 1999: 16; as accessed in translation in East View database (www.ebiblioteka.ru/browse/doc/19928457).

Yevnevich, Lt. Gen. V. G., "Features of Combat Training for the Changing Armed Forces," *Military Thought*, 4 (2010): 144–8; as accessed in translation in East View database (www.ebiblioteka.ru/browse/doc/24406314).

Yurkin, Anatoly, "Artillery Learning New Tactics in Chechnya," *Itar-Tass Weekly News*, November 1999; as accessed in translation in East View database (www.ebiblioteka.ru/browse/doc/3013283).

Zhilin, Aleksandr, "Boris Gromov: 'The Operation was Prepared in Deep Secrecy,'" *Current Digest of the Russian Press*, February 2, 1995: 6; as accessed in translation in East View database (www.ebiblioteka.ru/browse/doc/13582022).

Zolotov, Col. Gen. L. S., "Counter-Terrorist Operation in Dagestan and Chechnya: Main Lessons and Conclusions," *Military Thought*, May 2000; as accessed in East View database (www.ebiblioteka.ru/browse/doc/2449342).

PART TWO

Caucasian Consequences

CHAPTER FIVE

Russia's Canary in the North Caucasus' Mine: Stavropol'skii *krai*

Andrew Foxall

Bordering five of the seven North Caucasus republics, Stavropol'skii krai is uniquely placed for an assessment of the impact that these republics have had upon Russia as a whole. This chapter argues that instabilities in these republics have had both negative effects—as, for example, in instances of terrorism, in the rise of Russian nationalism, and in so-called kavkazofobiya (Caucasus-phobia)—and also positive effects—as seen, for example, in Stavropol's emergence as a regional financial center. In response to these instabilities, Stavropol'skii krai has come to occupy a prominent role in Russian politics. As Russia continues to struggle with North Caucasian instabilities, Stavropol'skii krai's importance is likely to increase.

Introduction

Writing on the second Chechen war, Vendina, Belozerov, and Gustafson[1] noted that the "effects of the war on the North Caucasus have been uneven and diverse." Although this observation applies to the North Caucasus, it is

clear that it also applies to wider spatial scales. Indeed, the impacts of instabilities in the North Caucasus republics on post-Soviet Russia have been
distinctive on each of the 89[2] federal subjects of the Russian Federation.
This chapter explores the impact of such instabilities on Stavropol'skii *krai*.
Stavropol'skii *krai* provides an interesting case study because of its contemporary geopolitical position at the center of the North Caucasus region,
bordering five of the seven republics. Historically seen as the most advanced
Russian outpost in the North Caucasus region, Stavropol'skii *krai* is notable as the only federal subject within the North Caucasus Federal District
that has an ethnic Russian majority population and that is not a republic.
As such, Stavropol'skii *krai* occupies a unique position in Russia's contemporary territorial development.

The impacts of instabilities in the North Caucasus republics on
post-Soviet Russia have been wide-ranging and multifaceted. This chapter focuses on the outmigration of population from the North Caucasus
republics, the widening of terrorism and insurgency, the rise of Russian
nationalism and so-called *kavkazofobiya* (Caucasus-phobia), the restructuring of the Russian federal system and institutional separation of the
North Caucasus from Russia "proper," and, the shifting economic geography of southern Russia. It suggests that the economic, demographic,
political, and social changes that have taken place in Stavropol'skii *krai*
since 1991 reflect broader changes in Russia as a whole. In many respects,
owing to its proximity to the North Caucasus republics, Stavropol'skii *krai*
serves as a frontline barometer of Russia's reaction to events in the North
Caucasus.

What's in a name? A note on terminology

Much ambiguity surrounds the position of Stavropol'skii *krai* within Russia
relative to the North Caucasus. This is, in part, because there has been
much ambiguity as to what constitutes the "North Caucasus."[3] While the
southern border of the North Caucasus connects the peaks of the main
range of the Caucasus Mountains, the northern border lies somewhere
in southern Russia. Thus, while some authors include Stavropol'skii *krai*
when discussing the North Caucasus, others distinguish it from the region.
Because this chapter focuses upon relations between Stavropol'skii *krai* and
other federal subjects in the North Caucasus, it will prove helpful to define
terms of reference.

"**North Caucasus**": The republics[4] of Adygea, Chechnya, Dagestan,
Ingushetia, Kabardino-Balkaria, Karachaevo-Cherkessia, and North
Ossetia-Alania, the territories of Stavropol'skii *krai* and Krasnodar
krai,[5] and the region of Rostov *Oblast'*.[6]

"North Caucasus republics": The republics of Adygea, Chechnya, Dagestan, Ingushetia, Kabardino-Balkaria, Karachaevo-Cherkessia, and North Ossetia-Alania.

"North Caucasus Federal District": The North Caucasus republics (with the exception of Adygea) and Stavropol'skii *krai*.

Demography: Migration and changing ethnic geography of southern Russia

Post-Soviet instabilities in the North Caucasus republics have had a very high cost in human lives, with more than 200,000 people dying from the effects of the violence since 1994.[7] At the same time, hundreds of thousands of people (including both ethnic Caucasians and ethnic Russians) have fled the republics, primarily Chechnya, to other parts of Russia.[8] While the impacts of this mass-migration were wide-ranging and felt throughout much of Russia, they were most acute in southern Russia. Here, the out-migration of ethnic Caucasians led to the development of significant Caucasian communities in territories traditionally occupied by ethnic Russians. Meanwhile, the out-migration of ethnic Russians has further intensified the long-term "de-Russification" of the North Caucasus republics.

It is estimated that between 400,000 and 600,000 people were displaced between 1994 and 1996 by the first Chechen war.[9] The majority of these people were ethnic Caucasians from Chechnya and Dagestan. While a small number settled in Moscow and elsewhere, the majority settled in ethnic Russian-dominated territories in southern Russia owing to their comparative stability and attractive opportunities for employment. As a result, in the 1990s the number of Chechens, Dargins, and Avars (from Dagestan) increased by between a fifth and a third in Stavropol'skii *krai* and Krasnodar *krai*, and by between a sixth and a quarter on the Volga. Such was the scale of this migration that Matveyev[10] noted "Ethnic migration in the Kuban region [Krasnodar *krai*] in the 1990s . . . does not have any analogy in the past." Stavropol'skii *krai*, as the primary destination for migrants fleeing the republics, was particularly affected: in the early 1990s, every twelfth migrant in Russia was registered there.[11]

After the 1996 ceasefire that brought a halt to the first Chechen war, some of these people were able to return home or resettle, but the second Chechen war also created a significant migrant population. According to statistics obtained by Memorial, between December 1999 and June 2002, 568,449 people left Chechnya as "Internally Displaced Persons" (IDPs).[12] Of these, however, less than three percent were recognized as "Forced Migrants" by authorities. Over a quarter of those who received "Forced Migrant" status did so in Stavropol'skii *krai* (3,250 people).

These patterns of migration were reflected in the 2002 Census, which recorded the largest Chechen populations outside of the North Caucasus republics in Rostov *Oblast'* (15,469 people), Stavropol'skii *krai* (13,208 people), and Volgograd *Oblast'* (12,256 people). With the official end of the second Chechen war in 2002, some ethnic Caucasian migrants began returning to the republics. It is estimated that around 255,000 IDPs returned to Chechnya from elsewhere in Russia between 1999 and 2009. While the majority returned to Chechnya from neighboring republics, there was also a process of return migration from Chechen communities in ethnic Russian-dominated territories. Accordingly, the Chechen populations in Rostov *Oblast'*, Stavropol' *krai*, and Volgograd *Oblast'* all decreased between the 2002 Census and 2010 Census.

At the same time that ethnic Caucasians have fled the republics since 1991, so too have ethnic Russians. According to census data, between 1989 and 2010 the ethnic Russian population fell in each of the North Caucasus republics, with an overall decrease of 466,484 people (see Table 5.1).[13] Within the republics, the greatest decrease was recorded in Chechnya (244,748 people) followed by Dagestan (61,290 people). It is estimated that 120,000 ethnic Russians fled Chechnya between 1991 and 1992 alone, while another 200,000 left following the outbreak of the first Chechen war.[14] In turn, the second Chechen war led to the further out-migration of around 50,000 ethnic Russians. Most fled to Russian-dominated areas, especially neighboring Stavropol'skii *krai* and Krasnodar *krai*. Official figures show that 78,000

TABLE 5.1 Change in the ethnic Russian population in the North Caucasus republics, 1989 to 2010.

North Caucasus republics	Ethnic Russian population		
	1989 census	2002 census	2010 census
Adygeya	293,640	288,280	270,714
Chechnya	269,130	40,645	24,382
Dagestan	165,940	110,875	104,020
Ingushetia	24,641	5,559	3,321
Kabardino-Balkaria	240,750	226,620	193,155
Karachaevo-Cherkessia	175,931	147,878	150,025
North Ossetia-Alania	189,159	164,734	147,090
TOTAL	1,359,191	984,591	892,707

ethnic Russians who fled Chechnya and Ingushetia between 1991 and 2010 settled in Stavropol'skii *krai*, although Markedonov[15] suggests that the real number may be twice as high. According to the 2010 census, ethnic Russians now constitute 9.3 percent of the population of the North Caucasus republics, down from 14.9 percent in 2002 and 26 percent in 1989.[16]

One impact of these demographic processes is that, in contrast to Russia as a whole, Stavropol'skii *krai* has registered an increase in its population over the post-Soviet period.[17] Indeed, while the population of Russia fell from 147.34m in 1989 to 145.30m in 2002 and 142.93m in 2010, the population of Stavropol'skii *krai* increased over this period from 2.41m in 1989 to 2.73m in 2002 and 2.78m in 2010. There are, of course, important ethnic differences within this population growth. While the ethnic Russian population in Stavropol'skii *krai* registered a modest increase from 2.19m in 1989 to 2.23m in 2002 and 2.23m in 2010, the nonethnic Russian population more than doubled over the same period, from 220,000 in 1989 to 500,000 in 2002 and 550,000 in 2010. As a result, the ethnic Russian proportion of the *krai* population decreased from 84 percent in 1989 to 81.6 percent in 2002 and 80.9 percent in 2010. While both of these trends reflect the large-scale in-migration of population into Stavropol'skii *krai* since 1991, they also reflect the difference between high levels of natural increase for ethnic Caucasians and low levels of natural increase for ethnic Russians.[18]

Within Stavropol'skii *krai*, there has been a marked shift in the ethnic geography of the *krai* with the Russian (and, more broadly, Slav) population moving to *raions*[19] in the north and west, furthest away from the North Caucasus republics. In turn, ethnic Caucasians have migrated to the south and east of Stavropol'skii *krai* and now constitute the majority populations in many rural settlements in these *raions*. While the patterns of migration taken by ethnic Caucasians since 1991 have followed well-established routes dating from the 1970s (owing, at least in part, to the availability of land in eastern Stavropol'skii *krai* compared to the North Caucasus republics[20]), they have been far more intense than in earlier decades.[21]

It is owing to the demographic differences between ethnic Russians and ethnic Caucasians in Stavropol'skii *krai* that Markedonov[22] argues the *krai* "... has become a frontier, a unique borderline dividing 'the Russian world' and 'the Caucasus world.'"

Terrorism: The widening of insurgency

Perhaps more than anything else, the spread of terrorism has been the most prominent way through which instabilities in the North Caucasus republics have affected Russia. Outside of the North Caucasus republics, Stavropol'skii *krai*, together with Moscow, has been one of the primary locations of such terrorism. Indeed, the first major terrorist attack in post-Soviet Russia took place in Budennovsk, Stavropol'skii *krai*, between June 14 and 19, 1995.[23] In many respects, the hospital siege in Budennovsk was a turning point in the first Chechen war and ultimately led to the Khasavyurt Accord (signed on August 30, 1996) that officially ended the conflict. Owing to his inept handling of the siege, the Russian State Duma considered a motion of censure against Prime Minister Viktor Chernomyrdin's government on June 21, 1995. Although the motion was rejected (189 of 226 members participated), the siege did cost Sergei Stepashin (Director of the Federal Security Service (FSB)) his job; he was dismissed at his own request on June 30, 1995. The same day, President Yeltsin announced the dismissal of: Viktor Yerin, Minister of Internal Affairs (MVD); Nikolai Yegorov, Minister of Nationalities and Regional Policy; and, Evgenii Kuznetsov, Governor of Stavropol'skii *krai*.

In the years immediately following the siege in Budennovsk, Russia was largely spared from terrorism. This changed with the apartment bombings in Buinaksk, Moscow, and Volgodonsk in September 1999, which, in part, gave rise to the second Chechen war. Within Stavropol'skii *krai*, the interwar period saw incursions by Chechen criminal gangs and militants into the *raions* bordering Chechnya and Dagestan in the east of the *krai*, in particular Neftemkumskii *raion* and Shelkovskii *raion*. This included reconnaissance by Shamil Basaev and militants loyal to him between April and August 1999 in preparation for the military invasion of Dagestan, which contributed to the launch of the second Chechen war (in October 1999). While these militants committed numerous terrorist acts in Stavropol'skii *krai*, including hijacking a bus in Nevinnomiskk in July 2001, the second Chechen war largely suppressed insurgent activity outside of the North Caucasus republics while it was being fought. Indeed, when Vladimir Putin officially declared the end of the second Chechen war in his April 2002 State of the Nation speech, Russia had not seen any significant insurgency related activity or terrorist attacks outside of the North Caucasus republics since the 1999 bombings.

As many scholars have noted,[24] Putin's 2002 pronouncement of the end of the second Chechen war was premature. Roughly a month later, in May 2002, the Riyadus-Salikhin Reconnaissance and Sabotage Brigade of Chechen Martyrs (RSRSB), led by Shamil Basaev, launched a two-year campaign of terrorism against civilian targets in Russia. Around 200 people were killed in a campaign of suicide bombings, including the 2004 Moscow metro bombing (40 deaths) and the 2004 Russian aircraft bombing (89 deaths). As part of the campaign, in September 2003 Chechen militants exploded a bomb on a train in Essentuki, Stavropol'skii *krai* killing 7 people and injuring more than 80 others. Months later, in December of the same year, a suicide bomber detonated him/herself in the carriage of a commuter train travelling on the same stretch of railway in Essentuki, killing over 45 people and injuring around 170 others. At the same time, the

RSRSB also used hostage taking in their campaign of terrorism. Here, the Dubrovka Theater siege (October 2002) and Beslan school hostage siege (September 2004) are particularly notable.

In the aftermath of the Beslan siege the RSRSB became less active and effectively disbanded after the death of Shamil Basaev in July 2006. Despite this, insurgency continued in Stavropol'skii *krai*. In August 2005, a large-scale police operation recovered armaments meant for Chechen militants hidden in a mosque in Tukuy-Mekteb, Neftekumskii *raion*. Less than a year later, in February 2006, a gunfight in the same village between the so-called Shelkovskii-jamaat and over 300 Interior Ministry special forces led to the deaths of 12 militants and 7 special forces officers.[25]

This pattern is reflected in data from the Open Source Data Center, which suggest that after a peak in the incidence of *jihadist*-related violence in the North Caucasus republics and Stavropol'skii *krai* between 2002 and 2004 there was a "lull" between 2005 and 2006. Beginning in 2007, however, the Center reported a notable increase in insurgency outside of Chechnya, particularly in 2008 and 2009.[26]

As a result of decreasing levels of insurgency and the wider stabilization of the republic under Ramzan Kadyrov, on April 16, 2009 the Kremlin officially declared the end of Russia's "counterterrorist operation" [*Kontrterroristicheskaya operatsiya*—KTO] in Chechnya. Like Putin's 2002 pronouncement, however, this was also premature. In the summer of 2009 Russian military and security forces undertook a number of *zachistki* ("cleaning-up") operations against alleged terrorists in Chechnya and elsewhere in the North Caucasus republics, and there were a number of major terrorist incidents in the republics, including the murder of Adilgerey Magomedtagirov (Internal Affairs Minister of Dagestan) on June 5 and an attack on Yunus-bek Yevkurov (President of Ingushetia) on June 22. These coincided with the reconstitution of the RSRSB by Doku Umarov (the leader of the Caucasus Emirate) earlier the same year.

In response to these attacks, on August 19, 2009 President Dmitri Medvedev convened a special session of the Russian Security Council in Stavropol' and spoke of the "terrorist and extremist threat" facing Russia.[27] Later the same day, Medvedev held a meeting with Valeri Gaevskii, Governor of Stavropol'skii *krai*, at which he expressed concern about the increasing frequency of terrorist attacks both within the North Caucasus republics and elsewhere.[28] For its part, Stavropol'skii *krai* subsequently established an "Anti-Terrorism Commission," which builds on initiatives of the National Antiterrorist Committee.

In an interview with the *Kavkaz Center* in January 2010, Doku Umarov explained that the recreation of the RSRSB meant: "The zone of military operations will be extended to the territory of Russia . . . Blood will no longer be limited to our cities and towns [in the North Caucasus republics]. The war is coming to their [Russian] cities."[29] Reflecting Umarov's call for insurgents to target civilians and to widen the geographic scope of insurgency away from the North Caucasus republics,[30] a series of terrorist attacks subsequently took place across Russia, including: two suicide bomb attacks in March 2010 on the Moscow metro, which killed 38 people and injured 60 others; and, the January 2011 suicide bombing at Moscow's Domodedovo Airport, which killed 37 and injured over 173 others. Within Stavropol'skii *krai*, there was an increase in insurgency-related incidents from 6 in 2009 to 11 in 2010. Included in this is the car bomb explosion outside a café in Pyatigorsk in August 2010, which injured at least 30 people. Much of the contemporary insurgency in the *krai* is linked to the "Nogai jamaat,"[31] based in Neftekumskii *raion* in eastern Stavropol'skii *krai*, who were linked to the failed bomb attack in Moscow on December 31, 2010.[32]

Society: The rise of *Kavkazofobiya* and Russian nationalism

While anti-Chechen sentiments have long existed in Russia as a result of the Caucasian Wars of the nineteenth century, post-Soviet geopolitical instabilities in the North Caucasus republics have exacerbated them. Laruelle[33] notes that sociological polls in Russia record a rise in xenophobia following "every terrorist act committed in Central Russia or the North Caucasus (explosions at markets, in trains, and at metro stations, violent physical attacks against the police forces, etc.)." These events serve, in the popular consciousness, to associate "Chechens" with "terrorists." As a result, in the post-Soviet years anti-Chechen sentiment has turned into a more generalized and hysterical aversion to all Caucasians regardless of their nationality (so-called Caucasus-phobia—*kavkazofobiya*). In turn, this has contributed to the spread of ethno-national violence.

According to the Levada Center, more than half of the Russian population agreed with the slogan "*Rossiya dlya Russkikh*" ("Russia for [ethnic] Russians") between 2001 and 2006. Data from the SOVA Center, the Moscow-based NGO, suggest that racist and neo-Nazi killings increased from 2004 (the first year for which data are available) to 2008, and have decreased each year since: from 50 in 2004 to 116 in 2008 and 20 in 2011. The same pattern is true of racist and neo-Nazi attacks in which individuals are beaten or wounded but not killed: rising from 218 in 2004 to 618 in 2007, before decreasing to 148 in 2011.[34]

There is, of course, a geography to Russia's violent xenophobia.[35] While racist and neo-Nazi violence is found in nearly all of Russia's regions, the majority (54 percent, or 2,042 incidents) of all racist and neo-Nazi attacks in Russia between 2004 and 2011 occurred in Moscow and St. Petersburg. Elsewhere, there were significant concentrations in Krasnodar *krai* (69 attacks) and Stavropol'skii *krai* (64 attacks).

In Stavropol'skii *krai*, reports from the NGO EAWARN (Network for Ethnic Monitoring and Early Warning) suggest that ethno-national discrimination and violence has been increasing since the late 1990s. In 1995, in response to the start of the first Chechen war and the high levels of in-migration of ethnic Caucasians, *krai* authorities established a law on the "Status of a Resident of Stavropol'skii *krai*," which stipulated that resident status could only be acquired after seven years residence in the *krai*.[36] However, the law was ruled unconstitutional by the Russian Supreme Court. As a result, *krai* authorities adopted a tightly controlled Immigration Code and undertook a number of local initiatives to limit the in-migration of ethnic Caucasians, including installing units of Cossack border guards on the *krai's* borders with Chechnya and Dagestan.[37] In the aftermath of the Budennovsk siege, the border between Stavropol'skii *krai* and Chechnya became a priority for the *krai* authorities, and Petr Fedosov, ataman of the Stavropol'skii *krai* Union of Cossacks (*Stavropol'skii kraevoi Soyuz kazakov—SKSS*),[38] was co-opted into the *krai* government.[39] With Chechnya's de facto independence from Russia between 1996 and 1999, the border between Stavropol'skii *krai* and Chechnya was formalized when Interior Ministry troops were stationed there in 1997. With the start of the second Chechen war in 1999, Cossack units and Interior Ministry troops were joined by Russian neo-nationalist groups, who found official support from the Stavropol'skii *krai* authorities, in patrolling the border between Stavropol'skii *krai* and Chechnya.

Given this institutional climate for supporting right-wing movements, there was a marked growth of Russian nationalist movements in Stavropol'skii *krai* (mirroring a growth in Russia as a whole[40]), with Russian National Unity (*Russkoe natsional'noe edinstvo*) particularly active in the late 1990s. Since 2000, interethnic tension has become widespread in Stavropol'skii *krai* and is primarily focused on Chechens.[41] While this has been manifest in localized interethnic conflict, particularly in the rural *raions* in the east of the *krai*, there are examples of large-scale conflict. Most notably, in May and June 2007 widespread interethnic tension led to the deaths of three youths (two ethnic Russians and one ethnic Chechen) during six weeks of intermittent rioting in Stavropol'. During the riots, special police forces (OMON) and local police forces joined with nationalists, including members of the now-banned Movement Against Illegal Immigration (*Dvizhenie Protiv Nelegal'noi Immigratsii—DPNI*), in attacking ethnic Caucasians.[42] Taking place less than a year after the riots in Kondopoga, Karelia, the riots led to the recentring of state security apparatus in Stavropol'skii *krai*.

More recently, the Union of Slavic Communities of Stavropol' (*Soyuz Slavyanskiki Obschestvennikh Organizatsii Stavropol'ya*—which emerged from a split within Russian National Unity) has been particularly active in coordinating Russian nationalist initiatives, supporting the actions of militant Cossacks, and violently opposing ethnic Caucasian migration into the *krai*. They were linked to the 2008 bomb hoax at the Nevinnomissk branch of the FSB, as part of a wider campaign by Russian nationalists to imitate Caucasian insurgency as a means of provoking xenophobia. Two years later, in May 2010, a bomb exploded outside the House of Culture and Sport in central Stavropol' just minutes before a Chechen dance ensemble (who enjoy the patronage of Ramzan Kadyrov, President of Chechnya) were due to perform, killing at least 8 people. In the aftermath of the attack, Vladimir Nesterov, head of the Union of Slavic Communities of Stavropol', blamed widespread ethnic Caucasian migration into the *krai* for provoking xenophobic and nationalist sentiments.

Politics: The restructuring of the Russian federal system

In response to the invasion of Dagestan by Chechnya-based militants in August 1999 and the apartment bombings of September 1999, Vladimir Putin (at the time, Prime Minster) launched the second Chechen war in October 1999. Putin's approvals ratings increased from 31 percent in August 1999 to 80 percent in November 1999, and he was subsequently elected President in March 2000 (with 53.4 percent of the vote). Two months later, Putin undertook a raft of reforms with the aim to reassert the authority of the federal center.

For example, Putin gave himself the authority to dismiss regional governors, banned governors from sitting in the Federation Council (the upper parliamentary chamber), applied pressure on governors to reverse regional laws that contradicted federal ones, and otherwise shifted the balance of power back from the regions toward the federal center. Given the early success of his militaristic approach to instabilities in Chechnya and Dagestan, Putin used the bureaucratic structure of the Russian military as the basis for his recentralization of power. He reorganized the Russian Federation on the model of Russia's seven military districts, and gave himself the power to appoint seven presidential plenipotentiaries to oversee each district.[43]

Stavropol'skii *krai* was included in the Southern Federal District (SFD), together with Astrakhan *Oblast'*, Krasnodar *krai*, Rostov *Oblast'*, Volgograd *Oblast'*, the Republic of Kalmykia, and the North Caucasus republics. Initially called "Northern Caucasian," the name of the federal

district was changed so that Moscow served as the primary point of geopolitical reference for the new entity.[44] The SFD was headed by General Victor
Kazantsev from its creation on May 18, 2000 to March 9, 2004, when he
was replaced by Vladimir Yakovlev.

Reflecting both his own approach as well as that of Kazantsev (who led
the Russian military response to the Chechen invasion of Dagestan in 1999,
and was a participant in both Chechen wars), between 2000 and 2004
Putin focussed on the use of violent repression as the primary means to calm
instability in the North Caucasus republics. At the same time, Putin spoke
about recreating the Soviet-era *vertikal* of power, with decision-making
dictated at the top.[45] The hostage siege in Beslan, North Ossetia-Alania, in
2004 presented Putin with the opportunity to put his plans into action. In
addition to a host of more minor security measures, Putin announced the
centralized appointment of Russia's regional governors and the overhaul of
the Russian electoral system, which effectively assured additional strength
for the party of power.

In Stavropol'skii *krai*, Putin reappointed the incumbent Alexander
Chernogorov as Governor of the *krai* despite widespread disdain for
Chernogorov in the wake of allegations concerning his predilections for
corruption and the finer points of billiards.[46] Following his reappointment,
Chernogorov left the Communist Party and became a member of Putin's
Edinaya Rossiya ("United Russia") political party.

In the aftermath of Beslan, Putin appointed Dmitri Kozak as Presidential
Envoy to the SFD. Kozak's appointment was interpreted as a sign of Putin's
desire to take productive steps to solve the relentless problems of the North
Caucasus republics.[47] In mid-2005 Kozak sent a classified report to Putin
and the Federal Assembly warning that the North Caucasus republics and
contiguous areas of southern Russia, including Stavropol'skii *krai*, had
become a "macro-region of sociopolitical and economic instability" that
could "unravel" through "permanent destabilization." The report, excerpts
from which were published in *Moskovsky komsomolets* newspaper, called
for serious and sustained efforts to address the economic, political, and
social problems in the region. Kozak's warnings, however, did not convince
Putin to alter his security-orientated approach to the republics.[48]

This changed when Dmitri Medvedev became President in 2008.[49]
Following his visit to Stavropol' in the aftermath of the terrorist attacks in
the North Caucasus republics during the summer of 2009, Medvedev used
his November 2009 Address to the Federal Assembly to criticize the lack of
progress achieved in "normalizing" the socioeconomic development of the
North Caucasus republics and described the security situation in the region
as "the most serious internal problem" in Russia.[50] Two months later, in
January 2010, Medvedev announced the creation of the North Caucasus
Federal District (NCFD).[51] The SFD was effectively divided into two parts.
The NCFD included six of the North Caucasus republics (Chechnya,

Dagestan, Ingushetia, Kabardino-Balkaria, Karachaevo-Cherkessia, and North Ossetia-Alania) and one territory (Stavropol'skii *krai*),[52] while the other regions remained in the SFD. The NCFD is administered from Pyatigorsk in southern Stavropol'skii *krai*. Alexander Khloponin (former governor of Krasnoyarsk *krai*) was jointly appointed Presidential Envoy to the NCFD and Deputy Prime Minister and, in 2010, was given wide-ranging powers to strengthen law and order in the district, develop the judicial system, and to take action to improve the social and economic situation.

The creation of the NCFD effectively marked the institutional separation of the North Caucasus from Russia "proper." Stavropol'skii *krai*, long seen as Russia's most advanced outpost in the North Caucasus, is the only territory within the NCFD with an ethnic Russian majority population (see Table 5.2). The decision to include Stavropol'skii *krai* in the NCFD has proved highly controversial in the *krai* itself, with the emergence in September 2010 of a grassroots secession campaign to restore the *krai* to the SFD.[53] The campaign suggested that since the *krai* was included in the NCFD there had been an increase in crime, levels of in-migration from the North Caucasus republics, and instances of terrorism. The

TABLE 5.2 Ethnic Russian population in the subjects of the North Caucasus Federal District, 1989 Soviet Census and 2002 and 2010 Russian Census.

Subjects of North Caucasus Federal District	Ethnic Russian percentage of population, by census		
	1989 (%)	2002 (%)	2010 (%)
Chechnya	24.8	3.7	1.9
Dagestan	9.2	4.7	3.6
Ingushetia	13.2	1.2	0.8
Kabardino-Balkaria	31.9	25.1	22.5
Karachaevo-Cherkessia	42.4	33.6	31.6
North Ossetia-Alania	29.9	23.2	20.8
Stavropol'skii krai	84	81.6	80.9

Note: Although Chechnya and Ingushetia were united as the Checheno-Ingush ASSR in 1989, these figures reflect the ethnic Russian populations within the *raions* that now constitute each republic.

campaign also suggested that many ethnic Russians in Stavropol'skii *krai* fear the inclusion of the *krai* into the affairs of the North Caucasus republics.[54] Days after the campaign began, Yuri Shepelin, Deputy of Stavropol' City authorities and Chairman of the "Advisory Council on National-Ethnic Relations in Stavropol' City" (*Konsul'tativnii sovet po voprosam natsional'no-etnicheskikh otnoshenii pri administratsii goroda Stavropolya*),[55] reported a sharp escalation in tensions between ethnic Russians and ethnic Caucasians in Stavropol'.[56] Subsequently, over the course of two weeks a number of large-scale interethnic riots took place in Stavropol' and order was only restored after the Stavropol' City Security Council introduced restrictions on movement in the city.

Economics: The changing economic geography of southern Russia

Instabilities in the North Caucasus republics have a major effect on the economic situation in Russia. Not only have they compounded the uneven geography of Soviet development—already one of the least developed regions of the Union of Soviet Socialist Republics (USSR), the regional economy of the North Caucasus republics contracted by between a quarter and a fifth during the post-Soviet "transition" of the 1990s[57]—but they have also led to a shift in the economic geography of southern Russia. In response to instabilities, regions in southern Russia have assumed dominant positions in industries (e.g. oil production and transportation) that were once held by Chechnya and other republics, and centers of economic activity and flows of finance, investment, and trade have moved to new locations. As a result, the economy of the North Caucasus republics' is the most underdeveloped in Russia and the republics are heavily dependent on federal subsidies. Between 2000 and 2011, these subsidies amounted to over 1,240 billion rubles (USD42.8 billion).[58] In 2010, each republic received over 50 percent of its budget from Moscow (both Chechnya and Ingushetia received 91%), compared with an average of 15 percent for Russia.[59] This has given rise since 2011 to the "Stop Feeding the Caucasus" campaign, led by Russian nationalists and Vladimir Zhirinovksy, leader of the Liberal Democratic Party of Russia (LDPR) and Deputy Chairman of the Lower House of the State Duma, which has led to major protests in Moscow and smaller protests across Russia. At the same time, there is little relation between the economic development of a territory and the amount of federal subsidy it receives (see Table 5.3).

Because of their wealth and comparative stability, ethnic Russian regions in southern Russia have avoided much of the economic dislocation that has characterized the North Caucasus republics since 1991. While Krasnodar

TABLE 5.3 Levels of Federal Subsidy, Gross Regional Product, and Unemployment in the subjects of the North Caucasus Federal District, 2010.[60]

Subject of North Caucasus Federal District	Percentage of Budget from Federal Subsidy, 2010 (%)	Gross Regional Product, 2010 (millions of roubles)	Level of Unemployment, April 2010 (%)
Chechnya	91	69,675.7	59.7
Dagestan	70	285,278.9	17.2
Ingushetia	91	21,536.7	53.0
Kabardino-Balkaria	53	76,056.5	14.3
Karachaevo-Cherkessia	66	43,324.1	11.7
North Ossetia-Alania	57	74,844.8	10.0
Stavropol'skii krai	38	316,888.9	7.5

krai and Rostov *Oblast'* have faired well, Stavropol'skii *krai* stands out. In many respects, Stavropol' acts as the financial center for the North Caucasus republics and much of the money flowing in and out of the republics has been channeled through the *krai*. For example, Sberbank, one of Russia's largest banks, maintains its major regional headquarters in Stavropol', from where it operates smaller operations in the republics. The adoption, in October 2010, of "The Strategy of Social-Economic Development of the North Caucasus Federal District until 2025" (hereafter "The Strategy"),[61] with its significant budget, will further cement this role.

During the 1990s, a significant shadow economy developed in the North Caucasus. According to data collected by the Southern Branch of the Russian Academy of Sciences in 2003, the shadow economy accounted for between 60 and 80 percent of all economic activity in the republics, compared with around 30 percent in Stavropol'skii *krai*.[62] Together with Khasavyurt in Dagestan, the Lyudmila Market on the outskirts of Pyatigorsk acts as a key point for trade and distribution of goods, not only in the republics and Stavropol'skii *krai* but also onward toward Moscow and elsewhere. In 2003 it was estimated that at least USD5 mn passes through both markets each month, although the actual figure is likely to be much higher.[63] Owing to this shadow economy, local and federal authorities fail to receive tax on trade and commodities, reducing income in the republics' budget. In 2010, the NCFD contributed only 0.9 percent to the tax budget of the Russian Federation.

As the situation deteriorated in the republics in the 1990s, regional energy and transportation infrastructure was redirected away from Chechnya. For example, both the Baku-Novorossiysk oil pipeline[64] and the Rostov-on-Don to Baku (Azerbaijan) highway were rerouted around Chechnya through Stavropol'skii *krai*.[65] At the same time, Mineral'nye Vody in southern Stavropol'skii *krai* has been developed as a major air transport hub for the North Caucasus and serves as the primary transportation hub for Chechnya, Ingushetia, North Ossetia, Kabardino-Balkaria, and Karachaevo-Cherkessia. While the airport first received international flights in 1980, since 1997 it has been redeveloped to increase its capacity: construction of a second runway began in 2006, and in 2011 construction of a new terminal began.[66] This recent development and investment is funded by a regional development bank, established in The Strategy, and is tied to improving infrastructure (in particular, transportation) in southern Russia as Russia prepares to host the 2014 Winter Olympics in Sochi, Krasnodar *krai* and the 2018 FIFA World Cup (four cities in southern Russia have bid to host matches: Krasnodar, Rostov-on-Don, Sochi, and Volgograd). Together with the planned upgrades for five other airports in the North Caucasus (in Beslan, Krasnodar, Maikop, Makhachkala, and Nalchik), announced by President Medvedev in March 2012 and linked to the development of the NCFD Tourism Cluster, the upgrade of Mineral'nye Vody airport will increase the capacity of the transportation infrastructure in the region from 20,000 passengers per day to 100,000 per day.[67]

Conclusion

The effects of geopolitical instabilities in the North Caucasus republics on Russia since 1991 have been wide-ranging and multifaceted—some more tangible than others. Since the mid-1990s, instabilities have spread from the republics of the North Caucasus to other regions in southern Russia and onward to Moscow, with an impact that has been felt throughout the federation.

As elsewhere, Stavropol'skii *krai* has seen these instabilities not only in instances of terrorism and an increase in the in-migration of ethnic Caucasians and ethnic Russians from the republics, but also in a marked growth of *kavkazofobiya* and Russian nationalism. Yet widespread economic dislocation throughout the North Caucasus republics has led to Stavropol's emergence as a regional financial center, and instability in Chechnya and a number of other republics means that Stavropol'skii *krai* is now key to the regional energy and transportation infrastructure. In this context, Stavropol'skii *krai* has assumed a prominent role in regional and national politics, not least because of its location of the headquarters of the NCFD, and serves as an intermediary between the North Caucasus republics and the rest of Russia. As the economic, demographic, and religious divide between the North Caucasus republics and the rest of Russia continues to widen, and as Russia continues to struggle with geopolitical instabilities in the North Caucasus republics, the importance of Stavropol'skii *krai* to Russia is only likely to increase.

Notes

1 Olga Vendina, Vitali S. Belozerov, and Andrew Gustafson. "The Wars in Chechnya and Their Effects on Neighboring Regions," *Eurasian Geography and Economics*, 48 (2007): 197.

2 In 1993, when the Constitution of the Russian Federation was adopted, there were 89 federal subjects. However, the number has since decreased because of several mergers. Since 2008 there have been 83 federal subjects. As defined in Article 5 of the Constitution, each federal subject is designated as one of the following constituent entities, which have equal rights under the Constitution: *respublik* (republic); *oblast'* (region); *krai* (territory); *avtonomnaya oblast'* (autonomous region); *avtonomnaya okrug* (autonomous district); and, *gorod federal'nogo znacheniya* (federal city). Currently, there are 21 republics, 46 oblasts, nine krai's, one autonomous oblast', four autonomous okrug's, and two federal cities.

3 See, Andrew Foxall, "Defining regions: introducing the Caucasus," *Central Asian Survey*, 30 (2011): 291–5.

4 The republics are nominally autonomous and each has its own constitution and legislature. Each republic is officially "home" to at least one specific ethnic group after which the republic is named (often referred to as the "titular nationality"). Only three republics are home to more than one titular ethnic group, all of which are in the North Caucasus; Dagestan, Kabardino-Balkaria, and Karachaevo-Cherkessia.

5 *Krai* is often translated as "territory." Historically, *krai*'s were territories located along Russia's frontiers, since the word can also mean "border." Constitutionally, a *krai* is essentially the same as an *oblast'*.

6 *Oblast'* is often translated as "region" and is the most common type of federal subject in Russia. Each *oblast'* has a federally appointed governor and a locally elected legislature, and is commonly named after its administrative center.

7 Freedom House. "The Worst of the Worst: The World's Most Repressive Societies 2006." Last modified September 6, 2006. www.freedomhouse. org/template.cfm?page=138&report=40www.freedomhouse.org/uploads/ WoW/2006/Chechnya2006.pdf

8 See, Olga Vendina, Vitali S. Belozerov, and Andrew Gustafson. "The Wars in Chechnya and Their Effects on Neighboring Regions," *Eurasian Geography and Economics*, 48(2007): 178–201.

9 Francis M. Deng, "Specific Groups and Individuals Mass Exoduses and Displaced Persons, Report of the Representative of the Secretary-General on internally displaced persons, Profiles in displacement: the Russian Federation," UN Commission on Human Rights, E/CN.4/2004/77/Add.2. February 24, 2004, 2006.

10   Matveyev (2002) quoted in Viktor Avksentiev and Ludmilla Lobova, "Ethnopolitical problems of Post-Soviet Russia: The Case of Northern Caucasus," in *Russia—Continuity and Change*, Gerald Hinteregger and Hans-Georg Heinrich (eds) (Wien: Springer-Verlag, 2004), 532.

11   Anna Matveeva, *The North Caucasus: Russia's Fragile Borderland* (London: The Royal Institute of International Affairs, 1999), 42.

12   See, Svetlana A. Gannushkina, "Memorial Human Rights Centre: The Internally Displaced Persons from Chechnya in the Russian Federation." Last modified June 10, 2002. http://refugee.memo.ru/For_All/rupor.nsf/839ac874eb0b559cc3 256a4a003bb69f/9bf376467e69ac49c3256bd3007a8b55!OpenDocument

13   While official figures state that the ethnic Russian population in the North Caucasus republics fell by 374,600 people between 1989 and 2002, experts suggest that these figures underestimate the number by almost 50,000 people. It is estimated that the ethnic Russian population more likely decreased by between 415,000 and 420,000 over this period, which brought the number of ethnic Russians in the republics down from 1.359 million in 1989 to between 940,000 and 945,000 in 2002. If this were the case, the 2010 population would be closer to 840,000 people. See, Valery Dzutsev, "'North Caucasus' Ethnic Russian Population Shrinks as Indigenous Populations Grow," *Eurasia Daily Monitor*, 6 (2010). Last modified November 13, 2009. www.jamestown.org/single/?no_cache=1&tx_ ttnews[tt_news]=35730

14   Oleg Tsvetkov, "Ethnic Russians Flee the North Caucasus," *Russian Analytical Digest*, 7 (2006): 9–12.

15   Sergei Markedonov, "Stavropol'yu nuzhna integratsiya [Stavropol' needs integration]," *Novaya Politika*, Last modified November 29, 2010. http://novopol.ru/-stavropolyu-nujna-integratsiya-text93089.html

16   The decline in the ethnic Russian (and, more broadly, Slav) population of the North Caucasus republics since 1991 is not solely due to the two conflicts in Chechnya or increasingly hostile policies in the republics, although these undoubtedly led to an increase in the levels of out-migration of ethnic Russians. Rather, it is part of a more long-term "de-Russification" of the republics: since 1959, the number of ethnic Russians in the republics has decreased between each census period. See, Vitali S. Belozerov, *Etnichesksaya karta Severnogo Kavkaza* [Ethnic Atlas of the North Caucasus] (Moscow: OGI, 2005).

17   See, John O'Loughlin, Alexander Panin, and Frank Wittmer, "Population Change and Migration in Stavropol' Kray: The Effects of Regional Conflicts and Economic Restructuring," *Eurasian Geography and Economics*, 48 (2007): 249–67.

18   See, ibid.

19   *Raion* is often translated as "district." It refers to an administrative district of a federal subject.

20   See Judith Pallot and Tat'yana G. Nefedova. *Russia's Unknown Agriculture: Household Production in Post-Soviet Rural Russia* (Oxford: Oxford University Press, 2007).

21   See Vitali S. Belozerov, *Etnodemograficheskiye protsessy na Severnom Kavkaze* [Ethno-demographic Processes in the North Caucasus] (Stavropol: Stavropol' State University Press, 2000).

22 Sergei Markedonov, "Na Stike Mirov Stavropol'skii Krai: fornost russkikh ili zone integratsii? [Stavropol Territory On a Join of Worlds: an advanced post of Russia or a zone of integration?]," *Chastnii Korrespondent*, Last modified June 25, 2009. www.chaskor.ru/p.php?id=7827

23 Prior to the Budennovsk siege there had been numerous other terrorist attacks in Stavropol'skii *krai*, including the hostage sieges in Mineral'nye Vody (November 9, 1991), Stavropol' (May 26, 1994), Mineral'nye Vody and Pyatigorsk (June 28, 1994), and Mineral'nye Vody (June 29, 1994).

24 See, for example, John Russell, "Terrorists, Bandits, Spooks and Thieves: Russian Demonization of the Chechens Before and Since 9/11," *Third World Quarterly*, 26 (2005): 101–116.

25 See BBC. "Fighting near Chechnya kills 19." February 10, 2006. http://news.bbc.co.uk/1/hi/world/europe/4700492.stm

26 See Jim Nichol, "Stability in Russia's Chechnya and Other Regions of the North Caucasus: Recent Developments," Congressional Research Centre, CRS-RL34613, Last modified December 13, 2010. www.fas.org/sgp/crs/row/RL34613.pdf

27 Dmitri Medvedev, "Soveshchanie s uchastiem chlenov Soveta Bezopasnosti o merakh po stabilizatsii sotsial'no-politichesckoi obstanovki i neitralizastii terroristicheskikh i ekstremistskikh ugroz v Severo-Kavkazskom regione [Meeting with members of the Security Council on measures to stabilize the socio-political situation and neutralize the terrorist and extremist threats in the North Caucasus region]," *kremlin.ru*, Stavropol', August 19, 2009, http://kremlin.ru/news/5236

28 Dmitri Medvedev, "Rabochaya vstrecha s gubernatorom Stavropol'skogo kraya Valeriem Gaevskim [Working meeting with Gubernator of Stavropol'skii krai Valerii Gaevskii]," *Kremlin.ru*, Stavropol', August 19, 2009. http://news.kremlin.ru/news/5237

29 Kavkaz Center. "Interview of the Caucasus Emirate's Emir Dokka Abu Usman." Last modified February 17, 2010. www.kavkazcenter.com/eng/content/2010/02/17/11434.shtml

30 See Mairbek Vatchagaev, "The Radicals Among the North Caucasus Rebels Appear to Have Gained the Upper Hand," *North Caucasus Analysis*, 11(0). Last modified September 10, 2010. www.jamestown.org/single/?no_cache=1&tx_ttnews%5Btt_news%5D=36816

31 See Mairbek Vatchagaev, "Warriors of the Nogai Steppe: A Profile of the Nogai Jammat," *North Caucasus Analysis*, 8(31). Last modified August 2, 2007. www.jamestown.org/single/?no_cache=1&tx_ttnews%5Btt_news%5D=4354

32 According to Russian authorities, an ethnic Kumyk woman from Chechnya, identified as "the wife of a Nogai Jamaat member arrested in Pyatigorsk," planned to blow herself up during the New Year's Eve celebrations in Manezh Square, Moscow. However, the martyrdom belt that she was wearing exploded early, killing another women near Kuzminski Park. See, www.themoscowtimes.com/news/article/suicide-bombers-strike-in-caucasus/431085.html

33 Marlène Laruelle, *In the Name of the Nation: Nationalism and Politics in Contemporary Russia* (New York: Palgrave/MacMillan, 2009), 40.

34 One reason for this recent positive trend is the increased focus of authorities on maintaining public order, in particular through monitoring the activities

of ultranationalist groups. In 2008 the federal government established a "Department for Combating Extremism" within the Interior Ministry, which has proved particularly efficient in combating neo-Nazi groups.

35 See Andrew Foxall, "Post-Soviet Ethnic Relations in Stavropol'skii krai, Russia: 'A melting pot or boiling shaft?,'" *Europe-Asia Studies*, 64 (2012): 1766–87.

36 Matveeva, *The North Caucasus*, 42.

37 This was part of the wider process marking the political rehabilitation of the Cossacks, which began in June 1991 when President Yeltsin issued a decree to this effect. The process gained momentum in March 1993 when Yeltin signed a further decree granting Cossacks state support. In August 1995, Yeltsin announced that Cossack units would be formed in the Border Guards of the Russian Army.

38 In 1994 this organization was renamed the Stavropol' Cossack Army (*Stavropol'skoe kazach'e voisko—SKB*). During the first Chechen war the SKB provided volunteer soldiers for the so-called Ermolov Battalion, which fought alongside the Twenty-first Airborne Brigade (now the 247th Air-Assault Regiment, but also known as the Caucasian Cossack Regiment).

39 Matveeva, *The North Caucasus*.

40 See Laruelle, *In the Name of the Nation*.

41 See Maiya Astvatsaturova, "Problemi etnicheskikh otnoshenii na Stavropol'e [Problems of Ethnic Relations in Stavropol'']," *EAWARN*, Last modified July 21, 2009. http://eawarn.ru/index.php?option=com_content&task=view&id=283&Itemid=40

42 See Andrew Foxall, "Discourses of Demonisation: Chechens, Russians, and the Stavropol' riots of 2007," *Geopolitics*, 15 (2010): 684–704.

43 See, for example, Richard Sakwa, *Putin: Russia's Choice* (London: Routledge, 2004).

44 See Robert Ware, "Has the Russian Federation Been Chechenised?" *Europe-Asia Studies*, 63 (2011): 495.

45 See Andrew Jack, "Putin rolls back regional freedoms of Yeltsin years," *Financial Times*, September 13, 2004. Last modified September 13, 2004. www.ft.com/cms/s/0/42c62680–05b1–11d9-bff2–00000e2511c8.html#axzz22UaG5rTw

46 See Izvestiya. "Supruga gubernatora Stavropol'ya Irina Chernogova: 'Muzh raz'ezzhaet ba "Bentli" i ne daet mne razvoda' [Wife of the governor of Stavropol' Irina Chernogorova: "My husband drives a 'Bentley' and will not give me a divorce"]." January 22, 2007. http://izvestia.ru/news/320882

47 See, for example, RIA Novosti. "Kremlin studying Kozak's recommendations for changes in the North Caucasus." June 21, 2005. http://en.rian.ru/analysis/20050621/40563954.html

48 See Mark Kramer, "The Changing Context of Russian Federal Policy in the North Caucasus," PONARS Policy Memo No. 416. Last modified December 2006. http://csis.org/files/media/csis/pubs/pm_0416.pdf

49 One of Medvedev's first acts after being elected President in May 2008 was to replace Chernogorov as Governor of Stavropol'skii krai with Valerii Gaevskii (former Deputy Presidential Envoy to the Southern Federal District). One of Medvedev's last acts as President in May 2012 was to replace Gaevskii with Valerii Zerenkov (a former Chairman of the State Duma of Stavropol'skii *krai*

between 1994 and 1997, and current Deputy of the State Duma of the Russian Federation for the "United Russia" party).

50 Dmitri Medvedev, "Poslanie Federal'nomu Sobraniyu Rossiiskoi Federatsii [Address to Federal Assembly of the Russian Federation]," *Kremlin.ru*, November 12, 2009. http://news.kremlin.ru/transcripts/5979

51 See Dmitri Medvedev, "V Rossii obrazovan novii federal'nii okrug— Severo-Kavkazskii [Russia has established a new federal district—North Caucasus]," *Kremlin.ru*, January 19, 2010. http://kremlin.ru/transcripts/6664

52 The borders of the NCFD are almost identical to those of the North Caucasus *krai* created in 1924 by Joseph Stalin.

53 Paul Goble, "Window on Eurasia: Stavropol's Russians Want Their Region Removed from North Caucasus Federal District," *Window on Eurasia Blog*. Last modified October 14, 2010. http://windowoneurasia.blogspot.co.uk/2010/10/window-on-eurasia-stavropols-russians.html

54 This was noted by Markedonov (Na Stike Mirov Stavropol'skii Krai: fornost russkikh ili zone integratsii? 2009) a year earlier.

55 See http://stavropol.stavkray.ru/bezop/pksovet/

56 Stavropol'skaya Pravda. "Uchastnikov massovikh molodezhnikh drak i podstrekatelei budut otchislyat' iz vuzov Stavropolya [Participants and instigators in the mass youth fights will be removed from Stavropol's universities]," September 20, 2010. www.stapravda.ru/20100920/uchastnikov_massovykh_molodezhnykh_drak_I_podstrekateley_budut_o_48164.html

57 There are, of course, regional-level geographical differences in the economic development of the North Caucasus that are not adequately captured in these figures. For example, distinctions between lowlands and highlands and between rural and urban areas are significant. See, Jean Radvanyi and Shakhmardan Mudyuev, "Challenges Facing the Mountain Peoples of the Caucasus," *Eurasian Geography and Economics*, 48 (2007): 157–77.

58 The amount of financial assistance increased over this period, from USD500 million per year in 2000 to USD9 billion in 2011. It should also be noted that particular assistance is targeted and thus not counted within these figures: Ingushetia, for example, receives a unique assistance package from Moscow worth USD1 billion.

59 See http://openbudget.karelia.ru/budnord/russian/fo_sevkav.htm

60 Budget statistics are taken from: http://openbudget.karelia.ru/budnord/russian/fo_sevkav.htm, and GRP Statistics are taken from: www.gks.ru/wps/wcm/connect/rosstat/rosstatsite/main/account/2b319e8044aba985b48df4db be9dd3a4#

61 See www.government.ru/media/2010/10/4/35578/file/1485.doc

62 Vendina, Belozerov, and Gustafson, "The Wars in Chechnya and Their Effects on Neighboring Regions," 186.

63 Rashid Yunusov, "Ekonomicheskiye i politicheskiye elity respubliki: Kak preodolet' razdelyayushchuyu ikh propast [Economic and Political Elites of Ethnic Republics: How to Overcome the Chasm between Them]," *Groznenskiy rabochiy*, 24(20879), October 10, 2003. Last modified October 10, 2003. www.admhohol.ru/news2/3351.php

64 This pipeline is central to Russia's transportation infrastructure in the region and is the main route for transporting oil from Kazakhstan's Tengiz field to Russia's Black Sea ports.

65 Vendina, Belozerov, and Gustafson, "The Wars in Chechnya and Their Effects on Neighboring Regions," 186–7.

66 Mineralnye Vody International Airport, "Istoriya Aeroporta [History of the Airport]," Last accessed August 3, 2012. www.mvairport.ru/article.php?id_article=17

67 Dmitri Medvedev, "Soveshchanie po voprosam razvitiya turisticheckogo klastera na Severnom Kavkaze [Meeting on the development of the North Caucasus Tourism Cluster]," *Kremlin.ru*, March 11, 2012. Last modified March 11, 2012. www.kremlin.ru/transcripts/14745

Bibliography

Astvatsaturova, Maiya, "Problemi etnicheskikh otnoshenii na Stavropol'e [Problems of Ethnic Relations in Stavropol']," *EAWARN*, last modified July 21, 2009. http://eawarn.ru/index.php?option=com_content&task=view&id=283&Itemid=40

Avksentiev, Viktor and Ludmilla Lobova, "Ethnopolitical problems of Post-Soviet Russia: The Case of Northern Caucasus," in *Russia—Continuity and Change*, Gerald Hinteregger and Hans-Georg Heinrich, eds,. Wien: Springer-Verlag, 2004, pp. 527–46.

Belozerov, Vitali S., *Etnichesksaya karta Severnogo Kavkaza* [Ethnic Atlas of the North Caucasus]. Moscow: OGI, 2005.

— *Etnodemograficheskiye protsessy na Severnom Kavkaze* [Ethno-demographic Processes in the North Caucasus]. Stavropol: Stavropol' State University Press, 2000.

Deng, Francis M., "Specific Groups and Individuals Mass Exoduses and Displaced Persons, Report of the Representative of the Secretary-General on internally displaced persons, Profiles in displacement: the Russian Federation," UN Commission on Human Rights, E/CN.4/2004/77/Add.2. February 24, 2004.

Foxall, Andrew, "Discourses of Demonisation: Chechens, Russians, and the Stavropol' riots of 2007," *Geopolitics*, 15 (2010): 684–704.

— "Post-Soviet Ethnic Relations in Stavropol'skii krai, Russia: 'A Melting Pot or Boiling Shaft?', *Europe-Asia Studies*, 64(2012): 1766–87.

Freedom House, "The Worst of the Worst: The World's Most Repressive Societies 2006," last modified September 6, 2006. www.freedomhouse.org/template.cfm?page=138&report=40www.freedomhouse.org/uploads/WoW/2006/Chechnya2006.pdf

Gannushkina, Svetlana A., "Memorial Human Rights Centre: The Internally Displaced Persons from Chechnya in the Russian Federation," last modified June 10, 2002. http://refugee.memo.ru/For_All/rupor.nsf/839ac874eb0b559cc3256a4a003bb69f/9bf376467e69ac49c3256bd3007a8b55!OpenDocument.

Kavkaz Center, "Interview of the Caucasus Emirate's Emir Dokka Abu Usman," last modified February 17, 2010. www.kavkazcenter.com/eng/content/2010/02/17/11434.shtml

Khoprov, Vladimir, "Boy s ten'yu [Shadow Boxing]," *Severnyy Kavkaz*, January 31, 2006, last modified January 31, 2006. www.sknews.ru/paper/2006/4/article.php?id=7&uin=1

Kramer, Mark, "The Changing Context of Russian Federal Policy in the North Caucasus," PONARS Policy Memo No. 416, last modified December 2006. http://csis.org/files/media/csis/pubs/pm_0416.pdf

Laruelle, Marlène, *In the Name of the Nation: Nationalism and Politics in Contemporary Russia*. New York: Palgrave MacMillan, 2009.

Markedonov, Sergei, "Na Stike Mirov Stavropol'skii Krai: fornost russkikh ili zone integratsii? [Stavropol Territory On a Join of Worlds: an advanced post of Russia or a zone of integration?]." *Chastnii Korrespondent*, last modified June 25, 2009. www.chaskor.ru/p.php?id=7827

— "Stavropol'yu nuzhna integratsiya [Stavropol' needs integration]," *Novaya Politika*, last modified November 29, 2010. http://novopol.ru/-stavropolyu-nujna-integratsiya-text93089.html

Matveeva, Anna, *The North Caucasus: Russia's Fragile Borderland*. London: The Royal Institute of International Affairs, 1999.

Nichol, Jim, "Stability in Russia's Chechnya and Other Regions of the North Caucasus: Recent Developments," Congressional Research Centre, last modified December 13, 2010. www.fas.org/sgp/crs/row/RL34613.pdf

O'Loughlin, John, Alexander Panin, and Frank Wittmer, "Population Change and Migration in Stavropol' Kray: The Effects of Regional Conflicts and Economic Restructuring," *Eurasian Geography and Economics*, 48 (2007): 249–67.

Pallot, Judith and Tat'yana G. Nefedova, *Russia's Unknown Agriculture: Household Production in Post-Soviet Rural Russia*. Oxford: Oxford University Press, 2007.

Riazantsev, Sergey V. "The Demographic Situation in the North Caucasus," *Sociological Research*, 42 (2003): 30–44.

Russell, John, "Terrorists, Bandits, Spooks and Thieves: Russian Demonisation of the Chechens Before and Since 9/11," *Third World Quarterly*, 26 (2005): 101–16.

Soldatov, Andrei and Irina Borogan, *The New Nobility: The Restoration of Russia's Security State and the Enduring Legacy of the KGB*. New York: PublicAffairs, 2010.

Tsvetkov, Oleg, "Ethnic Russians Flee the North Caucasus," *Russian Analytical Digest*, 7 (2006): 9–12.

Vatchagaev, Mairbek, "The Radicals Among the North Caucasus Rebels Appear to Have Gained the Upper Hand," *North Caucasus Analysis*, 11(0), last modified September 10, 2010. www.jamestown.org/single/?no_cache=1&tx_ttnews%5Btt_news%5D=36816

— "Warriors of the Nogai Steppe: A Profile of the Nogai Jammat," *North Caucasus Analysis*, 8(31), last modified August 2, 2007. www.jamestown.org/single/?no_cache=1&tx_ttnews%5Btt_news%5D=4354

Vendina, Olga, Vitali S. Belozerov, and Andrew Gustafson, "The Wars in Chechnya and Their Effects on Neighboring Regions," *Eurasian Geography and Economics*, 48 (2007): 178–201.

Yunusov, Rashid, "Ekonomicheskiye i politicheskiye elity respubliki: Kak preodolet' razdelyayushchuyu ikh propast' [Economic and Political Elites of Ethnic Republics: How to Overcome the Chasm between Them]," *Groznenskiy rabochiy*, 24(20879) (October 10, 2003), last modified October 10, 2003. www.admhohol.ru/news2/3351.php

CHAPTER SIX

Blowback? Chechnya and the Challenges of Russian Politics

Richard Sakwa

The complex relations that have developed between Moscow and Chechnya may be elucidated in terms of the Dual-state Model. In any given state, the Dual-state Model analyzes distinctions between normative or constitutional conceptions of that state on the one hand, and on the other hand, the arbitrary or prerogative nature of executive actions, which sometimes deviate from constitutional norms. This chapter argues that relations between Moscow and Chechnya have shifted the Russian Federation toward a more arbitrary and prerogative government. Yet continued balancing between the two orders makes possible the future extension of constitutional and legal norms to Chechnya.

Despite attempts to bracket the post-communist Chechen conflicts, Russian politics have been profoundly affected by developments in the North Caucasus.[1] The influence is complex, since the evolution of the Russian state has been fragmented at both the federal and regional levels, and developments in Chechnya have affected different parts of the Russian state in different ways. This chapter outlines the Dual-state Model for federal government, and notes the role of the various factions at the center and the differential way in which they interact with the local leadership in

Chechnya. The contrast between the *constitutional state* and the *administrative regime* defines contemporary Russia. The tension between the lofty principles declared in constitutional documents and the typically sordid practices inherent in the art of governing is characteristic of most societies, but in Russia these two assumed sharply delineated forms that have come to define the system as a whole.[2] Ernest Fraenkel described how in Nazi Germany the prerogative state acted as a separate law system of its own, although the formal constitutional state was not dismantled. Two parallel systems of law operated, where the "normative state" operated according to sanctioned principles of rationality and impartial legal norms; while the "prerogative state" exercised power arbitrarily and without constraints, unrestrained by law.[3]

In contemporary Russia the circumstances are very different, yet the tension between two systems of rule, and their normative and practical concomitants, checking and balancing each other, is the fundamental condition of everyday politics. To reflect the distinctive features of Russian development I use the terms "constitutional state" and "administrative regime" in place of Fraenkel's "normative" and "prerogative" states. In conditions where the balance of power has been pushed to an extreme, as in contemporary Chechnya, the latter term remains valid. The administrative regime took shape already in the early years of Boris Yeltsin's rule in the 1990s, and was exacerbated by the onset of the first Chechen war in December 1994. Under Putin the administrative element was raised to a whole style of governance, emphasizing technocratic rationality and insulation from popular and special interest pressures. This system was then emulated in some of Russia's regions, taking extreme form in Chechnya. However, as we shall see, given the extraordinary development of "emergency" forms of governance associated with the current Chechen leadership, the influence of the normative values of the constitutional state have been undermined to the point that the duality that remains prevalent elsewhere in Russia has been transcended in Chechnya to create a monocratic form of rule, a type of prerogative state.

The "chechenization" strategy focusing on the Kadyrovs (Akhmed-hadji Kadyrov, the former mufti of Chechnya, and his son Ramzan) is only part of a broader picture in which Moscow seeks to avoid being captured by a client regime; while the Kadyrov system is challenged by broader developments in Russia itself. If the constitutional state was strengthened, as proposed during his presidency from 2008 by Dmitry Medvedev and later when he became prime minister in 2012, then the Chechen Model would become increasingly anomalous, to the point that its viability would be called into question. Thus while there are elements of "blowback" in the interaction between Moscow and Chechnya, with Russia's policies toward the region enhancing the coercive and technocratic features of the administrative system, accompanied by its manipulations of media space and the micro-management of political processes as a whole, these are tempered by the countervailing policies intended to strengthen constitutionalism. To date, the country has been able to avoid such a stark choice because of the fragmented character of the Russian state, with various factions in the center cutting across each other depending on the issue area, accompanied by the broader problem of the segmented character of Russian regional politics as a whole. Instead of an ordered federal separation of powers, segmentation entails a series of *ad hoc* relations with regions, with very few institutional manifestations of collective behavior by the regions themselves.

A hollow victory

Although Russia may have "won" the second Chechen war, in that the insurgency in the Chechen Republic has, by and large, been defeated and the prospect of the republic leaving the Russian Federation are minimal in the near future, the war has ended on the basis of three fundamentally ambiguous outcomes.[4]

The first concerns the political status of Chechnya. Although now confirmed as part of Russia, the republic is tenuously part of the Russian constitutional space. Engagement between Russian and Chechen polities is mediated through a powerful "warlordist" figure, President Ramzan Kadyrov, and the Russian "strongman," President Vladimir Putin. The modes of interaction between Russia and Chechnya repudiate classical versions of modern state building. Instead, a type of neo-feudal relationship has emerged that, on one side, undermines the integrity of the Russian legal and constitutional space, while, on the other, effectively delivers the inhabitants of Chechnya to the rule of an individualized type of arbitrary power. The relationship between Moscow and Grozny becomes a personal one, centered on the relationships between the main actors, while the quality of social and political relationships in both Chechnya and Russia are degraded.

This type of anomalous and archaic state-building strategy does deliver tangible public benefits to both sides, but is not sustainable in the long term. All the region's rulers have adapted their norms to custom-based law (*adat*), but political demodernization now takes extreme forms and renders the whole region a type of internal abroad.[5] Indeed, Putin's policy of "Kadyrovization" exacerbated the problems across the region, while raising questions about Russia's development as a democratic state. With the etiolation of dualism in Chechnya, the defensibility of the norms associated with the constitutional state is weakened at the federal level. Kadyrov's pursuit of Oleg Orlov, the chair of the Memorial Human Rights Organization, in the courts where he was charged with defamation when he pointed the finger of responsibility at Kadyrov for the murder of Natalya Estemirova, a human rights activist and Memorial associate, on July 15, 2009, suggested that even in Moscow there would be no sanctuary for those seeking to defend human rights in Chechnya. The institutions of Russian constitutionalism were turned against defenders of the liberal principles that the constitution proclaims.

The second problem concerns the way that elements of what had originally been a Chechen insurgency have been generalized across the region. The Chechen relationship with Russia is part of the larger problem of the way that the North Caucasus as a whole is integrated into the larger polity. Kadyrov's strategy has been to undermine the legitimacy of, on the one hand, Chechen separatists, and, on the other, devotees of the radical Islamization of the North Caucasus who advance, in particular, the imposition of *shariah* courts.[6] The strategy of insurgency, while reduced in Chechnya, has become generalized across the region. Gordon Hahn reports that since the foundation of the *jihadi* Caucasus Emirate (CE) in late October 2007, the CE carried out some 1,600 terrorist attacks in Russia, 99 percent of which were in the North Caucasus, of which 23 percent were in Chechnya. These attacks killed over 1,100 state employees (civilians and security officials), and wounded 1,700 more. In addition, over 300 civilians were killed and another 900 wounded. In 2010 over half of the CE's violence was committed in Dagestan. Almost none of this, Hahn notes, is reflected in the Western media, who focus obsessively on Kadyrov's behavior.[7] In 2011 there was a 6.3 percent fall in the number of incidents, with 59 of the North Caucasian attacks taking place in Chechnya (compared to 80 in 2010 and 159 in 2009), while 315 of the 541 occurred in Dagestan.[8]

The CE's predecessor, the radically nationalist Chechen Republic of Ichkeria, had developed links with al-Qaeda by the mid-1990s, but it is not this link that is key today. Instead, the dynamism of a radical Islamist agenda (conventionally known as Wahhabism in Russia) challenges the various types of Islamic practice in the region, notably demotic forms of Sufism in Chechnya. Ambassador William J. Burns, in a cable to Washington dated May 30, 2006 revealed by the "cablegate" Wikileaks publications, in one of the most perceptive analyses of the Chechen and the broader North Caucasus situation, argued "The prospects for the nationalists would be poor even if Kadyrov . . . were assassinated."[9] The initiative has clearly passed to the post-nationalist insurgency. The remnants of the ethno-national independence movement, originally led by Dzhokhar Dudaev in the early 1990s, moved to Akhmed Zakaev, exiled in London. As far as Zakaev is concerned, the CE was little more than a Russian plot to destabilize the independence movement. Kadyrov, on the other hand, argued that the West was behind the insurgency, "interested in severing the Caucasus from Russia."[10]

This reflects the larger question, our third issue, about the form of Russian nation-building as a whole. As Shevel recently reminds us, there are several powerfully contending approaches to Russian nation-building.

In the Putin era, the authorities deliberately moved away from the Yeltsinite attempts to formulate a distinctive "national idea," and instead ruled with "purposeful ambiguity" within the framework of at least five identifiable models, not all of which are compatible.[11] This means that all sorts of different statements can be made about the nature of Russian state building, and most will capture an element of the truth, but few can hope to capture the entirety of the process. Thus the argument that Russia is drifting toward an "imperial" model of national development captures part of the reality; but it would be misleading to argue that the Russian Model of national development today is imperial. It may have elements of the imperial, but these are far from exclusive or predominant, and are contested by other models, notably the civic and the ethnic, and these in turn are fragmented by continuing debates about the extent of the nation in question; notably, whether it encompasses the whole East Slavic "nation," just "Russian speakers," or a variably defined community of "compatriots."

There remains a fundamental tension between various formulations of ethnic nation-building, but these are countered by a number of supranational projects— imperial, Slavic-Orthodox, a recreated Soviet Union, and even Dostoevsky's "universal man." For Zevelev, only some definition of a nation (whether ethnic or civic) can provide the foundations for a democratic polity. The chimera of some sort of supranational "civilizational" basis for state development, in his view, undermines the coherence of state institutions, quite apart from being perceived as a grave threat in the international arena. It was, after all, universalistic ideas (the defense of Christian sites in Palestine) that helped provoke the Crimean War in 1853.[12] The continuing debates over the compatriots law of May 1999 reflect the tensions in the definition of the Russian nation.[13] As Shevel concludes, "institutionalization and legalization of an ambiguous definition of Russia's "us" manifested in the compatriots law [of 1999] may be the only politically feasible, and also the most pragmatic, solution that serves a functional purpose."[14] It is not just that it allows Russian policymakers room for maneuver, but it reflects the real dilemmas and contradictions of Russian national development as a whole. Contradiction, indeed, became the operative mode of governance in the Putin–Medvedev era.[15]

To what extent has Russia been "Chechenized," and Chechnya "Russianized," let alone "Russified"? By Russianized in this context we mean the degree to which the cleavages and patterns of politics prevalent in Moscow are applicable to Chechnya. We have already argued that dualism is much weaker in Chechnya than in Moscow, yet the broader patterns of Russian politics may apply to Chechnya as well. As for the cultural process of Russification, this is certainly on the retreat. Only a tiny proportion of the population of 1,268,989 registered by the 2010 census are ethnic Russians, and various traditionalist forms of social identification and behavior are consolidating in Chechnya. Views veer from one extreme, in which it is argued that the outcome of the various conflicts in the region have provoked the full-scale Chechenization of Russia, to the opposed view that Russia has been able to insulate itself to a surprising degree from the conflicts in Chechnya and developments in the North Caucasus more broadly.

A middle view suggests that "today Chechnya is the Kremlin's success story," following the allocations of billions of dollars in reconstruction assistance that has seen Grozny emerge from the ashes, with a shiny new Putin Prospekt lined with banks and high-rise blocks.[16] Compared to the destitution in neighboring Ingushetia and the insecurity in Dagestan, Chechnya is indeed a relative success story, in terms of postwar recovery. But the physical rebuilding has been accompanied by the divergence in constitutional development, as well as in social practices. Polygamy, which is illegal under Russian law, is now practiced in unofficial ceremonies, women are forced to wear head covering (enforced by unofficial militia), civil servants have to adhere to a strict dress code, and the sale of alcohol is limited to two hours a day. Chechnya is thus engaged in a thorough process of de-secularization, through a range of policies and practices that run directly counter to the stipulations of the Russian constitution: and all of this at the Russian tax payer's expense. Of course, Russia is also becoming a partially post-secular society, but this organic process is not comparable to the aggressive imposition of elements of *shariah* in Chechnya.

Kadyrov has not only created a "state within the state," but also a parallel society that has grave implications for developments in the rest of Russia. As far as the North Caucasus is concerned, the three main Russian strategies for managing the region are: (1) the creation of "archaic khanates," to use Nikolai Petrov's term;[17] (2) the application of coercive policies, often including extra-judicial force; and (3) extensive investment in social programs that represents an attempt to "drain the swamp" of unemployment, social exclusion, and poverty that is seen as feeding the various insurgent movements. In Ingushetia, for example, the official unemployment rate is 57 percent with an average monthly salary of R7,000 (USD235). The bored and alienated youth are ready material for the "jihadization" of protest, which has already reached epic proportions in Dagestan, but the "loyalty for money" strategy, on its own, can do little to abate social and political conflict. Hahn is right to point to a regional dimension to the various outbursts of insurgency, reflected in the creation of the Caucasus Emirate.[18] In a region undergoing rapid urbanization and its accompanying dislocations, as well as a growth in student numbers, a segment of young intellectuals are attracted to Salafi ideas, including the view that *shariah* law provides a framework for moral order, while the poor and excluded see militant Islam as the antidote to poverty and corruption. Conflicts within officially organized Islam only reinforced the appeal of the radicals.[19] As Matveeva puts it in a recent study of the challenges facing the North Caucasus, "Islamism offers a ready response to those young people who feel a moral collapse of society, who are frustrated with poor performance of governing institutions, and who look for political participation and for opportunities to connect to like-minded groups worldwide and perform heroic deeds."[20] Of course, these region-wide processes assume local forms in each of the republics.

Sergei Markedonov argues that "In many ways the unity of Russia, the soundness of her political identity and the effectiveness of Russian Federation state and public institutions, are dependent on this region."[21] From this perspective the constitutional state should be strengthened: elections made genuinely competitive, the independence of the courts established, and corruption combatted. Equally, from the liberal perspective, appointments should be based on competence rather than ethnic affiliation. As the editors of *Nezavisimaya gazeta* argued, the Russian authorities "must learn to speak to society the truth about the war" in their country rather than to assume that they can ignore what Russian citizens are feeling.[22] These aspects remain on the agenda for both Russia and Chechnya.

Ramzanistan

The insurgency from 1991 and Russia's counterinsurgency operations provoked a spiral of degradation that sharply accentuated the powers of the arbitrary state. By the time Russia intervened with massive military force in December 1994 Chechnya had come to be seen as a threat to the very existence of the country.[23] The conduct of the war, moreover, combined elements of state "terrorism" and a full-scale conventional war. Russia claimed to be fighting "international terrorism," yet resolutely refused to internationalize the conflict.[24] The effective recognition of Chechen sovereignty following the Khasavyurt agreement of August 1996 was the most extreme example of segmented regionalism.[25] It pushed the logic of confederalism to the point that outright independence was on the cards after the stipulated five-year transitional period. Putin rejected this dynamic, and the second war from September 1999 in part reflected the new strategy. Provoked by the invasion of Dagestan by Chechen insurgents under Shamil Basaev and the Arab Islamist warlord ibn al-Khattab (an exemplary case of the foreign *mujahaddin* Islamist fighter in this conflict), as well as other attacks in Russia, the Putin leadership sought to overcome segmented regionalism, whose most extreme form was to be found in interwar Chechnya. Instead, radical asymmetrical "federalism" established a new balance between the center and the republic.

In the first instance this meant relying on Akhmed-hadji Kadyrov, who in the first war had fought with the separatists but threw in his lot with the federal forces, and in return on June 12, 2000 was appointed head of the federal administration in Chechnya. Kadyrov senior remained loyal to Chechnya's Sufi (tariqat, spiritual path) tradition of Islam, and rejected the growing power of militant Salafi forms represented by the so-called Wahhabi fundamentalists.[26] The social base of Kadyrov lay the traditional *virds*, or religious communities that form the Sufi tariqats (brotherhoods) Naqshbandi and Qadiriya, whose influence has often been underestimated, while the power of the traditional kinship groups, known as *teips*, has been exaggerated.[27] There are some 20 active *virds* in Chechnya, reflecting the profound integration of tariqatism into traditional community life. The Kadyrovs belong to the increasingly influential kunta hadji *vird*. The tension between the Qadiri tradition and the Naqshbandi Tariqah remains, although the former is dominant in contemporary Chechnya.[28] An important Russian study argues that Kadyrov tried to act as an ethno-national leader, but at the same time sought to portray himself as a champion of the "Islamic project" while curbing "the excesses of radicalism by counting on traditional approaches that oppose Wahhabism and Salafism." Against the background of a general crisis of ethno-nationalism in Russia, this was unlikely to succeed. The "socialization" strategy, already relatively successful in Russia's other Islamic regions such as Tatarstan, through the advancement of a far more active "Russian Model for Muslim education," to overcome the political passivity of official Islam, was advocated.[29] Chechenization represented an alternative approach, the retraditionalization of politics and society within the framework of Chechen national allegiances, rejecting what were considered alien forms of Islam while incorporating a spirit of patriotic militancy on behalf of both Chechnya and Russia.

It also entailed an exacerbation of the flaws in the Russian constitutional process. Chechenization entailed the extreme devolution of power to the republic's leader, but it also involved maximum derogation from the principles enunciated in the constitution. A degree of "Chechenization," defined as the subordination of law to power within the framework of segmented regionalism, was inherent in the Russian political system from the early 1990s; but this exercise of prerogative powers in Chechnya weakened the contrary drive for the rule of law and genuine constitutionalism. The Dual-state Model suggests that the constitutional state has defined political weight, meaning that such fundamental normative principles as the rule of law, liberal individual rights, the separation of church and state, and much more, are defended by broad constituencies, including jurists, civil society and human rights activists, and increasingly by a popular movement. These are challenged, as argued earlier, by the arbitrariness, personalism, and the informality of the administrative regime. Chechenization revealed duality at its starkest, and thus the term originally used by Fraenkel, the "prerogative state," is more appropriate than the somewhat softer term "administrative regime." The prerogative elements are far more extreme, accompanied by egregious ballot-rigging and the use of coercion. For example, the October

5, 2003 presidential elections in the republic, designed to re-establish a constitutional process, were manipulated to such an extent that vitiated the restoration of legality, which they were proclaimed to achieve.[30] As so often in the dual-state, the declared normative policy is directly repudiated by the administrative manner of its implementation. All the serious contenders were eliminated from the ballot even before the vote, ensuring that Kadyrov's election was a foregone conclusion. A powerful Chechen leader was created with Moscow's help, now buttressed by the legitimacy of elections; but this was a dangerous strategy since by definition a viable interlocutor is also an independent one.

Following Kadyrov's assassination on May 9, 2004 Putin shifted support to his son Ramzan, who in due course (on attaining the age of 30, the minimum allowed by the Chechen constitution) became president in March 2007. The Chechen "problem" was now contained through a form of political outsourcing: the classic combination of autonomy in exchange for loyalty. The emergence of an autonomous power system in Chechnya exposed the unstable foundations of the dual state nationally, with the regime at the center flouting the constitutional constraints on its behavior. It also introduced an independent force into the equation that could challenge the powers of the federal prerogative state on its own terms. It is for this reason that both the Russian military intelligence organization (the GRU) and mainstream *siloviki* (the "militocracy" based on the Federal Security Service (FSB), reflecting the security-oriented faction in Russian politics) such as Igor Sechin distrusted Kadyrov, and had earlier supported the interim president, Alu Alkhanov, who had taken over after Kadyrov senior's murder. The *silovik* faction understood the risks posed to their centralization drive by the creation of republican islands of separatism. They also understood that by taking the logic of the administrative regime to its prerogative extremes, the basis of their own power would be exposed, and thus ultimately threatened. A Kadyrovized Chechnya showed to Moscow one possible path of its own evolution.

However, Putin had come to the view that Chechenization would not work without Kadyrov *fils* as president; and that the program as a whole offered a route to some sort of stabilization of the region. This was not based on negotiation with the "separatists," to which Putin had a deep aversion because of the belief that concessions in the 1990s had only exacerbated problems. Instead of negotiation, the founding process for Kadyrovization is personal loyalty, bilateral relations, and deinstitutionalization. However, this meant that "Putin and Ramzan became hostages to each other." Kadyrov could only act by relying entirely on the support of his patron in Moscow, but as his client cleared the field in Chechnya of all opponents, Putin "fell into ever greater dependence on his client."[31]

Putin was supported in his strategy by the "democratic statists," the faction that advocated "sovereign democracy" and in particular the close management of political processes in their entirety. Vladislav Surkov, responsible for the management of domestic politics in the presidential administration, was one of the architects of the Chechenization strategy and a consistent supporter of Kadyrov personally. This no doubt was one of the reasons for the skepticism of the *siloviki*. His departure from office as deputy head of the presidential administration in December 2011 meant that the Chechenization strategy lost one of its most ardent proponents. The third main faction, the liberals, could only watch uneasily as their efforts to strengthen the constitutional part of the dual state were undermined in Chechnya.[32] For the liberals, the economic development of the regime would provide an effective platform for the republic's reintegration into the larger political community.

The liberal view that economic development could defuse separatist aspirations was one of the reasons for the creation on January 19, 2010 of a new North Caucasus Federal District, which split six republics and one region from the Southern Federal District.[33] Its capital was in Pyatigorsk in Stavropol region. Medvedev appointed Alexander Khloponin, who had been governor of Krasnoyarsk *krai* since 2002, to head the new body, and urged him to apply "primarily economic methods," rather than coercive strategies.[34] Regional leaders henceforth were to maintain contacts with the federal authorities exclusively through the new envoy, a stipulation that may well have been aimed against Kadyrov who had hitherto enjoyed direct access.[35] Khloponin was granted the power to dismiss the heads of any federal agency in the region. Medvedev insisted that "The roots of the majority of problems in this region [the North Caucasus] lie in a weak economy and an absence of prospects for the people living there," combined with a high level of corruption.[36] Medvedev acknowledged that "There is a lot of money in the region. That is why a financial manager is needed, as opposed to just a hard man."[37]

Khloponin's appointment was thus primarily motivated by his deserved reputation for effective economic management, and he was thus welcomed as such to the region by influential figures like the Lezgin billionaire Suleiman Kerimov. The move also had the effect of creating a supra-republican counter-balance to Kadyrov's power within Chechnya, and acted as a bulwark against his regional ambitions. Medvedev thus reasserted the liberal line that economic development offered a long-term resolution to the region's problems, and offered an alternative to the top-down Kadyrovization strategy while attempting to provide a broader institutional framework for relations with Chechnya. The tangible achievements were few, but at least represented acknowledgement of the line pursued by Dmitry Kozak when he was the federal representative to the region between 2004 and 2007: that security could be assured only when the other problems facing the region were tackled— corrupt elites, crime, human rights abuses, disputes over land use, interethnic tensions, economic stagnation, and unemployment.[38]

Chechnya policy was thus an issue that divided the factions in Moscow. The tensions were exacerbated during the succession in 2007–8, when Kadyrov sought to ensure that he retained Moscow's support into the new presidency. Putin was always ambiguous about Kadyrov personally; willing to award him various medals, but tended to speak in neutral terms about the rebuilding program in the republic. On his side, Kadyrov was never less than effusive about Putin: "Let me clarify. I'm not a president's man. I'm not an FSB, interior ministry, GRU or prosecutor general's office man. I'm Vladimir Vladimirovich Putin's man."[39] In the December 2007 Duma election Kadyrov delivered an astonishing 99.36 percent of the vote for the Kremlin's pedestal party, United Russia, on a 99.21 percent turnout (576,729 out of 580,918 registered voters).[40] Kadyrov was one of the most enthusiastic in favor of a third term for Putin, and was disappointed when he left office, commenting that presidency in Russia should be life.[41] Nevertheless, he delivered an exceptionally strong vote for Putin's nominee, Medvedev, in the March 2, 2008 presidential elections— again a stratospheric 88.7 percent.[42] Surkov reciprocated the sentiment, and argued that Kadyrov was indispensable for stabilization in the republic: "Stability in the Caucasus today rests on the shoulders of people like Ramzan Kadyrov. As long as people like Kadyrov are around, we can rest assured that constitutional order in the republic will prevail and every possible effort will be made to ensure peace, stability and prosperity in Chechnya."[43]

On April 16, 2009 the Kremlin officially announced the end of the "counter-terrorist operation" (KTO) in Chechnya, imposed on September 23, 1999 after the second invasion of Dagestan, in an attempt to draw the line under 15 years of conflict. The National Anti-Terrorism Committee (NAK), headed by the director of the FSB Alexander Bortnikov, lifted the security restrictions that had been in force in the region since the start of the second war. The move was welcomed by Kadyrov, arguing that it had "enormous moral and psychological significance" since the Kremlin "has officially confirmed the fact that the nest of terrorism has been crushed."[44] He stressed that the formal end of the war would facilitate economic development in the region, echoing the declaration of the committee, which stated that the end of operations was a chance for Chechnya to return to normal: "This decision aims to create conditions to further normalize the situation in the region, to restore and develop its economic and social infrastructure."[45] Both Moscow and Grozny colluded in a "normalization" discourse that sought to "desecuritize" relations between the two and within Chechnya.[46]

This did not mean, however, that dualism within Chechnya was overcome; indeed, the end of overt military operations allowed the extreme form to become consolidated in the republic. Instability was institutionalized in a set of personal relationships, while the retreat from modernity eviscerated the public sphere and privatized politics.[47] Conflict in the

North Caucasus had contributed to the development of the dual state at the federal level, and now Russia was only able to retain Chechnya by permitting extreme dualism, which inexorably reinforced the dualistic elements at the center.

Chechenization delivered certain tangible results, notably the relative containment of militant activity, which in Chechnya was now less than in Dagestan and Ingushetia. The crime rate in the republic was half the national average, although terrorist events still took place there.[48] The strategy of the former insurgents who were now running Chechnya was to push for as much autonomy short of declaring independence. This allowed the republic to be rebuilt. Grozny once again returned to life with busy boulevards and skyscrapers, accompanied by the construction of one of Europe's largest mosques, completed in 2009. The price to be paid was the creation of "Ramzanistan."[49] He was appointed for a new five-year term in April 2011, so even with the return of gubernatorial elections in 2012 Kadyrov would at the minimum remain president until 2016. In this space Kadyrov's preferences became law, media freedom was curtailed, the courts intimidated, and the population cowed. Elements of Kadyrov's "personality cult" were manifest nationally, with a glowing documentary broadcast on NTV on October 6, 2011 to mark his thirty-fifth birthday. Kadyrov is one of the few regional leaders with a national profile. Little mention was made of his alleged vast personal wealth and lavish lifestyle, with a newly constructed palace, a fleet of vehicles making up the "presidential cortege," as well as racehorses costing millions, and generous payments for footballers to play for Terek, his beloved Grozny football team.

Strains of Chechenization

It would not be so easy to undo the Faustian pact whereby in exchange for guaranteeing stability in the region and loyalty to Moscow, Kadyrov was basically granted a free hand in running the republic. The essence of a Faustian pact, however, is that the small print entails rather larger commitments than originally envisaged— the devil is indeed in the details. Gleb Pavlovsky, the former Kremlin "spin doctor," noted the broader consequences: "The Caucasus represents the failure of the model that demonstrated its success in building a power vertical from Moscow to Tuva, but only not here! This is what happens with any conception of power. It spreads nearly everywhere, but finds resistance in one little spot. And it is from that spot that signs of the end emerge."[50] However, before that could come to pass, the devil delivered on his side of the bargain.

In the light of the two wars that Russia has fought with the separatist territory of Chechnya since 1991, the spectacle of Chechen forces fighting on the Russian side in South Ossetia during the Five-Day War (August 2008) was quite extraordinary. The Vostok battalion, headed by Sulim Yamadaev, apparently was supported by the GRU, whereas Kadyrov, as we have seen, is supported by the FSB.[51] Thus the factionalism and inter-institutional rivalries that are rife in Moscow are played out in the Caucasus. Equally, Caucasian rivalries are played out in Moscow, as they had been with devastating effect in the 1990s when all sorts of cross-cutting personal links united Moscow and Grozny. Yamadaev in 2008 was the last remaining independent warlord who could challenge Kadyrov. Not surprisingly, they fell out (accompanied it appears by the withdrawal of GRU support, ordered possibly by Putin himself) and Yamadaev fled to Dubai. Even this was not far enough, and on March 28, 2009 he was murdered. According to the Dubai authorities, one of the assassins claimed to have received the murder weapon from a guard of Adam Delimkhanov, a United Russia Duma deputy from December 2007, a first cousin of Ramzan Kadyrov and a former Chechen deputy prime minister in 2006–7, who it was suggested was the mastermind for the murder.[52]

Already Umar Israilov, a Chechen then living in exile but who had formerly been part of the *jihadist* insurgency until captured in early 2003, gave written testimony about a pattern of brutality within Chechnya, including an alleged killing by a man with a shovel by Kadyrov and Delimkhanov.[53] Israilov himself was murdered in Vienna on January 13, 2009, and this was only one of a string of deaths, notably the murder of Movladi Baisarov, a former ally of Kadyrov's who had turned into his foe, in Moscow in 2006. In exile in London Zakaev, the last commander of the first Chechen war still alive and the head of the classical "nationalist" independence tendency (the "Ichkerians"), also felt threatened. As he noted, "For the past 12 years Putin has steered Russia in gangster direction.[sic] He first used these methods in Chechnya, and then in Russia. He's exporting them abroad."[54] Kadyrov also used the courts to intimidate his opponents, notably as we have seen against the head of Memorial. Orlov had castigated Kadyrov for Estemirova's murder, but in the event a Moscow court cleared Orlov of the libel charge in June 2011.[55] At that time Yuri Budanov, who had served eight-and-a-half years of a ten-year sentence for the killing of Elza Kungaeva in March 2000, was murdered, possibly in blood retribution for his earlier monstrous crimes. In 2004 Kadyrov had warned that unless Budanov was given a life sentence, other ways of punishing him would be found.

Kadyrov's views fit into a broad pattern of geopolitical contestation in the Caucasus. During a 2009 interview, he warned that Russia needed to be "wary of Georgia, which is under the wing of the USA." He advanced the audacious claim that when the Chechens were shown trust by Putin, "Chechnya saved Russia." Chechnya's role in the Georgian conflict had rehabilitated the republic. He warned of a decline in patriotism and moral standards, whereas in Chechnya he was doing everything a Muslim should do. He noted the consequences of the brain drain to Moscow, with the most able and active going to the capital, "only to find it is a free-for-all there and they get everything except an education." Chechnya now played a role in implementing Russian foreign policy, and "Chechnya has become the heart of Russian Islam." Asked whether "Chechens come up against the prejudices left over from the war?," Kadyrov launched into a broadside against various dark forces:

> No, on the contrary. We feel we are Russian citizens in Russia. We defended Russia. Chechnya took on the full force of international terrorism. The terrorist network opposed Russia's sovereignty and the terrorists chose our region as an arena to fight Russia. . . . Behind all this were certain circles who wanted to destroy the Russian Federation. What was the point of a war in Chechnya? Why was it necessary to arm the population to the teeth, give them sovereignty and then take it from them? The result was hundreds of thousands killed, destruction, billions of dollars wasted. Who needed this? The state? I think it was the other way round, it was done against the state. People trained by the special services were at work here. Why was it South Ossetia immediately after Chechnya? This was a staggered operation which was halted by Putin.[56]

It appeared that the wheel had turned full circle. Patrick Armstrong in this volume argues that the wars in Chechnya were, in part, consequences of fighting in South Ossetia and Abkhazia in the early 1990s. And now, these four wars have had the unanticipated effect of consolidating, in however distorted a form, the unity of the Russian state.

A new type of separatism without independence has been established in Chechnya. As long as Moscow keeps the subsidies flowing, then the ambitions of the Chechen leadership remain within the bounds of the bargain with Moscow. Between 2002 and 2006 the republic received R30.6 billion for postwar restoration, and R11.9 billion were transferred in 2007 alone.[57] In summer 2008 Putin, by now installed as prime minister, announced a four-year USD4.7 billion (R111 billion) program of reconstruction,[58] but already by the following spring this had been cut by 30 percent as the recession intensified. Chechnya provides only five percent of its budget from local resources,[59] with the rest covered from central subsidies, some R58 bn per annum. Over half the able-bodied population are unemployed, the highest proportion of any region in the country, although Ingushetia comes close at 45–48 percent, while the comparable figure in Dagestan is estimated to be 16 percent.[60] The transfer of resources became a matter of increasing concern to Russian public opinion, and prompted attempts to find a way of making the region more economically self-sufficient. However, the various modernization plans failed to engage with the complexity of social relations in the region.[61] Indeed, they are criticized as following the model of the 1930s, and failing to engage with contemporary challenges,[62] resulting in a type of "blocked modernization."[63]

Chechenization entails a constant tension between control and autonomy. The levers available for Moscow to exercise "control" are real, above all financial subventions, but this by no means can limit the appetite for autonomy. Kadyrov's announcement in May 2009 that no Chechens would be conscripted into the Russian armed forces for a year underlined that Chechnya remained a "special zone." However, Chechenization did not mean that Ramzan would get his way on all occasions, especially when it came to the "struggle for oil."[64] Malashenko notes that two factors define Moscow's relationship with Grozny: "Moscow's non-interference in strictly Chechen matters, and control over oil."[65] Chechnya's hydrocarbon reserves are estimated at some 60 million tons of oil and 3 bn cubic meters of gas. In 2011 Rosneft's Chechen subsidiary pumped 800,000 tons of oil. With such resources, the Chechen regime could do what the Russian one had done under Putin: use energy rents to secure elite power. Natural resource rents granted Putin's regime fiscal independence from accountability and parliamentary oversight; and if Kadyrov could secure oil revenues for himself, then his position would become virtually unchallengeable, freed from dependence on Moscow's subsidies.

In January 2000 Putin endorsed the plan whereby Rosneft would take responsibility for all reconstruction work in the Chechen oil industry, and in November the Grozneftegaz company was created, with a 49 percent stake owned by the Chechen administration and 51 percent by Rosneft, to implement the instruction. As Li-Chen Sim notes, "Rosneft acts as a surrogate for Putin's policy in Chechnya: in return for minimizing incidences of illegal siphoning of oil and reducing attacks on oil infrastructure by rival Chechen clans, the pro-Russian Chechen administration apparently receives part of the proceeds from the company's monopoly on oil sales there."[66] Disappointed that Rosneft did not take up its option to explore for oil in the troubled republic, the Chechen government offered the license to Azerbaijan's State Oil Company (SOCAR). The move challenged one of Putin's closest allies, deputy prime minister Sechin, the *silovik* who had long been Rosneft's curator. Already Kadyrov was angry at Rosneft for its plans to build an oil refinery in energy-poor Kabardino-Balkaria, and then when the plans changed, its failure to start construction in Chechnya in 2011. In the end SOCAR rejected the invitation: it had started investing abroad in 2007, but in rather more lucrative and stable markets. Attacks on oil facilities in the North Caucasus continue, while theft of oil from pipelines remains endemic.[67] Rosneft has now started work on building the refinery.

Putin's return to the presidency in 2012 meant that the established personalistic model of state building could continue indefinitely, but it is a fragile basis on which to build a polity. Chechnya was loyal to the Russian regime led by Putin, but the degree of loyalty to the Russian state—certainly, its constitutional part—is more questionable. In both the parliamentary elections of December 4, 2011 and the presidential election of March 4, 2012, Chechnya once again distinguished itself by the exceptionally high vote allegedly given to the ruling authorities. Chechnya usually finds itself top in the "loyalty" ratings to the representatives of the administrative regime, whereas loyalty to the constitutional state would mean conducting freer and fairer elections in the republic. The official figures show that in the presidential election there was an astonishing 99.61 percent turnout (compared to a national average of 65.25%), of whom 99.76 percent voted for Putin (compared to the national average of 63.6%). The other candidates each received less than one percent.[68] Such results make a mockery of the electoral process, but were designed to demonstrate that Kadyrov was the most loyal of the loyal. Undoubtedly cultural factors play a part in inflating the incumbent vote, with *teips* and families designating their political preferences in group forms as part of a ritualized exchange of recognition and acknowledgment of status and power that has nothing to do with individualized competitive elections of the standard liberal democratic sort, yet such egregious electoral malpractices undermined the legitimacy of the Russian elections as a whole.[69]

Already during the parliamentary election campaign and in the various mass demonstrations held in Moscow and some other Russian cities to protest against the flawed parliamentary election, the slogan "stop feeding the Caucasus" gained traction. The phrase reflected fear that Russia was pouring resources into the Caucasus, to little effect. Pavlovsky argued that this was necessary "In a system that does not allow public debate over the Caucasus, until a solution can be found. Budgetary funds for the Caucasus are to postpone problems, to dampen things down rather than to resolve issues."[70] In practice, statistics demonstrate that the funds devoted to the region are not dramatically out of line with the subsidies given to other depressed regions, and indeed less than in some.[71] Part of this is devoted to help victims of the wars, although it is alleged that at least half of compensation payments are "taxed" by Chechen officials before being released to the intended recipients.[72] Equally, the amount embezzled from state transfers to the North Caucasus is in line with that elsewhere. In 2011 about 2.5 billion roubles (USD84 million) were stolen, with only a tiny proportion recovered (2.8%), with a total of 1,400 corruption-related violations reported, of which some 1,000 led to criminal cases.[73] The slogan demonstrated a lack of national economic solidarity with the North Caucasus, and also resentment against cultural differences. In part, this represented a "blowback" by the center against this periphery, which had been the cause of so many problems for the Russian state for so long.

The upsurge of Russian nationalism was given voice by protest leaders such as Alexei Navalny, who calls himself a "national democrat."[74] He echoed Alexander Solzhenitsyn's sentiments that "Russia" (restricted to the ethnic heartlands) would be better off without troublesome regions such as Chechnya. However, as a critic of Navalny argued, "Only someone who does not know about Russia can be a Russian nationalist."[75] As I have argued elsewhere, Russia is more than multicultural; it is a pluricultural society, with well over 150 autochthonous peoples, and any attempt formally to prioritize one (however numerous) over the others, would threaten the integrity of the whole.[76] The murder of the Spartak supporter, Yegor Sviridov, in December 2010 by a group of Caucasians and their subsequent release by highly placed officials with a Caucasian background sparked one of the largest nationalist mobilizations since *perestroika*. The "Caucasus question" became the preserve not just of nationalists but also some leading representatives of the nonsystemic opposition, accompanied by polls demonstrating that at least a third of the population held negative attitudes to people from the region.[77]

Putin remained a supranational statist and argued that the secession of any of the North Caucasus republics would only bring disaster to Russia: "As soon as a country starts rejecting some difficult territories— even troubled ones— this is the beginning of the end of the whole country." He went on to argue that "They [the North Caucasus republics] cannot exist as independent states. In fact, they will be immediately occupied both spiritually and economically by some forces from the far or near foreign countries. Then they will be used as a tool for shaking Russia further."[78] He appeared to forget that in August 2008 Russia had recognized the independence of Abkhazia and South Ossetia. These two regions allowed Russia to extend its influence (with Abkhazia providing substantive geopolitical gains), whereas the loss of Chechnya or some other republic would lead to a diminution of Russia's power.

Experience of the 1990s and the bloody break-up of Yugoslavia suggest that Putin, despite inconsistency on the question of sovereignty, was quite right to stress the possibly calamitous consequences of Chechen independence in present circumstances. While the Russian leadership stressed that Russia was a multinational and multiconfessional society, the concept of multiculturalism (let alone pluriculturalism) was given little substantive content. Observance of the law is an essential condition for successful national integration, but with fragmented constitutionalism and segmented regionalism this remains a challenge.

Chechnya as mirror and foil to Russian politics

Souleimanov characterizes the Russian–Chechen conflict as an "endless war," but while the fighting has now stopped, the nature of the peace is highly ambiguous.[79] Chechnya has de facto achieved something like the status achieved by Puerto Rico in the "permanent union" established with the United States in 1975. Kadyrov brought Chechnya back into Russia's political framework, but constitutional order failed to be established. The legitimacy of the Russian constitutional order as a whole is placed in doubt if it is able to tolerate such a zone of constitutional and political arbitrariness. The current "peace" in Chechnya is evidently only a new form of a long-term, extra-constitutional "frozen" conflict.

A number of processes are combined in Russo–Caucasian relations: the "decolonization" factor, repudiating the region's incorporation by Russia in the nineteenth century; the "legacy" factor, arising from the Soviet construction of ethnic territories incorporated into an ostensibly federal system, but marred by deportations and the dominance of a unitary communist order; and above all Russia's contradictory "state-building" process today, in which the proclaimed allegiance to the creation of a constitutional state is vitiated by authoritarian tendencies practiced by the ruling regime and the latitude allowed to subnational authoritarianism, of which Chechnya is an extreme example.

Equally, the logic of Russian state building is challenged by the multi-faceted logic of Chechnya's own nation-building process. The Kadyrovs successfully exploited these contradictions, but the Chechenization option was unable to contribute to their resolution. Thus the present balance is at best a temporary solution, which does not resolve the fundamental underlying pressures. In that case, Putin is no de Gaulle;[80] and the struggle for resolution continues, which may in due course take the form of complete decolonization or the region's substantive integration into a democratized Russian polity. For the latter to succeed, the country will require a new federal "contract," allowing genuine autonomy to Russia's regions and republics but constrained by law and adjudicated by a respected independent constitutional court, with dynamic institutions at the center, notably the Federation Council (the upper house of Russia's bicameral parliament acting as a "senate"). The overcoming of duality at the center by consolidating the authority of the constitutional state would challenge the prerogative powers arrogated by the current Chechen leadership. This would be a most benign form of blowback, allowing the Chechen people to enjoy the constitutional rights to which they are entitled as citizens of Russia.

Chechnya under Kadyrov achieved a type of "secession without independence." Exaggerated loyalty to the forms of Russian state power disguised the substantial divergence from Russian constitutional norms. The rule of law had already taken a battering in Russia during the Yukos trials, but in Chechnya lip service to participation in the Russian political community allows centrifugal forces free rein. Both Russia and Chechnya are caught in a similar legal trap, but from opposite ends. The relatives of those victimized or killed by Russian forces during the conflicts continue to pursue their cases through the courts and in Strasbourg, and while Russia always pays the requisite compensation if ordered by the European Court of Human Rights (ECtHR), it has still failed to come to terms with the atrocities that its forces committed in the republic.

For example, Colonel General Aleksandr Baranov was seen ordering the execution of the son of Fatima Bazorkina in early 2000, and although she successfully took the case to Strasbourg, Baranov was subsequently awarded a Hero of Russia medal and remained in charge of Russian forces in the republic until 2008.[81] The Islamic insurgency throughout the region was stimulated by the denunciation of suspected militants and the brutal reprisals thereby triggered.[82] In Chechnya this activity has now been "republicanized" by forces loyal to Kadyrov. Moscow tolerated brutality in Chechnya, while Chechnya exacerbated duality in Moscow.

Chechenization was not accompanied by constitutional normalization, and instead relative desecuritization saw the intensified development of a prerogative state that began to transcend the imprecise yet substantive balance maintained by the dual state in Russia as a whole. The state of exception in Chechnya moved beyond the constraints implicit in the dual state, in which neither legality nor arbitrariness have the upper hand, to create a situation in which the latter is consolidated in the form of a developing prerogative state. While Medvedev in Moscow sought to transcend the dual state by strengthening liberal constitutionalism, in Chechnya the opposite process was at work: the overcoming of dualism but from the other end of the spectrum, the intensification of the prerogative powers of a dominant power system. Putin projected the prerogative part of the Russian state onto Chechnya (as Yeltsin had done before him), but the unbridled exercise of the arbitrary state in the republic undermined the balance between the two parts of the dual state at the national level.

This authoritarian transcendence of dualism, however, is far from being welcomed by the exponents of the prerogative state in Moscow. The Kadyrov system effectively instituted "systemic separatism" (the term used in Russia by those who proclaim loyalty to Moscow but practice *de facto* independence), "where Chechnya officially remains part of Russia, but actually lives of its own free will."[83] This was Zakaev's view, who in an interview with Radio Free Europe/Radio Liberty argued that "the decolonization of Chechnya is a *fait accompli*: Chechnya *de jure* and *de facto* absolutely did not become independent, but the very process of decolonization has already been completed."[84] "The Chechen people have won this war," he insisted. In his view Chechnya had achieved separation from Russia and achieved its war aims, but not in the way originally envisaged.[85] Indeed, Russia had removed rivals such as Aslan Maskhadov, Shamil Basaev, and Abdul-Khalim Sadulaev in the struggle for power, and marginalized Islamists like Doku Umarov, leaving the field free for "non-Ichkerian" ethno-nationalists and traditionalists such as Kadyrov, who in ideological terms have much in common with the national separatist Zakaev wing of the insurgency. It is for this reason that on a number of occasions Kadyrov invited Zakaev to return to Chechnya, noting that Zakaev had never been a fighter and thus had no blood on his hands.[86] Moscow even sanctioned Zakaev's participation in discussions in Norway in summer 2009 that prepared the ground for the merger of secular nationalists abroad and authoritarian statists in Chechnya. By removing all counter-forces to Kadyrov, however, Moscow became highly dependent on him, while weakening the instruments that could ensure his loyalty. While the operative political system in Moscow is permanent balancing between factions, in Chechnya political checks and balances have been systematically removed and a much simplified system of one-man leadership consolidated.

Conclusion

Chechenization has been a highly ambivalent process, resolving some problems while generating new ones.[87] On the one hand, it allowed the stabilization of the situation in Chechnya and for Moscow to be able to withdraw from direct engagement in the conflict. However, the consolidation of the power of a blatantly authoritarian leader in the republic was a visible sign of the fragility of the dualism of the Russian state. Chechenization weakened duality at the federal level, where the norms of the constitutional state were balanced by the shadow networks of the prerogative state. Chechenization transformed central–regional relations by creating an independent system at the regional level that had little in common with federalism and undermined the so-called power vertical while reinforcing the role of power at the expense of the normative-constitutional regulation of center-periphery relations. The transformation of vertical relations could not but affect the horizontal separation of powers.[88] The absence of a political conclusion to the Chechen conflicts and the bureaucratic imposition of a powerful leader means that a permanent civil war has been institutionalized in one republic. Although laboriously attending to the formal niceties of the constitutional order, constitutionalism and the rule of law have effectively been repudiated.

The highly centralized and personalized leadership exercised by Kadyrov is homologous to the power vertical strategy pursued by the federal leadership, but by definition undercuts the vertical power of the federal authorities. The Chechen conflict has been resolved through the development of a sultanist regime in a clientelistic relationship with Moscow. Chechnya represents an extreme example of the segmented regionalism characteristic of relations between the ethno-federal republics and Moscow in the 1990s. Although the Chechen elite was involved in separatist struggles for the best part of two decades, through Chechenization they have been able to achieve much of what they failed to win on the field. The reality is of a region that has in effect achieved separation by repudiating secession.

The official end of the counterterrorist operation effectively confirmed the special deal for Chechnya whereby in exchange for extensive autonomy (of the kind granted to no other region) the Chechen leadership renounced aspirations for independence, while granting it considerable scope to ignore Russia's constitutional provisions on human rights and the rule of law. However, loyalty was oriented not to the Russian state but to Putin personally, a very fragile basis to build a state. This was a classic case of stability being achieved at the expense of order. Even in Moscow many questioned whether concessions had gone too far. Chechenization entails not only granting the Kadyrov leadership *carte blanche* to rule the republic as he sees fit, but also illustrates the glaring duality of the Russian state. The fact that a whole republic was granted a type of "internal separatism" from the constitutionalism to which the rest of the country aspired threatened the viability of that constitutional order as a whole. If federal laws could be flouted with impunity in Chechnya, then what was their value elsewhere? By establishing a type of governmentality opposed to that formally espoused by the Moscow authorities, the whole process of constitutional development in Russia was weakened. Equally, Chechenization revealed the limits of governmental power emanating from Moscow, and thus weakened the authority of Moscow's rule. While the rudiments of stability have been achieved, the struggle for a genuinely constitutional order in both Russia and Chechnya is only beginning.

Notes

1 I am grateful for the editor's careful reading of the text, and for manifold useful suggestions for improvement.
2 Richard Sakwa, "The Dual State in Russia," *Post-Soviet Affairs*, 26(3) (July–September 2010): 185–206; idem, *The Crisis of Russian Democracy: The Dual State, Factionalism and the Medvedev Succession* (Cambridge: Cambridge University Press, 2011).
3 Ernst Fraenkel, *The Dual State: A Contribution to the Theory of Dictatorship*, translated from the German by E. A. Shils, in collaboration with Edith Lowenstein and Klaus Knorr (New York: Oxford University Press, 1941), reprinted by The Lawbook Exchange, Ltd, 2006.
4 This chapter develops arguments in my "The Revenge of the Caucasus: Chechenization and the Dual State in Russia," *Nationalities Papers*, 38(5) (September 2010): 601–22.

5   Alexey Malashenko, *The North Caucasus: Russia's Internal Abroad?*, Carnegie Moscow Center, *Briefing*, 13(3) (November 2011).

6   For a detailed analysis, see Domitilla Sagramoso, "The Radicalization of Islamic Salafi *Jamaats* in the North Caucasus: Moving Closer to the Global *Jihad*ist Movement?," *Europe-Asia Studies*, 64(3) (May 2012): 561–95.

7   Gordon M. Hahn, "There They Go Again: The Washington Post Attacks the Lesser of North Caucasus Evils," www.russiaotherpointsofview.com, April 4, 2011; in *Johnson's Russia List* (henceforth *JRL*), 61, 2011, Item 23.

8   Gordon M. Hahn, "Jihadist and Islamist Trends in Eurasia in 2011," CSIS, *Islam, Islamism and Politics in Eurasia Report (IIPER)*, 55, April 16, 2012.

9   Ambassador William J Burns, "Burns on Chechnya," Viewing cable 06MOSCOW5645, "Chechnya: The Once and Future War," http://213.251.145.96/cable/2006/05/06MOSCOW5645.html

10 "Kavkaz— strategicheskii rubezh Rossii: Beseduyut Prezident Chechenskoi Respubliki Ramzan Kadyrov i glavnyi redaktor gazety "Zavtra" Aleksandr Prokhanov," *Zavtra*, 39, September 23, 2009.

11 Oxana Shevel, "Russian Nation-building from Yel'tsin to Medvedev: Ethnic, Civic or Purposefully Ambiguous?," *Europe-Asia Studies*, 63(2) (March 2011): 179–202.

12 Igor Zevelev, "Russia's Future: Nation or Civilization?," *Russia in Global Affairs*, 4 (October–December 2009); Igor Zevelev, "Budushchee Rossii: natsiya ili tsivilizatsiya?," *Rossiya v global'noi politike*, 5 (September–October 2009).

13 For a discussion, see Igor Zevelev, "'Russkii vopros' posle raspada SSSR," *Pro et Contra*, 14(4–5) (July–October 2010): 67–79.

14 Shevel, "Russian Nation-building from Yel'tsin to Medvedev," 199.

15 A point I have argued earlier. See Richard Sakwa, "Putin's Leadership," in *After Putin's Russia*, 4th edn, Stephen Wegren and Dale Herspring (eds) (Boulder, CO: Rowman & Littlefield, 2010), 17–38.

16 Tom Parfitt, "A Journey Through Russia's Killing Zone," Part 6, "The Islamic Republic of Chechnya," *Foreign Policy*, March 15, 2011; in *JRL*, 48 (2011), Item 22.

17 Nikolai Petrov, "A Recipe for Success in the North Caucasus," *Moscow Times*, March 1, 2011.

18 Gordon M. Hahn, "The *Jihadi* Insurgency and the Russian Counterinsurgency in the North Caucasus," *Post-Soviet Affairs*, 24(1) (January–March 2008): 1–39. For a broader analysis, see his *Russia's Islamic Threat* (New Haven and London: Yale University Press, 2007).

19 In April 2012 the Spiritual Board of Muslims of the Chechen Republic left the Coordinating Center of Muslims of the North Caucasus (CCMNC), established in 1998 and headed by the mufti of Karachaevo-Cherkessia, Ismail Berdiev, Alexei malashenko, "All is Not Quiet in Russian Islam," Valdai Discussion Club, May 16, 2012, http://vladaiclub.com

20 Anna Matveeva, *North Caucasus: Views From Within* (London, Saferworld, March 2012), 24.

21 Sergei Markedonov, "Yeltsin's Complicated Legacy in the Caucasus," www.opendemocracy.net, February 19, 2011; in *JRL*, 31 (2011), Item 22.

22 Editorial, "Vy zveri— gospoda! Vlast' dolzhna nauchit'sya govorit' pravdu o voine," *Nezavisimaya gazeta*, February 28, 2011, 2; www.ng.ru/editorial/2011–02–28/2_red.html

23 This is at the heart of Tracey C. German's study, *Russia's Chechen War* (London: Routledge, 2003).

24 For a discussion of this, see John Russell, *Chechnya: Russia's "War on Terror"* (London: Routledge, 2007), chapter 8.

25 The recognition of South Ossetian and Abkhaz sovereignty on August 26, 2008 was by all accounts Medvedev's initiative, since Putin is more of a consistent Westphalian sovereignist. For a discussion of the Soviet view of multilayered sovereignty and its legacy on Russian thinking, see Ruth Deyermond, *Security and Sovereignty in the Former Soviet Union* (Boulder, CO: Lynne Rienner, 2007).

26 For a good study of the intra-Islamic tensions and their impact on the nascent Chechen state, see Vakhit Akiev, "Religious-Political Conflict in the Chechen Republic of Ichkeria," Central Asia and the Caucasus Press, www.ca-c.org/dataeng/05.akaev.shtml

27 Joanna Swirszcz, "The Role of Islam in Chechen National Identity," *Nationalities Papers*, 37(1) (January 2009): 59–88, in particular 79–80.

28 For a historical analysis, see Anna Zelkina, *In Quest of God and Freedom: Sufi Responses to the Russian Advance in the North Caucasus* (New York: New York University Press, 2000).

29 Evgenii Primakov and Vladimir Baranovskii, "Neotlozhnaya k resheniyu problema: Eksperty Tsentra situatsionnogo analiza RAN ob islame v Rossii i ugroze ego radikalizatsii," *Rossiiskaya gazeta*, April 4, 2012, 14.

30 Tanya Lokshina, Ray Thomas, and Mary Mayer (eds), *The Imposition of a Fake Political Settlement in the Northern Caucasus: The 2003 Chechen Presidential Election* (Stuttgart: Ibidem-Verlag, 2006).

31 Aleksei Malashenko, *Ramzan Kadyrov: rossiiskii politik kavkazskoi natsional'nosti* (Moscow: Rosspen, 2009), 34.

32 For a study of the factions, see Richard Sakwa, *The Crisis of Russian Democracy*.

33 Dagestan, Chechnya, Ingushetia, North Ossetia, Kabardino-Balkaria, Karachaevo-Cherkessia, whose total population according to the 2002 census was 6.2 million, and Stavropol region, with a population of 3 million, overwhelmingly ethnic Russian.

34 Dmitry Medvedev, "V Rossii obrazovan novyi federal'nyi okrug—Severo-Kavkazskii," www.kremlin.ru/transcripts/6664

35 Mairbek Vatchagaev, "Appointment of New Kremlin Envoy to the North Caucasus Causes Concern for Kadyrov," *Eurasia Daily Monitor*, 7(24) (February 4, 2010).

36 Dmitry Medvedev, "Rasshirennoe zasedanie kollegii Federal'noi sluzhby bezopasnosti," January 28, 2010, www.kremlin.ru/transcripts/6730

37 At a meeting with the FSB Collegium on January 28, 2010, Mairbek Vatchagaev, "New Federal District will not Stabilize the North Caucasus," *Eurasia Daily Monitor*, 7(20) (January 29, 2010).

38 Liz Fuller, "Why is the North Caucasus an Unholy Mess?," RFE/RL, *Russia Report*, August 15, 2011.

39 *Moskovskii komsomolets*, November 27, 2007.
40 Central Electoral Commission: www.cikrf.ru; www.vybory.izbirkom.ru.
41 Malashenko, *Ramzan Kadyrov*, 67.
42 www.vybory.izbirkom.ru/region.
43 www.ramzan-kadyrov.ru/position.php.
44 "Counter-Terrorist Operation in Chechnya Officially Ended," *North Caucasus Weekly*, 10(15) (April 17, 2009).
45 Luke Harding, "Kremlin Ends War Against Chechnya," *The Guardian*, April 17, 2009, 15.
46 Aglaya Snetkov, "When the Internal and the External Collide: A Social Constructivist Reading of Russia's Security Policy," *Europe-Asia Studies*, 64(3) (May 2012): 521–42, in particular, 532.
47 See Alexey Malashenko, *Losing the Caucasus*, Carnegie Moscow Center, *Briefing*, 11(3) (August 2009).
48 "Chechnya has Lowest Crime Level of all Russian Regions— Experts," RIA Novosti, August 18, 2011.
49 Marie Jego, "Welcome to 'Ramzanistan'," *Time.com*, October 31, 2011.
50 Gleb Pavlovskii, *Genial'naya vlast'* (Moscow: Evropa, 2012), 39.
51 Burns, "Burns on Chechnya."
52 Natalia Krainova, "Deputy Accused in Dubai Murder," *Moscow* Times, April 6, 2009.
53 C. J. Chivers, "Slain Exile Detailed Cruelty of the Ruler of Chechnya," *New York Times*, February 1, 2009.
54 Luke Harding, "Russia Wants to Eliminate Enemies, Say Chechen on 'Hitlist'," *The Guardian*, April 5, 2012, 24.
55 Andrew Roth, "Walking on Water," *Russia Profile*, June 16, 2011.
56 Regnum news agency, January 30, 2009, monitored by the BBC, in *JRL*, 23 (2009), item 36.
57 Editorial, *Vedomosti*, April 17, 2009.
58 Anatoly Medetsky, "$4.7Bln to be Invested in Chechnya," *Moscow Times*, June 24, 2008.
59 Nikolaus von Twickel, "Kremlin Ends Chechnya Operations," *Moscow Times*, April 17, 2009.
60 Of course, formal unemployment figures do not cover extensive engagement in the shadow economy.
61 For a detailed examination of the plans and their failings, see: I. V. Starodubrovskaya, N. V. Zubarevich, D. V. Sokolov, T. P. Intrigrinova, N. I. Mironova, and Kh. G. Magomedov, *Severnyi Kavkaz: Modernizatsionnyi vyzov* (Moscow: Delo, 2011).
62 Ibid., 305.
63 Ibid., 312.
64 Described by Malashenko, *Ramzan Kadyrov*, 78–81.
65 Ibid., 37.
66 Li-Chen Sim, *The Rise and Fall of Privatization in the Russian Oil Industry* (Basingstoke: Palgrave Macmillan, 2008), 112.
67 Robert Coalson, "Russia's Chechnya Invites Azerbaijan to Explore Oil Fields," RFE/RL, *Russia Report*, April 6, 2012.

68   www.vybory.izbirkom.ru; available as "Results of the Presidential Elections of
     4 March 2012," *Russian Analytical Digest*, 110 (March 16, 2012): 21.
69   Note that the February 1997 presidential elections were probably one of the
     most competitive and fair elections in Russia's post-communist history.
70   Pavlovskii, *Genial'naya vlast'*, 69.
71   "Russian Presidential Envoy [Khloponin] Dispels 'Myth' of High Subsidies for
     North Caucasus," Interfax, October 14, 2011.
72   Ivan Sukhov, "Bez anneksii i kontributsii," *Moskovskie novosti*, April 22, 2011, 3.
73   "USD80 Mln Embezzled in North Caucasus— Prosecutors," RIA Novosti,
     March 30, 2012.
74   For a portrait, see Alexander Bratersky, "Russian March Resists Navalny,"
     Moscow Times, November 7, 2011, 1, 2.
75   Elena Milashina, Editorial, *Novaya gazeta*, October 22, 2011.
76   Richard Sakwa, *Russian Politics and Society* (London and New York:
     Routledge, 2008), 216, 218. In a multicultural society the host community
     seeks to incorporate incomers on the basis of recognizing their differences;
     whereas in a pluricultural society these differences are an intrinsic part of the
     existing society, and thus no distinction can be drawn between incomers and
     some of host community. Of course, tensions remain between a dominant
     culture and that of ethnic and other minorities, but multiculturalism is an
     inappropriate policy response.
77   "Xenophobia Flourishes, Experts Warn Caucasus May Become Russia's
     Kosovo," ITAR-TASS, October 25, 2011.
78   Interview with Chechen media, "North Caucasus Republics Cannot Exist
     Without Russia— Putin," Interfax-AVN, August 24, 2011.
79   Emil Souleimanov, *An Endless War: The Russian-Chechen Conflict in
     Perspective* (Frankfurt: Peter Lang, 2006).
80   Matthew Evangelista, "Is Putin the New de Gaulle? A Comparison of the
     Chechen and Algerian Wars," *Post-Soviet Affairs*, 21(4) (2005): 360–77.
81   Claire Bigg, "NGO's Legal Woes Threaten Pursuit of Justice for Chechens,"
     RFE/RL, *Russia Report*, April 10, 2012.
82   "Daghestan's Mufti Slams "Indiscriminate" Violence by Security Forces," RFE/
     RL, *Russia Report*, April 10, 2012.
83   Ivan Sukhov, "Russian Federalism and Evolution of Self-Determination,"
     Russia in Global Affairs, 5(2) (July–September 2007): http://eng.globalaffairs.
     ru/numbers/20/.
84   "Zakaev Praises Kadyrov," *Chechnya Weekly*, 9(20), May 22, 2008.
85   Thomas de Waal, "Mysterious Shifts in Chechnya," *Moscow Times*, May 22,
     2008. For a redefinition of his statement that "decolonisation is now a fait
     accompli," repeated at a conference on May 14, 2008 at the Royal United
     Services Institute, see "Zakaev Denies Making Overtures to Kadyrov," no
     named author, *Chechnya Weekly*, 9(21), May 29, 2008.
86   Timofei Borisov, "Ramzan Kadyrov: Pristupaem k razvitiyu respubliki,"
     Rossiiskaya gazeta, February 10, 2009, 6.
87   For an overview, see Roland Dannreuther and Luke March, "Chechnya: Has
     Moscow Won?," *Survival*, 50(4) (August–September, 2008): 97–112.

88   See Simon Saradzhyan, "Chechnya Vow Cast a Long Shadow," *Moscow Times*,
     February 26, 2008, 1.

Bibliography

Dannreuther, Roland and Luke March, "Chechnya: Has Moscow Won?"
     Survival, 50(4) (August–September 2008): 97–112.
Deyermond, Ruth, *Security and Sovereignty in the Former Soviet Union*.
     Boulder, CO: Lynne Rienner, 2007.
Evangelista, Matthew, "Is Putin the New de Gaulle? A Comparison of the
     Chechen and Algerian Wars," *Post-Soviet Affairs*, 21(4) (2005): 360–77.
Fraenkel, Ernst, *The Dual State: A Contribution to the Theory of Dictatorship*,
     translated from the German by E.A. Shils, in collaboration with Edith
     Lowenstein and Klaus Knorr. New York: Oxford University Press, 1941),
     reprinted by The Lawbook Exchange, 2006.
German, Tracey C., *Russia's Chechen War*. London: Routledge, 2003.
Hahn, Gordon M., *Russia's Islamic Threat*. New Haven and London: Yale
     University Press, 2007.
— "The *Jihadi* Insurgency and the Russian Counterinsurgency in the North
     Caucasus," *Post-Soviet Affairs*, 24(1) (January–March, 2008): 1–39.
Lokshina, Tanya, Ray Thomas, and Mary Mayer (eds), *The Imposition of a
     Fake Political Settlement in the Northern Caucasus: The 2003 Chechen
     Presidential Election*. Stuttgart: Ibidem-Verlag, 2006.
Malashenko, Aleksei, *Ramzan Kadyrov: rossiiskii politik kavkazskoi
     natsional'nosti*. Moscow: Rosspen, 2009.
Malashenko, Alexey, *Losing the Caucasus*, Carnegie Moscow Center, *Briefing*,
     11(3) (August 2009).
— *The North Caucasus: Russia's Internal Abroad?* Carnegie Moscow Center,
     Briefing, 13(3) (November 2011).
Matveeva, Anna, *North Caucasus: Views From Within*. London: Saferworld,
     March 2012.
Pavlovskii, Gleb, *Genial'naya vlast'*. Moscow: Evropa, 2012.
Russell, John, *Chechnya: Russia's "War on Terror."* London: Routledge, 2007.
Sagramoso, Domitilla, "The Radicalization of Islamic Salafi *Jamaats* in
     the North Caucasus: Moving Closer to the Global *Jihadist* Movement?"
     Europe-Asia Studies, 64(3) (May 2012): 561–95.
Sakwa, Richard, *The Crisis of Russian Democracy: The Dual State,
     Factionalism and the Medvedev Succession*. Cambridge: Cambridge
     University Press, 2011.
— "The Dual State in Russia," *Post-Soviet Affairs*, 26(3) (July–September, 2010):
     185–206.
— "Putin's Leadership," in *After Putin's Russia*, 4th edn, Stephen Wegren and
     Dale Herspring (eds). Boulder, CO: Rowman & Littlefield, 2010, 17–38.
— "The Revenge of the Caucasus: Chechenization and the Dual State in Russia,"
     Nationalities Papers, 38(5) (September 2010): 601–22.

Shevel, Oxana, "Russian Nation-building from Yel'tsin to Medvedev: Ethnic, Civic or Purposefully Ambiguous?," *Europe-Asia Studies*, 63(2) (March 2011): 179–202.

Sim, Li-Chen, *The Rise and Fall of Privatization in the Russian Oil Industry.* Basingstoke: Palgrave Macmillan, 2008.

Snetkov, Aglaya, "When the Internal and the External Collide: A Social Constructivist Reading of Russia's Security Policy," *Europe-Asia Studies*, 64(3) (May 2012): 521–42.

Souleimanov, Emil, *An Endless War: The Russian-Chechen Conflict in Perspective.* Frankfurt: Peter Lang, 2006.

Starodubrovskaya, I. V., N. V. Zubarevich, D. V. Sokolov, T. P. Intrigrinova, N. I. Mironova, and Kh. G. Magomedov, *Severnyi Kavkaz: Modernizatsionnyi vyzov.* Moscow: Delo, 2011.

Sukhov, Ivan, "Russian Federalism and Evolution of Self-Determination," *Russia in Global Affairs*, 5(2) (July–September, 2007): http://eng.globalaffairs.ru/numbers/20/

Swirszcz, Joanna, "The Role of Islam in Chechen National Identity," *Nationalities Papers*, 37(1) (January 2009): 59–88.

Zelkina, Anna, *In Quest of God and Freedom: Sufi Responses to the Russian Advance in the North Caucasus.* New York: New York University Press, 2000.

Zevelev, Igor, "Budushchee Rossii: natsiya ili tsivilizatsiya?" *Rossiya v global'noi politike*, 5 (September–October, 2009).

— "Russia's Future: Nation or Civilization?," *Russia in Global Affairs*, 4 (October–December, 2009).

— "'Russkii vopros' posle raspada SSSR," *Pro et Contra*, 14(4–5) (July–October, 2010): 67–79.

CHAPTER SEVEN

Preparations for the Sochi Olympics

Walter Richmond

From the start, fundamental problems have beset Russia's preparation of the Black Sea town of Sochi for the 2014 Winter Olympics. This chapter examines three areas of concern. First, Moscow has created an extra-constitutional zone around Sochi, effectively stripping residents of legal protections. Although there have been attempts to communicate with the public, Moscow's approach generally has been autocratic rather than cooperative. Second, while initially promising special protection for the region's fragile ecology, Moscow has taken an increasingly hostile stance toward environmentalists. Third, the level of corruption involved in Olympic construction projects has been so extensive that it has threatened timely completion and affected the entire Russian economy with no promise of long-term economic benefit. Instead of inspiring political practices that are genuinely constitutional and participatory, the Russian government has grown more arbitrary and autocratic in its preparations for the games.

Moscow hailed the selection of Sochi as the host for the 2014 Winter Olympics as a multifaceted victory for the Russian people. In addition to enhancing Russia's international prestige, the Games promised to invigorate the economy and gave the administration an opportunity to expand Sochi's potential from a summer beach city into a year-round resort. As numerous similar projects were planned throughout the region, the Sochi Olympics appeared to be the first stage of a transformation of the entire North Caucasus into a haven for lucrative winter resorts.

As time passed, however, the complexity of the project began to overwhelm the government. When Moscow began to address the problems that arose, it revealed its limited ability to deal with such a major endeavor. Finances were fraught with waste and corruption, efforts to minimize ecological damage were amateurish at best, and despite some attempts to address local concerns federal authorities were either uninterested in or oblivious to methods of dealing with citizen groups. In fact, rather than face the challenges the Olympics posed in the manner of a representative democracy, Moscow has adopted strategies reminiscent of its Soviet and Imperial predecessors. These methods have both undermined constitutional legitimacy and made the federal government more rigid and heavy-handed in its dealings with the citizenry. Most seriously, the Sochi project is consuming enormous amounts of the Federal budget on facilities that may have a one-time economic benefit. It threatens to leave the Sochi area even less valuable as a resort than it currently is at a time when the entire nation's infrastructure is in need of dramatic improvement.

From the point of view of the International Olympic Committee (IOC), Sochi fulfilled a new goal to choose host cities where all Olympic events could be held in close proximity. However, Sochi also presented major challenges. First and foremost was the issue of the municipal infrastructure. The Soviets developed Sochi as a resort city for the Party elite and designed it to accommodate 250,000 residents. Sochi is now a city of over 400,000 but the infrastructure has remained unchanged since the 1930s.[1] A plan for the development of Sochi was proposed at the beginning of the decade, but once the city became a candidate for the Winter Olympics it was put on hold, and the infrastructure became even more overtaxed. Water systems are inadequate even for the current population, much less the increased population expected during the Olympics. Trash dumps are overfilled, and owing to the fragile environment locations for new dumps are limited. A recycling plant was planned, but it was delayed due to lack of expert analysis.[2]

Transportation is similarly inadequate. The Soviets generally built roads to carry limited industrial traffic, not to transport civilians, and Sochi was no exception. As a result of the increase in population and the dramatic rise in automobile ownership, much of the city is in a constant state of gridlock. Essential for the transportation of construction materials no less than Olympic spectators, the roads leading into Sochi are also woefully inadequate.

The terrain itself presented two other fundamental problems. First, the entire greater Sochi area is environmentally fragile and unique. A nature preserve established by the Bucharest Convention in 1994 is adjacent to Sochi and actually overlaps some of the land Moscow included in the construction projects. Second, the location selected for main Olympic complex is the Imereti Lowlands, a swampy and geologically unstable area that has presented serious challenges for construction.

In addition to political, infrastructural, and ecological problems, there are also ethnic and historical issues centering on the reaction of the Circassian community to the selection of Sochi as the Olympic host city. Sochi was one of the departure points for the Circassian deportation of 1864, an event that many Circassians and many scholars consider genocide. Furthermore, the Olympics will take place on the one-hundred-and-fiftieth anniversary of the deportation, and *Krasnaya Polyana* (Red Meadow), the location of many Olympic events, is precisely where the Russians held their victory celebration. Circassian activists saw this as an attempt by the Russian government to erase the memory of their people and the genocide.[3]

This chapter suggests that, while the federal government has been very aggressive in confronting individuals and organizations that threaten to slow down the project, it has wasted enormous amounts of money while falling behind schedule in nearly every sector of construction. Construction of buildings, ports, power stations, roads, and waste dumps have suffered from serious delays. There is concern in the Russian government that some may not be ready for the start of the Olympic Games, and all have consumed resources that might better have been allocated to other parts of the Russian economy. On May 13, 2012, Russian President Vladimir Putin visited Sochi to find that delays and price increases were "unacceptable." He warned contractors of stiff fines if deadlines continued to be disregarded.[4] These problems not only threaten the 2014 Games, but have ramifications for all of Russian society that may imply long-term social and political consequences.

Center-periphery relations

In dealing with concerns of the local population the Russian government has treated the Sochi project as a sort of laboratory for the violation of its own laws. The first step was Presidential Order 848, issued on July 5, 2007, which established measures for creating a budget for the Games. The problem was that the order directly violated the law "On the Federal Budget for 2007."[5] In order to circumvent this, the Duma passed Federal Law 310-F3 on January 6, 2008. This created an extra-constitutional zone around Sochi in which the Olympic Committee has virtually unlimited power.[6] The law was put in force retroactively from July 5, 2007, so that Order 848 would be included. Furthermore, 310-F3 remains in effect until December

3, 2016, nearly three years after the Games are scheduled. There is specu-lation that this has to do with the law's reference to "the development of Sochi as a mountain resort" in addition to preparations for the Games.[7] If this is the case, Moscow is apparently using an extraordinary situation to suspend federal law for a regular development project.

The Federal government's first use of 310-F3 was to acquire land owned by local residents for construction. Initially the authorities failed to con-sider their impact upon the residents, but quickly learned that angry civic groups can be disruptive. They modified their approach but still seemed incapable of considering the residents as partners in the project. The relo-cation of residents was typical of subsequent government actions. After an area was designated a construction zone the government assigned values to the properties it was expropriating. However, many were significantly lower than market value, and compensation for seemingly identical proper-ties has been inconsistent. For example, In March 2009, residents of the village Akhshtyr were told that they would receive the rouble equivalent of USD16,000 for each 1/100th of a hectare, but some residents inexpli-cably received nearly double that amount. Those who felt they had been cheated staged a hunger strike. Rather than communicate with the resi-dents, authorities refused to negotiate officially or to recognize that there was a dispute.[8]

A more poignant example concerns the Imereti Lowlands. Many of the residents are Old Believers, a sect of Russian Orthodox Christians who historically have been persecuted since their emergence in the seventeenth century. They refused to relocate, and when it became clear that the govern-ment would move them by force, they began to protest publicly. Ultimately, the decision was made that they could (a) be relocated to the village of Nekrasovskoe, (b) accept monetary compensation, or (c) take their mat-ter to the courts, where the government assured the residents they would lose. Furthermore, they would have to decide before a value was assigned to their land. Some continued to refuse to move, calling the entire process illegal. Indeed it would have been, but officials cited Federal Law 310-F3 and the standoff continued.[9]

On May 4, 2010 four families moved to Nekrasovskoe, but others found out at the last minute that *Olimpstroi*, the company given the lion's share of construction contracts, had decided not to move them as part of a "mini-mization" effort. While the sentiment was laudable, Olipmstroi's failure to inform the people originally scheduled for resettlement in a timely fashion that they could stay, created an atmosphere of acute uncertainty.[10] On May 19, ten residents went on a hunger strike, demanding to speak to President Medvedev and Prime Minister Putin. The protesters ended their strike on June 18, when authorities promised to examine each case individually.[11] The situation finally stabilized, and residents were eventually moved to Nekrasovskoe. Seven new villages were constructed for people being relocated from other construction sites, and the process became less stressful for everyone. In what turned out to be a rare exception, the Russian government seemed finally to deal responsibly with its citizens.

Such was not the case with evictions as a result of construction in Sochi itself. As Kurortny Prospekt is the only street that runs the length of Sochi, a second road is being built parallel to it. While some residents were relocated, others were evicted from their homes and left with literally no place to go. They were residents of a cooperative building constructed in 2004, which had been built "illegally," as they were informed, just before its demolition was scheduled. The construction firm is long gone, but since the residents were living in an "illegal" structure the authorities told them they had no responsibility to find them new housing. As a result, they had to seek shelter in garages and other makeshift locations throughout the city.[12]

Construction of the new road has caused other problems as well. As one might expect with a small city squeezed between the sea and a mountain range, nearly every square foot of Sochi either has been built up or is used for recreation. As it turns out, the new route goes through the city's most prized parks. Repeated petitions to address the issue failed to evoke any response from the Federal Government, so the citizens of Sochi formed the Territorial Society for Self-Government (TSS) to actively oppose the construction. On February 26, 2011, they invited the mayor and deputies of the municipal council to meet with the Society to deal with the evictions of the cooperative residents, but no one from the government attended.[13] In desperation, the residents who were made homeless have turned to the IOC for help.[14] As of this writing the problem is unresolved.

The creation of the new road is one step in the complete restructuring of the city mentioned in Federal Law 310-F3. In this context it is no surprise that new roads are displacing large numbers of long-term residents, or that the beaches have been cleared of long-standing homes to make room for resort hotels. What is somewhat puzzling and ominous, however, is the appearance of quarries in the mountains. The first was discovered accidentally when large amounts of toxins in the Psou River were traced back to the pit where they originated. Federal authorities explained that the quarry was created to exploit building materials in the area. This explanation did not suit residents, the Public Ecological Council, or Ecology Watch of the North Caucasus. The ecological groups pointed out that the quarry was illegal and was producing large amounts of waste that had nowhere to go.[15] Other quarries were soon discovered and Moscow was forced to admit that they were in fact illegal, but refused to halt the digging. Hundreds of old growth trees have been destroyed and the Psou River has been seriously polluted as a result. Meanwhile, Moscow has tied the evaluation of the project up in red tape.[16]

On the surface, the Federal Government seems to be interested in completely altering the nature of the city itself, transforming it from a summer resort that is open to the public into a combination summer/winter resort for a financially restrictive clientele.[17] Yet beneath the surface, there seem to be broader motives.

From the beginning, there was suspicion that submitting Sochi as a candidate for the Olympics was part of a comprehensive plan for restructuring the entire North Caucasus. In 2007, political analyst Stanislav Stremidlovsky postulated that the Sochi Olympics were part of a broader plan to deal with international matters (Georgia, Abkhazia, South Ossetia, the United States) and create a "super-region" that would be more firmly under Moscow's control.[18] The division of the Southern Federal District into two new administrative units—the North Caucasus and Southern Districts—seems to be part of this plan. Sochi is now disconnected from the "North Caucasus" in addition to being a separate "extra-constitutional zone" itself.

The division of the Southern District was seen in a completely different light by the Circassian community, who were already outraged by the IOC's selection of Sochi for the 2014 Games. The notion of medals being handed out to celebrate peaceful competition between nations on the very site where medals were handed out for the destruction of their nation, on the one-hundred-and-fiftieth anniversary of that event, filled Circassians with indignation. While ecological and financial concerns overshadowed the Circassian issue at first, increased activism and particularly Russian mishandling of the situation has brought international attention to the Circassians' concerns. This in turn forced the Kremlin to take the issue seriously, but rather than seek a compromise Moscow turned to more extreme tactics than it used against civic groups in Sochi.

As soon as Sochi was entered as a candidate for the 2014 Games, Circassians began expressing their dissatisfaction. Moscow seemed to be rubbing salt in the wound when a television chronicle of the "history" of Sochi, broadcast just before the IOC announcement, failed to mention the Circassians.[19] When President Vladimir Putin implied the original inhabitants of the Sochi area were Greeks in his acceptance speech, he unified the world Circassian community in a way unparalleled since the deportation.[20] This all happened at a time when Circassians in Russia were becoming more assertive in their efforts to create a unified republic and facilitate repatriation. Throughout 2009 Circassian groups issued declarations demanding that the three "Circassian" republics—Adygeya, Karachaevo-Cherkessia, and Kabardino-Balkaria—be united in one administrative unit along with a group of Circassian settlements along the Black Sea coast not far from Sochi.[21] It was shortly afterward, in January 2010, that Moscow divided the Southern Federal District, which had included all the Circassian-populated areas, into two districts. Karachaevo-Cherkessia and Kabardino-Balkaria were included in the North Caucasus Federal District, while Adygeya and the coastal Circassian settlements were assigned to the Southern Federal District.[22] Circassians worldwide saw this as an attempt to keep their community in Russia from unifying and as a response to their opposition to the Olympics.

While some Circassian groups in Russia announced that they would not officially oppose the Sochi Olympics, many in the diaspora adopted a more confrontational approach, and it is their movement that has turned the international spotlight on the Games.[23] The No Sochi 2014 Committee, founded in 2010, staged protests in Canada, the United States, Europe, and Turkey. The movement has gained some attention, including articles by *Reuters*, *Time,* and numerous other outlets around the world.[24] Websites in English, Turkish, Arabic, Russian, German, and other languages publicize the Circassian campaign to stop, or at least discredit, the Sochi Games.[25]

The Russian reaction has been a combination of repressive policies and propaganda intended to discredit the international movement. One part of this campaign describes the opponents of the Games as part of a US effort to disrupt the North Caucasus.[26] The Russian government portrays Circassian activists as extremists, and has gone as far as to file criminal charges against people who call the 1864 deportation genocide.[27]

While Moscow has not altered its plans for the Olympics construction, opposition has forced it openly to employ policies at odds with its broader claims of representative democracy. In some cases it has used a façade of cooperation to defuse particularly hot issues, but has taken few steps to accommodate the citizens. Particularly in the Circassian case, the Russian government has shown itself willing to use every possible means to quell dissent except compromise. While none of this will stop the Olympics, it is indicative of Moscow's attitude toward its citizens and particularly its ethnic minorities. How this will affect future relations with other minorities who have grievances against Moscow remains to be seen.

The "Green" Olympics

The Soviet environmental legacy was not impressive. Environmental costs were never figured into Soviet calculations, and for decades raising environmental concerns that might slow down production was considered "counter-revolutionary." The results were devastating: desertification in Central Asia, toxic salt storms rising from the bed of the Aral Sea, massive river pollution, and deforestation were just a few of the consequences. The first serious assessment of the environment came only under the administration of Mikhail Gorbachev, but with the fall of the Soviet Union the report was forgotten. The lawless Yeltsin years were accompanied by criminal exploitation of the environment: several species were hunted nearly to extinction throughout Russia, and in the Caucasus illegal logging operations shipped timber to Turkey with the blessings of the local leadership.[28] Nevertheless, when Moscow declared that the Sochi Games would be a "green" event there was hope among environmentalists that Russia would seek their help and conduct the Games in a manner that respected the unique ecology of the region.[29]

Early on, Moscow appeared to be living up to its pledge. The State Corporation for the Construction of Olympic Buildings and the Development of the City of Sochi as a Mountain Resort (*Olimpstroi*) placed ecologists in every department and promised to follow their advice.[30] The problem was that, first of all, the Sochi region is so environmentally fragile that experienced contractors would be challenged to complete the project by 2014—it could even be argued that Sochi's environment is so fragile that the area should never have been chosen as a site for such an enormous project.

The second problem was Moscow's failure immediately to begin construction so that any unforeseen environmental problems could be addressed. In fact, during the first year after Russia won the competition for the Games, virtually nothing was done.[31] When construction actually did begin, it was conducted at a pace that precluded the possibility of environmental responsibility.

Once the project started it quickly became clear that massive damage to the environment could be avoided only through actions far more extensive and expensive than either the government or the contracted companies were willing to undertake. Some of the sites that were central to the Olympic plan were so environmentally fragile that no amount of caution could deter serious damage or avert threats to the participants and spectators.[32] Nevertheless, construction continued unabated. By September 2008, residents of Sochi and environmental groups were complaining that the rapid pace of construction was violating both Russian federal and international laws. Yet while Russian officials continued to portray themselves as cooperating with environmental organizations, they intimidated local groups that protested specific projects.

The first incident occurred in October 2008 when Natalya Kalinovskaya, the director of a local civil oversight committee, complained to authorities that construction companies lacked required documentation. She and another local activist were invited to the regional governmental headquarters under the pretext of a dialogue with the construction company. When they arrived they were arrested, threatened by local authorities, and ultimately fined 2,500 rubles.[33] The first of many public confrontations took place in August 2009 over the construction of the Adler-Krasnaya Polyana Road, a joint auto-train route to Sochi. Early work on the rail portion of the project resulted in the destruction of many old-growth trees, and so on the eighteenth environmental activists from Sochi, Maikop, Krasnodar, and Nizhny Novgorod filed a statement with the Sochi Directorate of Internal Affairs declaring the activities of the company Stroidor-A to be an ecological crime. Not only were red book trees being destroyed, the construction project entered the supposedly inviolable Sochi National Park. On the morning of the nineteenth, the activists blocked the road and told the workers that the project was illegal. The government neither responded to the activists' statement nor came to negotiate with them, and so they ultimately had to back down.[34]

The Caucasus Nature Preserve moved the confrontation into the world arena, as the park is protected by both Federal and international treaties. Moscow had already encroached on the reserve in 2002 with the construction of a ski resort that the government labeled a "scientific center" to skirt the law. Ultimately, it became impossible to conceal the purpose of the resort and so Moscow resorted to a new strategy: "more accurately defining" the borders of the reserve. The result was the removal of 100 hectares from the reserve that were used for the construction of the resort.[35]

This ploy was used again when a similar situation arose in Sochi. When the city's development plan was finally approved, the municipal government declared that the original borders of the Reserve had been drawn inaccurately.[36] The areas removed from the Reserve as a result of the "redefining" of the park's borders coincided with the proposed route of the Adler-Krasnaya Polyana Road. As a result, environmentalists both in Russia and abroad asked the United Nations Environment Programme (UNEP) to visit the Sochi area. After their tour of the area in late January 2010, UNEP issued a carefully worded assessment. Noting several areas of concern, the main purpose of the report seems to have been to bring all parties to the negotiating table to develop a "comprehensive assessment of the overall impact of the Olympic and tourism projects" and "a strong monitoring program" that "should involve a third party."[37]

Apparently, UNEP's goal was to start a dialogue between environmentalists and the federal government. Yet the noncommittal tone of the report allowed Russian officials to read it as a justification of their position prior to the UNEP visit. On March 12, Vice-Premier Dmitry Kozak's statement seemed both to ignore the document's recommendations and to reaffirm the contractors' position, calling on ecologists "not to stall" the project. Rather than adopt UNEP's recommendations for a dialogue, Kozak focused on its statement that it "found no serious ecological problems." The point of this statement was that major ecological problems could still be averted, but only through cooperation by all parties. Kozak interpreted it to mean that environmentalists were exaggerating the potential risks and asserted that they were taking "a non-constructive position and (were) determined to simply stop the Olympic project."[38] By April, the Moscow Branch of the World Wildlife Fund (WWF) claimed that the situation was intractable and went from trying to stop environmental damage to simply reporting on it,[39] although the WWF made further attempts to advise *Olimpstroi* beginning only a month later.[40] In any case, UNEP put no further effort into reconciliation, and the environmentalists were left on their own.

Also in April a new controversy arose when the Russian press reported that geologist and former Olympics consultant Sergei Volkov told the BBC that the soil in some of the planned construction zones was contaminated with "radioactive and highly toxic elements."[41] Volkov's warnings included concerns over landslides that could endanger the lives of participants and spectators. He also accused the IOC of turning a blind eye to the impossibility of safely completing construction in Sochi within the given time frame, and asserted that officials had ignored all expert advice from the beginning. Volkov ultimately had to flee Russia for fear of his life.[42]

The Volkov affair marked the beginning of a change in Moscow's strategy. Up to this point the government restricted openly repressive tactics to local organizations with limited influence while continuing to portray itself as cooperating with international organizations. After the Volkov affair, all organizations that made objections to the project based on environmental concerns came under fire from multiple directions while international concerns were simply ignored. One of the most blatant examples of this new attitude concerned the activities of the Sochi Department of the Russian Geographical Society.

During 2011 large amounts of toxins—phosphates, fuel oil, nitrogen—began appearing in the Mzymta and Sochi Rivers. The Sochi Department had already been involved in monitoring ecological damage in the region and issued a statement concerning Sochi on January 7, 2012.[43] Moscow's response was quick: on the eighteenth the Sochi Department was informed by email that they were being shut down. Almost immediately afterward there was a distributed denial of service (DDoS) cyber attack on the department's website, as well as the sites of three other groups that regularly criticized the project's impact on the environment.[44] Most recently, the government has stepped up its tactics even more, arresting environmentalists and labeling them part of the widespread opposition movement currently challenging Moscow.[45]

Budgetary issues

Yet while Moscow's disregard for environmental concerns has been motivated by a desire to save money, its supervision of construction ironically has disregarded cost effectiveness. This and other major projects that promise only one-time benefits threaten long-term damage to the Russian economy. In the case of Sochi, the primary source of this waste is corruption.

In June 2010, Assistant Chairman of the Sochi Microregion Yury Reilyan stated that out of the USD39 billion that was expected to be spent on the

Sochi Olympics, a large portion was being wasted on "ineffective techniques and corruption: "we have huge outlays that accomplish nothing," Reilyan added, "and this is all corruption."[46] The enormous sum being spent on the Games—the equivalent of $200 per Russian man, woman, and child, and the equivalent of one-sixth the entire budget for the Russian Federation—is over ten times the amount spent on the Vancouver Olympics.[47]

As there is no transparency to the process it is difficult to determine where the money is going, but there seem to be two main channels. First, funds promised to subcontractors are being withheld and presumably funneled to local officials. Second, contracts are routinely transferred to non-Russian firms that cannot be monitored and frequently are under the control of Russian officials.

One example of abuse that involved both methods occurred in 2008, when the consulting firm InzhGeo was contracted to participate in the construction of numerous buildings. *Olimpstroi* head Semyon Vainshtok withheld payments to InzhGeo, and the subcontractor sued. Vainshtok was able to use his governmental contacts to transfer controlling interest of InzhGeo to a Dutch company that is directly tied to the Krasnodar Government. When InzhGeo protested, both local and district authorities ruled in Vainshtok's favor, while federal authorities removed government security forces from InzhGeo's local headquarters.[48]

The use of foreign firms to launder Olympic money is a widespread phenomenon. In June 2010 Valery Morozov, director of construction firm Moskonversprom, revealed that he had to pay Kremlin official Vladimir Leshchevsky a 177.6 million ruble bribe to receive a contract and use a Yugoslavian subcontractor that appeared to be at least partially owned by Leshchevsky himself. Morozov further noted that many Yugoslavian firms are subcontractors for the Sochi Olympics and alleged that they are being used in a similar manner to launder money.[49]

Another type of abuse involves judiciary misappropriation of beachfront property, mostly owned by people of modest means whose families were awarded the land nearly 100 years ago. In the same month as the Leshchevsky scandal former Krasnodar *Krai* judge Dmitry Novikov was indicted for using his position to obtain seventeen parcels of prime real estate. As the case proceeded, Novikov's attorney asserted that his client had first accused other regional judges, including Krasnodar *Krai* judicial chairman Alexander Chernov, of directing similar land acquisitions just before he was indicted.[50] Novikov was ultimately forced to retire, but continued to press the case. His appeal was scheduled to be heard in Moscow on March 29, 2012, and reporters from London, Paris, and the United States were expected to attend.[51] However, the government announced at the last minute that the appeal was cancelled and the case was closed.[52]

Widespread corruption is having an effect on construction projects. The business newspaper *Vedomosti* reported that 76 of the 393 proposed structures were behind schedule by the end of 2011. Vice-Premier Dmitry

Kozak blamed "private companies" and suggested that criminal proceedings might be conducted against some of them, but failed to give any reasons for the delays. A new electrical station in Sochi is seriously behind schedule, and another one in nearby Adler will almost certainly still be under construction by the time the Olympics begin. The main reason for the delay of the Adler project is repeated change of contractors, suggesting the same shell game that happened with the InzhGeo affair.[53] Simple bad planning has affected other projects, such as a shipping port that was begun in Sochi despite warnings that the frequent storms on the coast could easily destroy it. As it turned out, a massive storm struck in December 2009 and inflicted USD60 million damage on the construction project, dooming it to incompletion.[54]

The massive outlay of expenses to build additional roads to Sochi is perhaps the most serious consequence of poor planning. Nationwide, Russia's roads are in a state of near collapse and traffic jams stretching dozens of kilometers have become common.[55] Despite this critical situation, cuts in road construction have been planned as a result of the economic crisis while large amounts of money are being funneled to road and rail projects to reach Sochi.[56] Russian road construction is already highly inefficient; owing primarily to corruption, Russian roads are among the most expensive in the world.[57] Because of the mountainous terrain surrounding Sochi, the average cost of construction is even higher than usual, approximately USD200,000 per meter.[58]

In September 2010, the question of misallocation of resources for road construction reached Moscow, where at a hearing of the Social Chamber it was asserted that Moscow's overloaded traffic system would suffer as a result of funds being directed from the capital's infrastructure to the Sochi roads.[59] As Paul Goble points out, this report came at a time when anger at poor roads was escalating, and that "if a large number of [Russians] conclude that some of this money [earmarked for road construction in Moscow] is going to Sochi instead, they are likely to be furious."[60]

The combination of corruption and poor planning is complicating a project that already had promised to be a serious drain on Russia's budget. The extravagant expenses being incurred by Moscow for the Games seem all the more excessive when one considers that Russia is also hosting the 2013 Universiade in Kazan. As with the Sochi project, expenses for this event have gone far beyond original projections. As of March 2010, 23.5 million rubles had been invested, 18 times more than Belgrade spent on the 2009 Universiade, and 25 times the annual budget of Kazan. In Sochi, most of the expenses have been incurred on the creation of an infrastructure that can service the Olympic population. The fear is that much of this investment will have a one-time benefit but contribute nothing to the long-term development of the region: "'A long-term economic effect from the Olympics, as Salt Lake City demonstrates, is virtually non-existent.

Many of the sports stadiums built for the Olympics have not served any purpose after the Games,' explained Mikhali Khazin, president of [economic analysis firm] NeoKon." Khazin also noted that the new roads and rail lines will serve a one-time function and then become "roads to nowhere."[61] The ill-advised nature of the entire project, involving a fundamental, and unlikely, transformation of a highly unsuitable region that may or may not provide financial benefits while Russia's economy is struggling seems reminiscent of grandiose Soviet projects.

Conclusion

Rather than serving as an opportunity for the Russian administration to develop genuinely participatory or constitutional methods, problems associated with the Sochi Games have caused Moscow to become more entrenched in autocratic and arbitrary modes of government, much as Richard Sakwa argues in this volume. Unlike their Soviet predecessors federal authorities have tried to put up a facade of legitimacy. Events such as the recent "Direct Line" television show in which residents of Sochi were able to pose questions to Vladimir Putin give the impression that the administration is listening, but the reality is quite different.[62] The heavy-handed tactics used against civil organizations quickly escalated into coordinated efforts by local, federal, and private organizations to thwart all attempts to confront the abuse of the environment and the residents. This in turn has led to a broad assault on environmentalists, civil groups, and Circassian organizations.

The Moscow elite have been using the Sochi Olympics as a sort of testing ground for extra-constitutional methods that violate Russian laws and extract government funds. The employment of Federal Law 310-F3 has successfully demonstrated that the rule of law throughout the Russian Federation is subject to the needs of Moscow. The efforts of federal and local authorities, along with the collaboration of contractors, have eviscerated civil groups' abilities to confront violations of established law. In fact, as a result of federal heavy-handedness in Sochi it has become clear that the slightest challenge to the actions of the government could result in arrest and imprisonment. As construction has proceeded Moscow has become increasingly bold in the face of international objections. Initially expressing environmental concern while ignoring advice from environmental organizations, Moscow has begun blatantly to harass and imprison activists while flaunting its international agreements—especially with regard to the Caucasus Nature Preserve.

Perhaps most significant is the potential economic impact of Sochi Games. Certainly the Olympics, the Asia-Pacific Economic Cooperation Summit in 2012 in Vladivostok, and the Universiade in Kazan in 2013 are three internationally prestigious events, but they are significantly draining economic resources from projects that would be of more value to the average Russian citizen. In 2010 alone, the estimated expenses on construction in Sochi were 60 billion rubles.[63] Even there, the expenses have not been directed toward the real concerns of the citizens, and in many cases have worked against them. As retired mayor Vyacheslav Voronkov pointed out, if Moscow wanted to invest in Sochi for the sake of its residents, it should take into consideration that "Sochi doesn't have adequate schools, hospitals, and kindergartens." Instead, Voronkov noted, "recently the authorities took four hectares from a school . . . and gave it to investors, and control of the noted theater Stereo was given to Olimpstroi."[64] Vladimir Putin and other Russian officials have undertaken the challenge of the Sochi Games with a view toward Russia's international prestige, yet their disdain for domestic, international, and environmental responsibilities may shine a revealing light on some of Russia's deeper problems.

Notes

1   "Za Fasadom Olimpiady 2014: Doklad Komiteta Grazhdanskogo Kontrola," *Novaia Gazeta*, July 4, 2008, www.novayagazeta.ru/society/39502.html; "Naselenie Sochi k Olimpiade 2014 Mozhet Uvelichit'sia do Polumilliona," *Iuga*, June 15, 2009, www.yuga.ru/news/157558/

2   "Musornye Poligony Sochinskogo Regiona v Kriticheskom Sostoyanii," *RIA Novosti*, November 25, 2008, www.rian.ru/danger/20081125/155822883. html

3   Marshenkulova, Marina, "Outrage at 'Fake' Circassian Anniversary," *Institute for War and Peace Reporting*, October 5, 2007, http://iwpr.net/report-news/outrage-"fake"-circassian-anniversary

4   "Putin Calls Sochi Delays Unacceptable," *The Japan Times*, www.japantimes.co.jp/text/so20120513a1.html

5   "Za Fasadom Olimpiady 2014."

6   "Federal'nyi Zakon 310-F3," *Departament Krasnodarskogo Kraia po Realizatsii Polnomochii pri Podgotovke Zimnikh Olimpiiskikh Igr 2014 goda*, www.olympdep.ru/docs/ofdoc31

7   "Za Fasadom Olimpiady 2014."

8   Yevgeny Titov, "Reider, Olimpiiskii Vid," *Novaya Gazeta*, June 15, 2009, www.novayagazeta.ru/politics/44338.html

9   "Sobstvenniki Domov v Imeritinke Prepryatstvuyut Geologorazvedke na Meste Stroitel'stve Stadiona," *Kavkazskii Uzel*, April 21, 2010, www.kavkaz-uzel.ru/articles/167931

10 "V Sele Nekrasovskom Poselilis' Pervye Pereselentsy iz Imeretinskoi Nizmennosti Sochi," *Kavkazskii Uzel*, May 5, 2010, www.kavkaz-uzel.ru/articles/168475

11 "V Sochi Zhiteli Imeretinki Prekratili Golodovku," *Kavkazskii Uzel*, June 18, 2010, www.kavkaz-uzel.ru/articles/170369

12 "V Sochi Posle Snosa Doma Mnogodetnaia Sem'ia Pereselilas' v Garazh
    na Kladbishche," *Kavkazskii Uzel,* December 27, 2011, www.kavkaz-uzel.
    ru/articles/198366/; "V Sochi Lishivsheisia Zhil'ia Pensionerke Chubenko
    Vrucheny Kliuchi ot Komnaty," *Kavkazskii Uzel,* December 13, 2011, www.
    kavkaz-uzel.ru/articles/197525/; "V Sochi Chinovniki Otkazyvaiutsia
    Predostavit' Zhil'e Dvum Otselennym iz Chastnykh Domov Sem'iam,"
    Kavkazskii Uzel, August 24, 2011, www.kavkaz-uzel.ru/articles/191343/
13 "V Sochi Bolee sta Aktivistov Vystupili Protiv Zastroiki Zelenoi Zony,"
    Kavkazskii Uzel, February 26, 2012, www.kavkaz-uzel.ru/articles/201868
14 "Zhiteili Sochi, Lishivshiesia Zhil'ia iz-za Olimpiady, Obratiatsia za
    Pomoshch'iu v MOK, *Kavkazskii Uzel,* February 10, 2012, www.kavkaz-uzel.
    ru/articles/200948
15 "Tupikovyi Kar'er," *Sochinskie Novosti,* February 17, 2012, http://
    sochinskie-novosti.ru/articles/carier-tbo.html
16 "V Sochi Bolee sta Aktivistov."
17 Yevgeny Titov, "S Mesta v Kar'ery," *Novaia Gazeta,* January 15, 2012, www.
    novayagazeta.ru/politics/50441.html
18 Stanislav Stremidlovsky, "Organizator Olimpiady v Sochi Stanet Preemnikom
    Putina," *Agenstvo Politicheskikh Novostei,* May 7, 2007, www.apn.ru/news/
    article17373.htm
19 "Cherkesskii Kongress Vystupil Protiv Olimiady v Sochi," *Kavkazskii Uzel,*
    June 5, 2007, www.kavkaz-uzel.ru/articles/117988
20 "Real Snow Guaranteed: Putin," *Russia Today,* July 5, 2007, http://rt.com/
    news/real-snow-guaranteed-putin/
21 Zamir Shukhov, "Rezoliutsiia foruma cherkesskoi (adygskoi) molodezhi,"
    Justice for North Caucasus Groups Message Boards, September 12, 2009,
    www.justicefornorthcaucasus.com/jfnc_message_boards/russian.php?t
    itle=Резолюция-форума-черкесской-(адыгской)-молодежи&entry_
    id=1252947053&comments=comments
22 "Medvedev Creates New North Caucasus Federal District," *Radio Free
    Europe/Radio Liberty,* January 20, 2010, www.rferl.org/content/Medvedev_
    Creates_New_North_Caucasus_Federal_District/1934705.html
23 "'Adyge Khase' Adygei Vystupaet Protiv Prazdnovaniia Dvukh Iubileinykh Dat,"
    Kavkazskii Uzel, February 23, 2007, www.kavkaz-uzel.ru/articles/110816/
24 Thomas Grove, "Genocide Claims Complicate Russian Olympics Plans,"
    Reuters, October 13, 2011, http://af.reuters.com/article/worldNews/
    idAFTRE79C2XP20111013; Nathan Thornburgh, "Olympic Dreams: Will
    Sochi Rehabilitate Russia's Image?" *Time,* November 18, 2011, www.time.
    com/time/magazine/article/0,9171,2099428,00.html#ixzz1e4fpiSx5
25 See, for example, *No Sochi 2014,* http://nosochi2014.com/; "Genotsid
    Cherkesov i Olimpiada v Sochi," *Chechen News,* May 20, 2010, http://
    chechenews.com/world-news/breaking/363–1.html; Soçi Olimpiyatları Karşıtı
    Hareket ve Çerkes Soykırımı," *Çerkesnet,* April 12, 2012, www.cerkes.net/
    cerkes/index.php/ozel/haber/1449-soci-olimpiyatlar-kart-hareket-
    ve-cerkes-soykrm.html
26 Vladislav Gulevich, "Circasian Theme of Syria's Tragedy," *Strategic Culture
    Foundation,* February 16, 2012, www.strategic-culture.org/news/2012/02/16/
    circassian-theme-of-syria-tragedy.html

27 "Ubit Suadin Pshukov," *Adyge Sait*, April 10, 2011, www.elot.ru/main/index. php?option=com_content&task=view&id=2579&Itemid=1. A Circassian blogger in Russia who reproduced my interview with Voice of America concerning the Circassian genocide was subsequently charged with extremism in August 2011.

28 Arkady A, Tishkov, "Status Review of the Biodiversity Conservation in the Caucasus: Achieve C2010 Goals," *Countdown 2010*, www.countdown2010. net/caucasus/Russia%20Review%20Countdown%202010.pdf

29 "Olimpiada v Sochi Dolzhna Stat' 'Zelenoi,'" *Partiia Zelenikh Ukraini*, August 2, 2007, www.greenparty.ua/ru/news/news_15492.html

30 Strakhova, Tatyana, "Pri Stroitel'stve Ob'ektov Olimpiady-2014 Primenyat 'Zelenye Standarty,'" *RIA Novosti*, March 3, 2009, http://eco.rian.ru/ business/20090303/163733408.html; Strakhova, Tatyana, "Goskorporatsiia 'Olimpstroi' Uvelichit Shtat Ekologov," *RIA Novosti*, December 12, 2008, http://eco.rian.ru/business/20081212/157110623.html

31 "Za Fasadom Olimpiady 2014."

32 See, for example, Allenova, Ol'ga, "Vse Olimpiiskie Ob'ekty Mogut Uiti Pod Zemliu," *Kommersant' Vlast'*, June 15, 2009, www.kommersant.ru/ doc/1186885

33 Yevgeny Titov, "Zimnie Vidy Porta," *Novaya Gazeta*, October 16, 2008, www. novayagazeta.ru/society/38384.html

34 "V Olimpiiskom Bezumii 'RZhD' Unichtozhaet Derev'ya Patriarkhi," *APN Severo-Zapad*, August 19, 2009, www.apn-spb.ru/opinions/article5985.htm

35 Andrei Rudomakha, "Nakrylas' 'Lunnaia Poliana,'" *Novaya Gazeta*, June 12, 2007, www.novayagazeta.ru/society/34887.html

36 "Ekologi Prizyvayut Vlasti ne Prinimat' Genplan Sochi v ego Nyneshnem Vide," *RIA Novosti*, July 13, 2009, http://eco.rian.ru/ danger/20090713/177253772.html

37 "Report of the UN 2nd Expert Mission, January 28–30, 2010," United Nations Environment Programme, March 15, 2010, www.unep.org/PDF/PressReleases/ SOCHI_2014Jan28to302010_Mission_%20ReportFinal_%2015March.pdf

38 "Dmitrii Kozak Prizval Ekologov "ne zavalivat'" Stroitel'stvo Ob'ektov v Sochi," *Kommersant*, March 12, 2010, www.kommersant.ru/doc/1336581

39 Mitch Potter, "2014 Olympics in Sochi Face Terror and Environmental Concerns," *Toronto Star*, April 4, 2010, http://olympics.thestar.com/2010/ article/789905

40 Tatyana Strakhova, "Ekologi Podderzhivali Proekt Olimpiiskogo 'Zelenogo' Standarta," *RIA Novosti*, May 25, 2010, http://eco.rian.ru/ nature/20100525/238393156.html

41 "Rossiiskii Uchenyi Rasskazal BBC o Smertel'noi Opasnosti Olimpiiskikh Ob'ektov v Sochi," *allsochiinfo.ru*, April 16, 2010, http://forum.allsochi.info/ showthread.php?t=19234

42 Richard Galpin, "Russia Scientist Flees After Olympic Alerts," *BBC News*, April 16, 2010, http://news.bbc.co.uk/2/hi/europe/8624894.stm

43 "Ekologi Zaiavliaiut o Sbrose Mazuta v Reku Sochi," *Kavkazskii Uzel*, January 7, 2012, www.kavkaz-uzel.ru/articles/198888

44 "Chleny Sochinskogo Otdeleniia Russkogo Geograficheskogo Obshchestva Vystupali Protiv ego Zakrytiia," *Kavkazskii Uzel*, January 25, 2012, www.

kavkaz-uzel.ru/articles/199892; "Sochinskie Bloggery Proveli Aktsiiu Protesta v Sviazi s Atakami na Mestnye Saity," *Kavkazskii Uzel*, February 2, 2012, www. kavkaz-uzel.ru/articles/200417

45 James Brook, "Police Crack Down on Opposition in Post-Election Russia," *Voice of America*, March 19, 2012, www.voanews.com/english/news/Police-Cr ack-Down-on-Opposition-in-Post-election-Russia-143373276.html

46 Anastasiia Bashkatova, "Korruptsiia Ystanovila Olimpiiskii Rekord," *Nezavisimaia Gazeta*, July 6, 2010, www.ng.ru/economics/2010–06–07/1_ corrupciya.html

47 Allen Dowd, "Give a Home to Us not the Olympics, Say Protestors," *Reuters*, February 7, 2010, www.reuters.com/article/2010/02/08/us-olympics-poverty-id USTRE61705R20100208

48 Yevgeny Titov, "Zolota na Vsekh ne Khvatit," *Novaya Gazeta*, March 6, 2008, www.novayagazeta.ru/economy/41182.html

49 Roman Anin, "Kak ya Daval Vziatki Chinovnikam Upravleniia Delami Presidenta," *Novaya Gazeta*, June 4, 2010, www.novayagazeta.ru/politics/ 3252.html; "Genprokuratura RF Proveryaet Svedeniia o Korruptsii na Stroitel'stve v Sochi," *Kavkazskii Uzel*, June 11, 2010, www.kavkaz-uzel.ru/ articles/170853/

50 "Eks-Sud'ia Obviniaetsia v Raskhishchenii Vydelennykh dlia Olimpiady v Sochi Zemel'," *Kavkazskii Uzel*, June 28, 2010, http://kavkaz-uzel.ru/ articles/170864; "Eks-Sud'ia iz Sochi Obzhaloval Reshenie O Privlechenii evo k Ugolovnoi Otvetstvennosti," *Kavkazskii Uzel*, June 30, 2010, http:// kavkaz-uzel.ru/articles/170943/

51 "Verkhovnyi Sud RF Perenos Rassmotrenie Zhaloby Sud'I Novikova na 29 Marta," *Kavkazskii Uzel*, February 29, 2012, www.kavkaz-uzel.ru/ articles/202110

52 "Reshenie o Vosbuzhdenii Dela v Otnoshenii Eks-Sud'i Novkova iz Sochi Peresmatrivat'sia ne Budet," *Kavkazskii Uzel*, March 28, 2012, www. kavkaz-uzel.ru/articles/203861/

53 Natal'ia Kostenko, Maksim Tovkailo, Anton Filatov, and Kseniia Dokukina, "Za Opozdanie s Olimpiiskim Stroitel'stvom Edva ne Vveli Ugolovnuiu Otvetstvennost'," *Vedomosti*, January 13, 2012, www.vedomosti.ru/politics/ news/1473985/srok_za_olimpiadu

54 "Olimpiiskii Port Smylo Shtormom," *Stroyteh*, December 16, 2009, www. stroyteh.ru/publication/OlimpiiskiI_port_smylo_shtormom

55 Vladimir Turin, "Stoianke na 'Dony,'" *Nezavisimaia Gazeta*, March 26, 2010, www.ng.ru/economics/2010–03–26/4_don.html; "V Krasnodarskom Krae Gigantskie Probki Paralizuet Trassu 'Don,'" *Kavkazskii Uzel*, August 11, 2010, www.kavkaz-uzel.ru/articles/172850

56 Paul Goble, "Moscow's Forcible Consolidation of Schools Threatens Russia with New Pikalevos, Expert Says," *Window on Eurasia*, August 3, 2009. http:// windowoneurasia.blogspot.com/2009/08/window-on-eurasia-moscows-forcibl e.html

57 Egor Lysenko, "Vse Zakatali v Asfalt. Krome Dorog," *Novaya Gazeta*, July 19, 2010, www.novayagazeta.ru/data/2010/077/00.html

58 Igor Naumov, "Olimpiiskie Milliardy Zakatyvayut v Asfalt," *Nezavisimaya Gazeta*, June 28, 2010, www.ng.ru/economics/2010–06–28/1_sochi.html

59 "Olimpiady v Sochi Grozyat Moskovskie Probki," *Osobaya Bukva*, September 22, 2010, www.specletter.com/obcshestvo/2010–09–22/olimpiade-v-sochi-grozjat-moskovskie-probki-.html
60 Paul Goble, "Opportunity and Human Costs of Sochi Olympics Hitting Home With Russians," *Window on Eurasia*, September 22, 2010, http://windowoneurasia.blogspot.com/2010/09/window-on-eurasia-opportunity-and-human.html
61 Anastasiya Bashkatova, "Eshche Raz o Sochi," *Nezavisimaya Gazeta*, July 6, 2010, www.ng.ru/economics/2010–07–06/4_sochi.html
62 "Razgovor s Vladimirom Putinym," *Pravitel'stvo Rossiiskoi Federatsii*, December 15, 2011, www.government.ru/docs/17409
63 "V 2010 Godu na Stroitel'stvo v Sochi budet potracheno 60 mlrd. Rublei," *Kavakazskii Uzel*, April 14, 2010, www.kavkaz-uzel.ru/articles/167731
64 Yevgeny Titov, "Legendarny Mer Sochi—o Spasenii Milliardov," *Novaya Gazeta*, April 17, 2009, www.novayagazeta.ru/politics/45377.html

Bibliography

"'Adyge Khase' Adygei Vystupaet Protiv Prazdnovaniia Dvukh Iubileinykh Dat," *Kavkazskii Uzel*, February 23, 2007. www.kavkaz-uzel.ru/articles/110816/

Allenova, Ol'ga, "Vse Olimpiiskie Ob'ekty Mogut Uiti Pod Zemliu," *Kommersant' Vlast'*, June 15, 2009. www.kommersant.ru/doc/1186885

Anin, Roman, "Kak ya Daval Vziatki Chinovnikam Upravleniia Delami Presidenta," *Novaya Gazeta*, June 4, 2010- www.novayagazeta.ru/politics/3252.html

Bashkatova, Anastasiya, "Eshche Raz o Sochi," *Nezavisimaya Gazeta*, July 6, 2010. www.ng.ru/economics/2010–07–06/4_sochi.html

Brook, James, "Police Crack Down on Opposition in Post-Election Russia," *Voice of America*, March 19, 2012. www.voanews.com/english/news/Police-Crack-Down-on-Opposition-in-Post-election-Russia-143373276.html

"Cherkesskii Kongress Vystupil Protiv Olimiady v Sochi," *Kavkazskii Uzel*, June 5, 2007. www.kavkaz-uzel.ru/articles/117988

"Chleny Sochinskogo Otdeleniia Russkogo Geograficheskogo Obshchestva Vystupali Protiv ego Zakrytiia," *Kavkazskii Uzel*, January 25, 2012. www.kavkaz-uzel.ru/articles/199892

Denton, Karen, "The Olympics, Homelessness, and Civil Rights," *ACLU Reporter*, Fall 1999. www.acluutah.org/99fall.htm

"Dmitrii Kozak Prizval Ekologov 'ne zavalivat'' Stroitel'stvo Ob'ektov v Sochi," *Kommersant*, March 12, 2010. www.kommersant.ru/doc/1336581

"Ekologi Prizyvayut Vlasti ne Prinimat' Genplan Sochi v ego Nyneshnem Vide," *RIA Novosti*, July 13, 2009. http://eco.rian.ru/danger/20090713/177253772.html

"Ekologi Zaiavlaiut o Sbrose Mazuta v Reku Sochi," *Kavkazskii Uzel*, January 7, 2012. www.kavkaz-uzel.ru/articles/198888

"Eks-Sud'ia Obviniaetsia v Raskhishchenii Vydelennykh dlia Olimpiady v Sochi Zemel'," *Kavkazskii Uzel*, June 28, 2010. http://kavkaz-uzel.ru/articles/170864

"Eks-Sud'ia iz Sochi Obzhaloval Reshenie O Privlechenii evo k Ugolovnoi Otvetstvennosti," *Kavkazskii Uzel*, June 30, 2010. http://kavkaz-uzel.ru/articles/170943/

"Federal'nyi Zakon 310-F3," *Departament Krasnodarskogo Kraia po Realizatsii Polnomochii pri Podgotovke Zimnikh Olimpiiskikh Igr 2014 goda*, December 1, 2007 www.olympdep.ru/docs/ofdoc31

Galpin, Richard, "Russia Scientist Flees After Olympic Alerts," *BBC News*, April 16, 2010. http://news.bbc.co.uk/2/hi/europe/8624894.stm

"Genprokuratura RF Proveryaet Svedeniia o Korruptsii na Stroitel'stve v Sochi," *Kavkazskii Uzel*, June 11, 2010. www.kavkaz-uzel.ru/articles/170853/

Goble, Paul, "Moscow's Forcible Consolidation of Schools Threatens Russia with New Pikalevos, Expert Says," *Window on Eurasia*, August 3, 2009. http://windowoneurasia.blogspot.com/2009/08/window-on-eurasia-moscows-forcible.html

— "Opportunity and Human Costs of Sochi Olympics Hitting Home With Russians," *Window on Eurasia*, September 22, 2010. http://windowoneurasia.blogspot.com/2010/09/window-on-eurasia-opportunity-and-human.html

Greenpeace Russia. www.greenpeace.org/russia/en/news/

Grove, Thomas, "Genocide Claims Complicate Russian Olympics Plans," *Reuters*, October 13, 2011. http://af.reuters.com/article/worldNews/idAFTRE79C2XP20111013

Gulevich, Vladislav, "Circasian Theme of Syria's Tragedy," *Strategic Culture Foundation*, February 16, 2012. www.strategic-culture.org/news/2012/02/16/circassian-theme-of-syria-tragedy.html

Kostenko, Natal'ia, Maksim Tovkailo, Anton Filatov, and Kseniia Dokukina, "Za Opozdanie s Olimpiiskim Stroitel'stvom Edva ne Vveli Ugolovnuiu Otvetstvennost'," *Vedomosti*, January 13, 2012. www.vedomosti.ru/politics/news/1473985/srok_za_olimpiadu

Lysenko, Egor, "Vse Zakatali v Asfalt. Krome Dorog," *Novaya Gazeta*, July 19, 2010. www.novayagazeta.ru/data/2010/077/00.html. Accessed 7/22/2010

Marshenkulova, Marina, "Outrage at 'Fake' Circassian Anniversary," *Institute for War and Peace Reporting*, October 5, 2007. http://iwpr.net/report-news/outrage-"fake"-circassian-anniversary

"Medvedev Creates New North Caucasus Federal District," *Radio Free Europe/Radio Liberty*, January 20, 2010. www.rferl.org/content/Medvedev_Creates_New_North_Caucasus_Federal_District/1934705.html

"Musornye Poligony Sochinskogo Regiona v Kriticheskom Sostoyanii," *RIA Novosti*, November 25, 2008. www.rian.ru/danger/20081125/155822883.html

Naumov, Igor, "Olimpiiskie Milliardy Zakatyvayut v Asfalt," *Nezavisimaya Gazeta*, June 28, 2010. www.ng.ru/economics/2010–06–28/1_sochi.html

"Olimpiady v Sochi Grozyat Moskovskie Probki," *Osobaya Bukva*, September 22, 2010. www.specletter.com/obcshestvo/2010–09–22/olimpiade-v-sochi-grozjat-moskovskie-probki-.html

"Olimpiiskii Port Smylo Shtormom," *Stroyteh*, December 16, 2009. www.stroyteh.ru/publication/OlimpiiskiI_port_smylo_shtormom

Potter, Mitch, "2014 Olympics in Sochi Face Terror and Environmental Concerns," *Toronto Star*, April 4, 2010. http://olympics.thestar.com/2010/article/789905

"Razgovor s Vladimirom Putinym," *Pravitel'stvo Rossiiskoi Federatsii,* December 15, 2011. www.government.ru/docs/17409

"Report of the UN 2nd Expert Mission, January 28–30, 2010," United Nations Environment Programme, March 15, 2010. www.unep.org/PDF/PressReleases/ SOCHI_2014Jan28to302010_Mission_%20ReportFinal_%2015March.pdf

"Reshenie o Vosbuzhdenii Dela v Otnoshenii Eks-Sud'i Novkova iz Sochi Peresmatrivat'sia ne Budet," *Kavkazskii Uzel,* March 28, 2012. www.kavkaz-uzel.ru/articles/203861/

"Rossiiskii Uchenyi Rasskazal BBC o Smertel'noi Opasnosti Olimpiiskikh Ob'ektov v Sochi," *allsochiinfo.ru,* April 16, 2010. http://forum.allsochi.info/showthread.php?t=19234

Rudomakha, Andrei, "Nakrylas' 'Lunnaya Polyana,'" *Novaya Gazeta,* June 12, 2007. www.novayagazeta.ru/society/34887.html

Shukhov, Zamir, "Rezoliutsiia foruma cherkesskoi (adygskoi) molodezhi," *Justice for North Caucasus Groups Message Boards,* September 12, 2009. www.justicefornorthcaucasus.com/jfnc_message_boards/russian. php?title=Резолюция-форума-черкесской-(адыгской)-молодежи&entry_ id=1252947053&comments=comments

"Sobstvenniki Domov v Imeritinke Prepryatstvuyyut Geologorazvedke na Meste Stroitel'stve Stadiona," *Kavkazskii Uzel,* April 21, 2010. www.kavkaz-uzel.ru/articles/167931

"Sochinskie Bloggery Proveli Aktsiiu Protesta v Sviazi s Atakami na Mestnye Saity," *Kavkazskii Uzel,* February 2, 2012. www.kavkaz-uzel.ru/articles/200417

Strakhova, Tatyana, "Ekologi Podderzhivali Proekt Olimpiiskogo 'Zelenogo' Standarta," *RIA Novosti,* May 25, 2010. http://eco.rian.ru/nature/20100525/238393156.html

— "Goskorporatsiia 'Olimpstroi' Uvelichit Shtat Ekologov," *RIA Novosti,* December 12, 2008. http://eco.rian.ru/business/20081212/157110623.html

— "Pri Stroitel'stve Ob'ektov Olimpiady-2014 Primenyat 'Zelenye Standarty,'" *RIA Novosti,* March 3, 2009. http://eco.rian.ru/business/20090303/163733408.html

Stremidlovsky, Stanislav, "Organizator Olimpiady v Sochi Stanet Preemnikom Putina," *Agenstvo Politicheskikh Novostei,* May 7, 2007. www.apn.ru/news/article17373.htm

Taroshchina, Slava, "Eto Kruto!" *Novaya Gazeta,* February 17, 2010. www.novayagazeta.ru/arts/4849.html

Thornburgh, Nathan, "Olympic Dreams: Will Sochi Rehabilitate Russia's Image?" *Time,* November 18, 2011. www.time.com/time/magazine/article/0,9171,2099428,00.html#ixzz1e4fpiSx5

Titov, Yevgeny, "Legendarnyi Mer Sochi—o Spasenii Milliardov," *Novaya Gazeta,* April 17, 2009. www.novayagazeta.ru/politics/45377.html

— "Reider, Olimpiiskii Vid," *Novaya Gazeta,* June 15, 2009. www.novayagazeta.ru/politics/44338.html

— "S Mesta v Kar'ery," *Novaia Gazeta,* January 15, 2012. www.novayagazeta.ru/politics/50441.html

— "Zolota na Vsekh ne Khvatit," *Novaya* Gazeta, March 6, 2008. www.novaya-gazeta.ru/economy/41182.html
— "Zimnie Vidy Porta," *Novaya* Gazeta, October 16, 2008. www.novayagazeta.ru/society/38384.html
"Tupikovyi Kar'er," *Sochinskie Novosti*, February 17, 2012. http://sochinskie-novosti.ru/articles/carier-tbo.html
Turin, Vladimir, "Stoianke na 'Dony,'" *Nezavisimaia Gazeta*, March 26, 2010. www.ng.ru/economics/2010–03–26/4_don.html
"Ubit Suadin Pshukov," *Adyge Sait*, April 10, 2011. www.elot.ru/main/index.php?option=com_content&task=view&id=2579&Itemid=1. A Circassian blogger in Russia who reproduced my interview with Voice of America concerning the Circassian genocide was subsequently charged with extremism in August 2011.
"Verkhovnyi Sud RF Perenos Rassmotrenie Zhaloby Sud'I Novikova na 29 Marta," *Kavkazskii Uzel*, February 29, 2012. www.kavkaz-uzel.ru/articles/202110
"V 2010 Godu na Stroitel'stvo v Sochi budet potracheno 60 mlrd. Rublei," *Kavakazskii Uzel*, April 14, 2010. www.kavkaz-uzel.ru/articles/167731
"V Krasnodarskom Krae Gigantskie Probki Paralizuet Trassu 'Don,'" *Kavkazskii Uzel*, August 11, 2010. www.kavkaz-uzel.ru/articles/172850
"V Olimpiiskom Bezumii 'RZhD' Unichtozhaet Derev'ya Patriarkhi," *APN Severo-Zapad*, August 19, 2009. www.apn-spb.ru/opinions/article5985.htm
"V Sele Nekrasovskom Poselilis' Pervye Pereselentsy iz Imeretinskoi Nizmennosti Sochi," *Kavkazskii Uzel*, May 5, 2010. www.kavkaz-uzel.ru/articles/168475
"V Sochi Bolee sta Aktivistov Vystupili Protiv Zastroiki Zelenoi Zony," *Kavkazskii Uzel*, February 26, 2012. www.kavkaz-uzel.ru/articles/201868
"V Sochi Zhiteli Imeretinki Prekratili Golodovku," *Kavkazskii Uzel*, June 18, 2010. www.kavkaz-uzel.ru/articles/170369
"Za Fasadom Olimpiady 2014: Doklad Komiteta Grazhdanskogo Kontrola," *Novaia Gazeta*, July 4, 2008. www.novayagazeta.ru/society/39502.html
"Zhiteli Sochi, Lishivshiesia Zhil'ia iz-za Olimpiady, Obratiatsia za Pomoshch'iu v MOK," *Kavkazskii Uzel*, February 10, 2012. www.kavkaz-uzel.ru/articles/200948

PART THREE

Caucasian Crosscurrents

CHAPTER EIGHT

Islam and Orthodox Christianity in the Caucasus: From Antagonism to Partnership

Nicolai N. Petro

The Russian Orthodox Church has a long and often troubled history in the Northern Caucasus. Since the collapse of the Union of Soviet Socialist Republics (USSR), both Orthodox and Muslim leaders have looked for ways to heal old wounds and forge alliances against a new common enemy—secularism. To this end the Church has crafted a new approach to Islam that defines it not as a religion of an ethnic minority, tolerated but clearly subordinate to Orthodox Christianity, but as a full fledged partner in shaping the nation's social and political values. While these values are neither liberal nor secular, both the Russian Orthodox Church and its Muslim partners argue that they are modern and democratic. Moreover, they see this new "Russian Model" of religious and ethnic tolerance as one that could benefit the world.

This chapter looks at the impact that Russia's long and often troubled involvement in the Northern Caucasus has had on religious communities there. Many communities in the Caucasus have deep Christian roots. According to local lore the Apostles Andrew, Bartholomew, and Simon the Canaanite all visited the region, making it one of the earliest to receive the Gospel. The Abkhaz-Imretian and Albano-Agvan kingdoms were given their own diocese in the fourth century.[1] Meanwhile, Muslims from Middle East arrived in Dagestan and Azerbaijan as early as the eighth century, but Islam was not widely practiced until the seventeenth century. Some historians claim that it was the severity of Russian policies that caused the mountain people of the Caucasus to adopt Islam *en masse*.[2] The history of the Russian Orthodox Church in the region therefore cannot be separated from the history of Islam.

A brief history of Islam and Orthodoxy in the North Caucasus

How Islam came to the North Caucasus

The term North Caucasus is somewhat artificial, since it creates a division between the northern and southern sides of the Caucasus mountain range which are, in fact, interwoven historically and culturally. For the purposes of this discussion, however, the North Caucasus refers to the North Caucasus Federal District (NCFD), which was carved out of the Southern Federal District of Russia in January 2010. The NCFD contains the republics of Dagestan, Ingushetia, Kabardino-Balkaria, Karachaevo-Cherkessia, Chechnya, and Northern Ossetia-Alania, as well as Stavropol *krai*.[3]

Compared to the other seven federal districts, this one is the most recent, the smallest in size, and the most densely populated. It is also by far the poorest federal district, with five out of its seven members in the bottom 12 percent of all Russian regions in Gross Domestic Product (GDP) *per capita*. Finally, and most notably, it is the only federal district with a population that is overwhelmingly (more than 70%) non-Russian and non-Christian.[4] Approximately half of Russia's 15 million Muslims live in the North Caucasus.[5] Given these anomalies, it seems clear that the decision to create such a district is part of a broader effort by the Russian government to focus resources and attention on the region's particular problems.

Perhaps the most striking thing about this region is its astonishing ethnic and linguistic diversity. Roughly the size of Uruguay, or the US state of Missouri, it contains a greater variety of distinct ethnic and linguistic groups than any other region on earth.[6] It was the intervention of neighboring empires that, over the course of centuries, drove religious, and political consolidation in the region.

The first such intervention was the Byzantine Empire, which brought Christianity to the Georgians, Armenians, and Albanians (part of present day Azerbaijan and Dagestan) in the southern part of Caucasus, and to the Adygs, and Alanians (present day Ossetians) in the northern part of the Caucasus. As the Byzantine Empire declined, the region eventually fell under the influence of the Persian and then the Ottoman Empires. By the seventeenth century most of the peoples of the Northern Caucasus had converted to Islam, though a few, like the Ossetians, remain predominantly Christian.[7]

Russia's involvement in the Caucasus can be traced back to the fifteenth century, when the Christian kingdom of Georgia, besieged by the Persians, appealed to the Christian Tsar of Russia for support and protection, support that Russia was often reluctant to give. During the Time of Troubles (1589–1613), when Moscow itself was coping with Polish occupation, contact with the Caucasus all but ended. It revived in the seventeenth century, thanks to a military and political alliance with the Kabardins, then the dominant nationality in the North Caucasus. As a result of a treaty with the Ottoman Empire signed in 1739, the Kabardinian lands were relinquished to Russia and served for decades as a buffer zone between the two empires.

Russia's interest in the region once again lapsed during the Napoleonic Wars. It was not until 1856, with the signing of the Treaty of Paris that formally ended the Crimean War, that Russia committed itself to the pacification of the region and its incorporation into the Russian Empire (though by then there were influential voices that argued for leaving it on the other side of the border).[8] To this end, forts and settlements were established all along the so-called Caucasus Line along the river Terek. The area north of the river was settled by Cossacks, originally from the Don River region, who are now known simply as Terek Cossacks. It is in response to these settlements that Islam first becomes a rallying point for the people of the region.

The first major figure to declare holy war against the infidels was Sheikh Mansur Ushurma (1765–94), a Chechen mullah who had studied in Dagestan. He led a number of successful attacks against Russian forces, until he was captured in 1791. His cause was then taken up by Kazi Mullah (or Kazi Mohammed), the first Imam of Dagestan and Chechnya. He too was eventually captured and killed, along with many of his followers, one of whom survived Kazi Mullah's famous last stand in the tower of Gimry to become the third and most famous Imam of Dagestan and Chechnya, the legendary Shamil (1797–1871).[9]

From 1834 until his surrender in 1859, Shamil coordinated a campaign against Russian forces that united the North Caucasus. By teaching that Islam should take precedence over local tribal customs (*adat*), he unified the fractious clans and gave them a common, religiously inspired purpose—the creation of an independent Imamate of the Caucasus, a theocracy that was to be ruled according to the precepts of *shariah*, or Islamic law.

Russia fought Shamil by the brutal methods of the time. Stronger and more loyal populations, like the Kabarda and Karachay, were invited to join the Russian Empire by treaty and allowed considerable local autonomy.[10] With weaker and less organized communities, however, the Russian government simply eradicated their forests, forcing them into the mountains, and then repopulated their lands with Russian settlers.

Russian military governors sent to pacify the region had little interest in local attitudes and customs, ascribing them to backwardness and feudalism. The most infamous of these, Alexei Ermolov (1777–1861), fought a ruthless campaign of extermination against the rebels based on the assumption that the type of Islam they practiced was corrupt, and was being used by religious leaders to oppress the common people. Scarcely a century ago, he wrote, the local population had still been "idol worshippers" and so could not have gained a proper grounding in the Islamic faith.[11]

Oddly enough, the Russian government and the Islamic leaders who fought against it were not far apart in their critiques. Mansur opposed many *adat* (customary) traditions, and argued that feudalism and slavery were incompatible with Islamic *shariah*.[12] Kazi-Mullah and Shamil echoed the same reformist themes. One might almost have expected the Russian government to welcome their efforts to introduce a more contemporary and systematic form of Islam as social progress, but they had too little contact with the native population to grasp such nuances. When the call for *shariah* merged with calls for independence, it was interpreted as a corrupted religion bringing out the worst in people. And the worst of the worst, in the eyes of Russia's military commanders, were the Chechens.[13] General Ermolov refers to them as "the most evil bandits," adding, in terms that are chilling to read even today: "I have seen many peoples, but ones as arrogant and unbridled as the Chechens do not exist on this earth. The path to the conquest of the Caucasus lies through the subjugation of the Chechens, specifically, through their total annihilation."[14] Russia's conquest of Caucasus ultimately took nearly half a century, and cost the lives of over 25,000 Russian soldiers, and countless thousands of local residents.[15]

Although Shamil carried on bravely for more than two decades, he was eventually captured and given quite honorable terms. After he and his sons swore allegiance to Russia, he was allowed to settle in Kaluga, a town in central Russia, and granted the status of a minor nobleman. Toward the end of his life he was allowed to move to Kiev, for the climate. He lived to be 74 and died while on a pilgrimage to Mecca.[16] After his defeat the rebellion collapsed for want of a new charismatic leader. But during this prolonged struggle Islam and North Caucasian national identities had become one. Forged in a crucible of fire, it was preserved by the traditional clan system that survived the conflict.

Thanks to this linkage, the peoples of this region were better able than most in the Soviet Union to resist secularization and preserve their traditions. The Soviet government felt that it could ill-afford the bloody battles of the previous century, so while some in the region adapted to life under atheistic socialism, others made the decision to live part of their lives apart from the secular norms of Soviet society and to keep to the ways of *adat* and Islam in the Northern Caucasus.[17]

The historical role of the Orthodox Church in the North Caucasus

When the Russian Orthodox Church followed Russian settlers into the region, it did not see itself as a newcomer. Rather, it saw itself as restoring the traditional Christian faith to the peoples of the Caucasus. As early as 1742, an Ossetian Spiritual Commission had been established to help convert the region, though it relied heavily on Orthodox priests from Georgia.[18] Such conversions typically occurred when a clan elder entered Russian service as a nobleman. The following account, from the archives of the Stavropol diocesan news, describes the process:

> . . . a proprietor of lesser Kabarda, Korgo-Konchokin, adopted Christianity along with part of his subjects. The name of this proprietor of lesser Kabarda is tied to the establishment of Mozdok. Having adopted Christianity along with his subjects, Korgoko, who at baptism assumed the name Prince Andrei Ivanovich Cherkassky-Konchokin, appealed to the Russian government to be allowed to settle along the left bank of the Terek. He was given the right to select any location he might desire, and he chose the location of Mozdok. In 1763 a forward post was built at the site, and alongside it a settlement with an Orthodox church. Konchokin's subjects formed the backbone of the regiment's Cossack Mountain Line, so named because it was originally made up of mountaineers— Kabardins as well as other people of the Caucasus. Mozdok served for many years as a safe haven for those Kabardins, Ossetians, Chechens and others who adopted Christianity, and for all who suffered from Muslim oppression, as well as the occasional Georgian and Armenian.[19]

Despite the difficulties of wartime, Orthodox Church membership grew steadily through the early nineteenth century. Local church archives show that between 1817 and 1823 more than 60,000 people were converted to Christianity, including nearly all the Ossetians. Over the course of the next two decades conversions numbered 1,000–2,000 per year.[20]

After the end of major military operations in the region, the Ossetian Commission was replaced by the Society for the Restoration of Orthodox Christianity in the Caucasus, and its Georgian clergy replaced by ethnic Slavs. The government continued to settle the region with other nationalities, and supported the establishment of villages where soldiers and their families could retire. It was assumed that this strengthened the positions of both the Orthodox Church and the Russian Empire.[21] According to historian Pyotr V. Znamensky, the mission of local clergy became the construction of "Russian Christian citizenship" [*russkaya khristianskaya grazhdanstvennost*].[22]

As the Russian-speaking population of the Caucasus grew to over half-a-million, missionary work was replaced by pastoral care of the region's rapidly growing mix of immigrants. It ran almost all social work in the region, and did much to raise the status of women by encouraging their education.[23] It is also interesting to note that while the Cossacks are today considered a bulwark of Orthodox traditionalism, at end of the nineteenth century the Church grappled with the issue of how to bring them back into the fold. Years of long and often solitary service without regular pastoral care had led many of them to become Old Believers, a group that had split from the official Church in the seventeenth century, or even adepts of other sects.[24]

At the beginning of the twentieth century, therefore, a large group of Muslim spiritual leaders loyal to Moscow had arisen, so much so that the fifth Imam of Dagestan, sheikh Najmuddin Gotsinsky, whose father had once served as Shamil's deputy (*naib*), fought for the territorial integrity of Russia, and backed the White ("Volunteer") Army of General A. Denikin during the Russian Civil War.[25]

Following two decades religious persecution, Stalin appealed to Muslim religious leaders for support during the Second World War (as he did with the leaders of the Russian Orthodox Church). In return for their loyalty he allowed a Muslim Spiritual Directorate for the Northern Caucasus to be set up in the Dagestani town of Buinaksk in 1944. By 1988, however, there were still only 27 active mosques in Dagestan. Just three years later, Dagestan had its own Spiritual Directorate and transferred its seat from Buinaksk to the capital city of Makhachkala.[26] Conflicts that had cooled down considerably on the eve of the Russian Revolution, and been in deep freeze under Soviet rule, were about to heat up.

The resurgence of Islamic Tolerance in the North Caucasus

Although the term is used more often to refer to localized territorial conflicts, there is good reason to think of the entire Caucasus region as a "frozen conflict." The merger of national and religious identity that had served as a self-protection mechanism under both Russian imperial and Soviet rule, became an explosive combination in the chaotic years following the collapse of the Union of Soviet Socialist Republics. At the end of the 1990s, seven out of ten young Tatars identified themselves as believing Muslims, whereas in the three most Islamic North Caucasus republics (Dagestan, Ingushetia, and Chechnya) this number already approached 100 percent.[27] Despite its poverty, since the end of the Union of Soviet Socialist Republics the Northern Caucasus has led Russia in the construction of new mosques, and accounts for more than two-thirds of Russia's pilgrimages to Mecca (hajj).[28] The rise of repressed religious identity has accentuated national identity, and caused Islam to assume a pre-eminent role in the political and social life of the North Caucasus. It is now routine for local political leaders to refer to Islam as a founding principle of political and social life, or even, as the president of Tatarstan did recently on a trip to Dubai, to refer to themselves—mistakenly it will be observed—as "Muslim republics."[29]

At the same time that the collapse of the old order brought with it a re-traditionalization of public consciousness and behavior, it also loosened the floodgates of rebelliousness against the region's traditional religious leadership, especially after most of them chose to stand with Russia during the second Chechen military conflict (1999–2000). The impact of this conflict best can be seen in the region's two key republics—Dagestan and Chechnya.

As the birthplace of Islam in Russia, and the birthplace of Shamil, Dagestan occupies a unique place in the religious life of the North Caucasus. The current Mufti of Dagestan, and thus the nominal leader of its Muslim community, is Akhmed Haji Abdullaev. In 1992, at the young age of 33, Abdullaev was asked to head the North-Caucasus Islamic Institute. Six years later he was unanimously elected to head the Spiritual Directorate of Muslims of Dagestan, an appointment he had previously declined. In a region famed for revering its heritage, he has the benefit of coming from a line of religious leaders that can apparently trace its lineage back to the Prophet Muhammad himself.[30]

Abdullaev's erudition, youth, and willingness to reach out to dissatisfied religious constituencies have made him a consensus figure in Dagestan. He supported the 1998 decision by the Dagestani Council of alims (authoritative theologians) to not send students abroad to study theology, as they often came back radicalized.[31] He supervises an impressive network of local Islamic publications, institutions of higher education, and madrassahs (Islamic schools attached to mosques), as well as several Islamic websites (Islam.Ru, Sufism.Ru, Mufti.Ru). They all proclaim tolerance and respect for other religious beliefs as core principles of Islam.[32] He also supports the controversial notion that other religious traditions, such as Orthodox Christianity, should be taught at Islamic educational institutions.[33] On other matters, however, Abdullaev is quite traditional. He has even been criticized by some Dagestani officials for taking too hard a line on public morality, for suggesting that women should not be allowed to wander in public unattended, and for supporting polygamy.[34]

In 2011, Abdullaev took a bold step toward healing the deep rift between Dagestan's traditionally more hierarchical Sunni Sufis, and the more radical Sunni Salafists (Wahhabists) who call for the purification of Islam from external influence. He publicly denounced muftis who turned over the names of suspected radicals to authorities, and then did away with the Spiritual Directorate's review of religious material for extremist content. These moves were hailed by opposition figures as ushering in a new era of religious dialogue among Muslims, and in late April 2012 he hosted the first formal meeting of both groups in Makhachkala.[35]

In Chechnya the position of Mufti and chairman of the Spiritual Directorate of Chechnya is held by Sultan Hadji Mirzayev, a long-time associate of the former Mufti and president of the Chechnya, Akhmed-Hadji Kadyrov. Before this Mirzayev had served as religious affairs advisor to Aslan Maskhadov, president of the briefly independent Chechnya (Ichkeria). Under Maskhadov Mirzayev, then 35, was appointed chairman of the influential Supreme *Shariah* Court of Chechnya. He nevertheless publicly condemned what he saw as Maskhadov's pandering to criminals and, during Russia's second intervention, fought and was wounded, as he now puts it, "fighting for the territorial integrity of Russia."[36] He now strongly supports Chechnya as part of Russia, saying that, under Vladimir Putin, the government has done more to support Islamic youth, education, and science even than in some Islamic countries.[37]

Since the prolonged military conflict has resulted in the exodus of most of the Russian-speaking population of Chechnya, Mirzayev has made their return one of his top priorities. He therefore supports teaching the Foundations of Orthodox Culture curriculum in public schools, and has even donated money intended for the construction of a mosque for the re-construction of the Church of the Archangel Michael in Grozny.[38] The Chechen government supports religious life as an absolute priority, and Mirzayev insists that this includes all of Russia's traditional religions. In public speeches, he highlights the commonalities between Islam and the other "religions of the Book" and stresses that none of them justify religious enmity.[39] He is also on record as saying that how women dress in public is their own business, and that *shariah* law should not replace Russian law.[40]

Thus, as Islam has grown in strength and stature, it has also redefined its relations with the Russian Orthodox Church, once its traditional rival. Many local Islamic leaders have come to see the crisis of morality, the loss of direction among young people, and the fracturing of common social values as problems that cannot be escaped by simply declaring independence. They form part of the global fabric of modernity and will need to be addressed together by all people of faith. This realization, more than anything else, has forced traditional Islamic leaders to reassess their relations with Russia, and to view the Russian Orthodox Church as a valuable ally in the global struggle against secularism and immorality.

This alliance summed up in the motto: "two principle faiths, along-side several traditional religions."[41] The "two principle faiths"—Islam and Orthodoxy—bear the primary burden for restoring morality and harmony to the region. They are expected to take the lead in local councils and given pride of place at public gatherings. The Islamic leadership must also seek to control extremism, while the Russian Orthodox Church is expected to reign in the excesses of Cossacks and Russian nationalists. Russia's two other traditional religions, Judaism and Buddhism, and the handful of eth-nic/religious enclaves dotting the Caucasus, are expected to play a second-ary, but supportive role.

This agenda was aptly articulated at the First Congress of Religious lead-ers of the Northern Caucasus, which took place in Makhachkala in June 2011. Its concluding resolution highlights its ambitions:

We call upon religious leaders to strengthen peace and civic harmony in Russian society and affirm our willingness to cooperate with authorities at all levels in combating terrorism [and to preserve] the territorial integrity of the Russian Federation. . . . There is no room in Islam for violence against our neighbors [and] we firmly declare that in the Russian Federation all democratic conditions have been created for the resolution of existing social problems, especially for guaranteeing the right to freedom of conscience and faith, and that there is no basis for calls to military *jihad* or military conflict in Russian society.[42]

The new Islamic–Orthodox alliance against secularism

Meanwhile, the Orthodox Church has been undergoing a dramatic revival of its own fortunes. From 6,899 churches in 1987, it now has over 30,000, and its 15 monasteries have mushroomed to nearly 800.[43] To cite former president Medvedev, "The Russian Orthodox Church (ROC) is the larg-est and most authoritative social institution in contemporary Russia."[44] It seeks a modern version of the Byzantine ideal of *symphonia* in which both Church and state work together to promote social harmony, charity, and public morality.

Russia's political authorities have wholly embraced this partnership model. Yeltsin, Putin, and Medvedev have all spoken poignantly about the historical and cultural importance of Russian Orthodoxy, and called for it to be more actively involved in social affairs. When asked why they give so much prominence to the Church, Russian politicians often cite Vladimir Putin, in saying that they are "repaying the State's historical debts to the church."[45] Of course, it helps that the Church and its leaders consistently poll first or second among the most trusted institution of society.[46]

It is not surprising therefore that the ROC recently reorganized its administration of the North Caucasus in a way that more closely matches the contours of government administration there. Two new diocese have been added. There is now a new Bishop of Pyatigorsk and Cherkessk, Feofilakt, who oversees the more Orthodox areas of the Caucasus, as well as a new Bishop of Vladikavkaz and Makhachkala, Zosima, who serves as pastor to predominantly Muslim Dagestan, Ingushetia, and Chechnya, as well as Northern Ossetia. For the popular and well-respected Zosima this is a shift within the Caucasus, but the elevation of Feofilakt is noteworthy because he is of a younger generation (born in 1974), and because he was born and raised in Grozny and is one of the Church's leading experts on Islam.[47]

In the predominantly Orthodox areas of the North Caucasus, like Stavropol *krai*, the Church has a network of educational institutions, from theological seminaries and higher educational institutions in Stavropol, Armavir, and Rostov at the top, through several hundred lyceums, gymnasiums, all the way down to Cossack and Sunday schools that emphasize Orthodox heritage and culture.[48] The local Orthodox press has a circulation in the tens of thousands, and the Church has its own regional television channel ("Don" run by the diocese of Rostov and Novocherkassk), as well as control over religious programming on regional television. It goes without saying that local officials are eager to provide the Church with both land and public funding to build churches.[49]

Local Orthodox clergy tend to see social issues very much the way their Muslim counterparts do. They share the same concerns about how to improve religious education among young people, how to build more houses of worship, how to fight extremism (interestingly, the "traditionalists" help each other against their respective "extremists"—the Orthodox ally with Muslim clerics against Wahhabis, while Muslims support the Orthodox against Protestant evangelism). Spiritual poaching between Muslims and Orthdox Christians is strongly discouraged, and senior clerics on both sides have publicly supported the study of the other's religion. As of 2012, Archbishop Feofilakt has mandated that all Orthodox clergy under his supervision be required to take courses in Islamic theology.[50] In addition to providing deeper knowledge of their neighbors, he hopes that this will allow Orthodox to participate as equals in public discussions of faith. Archbishop Zosima, for his part, intends to expand the annual summer youth camps for Orthodox and Muslim youth, which have been a tradition in the region since 1998. At his initiative, the diocese recently signed an agreement with the Spiritual Directorate of Muslims in Kabardino-Balkaria to set up interconfessional youth clubs with chapters in all local institutions of higher education.[51]

These appointments and initiatives reflect the view within the highest levels of Russian Orthodox Church that Islam can be a valuable ally in rolling back secularism. Just as the Russian Orthodox Church has raised its voice in defense of Christian values in what it deems to be an overly secularized Europe, so senior Church officials have touted the virtues of Islam, saying that its values are closer to those of the Orthodox Church than those of Western secular culture.[52]

Patriarch Alexey II set the tone for this alliance in his October 2007 letter to 138 Muslim theologians, in which he referred to Islam and Orthodox Christianity as religions that both "witness to the interconnectedness of peace and justice, morality and the law, truth and love." He called for a regular dialogue on doctrine that could lead to practical prescriptions on how Muslims and Christians could work together to defend the role of religion in public life and morality.[53]

This outreach to the Muslim world has been pushed even further by his successor Patriarch Kirill, who has stressed that all of Russia's traditional religions speak with one voice in support of traditional moral values. "The future of humanity depends on the role that religion plays in society," Kirill says, "because if the enormous power that man has over nature, over the world, is separated from belief and morality, then our future is in danger."[54] For his part Archbishop Hilarion (Alfeyev), Kirill's successor as the head of Church's External Affairs Department, has remarked that the challenges posed by "aggressive Western secularism" amount to "a hidden war" against traditional values, and that the support of Muslims is vital in overcoming this challenge.[55]

Patriarch Kirill not only emphasizes the problems facing people of faith in the modern world, but also offers a common agenda about what to do: promote role of religion in international fora, increase its role in education, and condemn extremism and terrorism. Terrorism, he says, is an especially insidious foe because when secularists wish to undermine religion they claim that violent acts are religiously inspired. This gives Christians and Muslims a common cause, for the one thing that most distinguishes Russia and the Islamic world from the West today is the resurgence of faith, and the desire to see it become of central importance to life and society.[56]

Patriarch Kirill sees such a partnership as guided by historical precedent—in those regions where a particular religion has become the most prominent, it should not be expected to relinquish that pre-eminence to a secular state in the name of equality, for in reality, under a secular paradigm, equality subordinates all religions to the state. Instead, the dominant religion should create a welcoming environment for religious minorities, and expect reciprocity in other areas where it is the minority. He cites with approval the late Russian Empire where Orthodox Christianity was the official religion, but Muslims had the ability to practice their faith throughout

the empire. Conversely, in those areas of Russia where Islam has traditionally been dominant, they are expected to reciprocate.[57]

Hegumen (or Abbott) Philip (Ryabykh), who serves as the representative
of the Moscow Patriarchate to the Council of Europe, has expounded on
the advantages of what he calls "the Russian Model" of religious toleration.
Its success, he says, rests on four pillars. The first is recognition of the value
of religion and respect for the principle of religious freedom.

Hegumen Philip refers to the second as "the principle of justice
(*spravedlivost*)," by which he means the same respect for traditional religious attachments to which Patriarch Kirill referred. When considering
public policy it is, he says, a matter of "justice" that the historically established proportions of the religious communities be taken into account, and
that the largest communities be afforded due deference by the state and by
other religious communities. Proselytizing is therefore unacceptable, and
citizens have the right to ask their traditional communities to defend them
against the encroachments of foreign missionaries. Hegumen Philip recognizes that this may at times conflict with other freedoms, such as the
freedom of expression, but, he says, it has proved essential to preserving the
peace in Russia when it comes to matters of faith.[58]

A third pillar of the Russian Model is widespread support for a common set of social values. The fact that traditional religious see eye-to-eye
on most social issues has made interreligious dialogue fruitful.[59] Finally,
Hegumen Philip notes that Russian religious organizations are legally part
of civil society, and are therefore encouraged to work with both society
and government. Unlike some other countries, Russia has set up structures
to help coordinate interreligious dialogue, the most important being the
Interreligious Council of the Russian Federation established in 1997. These
interact with organs of the state from the federal down to the local level.

Anticipating those critics who argue that the Russian Model merely
serves to give the Russian Orthodox Church an advantage over other faiths,
and a privileged position from which it can exert undue influence over
society, Hegumen Philip counters that unbridled secularism has proven to
be even more socially destructive. The tragedies of the twentieth century,
he argues, stemmed not from flaws of individual nationalities, classes, or
people, but from the collective rejection of God. We must beware, therefore, "not only of the glorification of Nazism or Stalinism, but of what lay
at their heart—godlessness."[60] The proper solution is not to reject secularism outright, but to improve upon it. It is quite true, he says, that secularism arose to guarantee the rights of religious and other minorities at a
time when they were oppressed by dominant faiths. But now that there is
no such oppression, secular governments have become instruments of the
repression of religion per se.

The task before society therefore is to preserve the best aspects of secularism, such as protection for religious minorities, while insisting on a

more positive view of religion's social function. It would then be possible for religious people to view secularism not as something negative—as society and state divorced from religion—but as allowing religious groups to cooperate with the state in proportion to their presence in society, all the while underscoring that religious and state benefits differ fundamentally.[61] During his most recent presidential campaign, Vladimir Putin expressed a very similar sentiment to the members of Interreligious Council of the Russian Federation: "we must leave behind the primitive notion of separation of Church and state, and instead put into it an entirely new meaning—cooperation."[62]

Toward "One, Holy, Orthodox, and Islamic Russia"?

Concluding his review of the role of religion in the North Caucasus in the 1990s, Valery Tishkov, one of Russia's leading experts on the region, concluded pessimistically that "history is repeating itself." While religious differences were not the source of the region's conflicts, he felt that they would become increasingly significant for four reasons. First, because of the religious revival among both Muslims and Christians; second, because both religions were becoming increasingly politicized; third, because of Moscow's penchant for solving problems through the use of force; and fourth, because of the growing influence in the region of external actors from the Middle East.[63]

Thankfully, Tishkov was wrong. Although the factors he described remain, the way they affect the political stability of the region has fundamentally changed. At one point some 20,000 Russian students were studying in Islamic institutions abroad, but since 1998 the Spiritual Directorates of the North Caucasus have prohibited study outside of a handful of approved institutions.[64] The ability of external actors, most notably Saudi Arabia, to convert local youth to more radical interpretations of Islam has thus been sharply curtailed.[65]

The use of military force against rebels has also been on the wane, particularly in Chechnya, where all troops not ordinarily stationed there were withdrawn in 2009.[66] Sporadic acts of terrorism and murder still occur, but they no longer pose a serious threat to political stability in the region.

One consequence of the noted politicization of religion, as this chapter has shown, has been to encourage locals to forge new alliances, with each other and with the government, in the interests of promoting peace. The Mufti of Chechnya, Sultan Mirzayev has called this accepting "mutual responsibility [*sovmestnaya otvetstvennost*]." Islam and Orthodoxy, he says, must accept mutual responsibility for the well being of the Caucasus and, more broadly, for the fate of Eurasian civilization.[67] Finally, as this religious renaissance has continued, it has shifted from simply being an increase in gross numbers, to a deeper appreciation of the role that religion can play in forging new social values.

An example of this trend can be seen in the Republic of Tatarstan, where "traditional" Islamists have gone from merely opposing radical teachings, to developing an alternative to it—a more modern and multicultural form of Islam that has its roots in the writings of Muslim scholars from the early twentieth century.[68] Dubbed "EuroIslam" by Rafael Khakimov, director of the Institute of History at the Academy of Sciences of the Republic of Tatarstan and an advisor to former Tatarstan President Mintimer Shaimiev, it seeks to update the teachings of *jadadism*, which emphasize the cultural rather than ritualistic aspects of Islam, and apply them to the modern world.

In addition to Khakimov, the list of influential Islamic modernizers includes sheikh Ravil Gainutdin, chairman of the Council of Muftis of Russia, Tatar political essayist Gamer Bautdinov, and the rector of the Russian Islamic University, Rafik Mukhametshin, who argues that "by the mid-nineteenth century, Tatar society had already chosen a strategically correct path and by the beginning of the twentieth century [had] succeeded in creating a mini-model of civil society."[69] As a result of their efforts the Islamist movement in Tatarstan, which as Shireen Hunter reminds us, was "much stronger" than it was in Chechnya in the early 1990s, was nipped in the bud.[70]

Similar teachings have been slow to spread in the North Caucasus (although the head of the recently established Northern Caucasus Islamic University in Nalchik has also said that older interpretations of Islamic teachings need to be updated).[71] One possible reason for this is that religious awareness among local government officials has lagged behind the high level of public religiosity in the region. The hands-off approach taken by local officials to the Muslim religious conflicts of the early 1990s has been blamed for encouraging the rise of fundamentalism. It was only after the Russian government insisted that local government officials lend direct support to the traditional Islamic religious leadership that the situation began to turn around. The process began, Hunter notes, "with Russia [sic] blessing [Akhmed] Kadirov, is basically using Islam to legitimize his rule."[72]

Noting the many problems that continue to plague the region, some observers criticize Moscow for not having any strategy at all.[73] There is such a strategy, however, and it consists of three objectives. The first, as president Medvedev said during his remarks to the assembly of Muslim clergy of Russia in July 2011, is to state clearly that "our most important joint task is the dissemination of the ideas of tolerance, religious acceptance, and a caring respect for spiritual values."[74]

The second objective is to affirm publicly that Islam is a core component of Russian history and Russian identity, and thus allow Russia to reach a new level of cooperation with the Islamic world. At a Kremlin-sponsored conference in September 2011, high-ranking representative of 43 predominantly Muslim countries heard Russia's senior Muslim clerics not only affirm their allegiance to Russia, but say that they were eager to serve as Russia's ambassadors to the global Islamic *umma*. In his keynote address the Chairman of the Council of Muftis of Russia, Ravil Gainutdin, pointed out that Russian statehood had its roots in both the Islamic and Orthodox worlds, and that its current aspirations to be a truly multiethnic and multireligious state could be traced all the way back to the Golden Horde Kingdom of the thirteenth to fifteenth centuries.[75]

The final objective is the creation of a stable, multicultural state. With all the attention paid to Muslim extremists, it is easy to miss the fact that the vast majority of Russian Muslims are loyal citizens. They not only share with their non-Muslim neighbors an aversion to the chaos of the 1990s, but they are more likely than most to be thankful to Vladimir Putin for having restored law and order.[76] Being part of a powerful, influential, and stable Russia has been a constant refrain in the statements of senior Muslim leaders, and helps to explain the breadth of electoral support for Putin in the region.

In contrast to some Russian politicians who point to the "threat from the South," Russian presidents have consistently emphasized Russia's multicultural nature, perhaps never more eloquently or succinctly than president Medvedev did during his state visit to Egypt in 2009, when he said: "We do not need to reaffirm our friendship with the Muslim world because Russia is an indispensable part of it."[77]

Will such a strategy suffice to gain the allegiance of all of Russia's Muslims? Probably not. As long as the religious conflict between traditional Sufi–Sunni and radical Salafist Muslims continues to rage, there will be individuals willing to sacrifice their life for it. But even Russia's critics acknowledge that the current strategy has succeeded in marginalizing the most violent, by making the main Salafist premise—that violence was needed to preserve Islamic traditions—"irrelevant."[78]

Another criticism is that, while it is well and good for Russia to say that it will harness religious passion for the common good, rather than fight it by promoting religious apathy, many would say that this is simply not possible. On this point the position of Russia's two major faiths is very much at odds with that of the Western mainstream, so much so that it poses a fundamental challenge to the secular definition of modernity.

It is worth recalling that in 2011 French president Nicolas Sarkozy, German Chancellor Angela Merkel, and British Prime Minister David Cameron all nearly simultaneously repudiated multiculturalism, which had already become little more than cultural pluralism shorn of its religious identity.[79] This suggests that many in the West remain fundamentally committed to a society in which, as Yale law professor Stephen L. Carter put it, religion is "something without political significance, less an independent moral force than a quietly irrelevant moralizer, never heard, rarely seen."[80] What the West in its wisdom wishes to affirm, traditional religions in Russia very much wish to avoid.

Religious radicals see this as proof that the Western path to modernization leads inevitably to a loss of faith and rampant immorality. But if religious communities could be empowered and allowed to participate in the modern world in ways that allowed them to honor their traditional beliefs, it might defuse one of the major sources of hostility that modernization engenders in traditional societies. Allowing modernity to reach an accommodation with religion that does not explicitly reject religion, or hollow it out by privatizing it, would surely make it a much more attractive for a large portion of mankind.

At the same time that Western European leaders were repudiating multiculturalism, president Medvedev went out of his way to reaffirm Russia's commitment to both multiculturalism and modernization.[81] Only time will tell if Russia will be successful in forging a social compact that combines both religion and modernity, but there is a lot riding on the outcome. If a modern Russia does emerge, it will be because its Muslim and Christian communities find a balance that allows for a modern, civic, *and* religious society to emerge. Such a society might indeed provide an attractive alternative model for countries currently seeking to make the transition to modernity.

(Note: See the Appendix for an analysis of Russian Orthodox issues in connection with Patrick Armstrong's discussion of memes—RBW.)

Notes

1 "Pravoslavie na Kavkaze—vzglyad palomnika," *Khram sv. Nikolaya v Starom Vagankove*, May 7, 2010, www.s-nikola.ru/photos/108-photo.html, www.s-nikola.ru/photos/108-photo.html. A. N. Beldy, "O musulmanstve na Severnom Kavkaze," December 12, 2011, http://pravoslavrazgovor.mirtesen. ru/blog/43139873501/A.-N.-Beldyi-%22O-musulmanstve-na-Severnom-Kav kaze%C2%BB. For more on early Christian lore see: "Istoriya khristianstva na Servernom Kavkaze," 2004 at www.kmvline.ru/article/a_24.php; Gedeon, Metropolitan of Stavropol and Baku, *Istoriya Khristianstva na Severnom Kavkae do i posle prisoedineniya ego k Rossii*, www.um-islam.nm.ru/2gedeon. htm; and I. L. Babich and L. T. Solovyeva, *Khristianstvo na Severnom Kavkaze: istoriya i sovremennost* (Moscow: Institute of Ethnology and Anthropology, Russian Academy of Science, 2011). On the history of the diocese of Baku, which traces its origins back to the apostles, see Hieromonk Alexei (Nikonorov), *Istoriya Khristianstva v Kavkazkoi Albanii* (Sergiev Posad: Cathedra of Ancient

Church History, Moscow Spiritual Academy, 2004), http://baku.eparhia.ru/history/albania/

2 Vitaly Ulanov, "Severnyi Kavkaz v prostranstve russkogo diskursa," *Evrazia. org*, September 4, 2011, www.evrazia.org/print.php?id=1773

3 "Severo-Kavkazskii federalnyi okrug," *Wikipedia.Ru*, February 2, 2012, http://ru.wikipedia.org/wiki/СКФО

4 "Spisok rossiiskikh regionov po VRP," *Wikipedia.Ru*, May 25, 2012, http://ru.wikipedia.org/wiki/ВРП_регионов _России

5 Alexei Malashenko, "Islam in Russia," *Social Research*, March 22, 2009, www.thefreelibrary.com/Islam+in+Russia.-a0203482047. The other half are the Tatar and Bashkir, who live along the Volga in Central Russia.

6 Nina Sumbatova, "Dagestanskie dialekty," *Polit.Ru*, April 10, 2012, http://polit.ru/article/2012/04/10/sumbatova/

7 "Kakie narody zhivut na Severnom Kavkaze," *Pravmir.Ru*, March 17, 2011, www.pravmir.ru/kakie-narody-zhivut-na-severnom-kavkaze/

8 "Kavkazkaya voina," *Wikipedia.Ru*, March 16, 2012, http://ru.wikipedia.org/wiki/Кавказкая_война

9 Moshe Gammer, *Muslim Resistance to the Tsar: Shamil and the Conquest of Chechnia and Daghestan* (Abingdon, UK: Frank Cass and Company, 1994).

10 Ibid.

11 Ulanov, "Severnyi Kavkaz."

12 John Frederick Baddeley, *The Russian Conquest of the Caucasus* (London: Curzon Press, 1999).

13 "Kavkazkaya voina," *Wikipedia.Ru*, March 16, 2012, http://ru.wikipedia.org/wiki/Кавказкая_война

14 From Ermolaev's report to Tsar Alexander I, February 12, 1819. "Kavkazkaya voina," *Wikipedia.Ru*, March 16, 2012, http://ru.wikipedia.org/wiki/Кавказкая_война

15 "Kavkazkaya voina," *Wikipedia.Ru*, citing Rossiya I SSR v voinakh XX veka, Moscow, 2001, 568. For other assessments, see B. V. Sokolov, "Kavkazkaya voina," http://bibliotekar.ru/encW/100/69.htm and B. Ts. Urlanis, *Istoriya voennykh poter* 1800–1864, 131, www.noisette-software.com/priblizitelnye-poteri-russkoj-armii-v-vojnax-19-veka-tys-chelovek/

16 Gammer, Muslim Resistance to the Tsar.

17 Even in Soviet times Chechnya was thought of a "bastion" of traditional Islam. Valery Tishkov, "Religioznyi factor," in Valery Tishkov ed., *Puti mira na Severnom Kavkaze* (Moscow: Nezavisimyi ekspertnyi doklad, 1999), www.valerytishkov.ru/cntnt/publikacii3/kollektivn/putI_mira_/religiozny.html?forprint=1

18 Marina Daniliuk, "Rol Russkoi Pravoslavnoi Tserkvi v politike Rossii v Dagestane vo vtoroi polovine XVIII-nachale XX veka," dissertation for the degree of candidate of historical sciences (Makhachkala 2008), www.dissercat.com/content/rol-russkoi-pravoslavnoi-tserkvi-v-politike-rossii-v-dagestane-vo-vtoroi-polovine-xviii-nach

19 S. A. Razdolsky, "Monastyri Kavkazkoi eparhii I ikh rol v kulturnom rasvitii Severnogo Kavkaza," *Yuzhnorossiiskoe obozrenie* TsRIiP IPPK RGU I ISPI RAN, 33 (2006), http://apsnyteka.narod2.ru/r/monastirI_kavkazskoI_eparhiI_I_ih_rol_v_kulturnom_razvitiI_severnogo_kavkaza/index.html

20 "Monastyri Kavkazkoi eparkhii," *Yuzhnorossiiskoe obozrenie,* http://
    apsnyteka.narod2.ru/r/monastirI_kavkazskoI_eparhiI_I_ih_rol_v_kulturnom_
    razvitiI_severnogo_kavkaza/index.html
21 Daniliuk, "Rol Russkoi Pravoslavnoi Tserkvi."
22 Pyotr V. Znamenski, "Vosstanovlenie pravoslaviya na Kavkaze," *Istoriya Russkoi
    Tserkvi,* http://lib.eparhia-saratov.ru/books/08z/znamenskii/history4/251.html
23 S. A. Razdolsky, "Monastyri Kavkazkoi eparkhii I ikh rol v kulturnom
    rasvitii Severnogo Kavkaza," *Yuzhnorossiiskoe obozrenie* TsRIiP IPPK RGU
    I ISPI RAN, 33 (2006), http://apsnyteka.narod2.ru/r/monastirI_kavkazskoI_
    eparhiI_I_ih_rol_v_kulturnom_razvitiI_severnogo_kavkaza/index.html
24 Valentina Laza, "Opyt missionerskoi deyatelnosti Russkoi Pravoslavnoi
    Tserkvi na Kavkazskikh Minerralnykh Vodakh v kontse XIX-nachale XX vv.,"
    Pravoslavie.Ru, September 1, 2005, www.pravoslavie.ru/put/5294.htm
25 Murat80, "Islam v Dagestane," *Kavkazweb.Net,* August 3, 2007, http://
    kavkazweb.net/forum/lofiversion/index.php/t38902–200.html
26 Ibid.
27 Malashenko, "Islam in Russia."
28 Tishkov, "Religioznyi factor."
29 "Prezident Minnikhanov obyavil Tatarstan musulmanskoi respublikoi,"
    Regnum.ru, May 7, 2012, www.regnum.ru/news/polit/1526591.html
30 "Akhmed-hadji Abdulaev," *VsePortrety.Ru,* www.vseportrety.ru/info-abdulaev.
    html, n.d.
31 Gadzhimurad Murtazaliev, "Silovye metody polzy ne prinesut," *Chernovik.net,*
    October 5, 2011, http://chernovik.net/print.php?new=3435
32 "Akhmed-hadji Abdulaev," *VsePortrety.Ru.*
33 "V islamskikh vuzakh dolzhny izuchatsya I osnovy drugikh religii,"
    Informatsionno-prosvetitelskii portal YuGRY Khanty-Mansiisk, October 14,
    2009, www.eduhmao.ru/news/15/11477/
34 Marko Shakhbanov, "Zapozdalaya reaktsiya," *Chernovik.net,* February 11
    2005, http://old.chernovik.net/news/78/REPUBLIC/2005/02/11/870; "V
    Dagestane voiny ne mozhet byt'," *Chernovik.net,* December 3, 2010, http://
    old.chernovik.net/news/418/Others_SMI/2010/12/03/11333
35 "Dagestanu, kak vozdukh, neobkhodim dialog mezhdu islamskimi
    dzhamaatami," *Kavkaz.Ge,* April 10, 2012, http://kavkaz.ge/2012/04/10/da
    gestanu-kak-vozdux-neobxodim-dialog-mezhdu-islamskimi-dzhamaatami/
    print/; Abdulla Alisultanov, "Kebedov: vzryzy v Makhachkale," *Kavkaz-uzel.
    Ru,* May 4, 2012, http://ingushetia.kavkaz-uzel.ru/articles/206072/; VK,
    "Natsionalizm—problema obshcherossiiskaya," *VestiKavkaza.Ru,* April 13,
    2012, http://vestikavkaza.ru/articles/obshestvo/meznaz/55979.html"Vstrecha
    Assotsiatsii uchyonykh Akhlyu Sunna I DUMD," *Ucoz.com,* May 3, 2012,
    http://gimry.ucoz.com/news/vstrecha_associaciI_uchjonykh_akhlju_sunna_v_
    dagestane_I_dumd/2012–05–03–36. Many see the subsequent bomb attacks of
    May third as an effort to torpedo this dialogue.
36 Yana Amelina, "'Vahhabitam ne zhit na etoi zemle'," *RosBalt.Ru,* February 27,
    2007, www.rosbalt.ru/main/2007/02/27/287704.html
37 The amount of 2–4 billion rubles a year just to the DUM of Chechnya. "V
    Kiev pribyl mufti Chechnii—podpisyvat' dogovor o sotrudnichestve," *IA
    Novyi Region,* April 11, 2012, http://stmvl.livejournal.com/374583.html

38 "Sultan Mirzayev: mezhkonfessionalmyi dialog—zalog krepkogo gosudarstva," *Kavkazkaya politika*, February 22, 2012, http://kavpolit.com/sul tan-mirzaev-mezhkonfessionalnyj-dialog-zalog-krepkogo-gosudarstva/

39 "Sultan Mirzayev," *Kavkazkaya politika*.

40 Amelina, "'Vahhabitam ne zhit na etoi zemle'."

41 N. A. Neflyasheva, "Dukhovnye avtoritety Severnogo Kavkaza," *Idmenia.Ru*, n.d., www.idmedina.ru/books/materials/rmforum/3/teo_neflasheva.htm

42 "V Makhachkale sostoyalsya I Kongress religioznykh liderov Severnogo Kavkaza," *Ministry for National Policy, Religious Affairs and External Ties of the Republic of Dagestan*, June 28, 2011, www.minnaz.ru/news_open.php?id=511

43 "Russkaya pravoslavnaya tserkov," *Wikipedia.Ru*, May 25, 2012, http://ru.wikipedia.org/wiki/Русская_православная_церковь

44 Alex Anishyuk, "Russian Orthodox Church allowed to enter politics," *Reuters*, February 3, 2011, cited in Johnson's Russia List #2011-#20. www.cdi.org/russia/johnson/

45 Vladimir Putin, "President Putin's Speech at The Meeting With Participants of The Bishops' Council of The Russian Orthodox Church," *Kremlin.Ru*, October 6, 2004, cited in Johnson's Russia List #8398, www.cdi.org/russia/johnson

46 "Poll Shows Russians Trust Putin More Than Church," *ITAR-Tass*, January 13, 2004, cited in Johnson's Russia List #8012; "Russians Trust President and Church Most," *Rosbalt*, March 25, 2004, cited in Johnson's Russia List #8136, www.cdi.org/russia/johnson/; "Most Russians trust Church and the Patriarch—poll," *Interfax-Religion*, May 10, 2012, www.interfax-religion.com/?act=news&div=9342

47 He led the Orthodox delegation to the VIIth round of the Islam-Orthodox Dialogue with Muslim theologians in Iran, which began in 1995 at the initiative of the former Archbishop of Smolensk (now Patriarch) Kirill. "Intervyu zamestitelya predsedatelya Otdela vneshnikh tserkovnykh svyazei Roadiostantsii 'Radonezh' o dialoge 'Islam-Pravoslavie,'" *Patriarchia.Ru*, October 6, 2010, www.patriarchia.ru/db/print/1292096.html

48 Neflyasheva, "Dukhovnye avtoritety."

49 Ibid.

50 "Intervyu arkhiepiskpoa Vladikavkazkogo n Makhachkalinskogo Zosimy portalu 'Interfax-Religiya,'" *Patriarchia.Ru*, October 25, 2011, www.patriarchia.ru/db/print/1655714.html

51 "Pravoslavnye i musulmane na Severnom Kavkaze obedinyayut usiliya," *Agenstvo natsionalnykh novostei*, September 16, 2008, www.annews.ru/news/detail.php?ID=167486 www.annews.ru/news/detail.php?ID=167486

52 "Episkop Venskii Ilarion: 'Po mnogim ustanovkam islam gorazdo blizeh k khristianstvu, chem. sovremennaya zapadnaya ideologiya," *Strana.ru*, April 6, 2005, www.strana.ru/text/stories/01/12/04/2157/244758.html

53 "Otvet Predstoyatelya Russkoi Pravoslavnoi Tserkvi na otkrytoe pismo 138 musulman skikh bogoslovov," *Patriarchia.Ru*, April 14, 2008, www.patriarchia.ru/db/print/391673.html

54 "Sostoyalas vstrecha Svyateishego Patriarkha Kirilla s predsedatelem Upravleniya musulman Kavkaza," *Patriarchia.Ru*, November 21, 2011, www.patriarchia.ru/db/print/1750274.html

55 "'Aktualnost pravoslavno-islamskogo dialoga v sovremennom mire.'
   Vystuplenie predsedatelya OVTsS mitropolita Volokolamskogo Ilariona v
   Rossiiskom islamskom institute," *Patriarchia.Ru*, November 5, 2011, www.
   patriarchia.ru/db/print/1666727.html. One of his favorite phrases is by Swiss
   Archbishop Kurt Koch: "we should fear not a strong Islam, but a weak
   Christianity." "Episkop-strannik. Intervyu vladyki Ilariona (Alfeeva) zhurnalu
   'Foma,'" *Patriarchia.Ru*, March 5, 2007, www.patriarchia.ru/db/print/208655.
   html
56 "Slovo Svyateishego Patriarkha Kirilla n vstreche s glavami diplomaticheskikh
   missii arabskikh gosudarstv v Rossiiskoi Federatsii," *Patriarchia.Ru*, September 4,
   2009, www.patriarchia.ru/db/print/733551.html
57 Ibid.
58 Hegumen Philip (Ryabykh), "'Dialog v khristiansko-evreiskhikh otnosheniyah
   v sovremennoi Rossii i v mire'," *Patriarchia.Ru*, September 28, 2010, www.
   patriarchia.ru/db/print/1285461.html
59 Ibid.
60 Ibid.
61 Ibid.
62 "Stenogramma vstrechi predsedatelya pravitelstva RF V. V. Putina so
   svyateishim Patriarkhom Kirillom i liderami traditsionnkykh religioznykh
   obshchin Rossii," *Patriarchia.Ru*, February 8, 2012, www.patriarchia.ru/db/
   print/2005767.html
63 Tishkov, "Religioznyi factor."
64 Paul Goble; Shireen Hunter, "Russia's Muslims," A briefing for the
   Commission on Security & Cooperation in Europe: *U.S. Helsinki Commission*,
   December 17, 2009, http://csce.gov/index.cfm?FuseAction=ContentRecords.
   ViewTranscript&ContentRecord_id=465&ContentType=H,B&ContentRecord
   Type=B&CFID=25941239&CFTOKEN=36947033
65 "Sultan Mirzayev," *Kavkazkaya politika*; Neflyasheva, "Dukhovnye avtoritety."
66 "Russian Defense Minister Ivanov on Results of Past Year, Plans for 2007,"
   Izvestia, January 1, 2007, cited in Johnson's Russia List #2007-#1. Available at
   www.cdi.org/russia/johnson/. Accessed January 4, 2007.
67 Sultan Mirzayev, "Zadachi ukrepleniya svyazei Rossii s musulmanskim
   mirom," *PolitObraz.Ru*, January 30, 2011, www.lawinrussia.ru/node/28309
68 Goble; Hunter, "Russia's Muslims."
69 Malashenko, "Islam in Russia."
70 Goble; Hunter, "Russia's Muslims."
71 Malashenko, "Islam in Russia."
72 Goble; Hunter, "Russia's Muslims."
73 At a recent conference the deputy director of the sociological Institute of the
   Institute for History, Archeology and Ethnography of Dagestan Scientific
   center of the Russian Academy of Sciences, Zaid Abdulagatov, made this
   complaint, adding that "we do not even know the answers to basic questions."
   Artur Mamaev, "NeobDUMannye vykhodki," *Chernovik.net*, July 24, 201[1],
   http://chernovik.net/print.php?new=9084
74 Mamaev, "NeobDUMannye vykhodki."
75 Interestingly enough, Gainutdin was paraphrasing Putin's remarks at the
   millennium of the founding of the city of Kazan. Dilyara Akhmetova,

"Problemy Rossii i Blagorodnoe sobranie," *Idmedina.Ru*, n.d., www.idmedina. ru/books/history_culture/minaret/21/trables.htm
76 "Majority of Chechens Against Separatism—Poll," *Interfax*, February 2, 2006, cited in Johnson's Russia List #2006-#33, available at www.cdi.org/ russia/johnson/. Accessed January 4, 2007; Fred Weir, "Hopes for Stability in Chechnya Vote," *Christian Science Monitor*, November 25, 2005, available at www.csmonitor.com/2005/1125/p07s02-woeu.htm. Accessed November 27, 2006; and Robert Bruce Ware and Enver Kisriev, *Dagestan: Russian Hegemony and Islamic Resistance in the North Caucasus* (New York: M.E. Sharpe, 2010).
77 Mirzayev, "Zadachi ukrepleniya."
78 Mairbek Vatchagaev, "Chechnya is becoming an Islamic republic under Moscow's watch," *Jamestown Foundation Eurasia Daily Monitor*, May 10, 2012, cited in Johnson's Russia List #2012-#86. http//www.cdi.org/russia/ johnson/
79 "Nicolas Sarkozy joins David Cameron and Angela Merkel view that multiculturalism has failed," *Daily Mail*, February 11, 2011, www.dailymail. co.uk/news/article-1355961/Nicolas-Sarkozy-joins-David-Cameron-Angela-Me rkel-view-multiculturalism-failed.html#ixzz1vtyOEMPX
80 Steven L. Carter, *The Culture of Disbelief* (New York: Anchor Books, 1994), cited at: www.enotes.com/culture-disbelief-salem/culture-disbelief
81 Dmitry Medvedev, "V Ufe Dmitry Medvedev vstretilsya s rukovoditelyami natsionalno-kulturnykh ob'edineii Bashkirii," *Kremlin.Ru*, February 11, 2011, available at http://kremlin.ru/transcripts/10310. Accessed February 11, 2011.

Bibliography

"'Aktualnost pravoslavno-islamskogo dialoga v sovremennom mire.' Vystuplenie predsedatelya OVTsS mitropolita Volokolamskogo Ilariona v Rossiiskom islamskom institute," *Patriarchia.Ru*, November 5, 2011. www.patriarchia.ru/ db/print/1666727.html
"Akhmed-hadji Abdulaev," *VsePortrety.Ru*. www.vseportrety.ru/info-abdulaev. html. n.d.
Akhmetiva, Dilyara, "Problemy Rossii I Blagorodne sobranie," *Idmedina.Ru*, n.d. www.idmedina.ru/books/history_culture/minaret/21/trables.htm
Alisultanov, Abdulla, "Kebedov: vzryzy v Makhachkale," *Kavkaz-uzel.Ru*, May 4, 2012. http://ingushetia.kavkaz-uzel.ru/articles/206072/
Amelina, Yana, "'Vahhabitam ne zhit na etoi zemle'," *RosBalt.Ru*, February 27, 2007. www.rosbalt.ru/main/2007/02/27/287704.html
Anishyuk, Alex, "Russian Orthodox Church allowed to enter politics," *Reuters*, February 3, 2011. Cited in Johnson's Russia List #2011-#20. http//www.cdi. org/russia/johnson/
Babich, I. L. and L. T. Solovyeva, *Khristianstvo na Severnom Kavkaze: istoriya i sovremennost*. Moscow: Institute of Ethnology and Anthropology, Russian Academy of Science, 2011.
Baddeley, John Frederick, *The Russian Conquest of the Caucasus*. London: Curzon Press, 1999.

Beldy, A. N., "O musulmanstve na Severnom Kavkaze," December 12, 2011. http://pravoslavrazgovor.mirtesen.ru/blog/43139873501/A.-N.-Beldyi-%22O-musulmanstve-na-Severnom-Kavkaze%C2%BB. Available on the "Orthodox Dialogue" social network at http://pravoslavrazgovor.mirtesen.ru/. For more on early Christian lore see: "Istoriya khristianstva na Servernom Kavkaze" 2004, www.kmvline.ru/article/a_24.php

Carter, Steven L., *The Culture of Disbelief*. New York: Anchor Books, 1994. Cited in www.enotes.com/culture-disbelief-salem/culture-disbelief

"Dagestanu, kak vozdukh, neobkhodim dialog mezhdu islamskimi dzhamaatami," *Kavkaz.Ge*, April 10, 2012. http://kavkaz.ge/2012/04/10/dagestanu-kak-vozdux-neobxodim-dialog-mezhdu-islamskimi-dzhamaatami/print/

Daniliuk, Marina, "Rol Russkoi Pravoslavnoi Tserkvi v politike Rossii v Dagestane vo vtoroi polovine XVIII-nachale XX veka," dissertation for the degree of candidate of historical sciences (Makhachkala 2008). www.dissercat.com/content/rol-russkoi-pravoslavnoi-tserkvi-v-politike-rossii-v-dagestane-vo-vtoroi-polovine-xviii-nach

"Episkop-strannik. Intervyu vladyki Ilariona (Alfeeva) zhurnalu 'Foma,'" *Patriarchia.Ru*, March 5, 2007. www.patriarchia.ru/db/print/208655.html

"Episkop Venskii Ilarion: 'Po mnogim ustanovkam islam gorazdo blizeh k khristianstvu, chem. sovremennaya zapadnaya ideologiya," *Strana.ru*, April 6, 2005. www.strana.ru/text/stories/01/12/04/2157/244758.html

Gammer, Moshe, *Muslim Resistance to the Tsar: Shamil and the Conquest of Chechnia and Daghestan*. Abingdon, UK: Frank Cass and Company, 1994.

Gedeon, Metropolitan of Stavropol and Baku, *Istoriya Khristianstva na Severnom Kavkae do I posle prisoedineniya ego k Rossii*. www.um-islam.nm.ru/2gedeon.htm, n.d.

Goble, Paul and Shireen Hunter, "Russia's Muslims," A briefing for the Commission on Security & Cooperation in Europe: U.S. Helsinki Commission, December 17, 2009. http://csce.gov/index.cfm?FuseAction=ContentRecords.ViewTranscript&ContentRecord_id=465&ContentType=H,B&ContentRecordType=B&CFID=25941239&CFTOKEN=36947033

Hegumen Philip (Ryabykh), "'Dialog v khristiansko-evreiskikh otnosheniyah v sovremennoi Rossii i v mire'," *Patriarchia.Ru*, September 28, 2010. www.patriarchia.ru/db/print/1285461.html

Hieromonk Alexei (Nikonorov), *Istoriya Khristianstva v Kavkazkoi Albanii*, Sergiev Posad: Cathedra of Ancient Church History, Moscow Spiritual Academy, 2004. http://baku.eparhia.ru/history/albania/

"Intervyu arkhiepiskpoa Vladikavkazkogo n Makhachkalinskogo Zosimy portalu 'Interfax-Religiya,'" *Patriarchia.Ru*, October 25, 2011. www.patriarchia.ru/db/print/1655714.html

"Intervyu zamestitelya predsedatelya Otdela vneshnikh tserkovnykh svyazei Roadiostantsii 'Radonezh' o dialoge 'Islam-Pravoslavie,'" *Patriarchia.Ru*, October 6, 2010. www.patriarchia.ru/db/print/1292096.html

"Kakie narody zhivut na Severnom Kavkaze," *Pravmir.Ru*, March 17, 2011. www.pravmir.ru/kakie-narody-zhivut-na-severnom-kavkaze/

"Kavkazkaya voina," *Wikipedia.Ru*, March 16, 2012. http://ru.wikipedia.org/wiki/Кавказкая_война

Laza, Valentina, "Opyt missionerskoi deyatelnosti Russkoi Pravoslavnoi Tserkvi na Kavkazskikh Minerralnykh Vodakh v kontse XIX-nachale XX vv.," *Pravoslavie.Ru*, September 1, 2005. www.pravoslavie.ru/put/5294.htm

"Majority of Chechens Against Separatism—Poll," *Interfax*, February 2, 2006. Cited in Johnson's Russia List #2006-#33. Available at www.cdi.org/russia/johnson/ (accessed January 4, 2007).

Malashenko, Alexei, "Islam in Russia," *Social Research*, March 22, 2009. www.thefreelibrary.com/Islam+in+Russia.-a0203482047

Mamaev, Artur, "NeobDUMannye vykhodki," *Chernovik.net*, July 24, 201[1]. http://chernovik.net/print.php?new=9084

Medvedev, Dmitry, "V Ufe Dmitry Medvedev vstretilsya s rukovoditelyami natsionalno-kulturnykh ob'edineii Bashkirii," *Kremlin.Ru*, February 11, 2011. Available at http://kremlin.ru/transcripts/10310 (accessed February 11, 2011).

Mirzayev, Sultan, "Zadachi ukrepleniya svyazei Rossii s musulmanskim mirom," *PolitObraz.Ru*, January 30, 2011. www.lawinrussia.ru/node/28309

"Most Russians trust Church and the Patriarch—poll," *Interfax-Religion*, May 10, 2012. www.interfax-religion.com/?act=news&div=9342

Murat80, "Islam v Dagestane," *Kavkazweb.Net*, August 3, 2007. http://kavkazweb.net/forum/lofiversion/index.php/t38902–200.html

Murtazaliev, Gadzhimurad, "Silovye metody polzy ne prinesut," *Chernovik.net*, October 5, 2011. http://chernovik.net/print.php?new=3435

"Natsionalizm—problema obshcherossiiskaya," *VestiKavkaza.Ru*, April 13, 2012. http://vestikavkaza.ru/articles/obshestvo/meznaz/55979.html

Neflyasheva, N. A., "Dukhovnye avtoritety Severnogo Kavkaza," *Idmenia.Ru*, n.d. www.idmedina.ru/books/materials/rmforum/3/teo_neflasheva.htm

"Nicolas Sarkozy joins David Cameron and Angela Merkel view that multiculturalism has failed," *Daily Mail*, February 11, 2011. www.dailymail.co.uk/news/article-1355961/Nicolas-Sarkozy-joins-David-Cameron-Angela-Merkel-view-multiculturalism-failed.html#ixzz1vtyOEMPX

"Otvet Predstoyatelya Russkoi Pravoslavnoi Tserkvi na otkrytoe pismo 138 musulman skikh bogoslovov," *Patriarchia.Ru*, April 14, 2008. www.patriarchia.ru/db/print/391673.html

"Poll Shows Russians Trust Putin More than Church," *ITAR-Tass*, January 13, 2004, cited in Johnson's Russia List #8012. www.cdi.org/russia/johnson/

"Pravoslavie na Kavkaze—vzglyad palomnika," *Khram sv. Nikolaya v Starom Vagankove*, May 7, 2010. www.s-nikola.ru/photos/108-photo.html

"Pravoslavnye i musulmane na Severnom Kavkaze obedinyayut usiliya," *Agenstvo natsionalnykh novostei*, September 16, 2008. www.annews.ru/news/detail.php?ID=167486 www.annews.ru/news/detail.php?ID=167486

"Prezident Minnikhanov obyavil Tatarstan musulmanskoi respublikoi," *Regnum.ru*, May 7, 2012. www.regnum.ru/news/polit/1526591.html

Putin, Vladimir, "President Putin's Speech at The Meeting With Participants of The Bishops' Council of The Russian Orthodox Church," *Kremlin.Ru*, October 6, 2004, cited in Johnson's Russia List #8398. www.cdi.org/russia/johnson

Razdolsky, S. A., "Monastyri Kavkazkoi eparkhii I ikh rol v kulturnom rasvitii Severnogo Kavkaza," *Yuzhnorossiiskoe obozrenie* TsRIiP IPPK RGU I

ISPI RAN, 33 (2006). http://apsnyteka.narod2.ru/r/monastirI_kavkazskoI_eparhiI_I_ih_rol_v_kulturnom_razvitiI_severnogo_kavkaza/index.html

"Russian Defense Minister Ivanov on Results of Past Year, Plans for 2007," *Izvestia*, January 1, 2007, cited in Johnson's Russia List #2007-#1. Available at www.cdi.org/russia/johnson/ (accessed January 4, 2007).

"Russians Trust President and Church Most," *Rosbalt*, March 25, 2004, cited in Johnson's Russia List #8136. www.cdi.org/russia/johnson/

"Russkaya pravoslavnaya tserkov," *Wikipedia.Ru*, May 25, 2012. http://ru.wikipedia.org/wiki/Русская_православная_церковь

"Severo-Kavkazskii federalnyi okrug," *Wikipedia.Ru*, February 2, 2012. http://ru.wikipedia.org/wiki/СКФО

Shakhbanov, Marko, "Zapozdalaya reaktsiya," *Chernovik.net*, February 11 200[8]. http://chernovik.net/print.php?new=870

"Shamil," *Wikipedia.Ru*, May 25, 2012. http://ru.wikipedia.org/wiki/Шфмиль

"Sheikh Mansur," *Wikipedia.Ru*, May 25, 2012. http://ru.wikipedia.org/wiki/Шейх_Мансур

"Slovo Svyateishego Patriarkha Kirilla n vstreche s glavami diplomaticheskikh missii arabskikh gosudarstv v Rossiiskoi Federatsii," *Patriarchia.Ru*, September 4, 2009. www.patriarchia.ru/db/print/733551.html

Sokolov, B. V., "Kavkazkaya voina," http://bibliotekar.ru/encW/100/69.htm

"Sostoyalas vstrecha Svyateishego Patriarkha Kirilla s predsedatelem Upravleniya musulman Kavkaza," *Patriarchia.Ru*, November 21, 2011. www.patriarchia.ru/db/print/1750274.html

"Spisok rossiiskikh regionov po VRP," *Wikipedia.Ru*, May 25, 2012. http://ru.wikipedia.org/wiki/ВРП_регионов _России

"Stenogramma vstrechi predsedatelya pravitelstva RF V. V. Putina so svyateishim Patriarkhom Kirillom i liderami traditsionnkykh religioznykh obshchin Rossii," *Patriarchia.Ru*, February 8, 2012. www.patriarchia.ru/db/print/2005767.html

"Sultan Mirzayev: mezhkonfessionalmyi dialog—zalog krepkogo gosudarstva," *Kavkazkaya politika*, February 22, 2012. http://kavpolit.com/sultan-mirzaev-mezhkonfessionalnyj-dialog-zalog-krepkogo-gosudarstva/

— "Zadachi ukrepleniya svyazei Rossii s musulmanskim mirom," *PolitObraz.Ru*, January 30, 2011. www.lawinrussia.ru/node/28309

Sumbatova, Nina, "Dagestanskie dialekty," *Polit.Ru*, April 10, 2012. http://polit.ru/article/2012/04/10/sumbatova/

Tishkov, Valery, "Religioznyi factor," in Valery Tishkov ed., *Puti mira na Severnom Kavkaze* Moscow: Nezavisimyi ekspertnyi doklad, 1999. www.valerytishkov.ru/cntnt/publikacii3/kollektivn/putI_mira_/religiozny.html?forprint=1

Ulanov, Vitaly, "Severnyi Kavkaz v prostranstve russkogo diskursa," September 4, 2011. www.evrazia.org/print.php?id=1773. Published by the analytical and information web site "Evrazia."

Urlanis, B. Ts. *Istoriya voennykh poter* 1800–1864, 131. www.noisette-software.com/priblizitelnye-poteri-russkoj-armii-v-vojnax-19-veka-tys-chelovek/. This excerpt of Urlanis' classic is reposted on a site devoted to home assigments (www.noisette-software.com) but can be downloaded in its entirety from http://fanknig.ru/xictori/dokumentalnaja/12917-skachat-besplatno-knigu.-urlanis-b.-c.-istorija.html

Vatchagaev, Mairbek, "Chechnya is becoming an Islamic republic under Moscow's watch," *Jamestown Foundation Eurasia Daily Monitor,* May 10, 2012, cited in Johnson's Russia List #2012-#86. http//www.cdi.org/russia/johnson/

"V Dagestane voiny ne mozhet byt'," *Chernovik.net,* December 3, 200[7]. http://chernovik.net/print.php?new=11333

"V islamskikh vuzakh dolzhny izuchatsya I osnovy drugikh religii," Informatsionno-prosvetitelskii portal YuGRY Khanty-Mansiisk, October 14, 2009. www.eduhmao.ru/news/15/11477/

"V Kiev pribyl mufti Chechnii—podpisyvat' dogovor o sotrudnichestve," *IA Novyi Region,* April 11, 2012. http://stmvl.livejournal.com/374583.html

"V Makhachkale sostoyalsya I Kongress religioznykh liderov Severnogo Kavkaza," Ministry for National Policy, Religious Affairs and External Ties of the Republic of Dagestan, June 28, 2011. www.minnaz.ru/news_open.php?id=511

"Vstrecha Assotsiatsii uchyonykh Akhlyu Sunna I DUMD," Ucoz.com, May 3, 2012. http://gimry.ucoz.com/news/vstrecha_associaciI_uchjonykh_akhlju_sunna_v_dagestane_I_dumd/2012-05-03-36

Ware, Robert Bruce and Kisriev, Enver, *Dagestan: Russian Hegemony and Islamic Resistance in the North Caucasus.* New York: M.E. Sharpe, 2010.

Weir, Fred, "Hopes for Stability in Chechnya Vote," *Christian Science Monitor,* November 25, 2005. Available at www.csmonitor.com/2005/1125/p07s02-woeu.htm (accessed November 27, 2006).

Znamenski, Pyotr V., "Vosstanovlenie pravoslaviya na Kavkaze," in *Istoriya Russkoi Tserkvi.* http://lib.eparhia-saratov.ru/books/08z/znamenskii/history4/251.html. This text is available on the library web site of the bishopric of Saratov, and is taken from a reprint, published in 2000, of the original. No pages are indicated.

CHAPTER NINE

The Northeastern Caucasus: Drifting Away from Russia

Anna Matveeva

This chapter questions the extent to which the Muslim-majority republics of Ingushetia, Chechnya and Dagestan are still parts of "Russia." Do these areas share a common Russian political, cultural, and social space, or do we witness an emergence of a new "Inner Abroad," that is, unintegrated territories which are "Russia" in form but not in daily practice. It outlines several factors that are contributing to the ongoing transformation of this region: changing social environment due to the growing influence of religious conservatism, spread of Islamist ideology among young people, near-absence of ethnic Russian population and emergence of a "North-Caucasian" identity as an opposition to an "all-Russian" identity. Moscow does not have a policy to address this precarious trend – a trend with increasing national consequence as Russians question whether diversity is tolerable up to the emergence of Islamic quasi-states within Russia's borders.

Introduction

Three autonomous republics of the North Caucasus—Ingushetia, Chechnya, and Dagestan,—have different political histories. Chechnya survived two devastating wars, Ingushetia—an ethnic conflict with North Ossetia, its neighbor, and Dagestan has been suffering from criminal violence. Together they have been emerging as Russia's "Inner Abroad," a distinct entity where social processes are radically different from those in the mainstream Russian Federation,[1] as the autonomous republics drift further away from Russian cultural and social space. Others, such as Kabardino-Balkaria and North Ossetia, are also affected by the trend, but on a much reduced scale. These distinctions matter, especially when people migrate northward and enter into direct contact—and often confrontation—with the mainstream Russian population.

This chapter begins with a look at how social and cultural milieu has changed with increased religiosity and the exodus of ethnic Russians. It goes on to consider why young people are attracted into Islamist movements, and the dialectic tension between North-Caucasian and all-Russian identities. In its final part the chapter focuses on the federal responses in policy and practice.

The chapter draws upon field work conducted by the author in Ingushetia in December 2011 and material of the Saferworld project, for which she has authored the research report "The North Caucasus: Views from Within."[2] The study included qualitative methods of social research to allow accumulation of grassroot voices.[3] The research design centered around: (1) sources of social tensions and challenges facing society, including the roles of ethnicity, religion, and age; (2) migration and the relationship between communities and political institutions; and (3) republican and federal responses to these challenges. Data collection included key informant interviews, focus groups with pre-defined population categories in each republic, engaged field observation and study of official documents.

Target populations for the focus groups were selected using the criteria of age, gender, employment, ethnic origin, and regional location. Younger participants were identified as students of elite universities and less educated youth. Older participants were selected by occupational categories: NGO activists and journalists, public sector workers, small and medium entrepreneurs, and rural communities. Respondents for in-depth interviews were civilian and security officials, established academics and experts, and religious figures. Guiding questions for focus groups and interviews were developed and supplied to the researchers in the republics together with guidance on how to conduct focus groups and interviews. Formats for recording interviews and focus groups were developed and supplied. Researchers were asked to record their own impressions of focus group sessions.

All researchers noted positive dynamics of the group interactions that enabled rich discussions to take place. The method enabled open and candid debates about difficult and contentious issues. All respondents were guaranteed anonymity, but types of respondents (younger and older generation, urban/rural, and so forth) were recorded. Most of the interviews and focus groups have audio records.

The field research phase took place in August—December 2011. Altogether 30 focus groups and 50 key informant interviews were held, in which about 250 respondents from five republics participated, including 7 focus groups and 10 interviews in Ingushetia, 6 focus groups and 11 interviews in Chechnya, and 3 focus groups and 8 interviews in Dagestan.

Analysis of the qualitative data—descriptive accounts and explanatory accounts—was carried out at a Pyatigorsk seminar in October 2011 that brought together the researchers and representatives of civil society from each republic. "Brainstorming exercise" included development of "outlooks" (short-to-medium term scenarios) for each republic and the region in general elaborated through collective reflection.

Generalization from the qualitative research was conducted on completion of field work. This approach involved reassessment of the original hypotheses, along with cross-referencing material against findings in different republics and against the original research agenda. An important part of the generalization process was an identification of the new trends versus previously existing knowledge.

Social and economic settings

These three republics vary in territory and population: in 2010 Dagestan's population numbered 2,910,249, Chechnya's—1,268,989, and Ingushetia's was 412,529.[4] Ingushetia is the youngest republic, established on June 4, 1992 as a result of the separation from the dual-nationality Checheno-Ingushetia—though Chechens and Ingush belong to a larger Vainakh group. Chechnya and Ingushetia demonstrate tendencies toward monoethnicity, while Dagestan is populated by 32 ethnic groups, none of which occupies a dominant position.

The republics are heavily subsidized. Vladimir Putin stated that in the 2000–2010 period the federal authorities allocated 800 billion roubles (USD25 billion), increasing budgetary subsidies throughout the decade. The share of federal subsidies varied in Ingushetia from 82 to 90 percent of the republic's budget, in Dagestan—75 to 80 percent, and in Chechnya, 87 to 92 percent. In 2011 federal budget allocation to Dagestan included 31 billion roubles (USD968 million), while Stavropol *Krai* of the same population size got only 8.8 billion (USD275 million). The same budget provided 7 billion roubles (USD218.5 million) to Ingushetia and 13.2 billion roubles (USD412 million) to Chechnya.[5]

Massive financial transfers from the central budget, which provides funding for educational facilities, public sector salaries, and unemployment benefits, led to social and economic improvements, but failed to bring desired security and stability. Formal unemployment was higher than nationwide figures in 2011: the North Caucasus Federal District average was 14.3 percent against Russia's average of 6.1 percent. The worst situation was in Ingushetia with 48.9 percent and in Chechnya with 27.2 percent unemployed.[6] In Dagestan the average salary is the lowest in the Federation (R11,479 and 2 kopeks or USD364 per month) and it is one of the few subjects, in which registered unemployment is rising.

Federal subsidies mitigate the effects of unemployment. Society capitalizes on the informal employment, when it is possible to evade taxes and play by different rules, which vary according to the circumstances. Public discourse does not refer to unemployment as a reason for poverty, but relates it to a sense of injustice and lack of self-fulfillment for young people. The research did not unveil evidence that unemployment and poverty are linked to Islamist appeal, although such sentiment forms the prevailing discourse.[7]

The republics' authorities echo the unemployment discourse, because it enables them to claim subsidies, as well as to avoid responsibility for allowing the grey economy to flourish, and for countenancing corruption and nepotism. Subsidies allocations are dependent on population. In this respect, the 2010 census proved controversial because the censors counted the de facto population that differs from the official permanent one based on residency registration because of high out-migration. Difference can be substantial and lead to a decrease in subsidies. For instance, in Ingushetia's Ekajevo village administrators believed that they had 31,600 residents versus 15,600 counted by the census, which means a reduced budgetary allocation.

Subsidies are producing an impact. Field observation in Ingushetia showed significant improvements in infrastructure between 2006 and 2012: roads have been constructed, communication systems work, and housing is of good standard. Older generation respondents assessed what had changed for the better in the post-Soviet times as: (1) increased consumerism—one can possess things that were inaccessible before; the acquisition of the republic's own government; (2) improved roads; (3) regular payment of federal subsidies; and (4) enhanced information flow.[8] However, there are fewer public buildings and facilities, such as social clubs and libraries. With the decline of *kolkhoz*,[9] most women in rural areas do not enter formal employment. Instead they tend their children and garden plots, and lose former means of public participation. Women's rights and interests are continuously violated.[10] Moscow does not interfere with Ramzan Kadyrov's orders for compulsory headscarves for women in state employment in Chechnya, does not try to combat polygamy, bride nappings, gross violations of maternity rights, and honor killings spreading in the region. Cultural, educational, and language policies work toward strengthening identification with respective republics and weakening identification with all-Russian identity and culture." Most evident is the decline of Russian language.

Ingushetia and Chechnya found themselves on the international frontier with Georgia, which places them effectively at a dead end of the Federation, as land routes to Georgia are mostly closed. This contributes to isolation. Ingushetia remains the most isolated, as there is little there to attract visitors and also because the administrative border with North Ossetia is heavily fortified. Educated people of the older generation regret the loss of access to Vladikavkaz with its developed city life and urban infrastructure. Dagestan, by contrast, benefits from trade with Azerbaijan, though security of rail transit has become precarious, making social interaction less intense.[11]

Heavily militarized settings dominate the visual space, defining what societies see as a "normal" picture of their world. A young middle-class woman who moved to Ingushetia from Kazakhstan, reacted with initial dismay to the sight of armored vehicles, reinforced checkpoints, special forces with machineguns and discussions of violence as of mundane experience, but got used to it. Societies get accustomed to living in conditions of insecurity. Respondents noted that a persistent feeling that one may be in a wrong place at a wrong time, and the sadness of attacks and killings creates a joyless, depressive atmosphere. People avoid travelling by road after dark.

Despite increase in formal freedoms in Russia in general, life opportunities for young people narrowed as compared to the Soviet times. They include (1) the law-enforcement sector for men, (2) teaching profession and other low-level public service for women, (3) private business organized through family networks, (4) agriculture, and (5) crime. The older generation had other options, such as belonging to all-Union professional networks, work at industrial enterprises, or service in the Soviet army. The ways of reaching social success have altered for the younger generation, as nepotism plays a bigger role in securing careers.

Russian minorities

The ethnic composition of the North Caucasus in the last two decades has been changing. Accelerating emigration of ethnic Russians brings a new set of problems of its own as the republics acquire greater autonomy. According to the 2010 census data, Russians constituted 3.6 percent of population in Dagestan (104,000), 1.9 in Chechnya (24,382), and 0.8 in Ingushetia (3,200). Russians are still 20.8 in North Ossetia and 22.5 in Kabardino-Balkaria, although their population is declining in both.[12]

In Ingushetia, the mono-ethnicity of the republic is not viewed as an asset, but as a handicap. A regret that minorities departed comes across ages and social groups. Some respondents viewed Russian departures as a loss and said that it would be good if they returned. Russians are seen as a symbol of good old times, and do not present a competitive threat, as professions open for Russians—such as teaching and medicine—pay too little to be attractive.

The remaining Russian communities are small and dispersed, and mostly consist of women, middle-aged and old. In Pokrov church—the Orthodox church in Ingushetia in stanitsa Ordjinikidzievskaya (Sleptsovkaya),—there is roughly one christening per month and seven weddings occurred in two years. The funerals, however, are plenty.[13] There are hardly any young men left and women, who wish to marry, have to look outside.

The local authorities and police take steps to enable Russians to stay, but this is insufficient to counterbalance the social pressures. It does not take much to scare the Russian communities into leaving if they believe that they have no future in the republics. The environment grows more Muslim and less tolerant. People do not venture out after 8 pm, even to visit friends or relatives. The Pokrov church was shot at three times with a grenade launcher in 2009–11. When two Ingush young women converted to Christianity, one was killed and the other went into hiding.[14] An initiative to build interconfessional rapprochement by Muslim and Christian Orthodox clergy ended in fiasco when the mosque and the church from where the respective clergy came from, were set on fire. Explosives were thrown into the courtyard of a house occupied by an interviewed Russian family. The Russian cemetery has been booby-trapped and an explosion took place at the burial of a Russian teacher, in which the funeral procession members had been maimed. Federal troops conduct a mine-sweeping operation at the cemetery on the eve of major Christian holidays to enable families to visit. Many are still afraid, as the notice from families on the gates apologizing for being unable to care for their dead shows.[15]

The effect of the diminished numbers of Russians led to a declining knowledge of the Russian language among children who have to enter schools where the official medium of instruction is Russian, while they speak only their local language. Teachers are also mostly from the same ethnic group. In practice, the teachers use a mixture of two languages, trying to explain the material. Sometimes pupils read a text without understanding the meaning.

The Russian respondents were very grateful to the federal and republican authorities for the support they receive, and stressed that local police looks after their interests.[16] Still, the prospects for maintaining viable communities which perform a role of a cultural continuity are feeble.

Growing religious conservatism

Cultural norms typical in Russia—for example, that men and women can share the same cinema hall or that young people of both sexes go to a café together, do not apply in Chechnya and Ingushetia, and are in decline in Dagestan outside of the capital.[17] Affected by isolation, low urbanization, and virtual mono-ethnicity, Ingushetia is increasingly adopting an Islamic way of life where the secular constituency does not dare to raise a voice. In Nazran and elsewhere in Ingushetia, there is almost nothing which stays open in the evening, apart from a theater, because most other facilities, such as poolrooms or restaurants, are considered non-Islamic. Recreation activities for male youth concentrate around sports clubs, mosques, the internet, and visiting relatives. Leisure opportunities for young women and girls mostly revolve around the family. In Dagestan, agricultural decline and an absence of special measures to keep the rural population at home, increases migration of young people from the countryside into the cities, which, in its turn, leads to a ruralization of urban environments.[18]

Drinking and selling alcohol in Chechnya and Ingushetia is made impossible by social pressure. Restaurants that served alcohol have been attacked, and Dagestan is now heading in the same direction. The only cinema in Ingushetia was attacked three times before it finally closed. In Dagestan Patimat Magomedova, a headmistress at a school in the village of Shahmal was shot dead in September 2010 for her uncompromising stand against the *hijab* at school, and on behalf of physical education lessons for girls.[19]

In Chechnya the situation is better due to facilities that comply with Islamic norms, including an Aqua park with separate sections for men and women, shopping malls and pop music concerts. The Head of Chechen Republic Ramzan Kadyrov is praised by many among the inhabitants of Ingushetia and Dagestan for his success in combining Islamic and secular ways of life, such that adherence to religion does not mean a ban on public entertainment and leisure. Kadyrov is seen as a good manager who succeeded in extracting funds from Moscow and building a miracle out of the rubble. Youth respondents in Ingushetia expressed: "I wish that here were like Chechnya. It is beautiful, ideal in Chechnya."[20]

Communities are caught between *shariah, adat* (customary law), and the Russian secular system. Clash between tradition and modernity creates a dynamic tension between Soviet and post-Soviet generations. The younger members use modern means, such as internet, email, and mobile technology, albeit to revive social norms of nineteenth century. *Adat* forms an important reference system in which the society develops. Certain customs against which the Soviet system pursued an uncompromising fight, are making a comeback, such as blood revenge and honor killings.

Religion plays an increasingly important role as a form of social organization and a growing force which consolidates societies, and becomes more powerful as compared to ethnic affiliation. The prevailing leitmotif in the focus groups was that "the ethnic cause has outlived itself, while the religious cause has moved to the forefront."[21] Organized religion looms large in public space and receives state support. The main interface between the mosque and the state are spiritual boards of Muslims [DUMs or muftiyats], although it is possible to register a separate mosque at the Ministry of Justice, if it adheres to a certain Sufi *vird* (Sufi fraternity) and is autonomous of the muftiyat. Madrassas, mosques, and Islamic institutes proliferate. Home-based informal religious education apparently exists, although the official clergy denies it. *Quaziyat* (*Shariah Court*) functions under the auspices of the muftiyat in Ingushetia. It mostly considers civil cases and provides arbitration, settles compensation claims, recovers debts and reconciles sides in disputes. It does not have enforcement powers and both sides should agree to refer their dispute to the *Quaziyat*.[22]

State-sponsored religious policies were assessed by the older respondents as contributing to the needs of the society which grows more religious. At the same time, the respect for DUMs in Ingushetia and Dagestan is low across different social groups, whereas the Salafi movement and forces of radicalization have been strengthening. Tension and violence persist in Dagestan between Sufi *tariqats* (brotherhoods),[23] supported by the republican government, on the one hand, and *jihadists* and non-violent Salafi, on the other hand. Muslim scholars and DUM periodically call for use of force against Salafis, which exacerbates the gap between the two Muslim constituencies. The state-masterminded Sufi–Salafi negotiations and agreements in Dagestan that were reached in April 2012 failed already in May when suicide bombings restarted. The public in the meantime believes that it is convenient for the authorities to defame Salafis, in order to seek funds from the center for a struggle against them, and also to explain away the republic's problems through the continuous troubles with Salafis.[24]

Secularism, on the contrary, is in retreat, withering away amidst the public expressions of religious ways of life. This is especially evident in how the mechanisms of social control have altered. The North-Caucasian societies experience a crisis of traditional authority. Although the custom is that the young defer to the old, in reality the younger generation exercises control over the older who are more tolerant of drinking, smoking, socializing with the opposite sex and generally are too much drawn to the "European culture." In an absence of a vocal and assertive secular constituency, there are no barriers to oppose the religious advance, even if privately some are not happy.[25]

The social environment is characterized by the lack of alternatives. Emigration of non-Caucasian groups made the environment less diverse and less tolerant to differences. Adherence to religion is compulsory: it is impossible to be an Ingush and not be a Muslim: "If you are outside religion, you are outside of society."[26] The religious factor produces various social restrictions and creates psychological pressure on individuals. In contrast to mainstream Russia with its political and social diversity, the three republics strive toward uniformity when everybody has to comply with certain behavioral norms.

Socialization at the workplace among diverse groups has also been reduced due to a decline in public sector employment. Alternatives to socialization at workplace—or colleges for the young people,—are few. Propaganda of internationalist values, typical for the Soviet times, subsided at school and workplace. As the respect toward different opinions and tolerance to diversity is low, culture of dialogue and dissent is underdeveloped.

Socio-psychological traits typical for the youth—for example, linear thinking, intolerance toward divergent opinions and ways of life, and a tendency to see the world as black and white—work in the same direction. The mental grounds are reinforced by combative sports that prevail in the Caucasus, which breed discipline, determination and the will to win, but do not encourage diversity and reflection. In such conditions young people have plenty of pent-up energy, which does not find ready relief.

Islamism

Social dislocation of modern times produced new problems, but also opened new opportunities. The expanding young contingent is simultaneously influenced by the forces of globalization and is locked in their own milieu detached from Russia proper. One powerful influence is that of Islamism.[27] Intra-confessional tensions between the traditionalists who adhere to Sufi *tariqats* (orders), and the Islamists, are not that pronounced among the youth as in the older generation. The most acute tensions are between the secularists, who are associated with the authorities, and the Islamists, associated with armed opposition to the ruling establishment and to the secular order.

As religion regulates social relations, protest takes the form of religious ideology, as religion forms the only possible alternative interpretation of the world opposing corrupt secularism. It plays a formative role in the ideology of struggle against social and political injustice, moral permissiveness and social evils, such as drinking and promiscuity. Young people, already more devout than their fathers and grandfathers, are attracted to bigger causes at the time when society is changing. The ideological component prevails in the appeal of Islamism, encompassing other elements, such as religious forms, political dissent, social problems or an absence of interesting ways of spending time. There is no equally appealing ideology on the secularist and/or traditional Muslim side to counterbalance it. Young respondents expressed that the Islamist idea is "more powerful," integrates different ingredients, and carries with it a sense of the cause worth dying for:

Each person lives for some idea, whether he lives peacefully or goes to war. And if that idea prevails in the person, he will go to the end.[28]

The discourse of discontent concentrates around injustice, corruption, dishonesty in official structures, inability to get a job on merit. At the same time, there is a lack of ideas and initiative on how this can be changed, and how young people can be part of that change. Many young people are at crossroads, as their minds can be turned into different directions, from positive to destructive. Rebellion that entails a degree of risk is seen as prestigious among young people who have to impress their peers. As young people lead fairly restricted lives, they have a plenty of energy which does not find easy expression. This is one of the traits on which Islamist movements capitalize:

> Today, I think, every young person is full of energy, and in [mainstream] Russia there are different ways of letting it out, because there are various groups and interests, but in our republic, unfortunately, there are few. There is sport where competition is ferocious, I have been there and I know.[29]

Youth respondents explained the reasons for appeal in the following terms. First, the lack of opportunities for promotion, self-fulfillment, and exciting life is one of the reasons. An example was given that several young men, who were training in wrestling, went to join the armed opposition, when they realized that they would not become champions and saw no other opportunities for self-realization. Group solidarity, camaraderie, romantic fascination with resistance, and a chance to bear arms all contribute to the attraction. Poverty and social deprivation, a routine explanation in western academic discourse, does not hold water and is, in fact, misleading. According to discussions held during focus groups and key informants interviews in Ingushetia, Islamist propaganda works mostly for people who come from privileged families, have jobs, and went to good universities, and who did not have to struggle for survival. The examples cited by respondents of different age and occupational groups in Ingushetia included a prosecutor's aide, a bailiff, sons of a leading doctor and of a supermarket chain owner, a relative of a minister, and students of prestigious universities in Moscow. Similar examples were given by an elderly Kumyk NGO activist from Dagestan during October 2011 brainstorming seminar in Pyatigorsk.

Secondly, the messages of Islamists resonate in society, as they point out to real grievances: "the authorities monopolized everything, sell jobs for big money," "officials are getting rich, the powers are corrupt," "security structures de facto reign everything, they are brutal, destroy, kill, abduct." This propaganda is persuasive, as examples are ready at hand. In Dagestan corruption among the older generation was named as one of the reasons, indicating a decline of values in society. An example was cited of a young man who had been watching his father accepting bribes, then turned to a search of a spiritual alternative, and was drawn into an Islamist group. He presented his parents with an ultimatum: either an Islamic wedding with no alcohol, or he would leave home and get wedded in a field.[30]

Thirdly, the symbolic domain is highly developed. Islamist movements have developed a subculture with its symbols and language which, on the one hand, connects with global Islamic heritage, and uses modern popular culture and ways of expression on the other. They include songs, *nash-eeds* (Islamic chants), articulate preachers, ability to discuss global and local events, and have heroic martyrs who lived exciting lives, promoted as role models. Islamist groups provide freedom from blood family ties and a chance to join a new family of choice. Joining underground "is prestigious," video recordings of Said Buryatsky[31] prophecies are exciting and popular, and Internet discussions on Islamist sites are engaging.

The role of internet and mobile technology is prominent in gaining new ideas, creation of new linkages and forms of solidarity. In a society where social interaction is limited, virtual participation becomes more important. Some students have been said to be willing to go and fight for the right cause in the Middle East, a sentiment apparently derived from the internet.

Fourthly, young people do not trust religious authorities who do not live according to the rules, and are frustrated with the lack of commitment and communication skills among the official clergy. They expressed views that propaganda administered by the traditional religious authorities associated with the state is dull.

> There exist two ideas—one which calls for peaceful Islam and the other—for militant Islam. If one evaluates both ideas objectively, one has to admit that the "forest" idea is stronger. The system of education of [official] spiritual leaders is weak. We all see that [they] read monotonously in mosques, but if one wants to convey a message, one should know how to do this. Such leaders are few and they are seldom allowed to practice. There must be leaders whom young people would listen to.[32]

All respondents who had direct contacts with Islamists stressed that, in their view, they had been lost to mainstream society. According to the discussions held during two focus groups in Nazran: (1) with Polytechnic college students (age group 16—20) and (2) with Law Faculty students, State University of Ingushetia (age group 20—23) and confirmed by the author's interview with a senior security official of the republic, it is virtually impossible to break away from an Islamist cell; people who join the groups realize that even if they regretted having done it, there is no return, because their families may be punished in revenge.

> When we tried to persuade him to stay, he said that there is no way back. He always has been going out together with our boys, but on this day he did not take them along. Men in vests with weapons came for him.

He knew that he would be killed. He did not want to go there. But he knew that if he does not go back, his family would suffer. He said that those who recruit there, are not in any way different from us. They are ordinary people, study, work, but in reality they have a different life.[33]

Many respondents noted a certain psychological atmosphere created by Islamists, which draws new people in. They could not articulate what it exactly was, but found it hard to resist: "they are making people zombified."

This is like hypnosis. Sometimes I find myself among people from that circle, although I am not one of them, I mean the Wahhabis. It happened to me a few times that when I am among those people I feel confused and lost, and sometimes even think that maybe they are right. I get possessed then with such fear that I pull myself together to leave and decide not to be near them ever again. For instance, they say that things that every Muslim should do, are not necessary. What is prescribed by religion, they distort. Say, this is not compulsory, that tomorrow you would not be judged for this, lead people into delusion. And then you get lost and do not know what to say. It is better never to talk to them and keep away.[34]

An idea of "fighting the Russian power which always oppressed us" forms a streak in the Islamist appeal, but arguably, not a main sentiment. This is confirmed by relatively scarce attacks on the federal representatives and security forces.

Kinship ties, strong in other aspects of the Caucasian life, do not work the same way when the ideological cause is at stake. Islamist groups are capable of attacking police in full knowledge that their relatives serve at a post or a checkpoint which is being attacked and most likely would be killed as a result. There are instances when siblings from the same family get drawn into a group, or when a brother joins to seek revenge for a brother slain by security forces. However, they are rare. More common is the pattern when the family is oblivious to their offspring getting involved and often refuses to believe that he or she participated in the movement, when they are detained or killed in raids. Cases are known when fathers turned their sons [over] to security forces, and two fathers in Ingushetia in two separate incidents killed their sons because they turned to Islamist groups. One father was later murdered by his son's comrades-in-arms in revenge.[35]

Communities do not feel themselves responsible for radicalization of some of their members, as they do not comprehend the reasons why they are drawn into such groups and do not see themselves as capable of influencing them. They tend to typify these reasons through socioeconomic hardship and Islamic education abroad. Older community members do not notice when young people become radicalized. Local administrators in Ekajevo in Ingushetia, where in 2010 Said Buryatsky's group was successfully taken on by the federal forces, described the militants who came from the village as ordinary young men, sociable, not reclusive, doing sports, shopping, attending the administration for various papers, "one family was just so nice." Their parents refused to believe that they had been involved with armed struggle. At the same time, there is no wider community support for any Islamist cause—on the contrary, the families of Islamists are ostracized by other community members after anti-terrorist raids. Their family occasions, such as weddings and funerals, are not attended and neighbors avoid dealing with them. Some had to move away as a result.

Formal institutions rather than local communities are seen by the public as the main agent of responding to the challenge of Islamism. In their view, they should be made to work properly, but instead societies have low trust toward civilian and security authorities. The main reasons are corruption and nepotism, arbitrary, non-transparent actions of security structures, and the situation when republics' authorities are unaccountable to the local constituency but are only motivated by pleasing Moscow. Security authorities are blamed for shooting Islamist suspects on the spot without trial and for detention of relatives of known militants. According to human rights' groups, parents are pressurized into keeping quiet under a threat that other children could be taken. It was reported that security agencies use torture, unsanctioned arrests, and searches.[36]

Continuous security threat

Islamist insurgency moves from one republic to another, depending on the receptivity of the local context and on the prowess of a republic's security forces. Overall, the period from December 2011 to June 2012 witnessed 260 attacks, which represent a sharp 32 percent decline from the same period last year.[37] Still, arrivals of new money bring new bouts of insecurity.

While there are significant gains in security in Chechnya, Dagestan became the epicenter of the Caucasus Emirate's (CE) *jihadi* operations and the locus of a growing Salafi movement. CE *mujahaddin* are the main perpetrators of violence. Their declared goals are the establishment of a *shariah* law-based Islamist state as part of the global *jihadi* revolutionary project to re-create the Caliphate.[38] CE is headed by amir (commander) Doku Umarov, a Chechen, and has *vilayats* (regional branches) throughout the North Caucasus and mainstream Russia.

Dagestan has seen sharp rises in *jihadi*-related violence since 2010, for which the Dagestan *Vilayat* (DV) network claimed responsibility. The number of attacks nearly doubled from previous years. In 2011, the DV continued its rise in operational capacity. During the first half of 2012, the DV carried out 63.5 per cent of CE's attacks in Russia.[39] According to Russia's Ministry of Interior, 70 percent of terrorist incidents in the North Caucasus took place in Dagestan in 2011, and 368 militants were killed and 804 detained. The largest act—an explosion in Makhachkala in May 2012—killed 14 people and injured over 100. The prevalence of violence is characteristic for the cities of Makhachkala, Izberbash, and Kaspiysk, and for the rural districts of Kizlyar, Tsuntinskii, Karabudakhkenskii, Khasavyurt, and Sergokalinskii.

Police and members of security agencies, and civilian authorities are the primary targets of the terrorist operations, but bystanders randomly became victims when spectacular acts were staged. Figures of state agents, civilians, and *mujhaddin* killed or wounded all went up. About 150 state agents were killed in 2011 in shoot-outs and explosions. The number of *mujhaddin* captured is also on the rise, showing that some of them are more willing to go to prison than to paradise. Recent tactics include a surge in the use of improvised explosive devices and of cars packed with explosives.

As noted by Gordon Hahn, "the conflict between traditionalist and Russia-loyal Islamic clergy, on the one hand, and the radical Islamist Salafis and the *jihadis* is now becoming a fact of life. The *jihadists* seem intent on blocking any rapprochement, which would perhaps reduce their prospects for recruiting."[40] As a result, distinguished Sufi clerics have come under heavy attack from *jihadists* in Dagestan, who have successfully "beheaded" their spiritual leadership. On June 7, 2011 Maksud Sadikov, a member of the Council of Muftis and Rector of the Institute of Theology and International Relations, was murdered; Sheikh Sirajjudin Khuriksky (Israfilov) was shot dead on October 28, 2011 at his home in the Tabassaran District. The most significant was the killing of the influential Sufi sheikh, 74-year old Said Atsaev Afandi Chirkeiskii, who died on August 28, 2012 together with six others in a suicide attack at his home. Atsaev's funeral was reportedly attended by some 150,000 people.[41] In March 2012, the chief mufti of the Muslim Spiritual Board of Dagestan (DUMD) Akhmed-Haji Abdullaev issued a statement calling for mutual respect between the republic's various Islamic currents and restraint on the part of law enforcement as a way of preventing the *mujhaddin* from finding more recruits. Abdullaev also denounced rumors that imams are handing over lists of Islamists to law enforcement which is widely believed to be the case.

Security authorities in Ingushetia record an overall reduction in numbers of armed groups' new recruits. Compared to the period of Murat Zyazikov's presidency (2001–2008), bomb explosions, armed raids, and killings of administrators and police became less frequent under president Yunus-bek Yevkurov (2008–present), and incidents of ordinary crime scaled down. Currently people born in 1980s prevail among the militants. In 2011, 40 militants were shot dead by security forces. At the same time, it was expressed that "we acquired the first suicide bombers from among the Ingush [in the Yevkurov period—AM]."[42]

Suicide attacks have been a huge security problem, since this is a tactic most difficult to counter. Seven successful suicide attacks in Russia took place in the first eight months of 2012; one more than in all of 2011. There were 16 in 2009 and 14 in 2010.[43] Dagestan leads in the number of attacks. The DV created its own *Riyadus Salikhiin Jamaat* (suicide bomb squad) in 2010 and the late DV amir Magomedali Vagabov strongly supported the use of suicide bombers. Dagestan presents a breeding ground for female bombers. Vagabov's wife blew herself up in Moscow in the 2010 metro bombing, and the wife of amir Daudov was to perform a suicide attack on Red Square on December 31, 2011, but the plot failed. Women were used in three attacks in 2012 in the republic, one of them being an ethnic Russian.

Russian security operations became more successful in uncovering arms' caches in the woods and interrupting Islamists' financial flows, and more efficient at killing amirs across the CE's *vilayats*. Killings of leading Dagestan's amirs and operatives such as Magomedali Vagabov (Seifullah) of Gubden and Ibrahimhalil Daudov (Saleh), the DV amir who was killed on February 14, 2012, have an effect on the CE mujahaddin operational command. At the same time, a chain of hierarchy is worked out in advance and it is known who would take the reins, should an amir be suddenly killed. Following Daudov's killing, his first *naib* (deputy) and the amir of the DV's central sector Rustam Asildarov (Abu Mukhammad) became the DV's amir and *vali* (governor). He renewed the *bayat* (Islamic loyalty oath) to CE amir Doku Umarov on behalf of himself and all of the DV's amirs and mujahaddin.[44]

Security forces made inroads toward greater transparency and community cooperation. Photographs of suspected members of illegal armed groups are available on the Ingush Interior Ministry website[45] and are placed on billboards at administrations and public places.[46] Field observation showed that these measures are executed formally.

Local police furnish the main community interface. They work with the Muslim clergy, elders, and municipal administrations to keep track of the population. As a result of the association with police and sometimes—physical proximity, administrators come under attack from members of armed groups. The premises of the Ekajevo municipal administration, visited by the author during her research in Ingushetia, which also hosts a police post, have been blown up twice. The police in charge of their territorial areas estimate the numbers in armed opposition through recordings of missing persons. The pattern is such that a policeman responsible for the area reports if a young person has disappeared, and then the family is questioned. In case no details of a "son gone abroad" are given, the police assume that the missing person has joined an underground group. It is more difficult to identify those who continue to live an ordinary life. For this reason the whole population, especially young men, come under suspicion. Reasons may be solid or random, but in most cases remain opaque. Asked how fathers can protect their sons from an arbitrary detention, respondents of the older generation replied : "get him a job with police."

Heads of the republics in Dagestan, Chechnya, and Ingushetia launched initiatives to enable those willing to surrender, to join civilian life. Establishment of conciliation commissions was an important public relations exercise. It was noted by the respondents that Yunus-bek Yevkurov, the president of Ingushetia, applies more humane methods to combat Islamism, and in this sense compares favorably to rough treatment by Chechnya's Ramzan Kadyrov. Civilian authorities in Ingushetia and Yunus-bek Yevkurov personally were reported to have rescued young men during the security forces' attempts to unlawfully kill or abduct them. Thirty-one persons were persuaded to submit themselves to the republic's Anti-terrorist Commission. Twenty of them had the charges against them of participation in the illegal armed formations dropped. The Commission amnesties people from this charge, but not from other crimes, committed in the course of being a member of an underground armed group, such as abduction or murder. Such crimes entail a prison sentence, but voluntarily giving oneself to the authorities may reduce the term.

Effectiveness of the commissions has been questioned. "When they get involved into Islamist groups, there is no way out," was a common opinion of those who had a personal experience of dealing with Islamists, "they are destined for death, and they know this."[47] Officials and civil society representatives involved in conciliation commissions expressed private doubts that any significant numbers can be persuaded to give up arms. They conceded that some individuals get involved for accidental and personal reasons, rather than following the ideological cause, and they may be able to reintegrate, if their families stand up for them. In such cases they and their families would have to leave a republic and start life elsewhere under new names. Moreover, reintegration into society is handicapped by blood vengeance from relatives of those killed by armed groups.

"Them" and "Us" all-Caucasian versus all-Russian identity

Given profound differences in security, social, and cultural conditions, it is unsurprising that North-Caucasian migration into Russia's major cities leads to social tensions. Although they are integrated into mainstream Russian society in terms of lifestyle, fashions, popular entertainment, and social intermix, distinct "Caucasian" behavioral patterns become more noticeable in public spaces. The Russian public views North Caucasians with apprehension, and the "us and them" paradigm becomes increasingly a fault-line in society. Since Caucasians are accustomed to their higher status and to a lower status of local Russians in their own republics, it is natural for them to continue to behave in the same way when they migrate. However, such attitudes increasingly encounter resistance outside the republics from a contingent that is predominantly Russian, young, male, and mostly working class—a contingent without sizeable representation in Caucasian homelands.

Focus groups respondents throughout the republics noted that a "North-Caucasian" identity is being formed as a reaction and opposition to the rise of anti-Caucasian attitudes in Russian-majority regions, and that they solidify more with other Caucasians than they had before. Anti-Caucasian attitudes in mainland Russia, populist discourse, "Russians, go forth!" football chants, use of derogatory terms, and the way central media reports on "Caucasian cases" were passionately condemned by the respondents in the Caucasus. They were adamant that they are Russian citizens just as everybody else, and are not separatists. However, there is little reflection in the region on the reasons for emergence of anti-Caucasian moods.

An all-Russian identity is stronger among the older generation. An uneasy mix of an all-Russian and North-Caucasian identity explains the formation of the "own and other" dichotomy among the younger generation, an issue laden with internal contradictions. For example, one focus group wished that Moscow created a center for conflict resolution in the Caucasus and at the same time wanted the term "Caucasian" to be banned. It was remarked that if Russia's state identity is based on multi-confessional character of the Federation, the state leadership should not be overtly Christian: "Putin and Medvedev should not be shown on the TV with a candle in the church. If they wish to be Christian, they should keep it private."[48] However, people do not see anything strange in very public display of Islam in their own republics.

The politics of identity remain complicated, combining elements of Russian citizenry with Caucasian affiliation. Discourse on the juxtaposition of Caucasian and all-Russian identities revolves around the notion that people regard themselves as Russian citizens in whatever manner appeals to them personally. The gist of it is that the Caucasian identity is distinct and more sophisticated, as it demands a certain type of behavior from an individual, such as respect for elders or healthy way of life, not typical for Russians, who smoke, drink, swear, etc. In addition, they are entitled as Russian citizens to the same rights as everybody else, but the citizenry responsibilities are somehow special. There is little understanding that this is not quite an all-Russian identity and therefore incomprehension why Russians have a problem in accepting it. Not all North Caucasians are ready to accept the same rules of the game for everybody without a special status.[49]

Because Chechnya suffered greatly in the two wars, there is a sense of entitlement that it is "being owed." Society in Ingushetia, affected by two Chechen wars, influx of IDPs (Internally Displaced Persons) and by the conflict in the disputed Prigorodny district (part of the republic of North Ossetia-Alania), partly share the same sentiment. The problem is that when people who think this way, migrate outside the republics, they find out that such ideas are unwelcome in Russian mainstream.

> Other Russian citizens did not suffer as we did during the military campaigns. They have not lost so many people. They are obliged to return lost housing to our population.[50]

Apart from the anti-Caucasian sentiment, views of Caucasians on "Russia" are largely positive. Many Caucasians compare standards in the rest of the Federation with their own situation which fares worse. In Ingushetia respondents remarked that the scale of compensation for families who lost relatives in terrorist acts in Moscow was ten times higher than in their republic. Young people believe that in central Russia employment opportunities are fairer. In Ingushetia "the only job I've ever seen openly recruited for, was of an office cleaner," said a student. Out of nine respondents in a youth focus group five declared their willingness to leave the republic after graduation from college. Integration into big cities of the Federation was not perceived as a problem by the would-be migrants.

Graduates of the republics' universities are disadvantaged in the local job market as bribe-taking is so widespread that employers do not trust their degrees. Education and behavior of teaching staff is a cause of dismay and again differs from standards in Russia, in the view of those who studied outside the Caucasus:

> Bribes are given and taken at the Chechen State University. First-year undergraduates are convinced that this is the norm. That if you study, you have to pay. In my third year I paid to pass an English exam, although I don't know the language. In my fourth year I had to pay again. Some lecturers talk openly that they should be given money. I have a recording at home where I bargain with a lecturer over the price. They demand either the knowledge of the whole curriculum or pay.[51]

Another indicator of differences in education system are the school final grades where standards in theory should be universal across the country. In 2010, Dagestan was in third place nationwide in the number of exam-takers who achieved the 100 percent grade in Russian language, despite having only 3.6 percent of ethnic Russian population. Fifty-four students achieved a 100 percent result, outdoing St. Petersburg, where only 29 students got the top grade out of 34,000 school exam-takers.[52] Deputy prime minister for social issues Olga Golodets was publicly questioned as to why, in her view, students from heartland Russia in their final year seek a transfer to schools in the North Caucasus where they would then sit the exams.

Outside the republics, views on representatives of Chechnya, Ingushetia, and Dagestan are largely negative. Intra-Caucasian migration from Chechnya and Dagestan causes friction in the republics of the Northwest. North Ossetia feels it more, and newcomers from Chechnya and Dagestan are met with apprehension.[53] There are tensions between Kumyk immigrants and the local population in Mozdok district in North Ossetia.[54] The same applies to migration of Chechens and Kumyks into Kabardino-Balkaria.[55] Moreover, in mostly Christian Ossetia there is a sense of resentment of being equated in the eyes of the Russian public with people from Chechnya, Ingushetia, and Dagestan by the virtue of being included into the same stereotypical "North-Caucasian" category.[56]

Since 2010 the beginnings of Russian nationalist consolidation has started to emerge. Catchy slogans have appeared, such as the "Enough Feeding the Caucasus" [Хватит кормить Кавказ!] campaign. Dmitri Medvedev and Vladimir Putin both felt the need to speak out against the campaign during their visits to the Caucasus.[57] Nevertheless, there is a growing conviction that state institutions and politicians work to disfavor the majority nation.

According to the poll of the "Public Opinion" Foundation of May 2012, 62 percent of ethnic Russians outside the Caucasus were against having neighbors from the North Caucasus. This is the least welcome group: 57 percent were against neighbors from Central Asia and 59 percent— neighbors from Southeast Asia.[58] Polls suggest that up to 50 percent would like to separate the Caucasus, wholly or partially, from the Federation.[59] Russia's Public Chamber initiated a poll in 2011, according to which 39 percent stated their negative feelings toward Caucasians and 26 supported the idea of separating North Caucasus from mainland Russia. Another 14 percent supported this measure on condition that the Caucasians go back to their home republics and do not stay in Russia. A Levada-Centre's poll showed similar results: 41 percent of Russians somewhat supported the idea of "Russia for Russians!" and 19 percent wholly support it. In November 2011 "Public Opinion" Foundation published its poll data, according to which 44 percent supported the "Russia for Russians' idea and 49 per-cent—the call "Enough of feeding the Caucasus."[60]

"Russian-on-Caucasian" confrontations acquired significant public resonance. In December 2010, large-scale protests by Moscow city resi-dents took place against unfair applications of the law by police. The action was initiated by a group of *Spartak* football fans who rebelled against the release of detainees, originally from Kabardino-Balkaria, accused of killing an ethnic Russian football supporter. Anti-Caucasian slogans were heard.

The protesters were joined by other Moscow residents, altogether numbering 10–15,000 people. They demanded equal criminal liability for everybody and protested against pressure on police investigation from ethnic
communities to reduce punishments for their members. Some protesters
clashed with the special police troops (OMON) and over 30 people were
injured.

Resentment by the ethnic Russians of behavior of some members of
Caucasian communities, which they regard as being above the law feeds
"Russian nationalism." A high profile case involves Dagestani wrestler,
Rasul Mirzaye. In August 2011, Mirzaye accidentially killed Ivan Agafonov,
a 19-year-old Moskovite student outside the Garage night club in Moscow,
following a clumsy joke made by Agafonov. The case became high-profile,
when the deputies of Dagestan's People's Assembly appealed to Moscow's
Zamoskvoretskiy court, asking for Mirzayev release under the deputies'
personal guarantees.[61] The "manslaughter" charge was changed to a lighter
charge of "causing death by accident," and Mirzayev was released on bail.
This caused a media outcry and protests outside the court, in which 50 people were arrested. Dagestan's president Magomedsalam Magomedov said
in March 2012 that the republic's government would stand in Mirzayev's
defense.[62] When in August 2012, members of the feminist punk band,
known as Pussy Riot, received a two-year jail sentence for performing a
stunt, while Rasul Mirzayev could walk out of the court as a free man, passions in Moscow rose up again.

The main arguments of the popular discourse are as follows. The North
Caucasus is the privileged territory in Russia, while Caucasians are privileged people. The status of North-Caucasian republics is higher than the
more "Russian" regions, they enjoy financial subsidies and preferential economic treatment. Subsidies are unfair and counterproductive, since they
increase appetites of local elites and encourage assertiveness among these
groups who feel that they can hold Moscow to ransom. Some of the federal
money ends up in the hands of militants. It is a territory where a de facto
civil war is going on,[63] and serves as a source of terrorism, threatening the
rest of the Federation. North Caucasians constitute the bulk of the most
ferocious, "stop-at-nothing" organized criminal gangs, while influential
ethnic clans save criminals from investigations and prosecutions.[64] They
violate Russian cultural standards, for example in treatment of women,
and the norms of "civilized behavior."

It does not escape attention of the Russian public that the heavily subsidized region is the homeland of some the richest people in Russia, such as
billionaire oligarch and Federation Council member Suleiman Kerimov—a
Lezgin from Dagestan—and brothers Mikhail and Sait-Salam Gutseriyevs
from Ingushetia. Mikhail Gutseriyev is co-owner of Russneft and the brothers own the most lucrative commercial real estate in Moscow. Kerimov owns
"Nafta-Moskva" company and Anji football club, among other assets, and

acts as an influential oligarch in Dagestan, shaping the republic's relationship with Moscow.[65]

This so-called Russian nationalism and Caucasian behavior are essentially two sides of the same process, which derives from the decay that occurred throughout the 1990s of state institutions as viable universal mechanisms. People on the country's periphery, especially in the Caucasus, found an alternative in ethnic mobilization and developed structures for lobbying the local interests, which worked well behind the scenes. The Russians who do not have traditional kinship structures, preserved their faith in the non-ethnic character of state institutions for a long time, but recently this has been changing. The essence is the same: if ethnic affiliation serves as a potent mechanism, then it should "work for us as it works for them."

Valerii Solovei, the leader of the emerging *Novaya Sila* (New Force) pro-nationalist party, dubs the region a "political, legal and financial-economic off-shore" in Russia and calls for a radical revision of the Kremlin policies, which only exacerbate the problem.

Federal efforts toward stabilization

During Dmitri Medvedev's presidency federal policy transitioned from a "stability-first" to a developmental maxim, in a belief that raising economic and social standards would bring about more harmonious North-Caucasian societies. At the same time, Moscow is constrained by its own apprehension of the region after the disasters of the 1990s. It is reluctant to intervene decisively into internal political developments, enforce uniform standards, and act against vested interests. The federal authorities leave internal politics in the hands of the Heads of Republics where they have a free reign, a pattern consistent in all three republics rather than being an exceptional practice in Chechnya.[66] In such circumstances, it is difficult for Moscow to pursue a consistent set of policies based on coherent principles.

Leaders of the North-Caucasian republics typically have an upper hand in their arguments with the center, largely because they successfully have framed their relations with Moscow as an exchange of their *loyalty in return for subsidies*. They delivered the "correct" electoral results in December 2011 elections to Russia's State Duma. In Chechnya, the ruling United Russia party received 99.5 percent of the vote, with a 99.45 percent voter turnout. In Dagestan, the party improved its performance from 89.4 in 2007 to 91.4 percent. Ingushetia recorded a 90 percent turnout, of which 78.1 percent voted for United Russia.

The major initiative was the October 2010 adoption of the "Strategy of Social and Economic Development of the North Caucasus Federal District until 2025." The North Caucasus Federal District Office created a new institutional infrastructure to support its implementation. The Strategy is expansive in scope, seeks to achieve various worthy objectives, and suggests wide-ranging policies in response to genuine challenges. However, it targets so many priorities which are so loosely defined that essential focus of the strategy remains unclear, unless it is simply to provide a justification for financial transfers.

Moscow's main problem is its patent ideological failure, when it comes to promotion of all-Russian identity or prevention of radicalization. Its propaganda measures are clichéd and formally implemented, with little conviction behind them, and their impact is not monitored. Unlike in the Soviet era, the center lacks a dedicated structure to provide guidance in religious, ethnic, and youth affairs, and to pursue a public awareness strategy. The federal ministry for nationalities was disbanded, while the Ministry of Regional Development deals primarily with social and economic matters. Spiritual Boards of Muslims are the main agent of influence, but are viewed by the public more as a problem than a solution because of their less-than-holy lifestyles and formal attitude to their religious duties. Moscow funds the republics' programs on "Spiritual and Moral Education" implemented by the local ministries of nationalities mostly through muftiyats. However, the lack of authoritative Muslim leaders who could motivate the communities accordingly undermines the effort.

Visibility of the federal authorities other than those in uniform is low. Central officials and experts seldom visit and spend little time in the region. Rules, regulations, and conventions, normal for the rest of the Federation, often are not applied in the republics. Control over implementation of the federal programs is mostly formal: Moscow expects regular activities reports, but does not examine in any depth whether the programs produce the intended impact.

The de facto responses consist of allocation of subsidies, security presence, occasional appointments of non-Caucasian outsiders into key public administration jobs and a "Russian-speaking population" return program. Security remains the main pillar. Chechnya has its own security sector accountable to the Head of the Republic, and conscripts are not drafted into the federal army, but serve locally. In others security agencies are the branches of the federal ministries, such as the Ministry of Interior and the Federal Security Service (FSB). There are Russian servicemen brought from outside in FSB and OMON police special forces. Heads of security agencies are staffed by appointees from the center, mostly Russians. The respondents in Ingushetia noted this as positive, since "when Russians are in top jobs, there is less suspicion of clan rule, and the information which goes to Moscow, comes across as more plausible if signed by a Russian."[67] Ethnic Russians can only act in the republics through collaboration with the indigenous cadre: "without locals, the federals would not have been able to do much here."[68]

Moscow has regarded budgetary subsidies as an essential payment for security, which has worked in Chechnya and started to show results in Ingushetia. Ramzan Kadyrov delivers security as he is paid to do, and Chechnya no longer serves as a source of terrorism destabilizing the rest of Russia. By contrast, Dagestan's leadership of Magomedsalam Magomedov and his predecessor Mukhu Aliev failed spectacularly. The republic requires massive federal security presence. Interior Ministry troops numbering 3,000 are stationed in the vicinity of large population settlements: the one-hundred-and-second brigade is stationed near Makhachkala and another base is at Kizlyar. The army regiments are located in the forested and mountainous terrain on the border with Chechnya, where three major operations took place in 2012 and 25 servicemen died. Border troops are stationed on the border with Azerbaijan, which in 2012 mounted a large anti-terrorist operation in the North with a Dagestani connection.

Exclusion of men from the republics from the Russian Armed Forces is a noteworthy development. The Ministry of Defense managed to realize its long-held aspiration not to deal with North-Caucasian conscripts. Conscription from Dagestan and Ingushetia, and conscription elsewhere in Russia of representatives of the ethnic groups that originate from these republics was temporarily suspended in 2011. The ban was extended to 2012 because of hazing and tendency to form ethnic gangs that harass other conscripts.[69] As a result, it is difficult for young men to be drafted into the military. In Ingushetia and Dagestan some men attempted to bribe conscription officers to join the army, because completion of the army service makes men eligible for jobs in the law-enforcement sector.[70]

Moscow periodically appoints top civilian administrators, such as Ingushetia's ex-premier Alexei Vorobiyev (October 2009–March 2011), and fills senior positions in audit, tax inspectorate, and other oversight bodies. Although field research showed that ordinary people appreciated their strict but fair approach to management, they typically do not last long in their jobs. External appointees who do not enjoy federal support if they face pressures from local power-holders. Moscow also engages with resolution of ethnic and land conflicts, which derive from conflicting ethnic claims over territory.

The Kremlin belatedly reacted to the glaring fact that ethnic Russians—its loyalist constituency—were emigrating from North-Caucasian republics in droves. A phantom federal program on repatriation of Russians who had left the region was adopted, and nominally implemented by the republics' ministries of nationalities. For example, the Ministry of External Relations, Nationalities, Press, and Information of Ingushetia implements the "Return and Arrangements for the Russian-speaking Population, 2010–2015" program, for which R81 million (USD2,529,471) were allocated for six years. However, the ministry privately believes that return is unrealistic and the best they can do is to preserve the remaining community.[71] Moreover, it is unclear who fits into the "Russian-speakers" category. The Ministry appealed to the Prosecutor's office for explanation, and was told that a definition does not exist and that the program may target all peoples apart from Ingush and Chechens.

Research data shows that Moscow's efforts to solve the republics' problems meet little appreciation on the ground. In Ingushetia no gratitude was expressed for the repatriation program to the Prigorodny district and for payment of compensation for the lost housing during the 1992 Ingush–Ossetian conflict. Federal efforts resulted in the return of 28,000 Ingush to Prigorodny, their houses rebuilt with money from the central budget. In October 2010, a federal law was adopted that offered financial compensation enabling those who did not wish to wait for return to Prigorodny to buy new homes elsewhere. Still, the federal authorities are held responsible for not pressuring the North Ossetian government to allow free settlement for the Ingush in Prigorodny.

The public believes that decisions to keep or replace the republic's politicians are made by Moscow based on its own criteria irrespective of local preferences. Perceptions are that Moscow is not dealing with eradicating corruption and is prepared to close its eyes on embezzlement of the federal transfers, as long as the federal security structures are allowed to operate unimpeded by the leaderships. The presidents/heads of republics are often regarded,—when it suits the circumstances,—as "Them"—an alien power accountable to the bureaucratic center, but not to the constituency at home. There is some truth in this argument given that these presidents were not genuinely elected. However, when these leaderships stand for the interests of their ethnic kin in mainland "Russia," then they are viewed as "Us."

Conclusion

In the words of the famous Dagestani poet Rasul Gamzatov, "we [North Caucasians] did not voluntarily join Russia, and would not leave it voluntarily. [мы добровольно в состав России не входили и добровольно из нее не выйдем]." Moscow has found itself in an awkward position vis-a-vis the North Caucasus and the three republics in particular. The choice it has is between further integration and further separation. The proclaimed federal policy that is supported by financial resources is staunchly pro-integration, but the reality is more complicated. Moscow substantially engages only in the security field, does not interfere decisively into internal affairs, and rather passively watches how the republics are drifting away by default. Implicitly, the leadership seems to appreciate that re-integrating the republics into Russia's political and social space would require a massive effort beyond funding, such as deployment of federal, mostly ethnic

Russian, personnel into public sector jobs. It also would mean enforcing rules, regulations, and practices common elsewhere, and opening serious investigations and prosecutions. This option is likely to be costly and unpopular.

However, even if Moscow contemplated formal separation of these territories, it is difficult to envisage how this could be done in practice. Excluding the republics for "bad behavior" would be an unprecedented step. The opportune moment of the early 1990s, when coherent secular independence movements existed, has been lost due to the fear of further federal breakdown. Presently, there are no indigenous pro-nationalist agents to articulate separation bids, and Czechoslovakia-style peaceful divorce is unlikely.

Instead, measures toward distancing from the republics are underway—such as suspension of conscription—and are likely to progress in the same direction. The losers in this paradigm are Stavropol *krai*, which could end up as a buffer between the republics and Russia's territory northward, and North Ossetia on the border with its nemesis Ingushetia. These territories have already taken a heavy toll in terrorist acts and casualties compared to the rest of the country, and frustration with Russia's leadership for placing them in this role and for failure to offer adequate protection is high. Still, Moscow's immediate problem is the situation in major cities, where protest moods do not subside and the issue of "Caucasians" is one to rally around. The Kremlin's best hope would be to limit Caucasian migration into Russia's big cities, but since the abolition of the Soviet-era residency permits, population movement is difficult to control.

The "North-Caucasian" debate has turned ethnicity into an emotionally charged political cleavage in modern Russia, and has raised issues of Russian nationalism to a pitch unprecedented in recent decades. This can be explained by the decline in universality of public institutions and surfacing of informal ways of problem-solving in the last 20 years. Ethnic solidarity mechanisms and networks characteristic for the Caucasian groups turned out to be effective in those circumstances. Presently—in the eyes of the Russian public—membership in a Caucasian group renders unfair advantages. It is unsurprising that this "injustice" subsequently caused resentment among the majority group. Thus, an all-Russian identity has a chance to become a reality only when state mechanisms became universally accessible and effective for all citizens.

Since the separation of the North Caucasus from Russia has been openly raised as an issue of public discourse, Moscow has been pushed toward a substantive (as opposed to a rhetorical) response. However, the options do not look good. Admitting that it cannot or does not want to exercise effective power over regional developments would risk Russia's appearance as a "weak" or even "failing" state, unable to control its own territory. Russia's leadership clearly does not wish to be considered as such. Therefore, it must pretend, in some plausible way, that the situation is under control. This is increasingly difficult to do.

Notes

1 Matveeva, Anna, "Chechnya in the North Caucasus: how much is it an exception to a rule?" in *Chechnya i Rossiya: bshchestva i gosudarstva*, Dmitrii Furman (ed.), 372–98. Moscow: Polinform-Talburi, 1999.

2 The project presented one of 18 case studies under *People's Peacemaking Perspectives*, funded by the EU Instrument for Stability. The author was the lead researcher and the author of the report "The North Caucasus: Views from Within: People's Perspectives on Peace and Security" (London: Saferworld, 2012).

3 Explanation of qualitative methods see in J. Ritchie and J. Lewis (eds), *Qualitative Research Practice: a Guide for Social Science Students and Researchers* (London: Sage, 2003).

4 "Информационные материалы об окончательных итогах Всероссийской переписи населения 2010 года," State Statistics Committee of the Russian Federation, Moscow, 2012.

5 Cited in "Русско-кавказские взаимоотношения в Северо-Кавказском федеральном округе," Вопросы Национализма, 2 (2010), http://vnatio.org/arhiv-nomerov/node86

6 Figures articulated by Vladimir Putin during his visit to Gudermes, Chechnya, December 20, 2011, reported in Latukhina K, "Kavkazskii Marshrut," *Rosskiiskaya Gazeta*, December 21, 2011, no. 287, 2.

7 See, for instance, in the present volume, Richard Sakwa, "Blowback? Chechnya and the Challenges of Russian Politics" and Domitilla Sagramoso and Akhmet Yarlykapov, "Caucasian Crescent: Russia's Islamic Policies and Its Responses to Radicalization."

8 Ekajevo focus group with village administrators, Ingushetia, December 2011.

9 *Kolkhoz* was a collective farm administered by state management, with inputs and outputs guaranteed by the state.

10 See "Stories you weren't meant to hear: Women, Tradition and Power in Russia's North Caucasus," *OpenDemocracy*, July 19, 2012, http://opendemocracy.net/russia

11 Author's interviews in Pyatigorsk with ethnic Russian and Dagestani respondents, October 2011.

12 "Информационные материалы об окончательных итогах Всероссийской переписи населения 2010 года," State Statistics Committee of the Russian Federation, Moscow, 2012, www.gks.ru/wps/wcm/connect/rosstat/rosstatsite/main/population/demography

13 Interview with Russian Orthodox priest, Pokrov church, Ingushetia, December 18, 2012.

14 Anonymous interview in Ingushetia, December 2011.

15 Visit to the Russian cemetery, stanitsa Ordjinikidziyevskaya, December 18, 2011.
16 Opinions expressed in the interview with Tamara Yandiyeva and by focus group respondents at stanitsa Ordjinikidziyeskaya, December 18, 2011.
17 The changes to make social environment more compliant with Islamic rules were already noted by Alexei Malashenko in 2007.
18 Akhmet Yarlykapov, "Dagestan: Stable Instability," in "The North Caucasus: Views from Within: People's Perspectives on Peace and Security" (London: Saferworld, 2012). Overall edit by Craig Oliphant with contribution by Luitgard Hammerer. The chapter in English exists only in electronic form and can be found at Saferworld website which is www.saferworld.org.uk The Russian edition contains the chapter in hard copy entitled "Республика Дагестан: Стабильная Нестабильность". The details of the Russian edition are "Северный Кавказ: Взгляд Изнутри: Вызовы и Проблемы Социально-Политического Развития» Anna Matveeva, Alexander Skakov and Igor Savin (eds.) (Moscow: Saferworld and Institute of Oriental Studies of Russian Academy of Sciences, 2012), pp. 137–53.
19 Oleg Ionov, "Makhachkala headmaster became a victim of contract killers," *Kavkazkii Uzel* www.kavkazuzel.ru/articles/174704/, cited by A. Yarlykapov.
20 Focus group with students of Polytechnic College, Nazran, December 2011.
21 A respondent at the university focus group, Nazran, December 2011.
22 Interview with a person among the respondents who had an experience of using quaziyat, Nazran, December 2011.
23 Anna Zelkina, *In Quest of God and Freedom: Sufi Responses to the Russian Advance in the North Caucasus*. New York: New York University Press, 2000.
24 Absallitdin Murzayev, presentation at Pyatigorsk seminar, October 2011.
25 Interview with Marem Yalkharoyeva, Nazran, December 2011.
26 Focus group with Law Faculty students, Ingush State University, Nazran, December 2011.
27 Domitilla Sagramoso, "The Radicalization of Islamic Salafi *Jamaats* in the North Caucasus: Moving Closer to the Global *Jihad*ist Movement?" *Europe-Asia Studies*, 64(3) (May 2012): 561–95.
28 Focus group with Law Faculty students, Ingush State University, Nazran, December 2011.
29 Ibid.
30 Absalitdin Murzayev in remarks at Pyatigorsk seminar, October 2011.
31 Said Buryatsky (real name Alexander Tikhomirov born in Buryatia) was considered the rebels' "no. 1 ideologist." He made his mark on the internet, posting dozens of videos of his sermons online and surging in popularity among young Russian Muslims—*Global Jihad 21st Century Phenomenon*, www.globaljihad.net/view_page.asp?id=1876
32 Young man—a student of Law Faculty, Ingush State University, focus group discussion, Nazran, December 2011.
33 Young woman—participant in a focus group discussion, Polytechnic College, Nazran, December 2011.
34 Focus group with students of Polytechnic College, Nazran, December 2011.
35 Interview with Akhmet Kotiyev, Secretary of the Security Council, Magas, December 2011.

36 Amnesty International, *The Circle of Injustice. Security Operations and Human Rights Violations in Ingushetia*. London: Amnesty International, 2012.

37 Gordon M. Hahn, *Islam, Islamism and Politics in Eurasia Report* (IIPER), no. 59, July 23, 2012.

38 Gordon M. Hahn, *Russia's Islamic Threat*. New Haven and London: Yale University Press, 2007.

39 *IIPER*, no. 59, July 23, 2012.

40 *IIPER*, no. 60, August 31, 2012.

41 *IIPER*, no. 60, August 31, 2012.

42 Interview with Magomet Musol'gov, director of *Mashr* human rights organization, Karabulak, December 2011.

43 *IIPER*, no. 60, August 31, 2012.

44 *IIPER*, no. 57, June 1, 2012.

45 Ministry of Interior of Ingushetia, http://mvd-ing.ru/finder/crime/

46 Interview with Akhmet Kotiyev, Secretary of the Security Council, Magas, December 2011.

47 Ibid.

48 Focus group with students of Polytechnic College, Nazran, December 2011.

49 The author is grateful to Igor Savin for pointing this out.

50 Focus group "Formation of civic institutions: prospects for establishment of partnership and dialogue with the authorities," Chechnya, conducted by Musa Yunusov for Saferworld study, September 2011.

51 Focus group with business people, Chechnya, conducted by Musa Yunusov for Saferworld study, September 2011.

52 Cited in "Русско-кавказские взаимоотношения в Северо-Кавказском федеральном округе," *Вопросы Национализма*, 2(2010), http://vnatio.org/arhiv-nomerov/node86

53 Igor Dulayev, Igor Savin, "What Next For North Ossetia – Complications Or Stability?" in "The North Caucasus: Views from Within: People's Perspectives on Peace and Security" (London: Saferworld, 2012). Overall edit by Craig Oliphant with contribution by Luitgard Hammerer. The chapter in English exists only in electronic form and can be found at Saferworld website which is www.saferworld.org.uk The Russian edition contains the chapter in hard copy entitled "Северная Осетия на Перепутье: Ситуация Сложная или Ситуация Стабильная?". The details of the Russian edition are "Северный Кавказ: Взгляд Изнутри: Вызовы и Проблемы Социально-Политического Развития» Anna Matveeva, Alexander Skakov and Igor Savin (eds.) (Moscow: Saferworld and Institute of Oriental Studies of Russian Academy of Sciences, 2012), pp. 78–98.

54 Ibid.

55 Janna Khamdokhova, "The Republic of Kabardino-Balkaria: Has the Sleeping Beauty Been Awoken?" in "The North Caucasus: Views from Within: People's Perspectives on Peace and Security" (London: Saferworld, 2012). Overall edit by Craig Oliphant with contribution by Luitgard Hammerer. The chapter in English exists only in electronic form and can be found at Saferworld website which is www.saferworld.org.uk The Russian edition contains the chapter in hard copy entitled "Кабардино-Балкария: "спящую красавицу» разбудили?" The details of the Russian edition are "Северный Кавказ: Взгляд Изнутри:

Вызовы и Проблемы Социально-Политического Развития» Anna
Matveeva, Alexander Skakov and Igor Savin (eds.) (Moscow: Saferworld and
Institute of Oriental Studies of Russian Academy of Sciences, 2012), pp. 49–77.
56 Author's interview with Igor Dulyaev, Vladikavkaz, North Ossetia—Alania,
December 2011.
57 Dmitri Medvedev on November 21, 2011, at a meeting with civil society and
media representatives in Rostov-on-Don, www.kavkaz-uzel.ru/articles/196208/
and Vladimir Putin in Gudermes, December 21, 2011.
58 "Отношение к мигрантам-соседям и мигрантам-коллегам. ФОМ
выяснил, как относятся россияне к мигрантам из других регионов и
других государств," Fond Obshestvennoye Mnenie, May 25, 2012, http://
fom.ru/mir/10442
59 *Rex Information Agency*, September 1, 2011, www.iarex.ru/news/19113.html
60 Ilya Roslyakov, "Вызовы кавказофобии и нетерпимости," May 28, 2012,
http://kavpolit.com/vyzovy-kavkazofobii-i-neterpimosti/
61 "Депутаты вступились за самбиста Р.Мирзаева, убившего студента," *RBK
daily*, August 22, 2011, http://top.rbc.ru/society/22/08/2011/611636.shtml
62 www.apn.ru/news/article26172.htm
63 This view is shared by experts; see, for instance, Alexei Malashenko, "What
the North Caucasus means for Russia," *Russie. Nei. Visions*, no. 61, IFRI,
Paris, July 2011, www.ifri.org
64 "Вызов Северного Кавказа. Наш ответ," May 2012, http://novayasila.org/
position/node25/
65 Robert Bruce Ware, "Has the Russian Federation Been Chechenised?"
Europe-Asia Studies, 63(3) (2011): 493–508.
66 As argued by Richard Sakwa in "Blowback? Chechnya and the Challenges of
Russian Politics," in the current volume.
67 Focus group, anonymous respondents, Nazran, December 2011.
68 Human rights' activist interview, December 2011.
69 According to the Ministry of Defense, cited by *RIA Novosti*, June 18, 2012,
http://ria.ru/society/20120618/675902719.html
70 "Four Ingush keep the whole company in terror," video clip cited by the
respondents at the Polytechnic College focus group, Nazran, December 2011.
71 Interview with Yakub Patiyev, Nazran, December 19, 2011.

Bibliography

Amnesty International, *The circle of injustice. Security Operations and Human
Rights Violations in Ingushetia*. London: Amnesty International, 2012.
Hahn, Gordon M., *Russia's Islamic Threat*. New Haven and London: Yale
University Press, 2007.
Malashenko, Aleksei, *Islam dlya Rossii*, Carnegie Moscow Centre. Moscow:
ROSSPEN, 2007.
Matveeva, Anna, "Chechnya in the North Caucasus: how much is it an exception
to a rule?" in *Chechnya i Rossiya: obshchestva i gosudarstva*, Dmitrii Furman
(ed.), 372–98. Moscow: Polinform-Talburi, 1999.

— "The North Caucasus: the Russian Inner Abroad," in *Borderlands in Transition*, Nikolai Petrov (ed.), Moscow: Moscow Carnegie Center, 2000.

Sagramoso, Domitilla, "The Radicalization of Islamic Salafi *Jamaats* in the North Caucasus: Moving Closer to the Global *Jihad*ist Movement?" *Europe-Asia Studies*, 64(3) (May 2012): 561–95.

Ware, Robert Bruce, "Has the Russian Federation Been Chechenised?" *Europe-Asia Studies*, 63(3) (2011): 493–508.

Zelkina, Anna, *In Quest of God and Freedom: Sufi Responses to the Russian Advance in the North Caucasus*. New York: New York University Press, 2000.

CHAPTER TEN

Conclusion: How Has the Caucasus Shaped Russia?

Robert Bruce Ware

The title of this concluding chapter is the question that I posed to those colleagues who graciously have offered their responses throughout this volume. Once asked, the question seems so natural that scholarship of these regions could not be considered complete without its investigation. Yet while Caucasian instabilities have played a prominent and continuing role in the evolution of the Russian Federation their influence remains under-studied and largely opaque.[1] On the other hand, the question's converse—-*how has Russia Shaped the Caucasus?*—has been an underlying theme in thousands of reports, both scholarly and journalistic.[2] Hence there has been a tendency to view the peoples of the North Caucasus in primarily passive roles, receiving policy directives and reacting to changes imposed upon them from Moscow, rather than as reciprocally causing important changes in the Russian Federation itself. Some may feel reassured by simple preconceptions of Russia as an aggressive, unenlightened hegemon that has forced Caucasian peoples to a stark dilemma of helpless victimization or desperate self-defense. But the reality of this relationship is more complex. Ultimately, these stereotypes have helped no one, and they have harmed the interests of all concerned. In an effort to address that deficit, this volume considers some of the complex causal relationships that have shaped Russia in recent decades.

Caucasian causation

The first part of this book presents a set of three historical surveys of Caucasian instabilities. Patrick Armstrong opens this segment with an argument that Western journalistic and scholarly reports on the Caucasus often have been based on presumptive memes, which precede factual information and which sometimes have precluded serious investigation. Directly contrary to the causal explanations that have been offered by these conventional views, Armstrong argues that Russia has reacted to problems that are Georgian in their origin.

On Armstrong's analysis, Georgian chauvinism played a role in ethnic frictions that sparked flames in South Ossetia (1991–2) and Abkhazia (1992–3). Among the historical data that he presents, Armstrong's observation that Western accounts generally have overlooked the perspectives and desires of Abkhazians and South Ossetians is particularly striking.

In Abkhazian flames, North Caucasian volunteers saw visions of the Mountain Republic that ephemerally had united North Caucasian nationalities from 1918 to 1922.[3] Volunteers such as Shamil Basaev, from Chechnya, answered Georgian aggression with atrocities of their own.

Meanwhile, South Ossetians displaced by conflict fled northward across the mountains, where many were settled in the Prigorodny *raion*. Prigorodny was formerly part of the Chechen-Ingush ASSR. It was annexed to North Ossetia in 1944 after Joseph Stalin deported the Chechens and the Ingush to Central Asia, dissolving their homeland into neighboring territories. In 1957, when Nikita Khrushchev rehabilitated the Chechens and Ingush, and restored some of their traditional lands, Prigorodny remained with North Ossetia.[4]

Frictions developed as Ingush returned to their homes to find them occupied by Ossetians. Though some of the Ingush repurchased their homes, the situation smoldered up to the early 1990s, and sparks flew when refugees from South Ossetia were settled into Prigorodny. Fighting broke out on October 30, 1992 and lasted until November 6. With support from Russian Interior Ministry forces, Ossetian militia waged a campaign of ethnic cleansing that killed over 600 Ingush civilians, and it was not for several days that Russian peace-keeping operations began.[5] More than 60,000 Ingush were pushed into squalid camps, which fester to this day, while refugees from South Ossetia settled into some of their homes.[6]

All of these events resonated in neighboring Chechnya, where recently elected president Dzhokhar Dudaev cherished nationalist aspirations. Not only did he advocate Chechnya's separation from Russia, but he promoted his republic as the rightful center of a North Caucasian state. Though Ingushetia had broken off from Chechnya in 1992, Chechens and Ingush share Vainakh language and culture. For many Ingush and Chechens, the flames of Prigorodny illuminated Moscow's favoritism of Christian Ossetia. Armstrong argues that Chechens such as Dudaev and Basaev aimed to follow Abkhazian and South Ossetian independence with that of Chechnya and Ingushetia as the next step in the reestablishment of a North Caucasian state, this time stretching from the Caspian to the Black Sea.

In this way, Armstrong traces a causal chain from Georgian chauvinism in the late 1980s to the first of the recent Russo-Chechen conflicts from 1994 to 1996. His is an argument of neither necessary nor sufficient, but rather of contributing causation. That is, Armstrong does not argue that this sequence inevitably connected all of the causes involved in these events. Abkhazia and South Ossetia may have split from Georgia even without Tbilisi's instabilities and the pressures of Georgian nationalism. Yet while these conflicts remain controversial, and while there is plenty of blame to go around, it is difficult to deny that Georgian nationalism and Georgian aggression were significant contributing factors.

Similarly, Prigorodny had been smoldering since the 1950s. The Ingush-Ossetian conflict might have ignited without inspiration from Abkhazia and South Ossetia and without additional pressures of South Ossetian refugees. Without conflicts in Abkhazia and Prigorodny, Dudaev and Basaev still probably would have advocated Chechen independence. The first Chechen conflict might have been avoided had Yeltsin managed Dudaev more wisely, or had Russian forces stayed away in December 1994. Yet it cannot be denied that the South Caucasian ethnic conflicts from 1991 to 1993 were factors that contributed to ethnic conflicts in the North Caucasus from 1992 to 1996.

Meanwhile, Domitilla Sagramoso and Akhmet Yarlykapov provide a historical look at influences arriving in the North Caucasus from the Islamic South and East. Their chapter is insightful in its balanced account of the contemporary Salafist insurgency and some of the causal reciprocity that ensues between the Russian Federation and this, its most-Muslilm region.

Islamist influences contributed only peripherally to frictions that were couched primarily in ethnic terms during the early 1990s. Yet as with ethnic violence, Islamism was a trend that arrived in the North Caucasus by way of many paths. After the collapse of the Soviet Union, there was a sharp rise in the number of Caucasians making the *hajj* to Saudi Arabia. More young men sought Islamic education outside of Russia, particularly in South Asia and the Arabian Peninsula. Islamist organizations expanded their operations globally. For example, Ayman al-Zawahiri, the high-level Al Qaeda leader, spent months in a Dagestani prison in 1996.[7] By these and other routes, Islamist influences converged on the North Caucasus from the South and from the East.

Salafism became an active force in the Soviet Union during *perestroika* when the Islamic Renaissance Party (IRP) organized in Tajikistan and immediately attracted attention with its publication of an influential manifesto entitled "Are We Muslims?" A Dagestani Avar named Akhmed-hadji Akhtaev, who was residing in Tajikistan, became the IRP Chair. Akhtaev, who was a trained physician and a self-taught theologian moved to Dagestan, where he founded a spiritual and educational organization known as *"Al-Islamiyya."*[8]

Chechen political leaders regarded Akhtaev as a religious authority. Akhtaev served as a deputy to Zelimkhan Yandarbiev, a radical Chechen leader, in organizing the Caucasian Conference, where Dudaev and Basaev advocated an Islamic pan-Caucasian state. He was also a deputy to Movladi Udugov in his movement "Islamic Nation." On an invitation from Udugov, Akhtaev became head of Islamic Nation's *Shariah* Court.[9]

The IRP was organized at the Union level in 1990 at a convention in Astrakhan, on the authority of Akhtaev and through the efforts of leading Dagestani Islamists, including the brothers Abbas (a.k.a. Illyas and Bagautdin Kebedov). The organization was registered in Moscow as the All-Soviet Union Moslem Political Organization. Among its goals were the "spiritual revival" and the "political awakening" of Muslims, and the realization of their rights to construct their life on the basis of the Koran. The constitutive documents of the organization referred to the need for "the broad education of all peoples concerning the basis of the Islamic religion, the need for training of Moslem leaders, who can understand the essence of Islam and are capable of giving answers to the vital problems of contemporary world."[10]

Akhtaev's program, in many ways, resembled that of the Muslim Brotherhood, which was at this time moving into the South Caucasus from North Africa and the Middle East. He practiced a "pure" form of Islam, regarding Sufism as a deviation, advocating the moral and spiritual superiority of fundamentalist Islam, and insisting upon its role in the economic modernization of Dagestan. Dagestan must become an Islamic state, he argued, because the interests of Russian Muslims required political support. Akhtaev believed that a united Islamic North Caucasus would gain greater respect from Moscow, along with greater economic and political autonomy.

His calls for Russian devolution along confederal lines attracted the attention of Chechen separatists, who repeatedly offered him positions in the Chechen government. However, Akhtaev affirmed that Dagestan was situated historically in both Islamic and Orthodox Christian civilizations and therefore rejected *jihad* against Russia. He sought a fundamental political transformation along Islamist lines, but he was prepared to work within established political structures, and he held political office in Dagestan.[11]

By 1998, Akhtaev had fallen afoul of both the Makhachkala authorities and the radical Salafist "Wahhabis." In Dagestan, either one of these difficulties is typically fatal. In the heat of the electoral race, the vigorous 56-year-old Akhtaev suddenly died, amid widespread rumors that he had been poisoned.[12] In that same year, foreign Islamist funding shifted from Akhtaev and *Al-Islamiyya* to Bagautdin Kebedov and his *Jamaat*. It was also in 1998 that Dagestani officials accused unspecified Persian Gulf organizations of waging *jihad* against Dagestan.

Though Kebedov had cooperated with Akhtaev in the early days of the IRP, and while they were similarly favored by Chechen separatists as late as 1993, their paths diverged as Bagautdin became immersed in the violence that overwhelmed Chechnya after the summer of 1994. Before the end of the first Chechen war in 1996, Bagautdin was organizing Wahhabi cells in Chechnya. Meanwhile in Dagestan he organized, and became the *amir* (spiritual leader) of, the *Jamaat*[13] *ul-Islamiiun ad-Dagestaniia* (Islamic Community of Dagestan).[14]

During those early years, Baugdtin was competing with Akhtaev to attract those Muslims who were alienated from Dagestan's politico-religious establishment. Hence, he staked out a particularly uncompromising approach toward the new Sufi Islamic authorities. His Dagestani followers rejected all official Islamic structures as complicit in the corruption of the local government and the hegemony of the Russian state. They rejected all legitimate political activities, including the formation of political parties, and they ruled out any form of cooperation or compromise with officials in Moscow or Makhachkala. They were fiercely hostile toward Russia and were committed to the foundation of an Islamist state to span the North Caucasus as a prelude to its unification with the Muslim *umma*. They aimed to replicate the political ascents of Islamists in Afghanistan and Sudan.[15]

By the end of the 1990s Dagestan's Wahhabis were flexing their muscles. With generous foreign assistance they built many of their own mosques and controlled no less than 14 *madrassahs*. They distributed religious literature from their own publishing house, and they operated a satellite uplink in Kizilyurt (where Bagautdin was based) through which they communicated with one another, and with their supporters abroad. Each year, they sent dozens of young men to study in Islamic *madrassahs* and universities in Saudi Arabia, Egypt, Algeria, Malaysia, Jordan, and Pakistan. Moreover their political significance extended beyond their organizational achievements. They were often well-armed, and by their very presence they polarized village life and provided an incentive for mountain populations to arm themselves for their own security. Religious schisms often occurred within a family, where children were at odds with parents or brothers were opposed to brothers.[16]

In December 1997, an alliance was established with a "Military Mutual Assistance Treaty" signed by the Chechen commander, Salman Raduev[17] and representatives of the "Fighting Squads of the *Djamaat* of Dagestan." The Treaty affirmed that Chechen government forces and the Islamic *Djamaat* of Dagestan were unified in the struggle for an independent Islamic Caucasian state.[18]

On December 22, 1997 Wahaabis from this *djamaat* joined with Chechen and foreign fighters from Chechnya's International Islamic

Battalion (comprising a total party of 30 to 120 gunmen according to various sources) to attack the 136th Armored Brigade based in the village of Gerlakh, near Buinaksk.[19]

The joint attack on the 136th Armored Brigade resulted in three civilian fatalities and 14 casualties, though the raiders' claims were far higher. According to various Russian and Chechen accounts anywhere from 10 to 300 vehicles were damaged or destroyed. The "Central Front for the Liberation of the Caucasus and Dagestan" claimed responsibility for the incident, and the subsequent investigation placed the blame on Dagestani Wahhabis—from a nearby Islamist enclave consisting of the ethnic Dargin villages of Karamakhi, Chabanmakhi, and Kadar—in concert with their Chechen allies.[20]

Their allies also included a Saudi *jihadist* known locally as Emir al Khattab. He was born in 1969 to a Saudi father and an Adyghe mother who named him Saleh Abdullah Al-Suwailem. From the age of 17, he fought the Soviets in Afghanistan, where, by his own account, he came into contact with Osama bin Laden. From 1993 to 1995 he fought for the Islamist opposition in Tajikistan's civil war. He entered Chechnya in 1995 as a television reporter and pioneered films of the Chechen conflict that were used for purposes of international recruitment and fund raising. While acting as an intermediary for Islamist funding, he increasingly filmed his own military exploits. Khattab achieved notoriety in April 1996, when he led an ambush on a Russian armored column near the Chechen mountain town of Shatoi. By the end of the first Chechen war he was the commander of the International Islamic Battalion, consisting primarily of Arab and other foreign fighters. He married a Dagestani woman from Karamakhi, where he resided intermittently.[21]

On July 5, 1998 a meeting of approximately 1,000 armed men took place in Karamakhi, which was variously advertised as the "United Congress of the Orthodox Muslims of Dagestan" and as the "Congress of the of the Military and Political Leadership of the Central Front for the Liberation of Dagestan." What was certain was their declaration of an independent political authority, the principal effect of which was to shift the forefront of anti-Russian agitation from Chechnya to Dagestan. Their demands included the resignation of the entire Dagestani government, union with Chechnya, and the withdrawal of all federal troops from Dagestani soil. In a published statement the Dagestani government responded that it would "do everything to protect the constitutional system, social rights and freedom of the citizens."[22] Throughout the next month tensions continued to increase.

After July 14–15, when fighters from this self-styled "Islamic *Djamaat*" (or "liberated Dagestan") participated in an attack upon Chechen forces in the Chechen town of Gudermes, it was denounced by the Presidents of both Chechnya (Aslan Maskhadov) and Ingushetia (Ruslan Aushev).[23] Yet some young men were attracted to military training camps operated in Chechnya by Khattab and Basaev with funding from abroad. In these camps rural Dagestani disaffection met Chechen militancy and the international *jihadist* movement. Meanwhile Wahhabism grew increasingly influential in Chechnya as rival political leaders appealed to puritanical Islam in order to transcend clan differences and to bolster their claims to authority.

In Grozny, on April 17, 1999, the second Congress of the Peoples of Ichkeria and Dagestan took place. In some circles the event was described as the "Congress of the Moslems of the North Caucasus." As reported by E. Kozhaeva in *Molodezh Dagestana,* the Congress included 297 delegates from 25 Dagestani *djamaats.* From Chechnya there were 195 official representatives plus over 200 invited guests. At the Congress, Basaev announced that he had founded the "peace-keeping Caucasian forces" that were amassing in training camps that he operated in conjunction with Khattab and Bagautdin Kebedov. In Basaev's words, "the military-political Council and the Security Council are formed, as well as the Islamic legion and peace-keeping brigade, which consists of several thousands of well-trained soldiers." These forces, according to Basaev, "are necessary for the realization of the resolutions of the Congress, the main purpose of which is the formation of the independent Islamic state in the range of Chechnya and Dagestan. . . ." The same forces were among those that invaded Dagestan less than four months later. A resolution of the Congress stated that the situation in the North Caucasus was "critical," and there was a need "to commence the process of the decolonization of Dagestan." Russian authorities were "offered the opportunity to start pulling their troops from the republic."[24]

Beginning on August 2,[25] and again on September 5, 1999, insurgents led by Basaev and Khattab invaded Dagestan from bases in Chechnya. In August they crossed the border into Dagestan's Botlikhsky and Tsumadinsky *raions.* On August 10 they declared the Independent Islamic Republic of Dagestan under the leadership of Siradjin Ramazanov, a relative of Akhmed-hadji Akhtaev, who lacked the latter's propensities toward intellectualism and moderation. By that time they had seized the villages of Ansalta, Rakhata, and Shadroda and reached the village of Tando, close to the district town of Botlikh. The fighting in these villages endangered the entire population of Andis, an ethno-linguistically distinctive group of about 30,000 that are counted administratively, along with other small groups, as Avars.[26]

To the evident surprise of the insurgents their invasion was fiercely resisted both by the local villagers and by an overwhelmingly majority of the population of Dagestan, who spontaneously formed citizen militias. Dagestani officials repeatedly requested federal military assistance before the Russian troops were finally dispatched under the leadership of Colonel-General Viktor Kazantsev, commander of the North Caucasus Military District.[27]

Faced with a hostile civilian population, an unanticipated counter attack from citizen militias, approximately 1,000 Dagestani special purposes mobile OMON troops, air-mobile Russian infantry, and a ruthless Russian bombardment that did not hesitate to obliterate Dagestani homes, and that saw the introduction of fuel-air explosives, Basaev and Khattab withdrew on August 22. They declared that their subsequent efforts to unite Dagestan with Chechnya would be "political not military." By August 26, all fighting in the region had ceased.[28]

Three days later Dagestani OMON troops initiated an offensive against the Islamist enclave in the villages of Karamakhi, Chabanmakhi, and Kadar. On September 5, Basaev and Khattab invaded Dagestan a second time, this time driving toward Buinaksk in an apparent attempt to relieve Karamakhi. The invasion was preceded by an explosion of an apartment block in Buinaksk on September 4. Soon thereafter two apartment block blasts occurred in Moscow on September 9 and 13, and then in Volgodonsk on September 16. Karamakhi capitulated to federal forces on that same day. In *Lidove Novingy* (Prague, September 9, 1999) Petra Prokhazkova offered the following quote from Shamil Basaev:

> The latest blast in Moscow is not our work, but the work of the Dagestanis. Russia has been openly terrorizing Dagestan . . . For the whole week, united in a single fist, the army and the Interior Ministry units have been pounding three small villages . . . And blasts and bombs—all this will go, of course, because those whose loved ones, whose women and children are being killed for nothing will also try to use force to eliminate their adversaries. This is a natural process and it is yet more evidence of Newton's third law, that each action generates a reaction . . . What is the difference between someone letting a bomb go off in the centre of Moscow and injuring 10–20 children and the Russians dropping bombs from their aircraft over Karamakhi and killing 10–20 children? Where is the difference?

Among those whose women and children were in the village was Khattab, who was married to a Karamakhi woman. On September 15, Greg Myre, an Associated Press reporter, quoted Khattab as saying

> From now on, we will not only fight against Russian fighter jets (and) tanks. From now on, they will get our bombs everywhere. Let Russia await our explosions blasting through their cities. I swear we will do it.

A total of 294 civilians died in the four apartment block blasts that occurred during the days that Karamakhi was under attack by federal forces. Yet despite the statements by Basaev and Khattab, and despite the correlation of the dates of the blasts with the fighting in Karamakhi, this connection has received nearly no attention from Western scholars and journalists.[29]

On September 29, 1999, Putin offered to open negotiations with Chechen leadership on condition (1) that Aslan Maskhadov condemn terrorism "clearly and firmly;" (2) that he eject armed bands from Chechen territory; and (3) that he agree to the extradition of "criminals." Maskhadov declined the overture.[30] On October 1 Russian troops crossed the Chechen border.

These events climaxed years of lawlessness in Chechnya. After Chechens achieved de facto independence from Russia in 1996, they elected a moderate—Aslan Maskhadov—to their newly created presidency. Yet Maskhadov quickly proved unable to control warlords such as Shamil Basaev, Salman Raduev, and Arbi Baraev. These and other commanders operated with Chechen criminal gangs that terrorized other Chechens and citizens of the surrounding territories. Livestock was rustled, money was counterfeited, petroleum was pilfered from numerous illegal taps on the—Baku-Novorossiysk pipeline, and automobiles that were stolen across Russia were funneled into Chechnya where they were out of the reach of Russian authorities.

Chechen gangs, under leaders such as Baraev, established a hostage industry that had thoroughly terrorized citizens of neighboring republics by the summer of 1998. Approximately 3,300 Russian citizens were kidnapped and taken into Chechnya, where they were beaten, starved, and confined in cellars and cages.[31] Kidnappers routinely videotaped themselves sawing off the appendages of hostages, so that they could send both videos and appendages along with demands of exorbitant ransoms that even extended Caucasian families were unable to pay. There were two slave markets that operated openly during those years, one in Grozny and one in Urus-Martan.[32] Child hostages too were tortured, mutilated, and sold into slavery.[33] On my visits to Dagestan, I saw the terror that the hostage industry inflicted upon all Dagestanis.

Chechnya's hostage industry took further tolls on the people of this region. In December 1996, six Red Cross staffers were murdered as they slept in Grozny.[34] Several employees of nongovernmental organizations(NGOs) were kidnapped from around the North Caucasus and transported to Chechnya, where they were abused and mutilated while awaiting enormous ransoms. I saw the videotape in which Chechen kidnappers sought to ransom an American by cutting off his finger with a crude knife.[35] The United Nations High Commissioner for Refugees (UNHCR) paid USD5 million to free the head of its North Caucasus operation after months of captivity. By 1998, after many similar incidents, every major international relief organization—including the United Nations—pulled out of the North Caucasus.

It was telling that these NGOs did not return to the region until after the Russian military had begun to make it safer for them to do so.[36] No sooner did groups such as Amnesty International, Human Rights Watch, and Médicins Sans Frontières venture back to the region than they began to issue reports condemning Russian brutalities and human rights abuses.

Generally, they did this without acknowledging[37] that before the Russian military returned, the situation had been so much more brutal, and that human rights abuses had been so much more extensive, that those organizations were unable to work in the region at all.

The conduct of Western journalists was all the more ironic. From the end of 1997 to the autumn of 1999, they almost entirely avoided this dangerous region. After Russian forces took Grozny in February 2000, Western journalists were brought to Chechnya under protection of Russian military forces. While they were ferried in and out of Grozny in Russian military helicopters, they wrote stories about the devastation and brutalities that Russian forces had inflicted.[38] The extremity of the situation before Russian troops arrived was mentioned much less frequently, much more briefly, and generally toward the end of their reports.[39]

Robert Schaefer and Andrei Doohovskoy examine Russia's underpreparation for the first Chechen war, and the military reasons for its desperation in the second. They show how the wars in Chechnya triggered a revolution in the Russian military, fundamentally altering its approaches to formations, tactics, training, and personnel. The authors argue that this transformation has had ramifications "throughout the social and political fabric of the Russian nation" because the military is among the most important socializing influences in Russia, calling, as it does, "at every young man's door." Schaefer and Doohovskoy show that Russia's military transformation is revolutionary not only because it is fundamental and sweeping, but also because it is unfinished. They suggest that the Caucasus will continue to cause deep changes in the Russian military.

Caucasian consequences

The first section of this book provides the basis for an argument that Georgian instability and chauvinism were among factors that contributed to conflicts in the South Caucasus, which contributed to conflicts in the North Caucasus, which, when combined with Islamist influences from the South and East, contributed to regional instabilities that cascaded into the near inevitability of the second war in Chechnya.

The second part examines the effects that Caucasian instabilities have had upon the Russian Federation. In neighboring Stavropol'skii *krai*, Andrew Foxall shows that these effects include out-migration, the rise of Russian nationalism, the spread of anti-Caucasian sentiments; and the transformation of southern Russia's economic and political geography. He argues that social, economic, and political changes taking place in Stavropol since 1991 reflect broader changes in Russia as a whole. Foxall's analysis is particularly helpful in tracing the effects that conflict and terrorism have had upon the evolution of the Russian federal system.

Beginning with the Yeltsin administration, this section examines that evolution more closely in order to connect it with Richard Sakwa's Dual-state analysis of influences of Chechenization on the Russian Federation. The result is a model of Russian political development that is subsequently elucidated through an interpretation of Walter Richmond's study of preparations for the Sochi Olympics.

Throughout his terms as Russia's president, Boris Yeltsin veered erratically through a series of prime ministerial appointments, tossing the title to Sergei Stepashin in May of 1999. Yet when militants from Chechnya invaded Dagestan on August 2 of that year, the chaotic federal response was uncomfortably emblematic of Yeltsin's bumbling administration. The stakes could not have been higher for the Russian Federation, when—just one week after the invasion of Dagestan began—Yeltsin tapped the obscure director of the Federal Security Service (FSB). At the time, Vladimir Putin seemed an unlikely prime minister; yet his self-assured approach to the military operation in Dagestan won immediate public approval, as did his belligerent reaction to apartment bombings in Buinaksk, Moscow, and Volgodonsk that September.[40]

Whatever the tendency in Putin's earlier career toward values of national security, military strength, and centralized control, these were brought to the fore as critical imperatives during Russia's defense of Dagestan in August and September of 1999, and in its subsequent invasion of Chechnya. By the time that Boris Yeltsin resigned from the Russian Presidency, such priorities were clearly ascendant over policies of decentralization and local democratic control that characterized the Yeltsin years. Indeed Yeltsin's long-term waffling on these points had much to do with the start of the first Chechen conflict, and contributed to the vicious cycle of Russian federal evolution and North Caucasian conflict that had begun even before the collapse of the Soviet Union.[41]

From his first weeks in power, both Putin's administration and popular perceptions thereof were indelibly stamped by imperatives in the northeast Caucasus. His leadership style and administrative priorities were arguably cast during the military and political trauma of those initial months. It is emblematic of his dramatic ascent that at the stroke of the New Year 2000, the very moment of Yeltsin's surprise resignation, Putin was not seated at the feet of his disgraced superior, but at the table of his new-found allies in Dagestan. "I love the people of Dagestan," he toasted.[42]

If Yeltsin had set his initial course for decentralization, Putin quickly swung the Federation back in the opposite direction with the May 2000 launch of his program for the recentralization of the Russian government. Given the early success of his militaristic approach to Dagestan and Chechnya, it came as little surprise that his bureaucratic model was Russian military organization. Just as the latter was organized through its central command of seven districts, so was the new federal state. The

North Caucasus fell into the nascent Southern Federal District, which was headed by General Victor Kazantsev from its inception on May 18, 2000 to March 9, 2004. Kazantsev led the federal military response to the invasions of Dagestan in 1999, and was a participant in both Chechen wars.[43]

Initially this federal district was called "Northern Caucasian," but the name was changed at Kazantsev's request. The name was altered ostensibly to reflect the fact that in addition to traditionally North Caucasian Republics (Dagestan, Chechnya, Ingushetia, North Ossetia, Kabardino-Balkaria, Karacheyvo-Cherkessia, and Adygeya), other southern Russian areas, such as Krasnodarsky, and Stavropol *krai*, the Rostovskaya *oblast* and two other territories were also included. However, the revised title also indicated an altered geopolitical orientation wherein Moscow served as the point of reference. Thus the district may have been north of the main range of the Caucasus Mountains, but more importantly it was also south of Moscow. The process of federal recentralization had a distinctive effect on each of these members of the Southern District. Andrew Foxall and Richard Sakwa emphasize that the effects of Russian recentralization in the North Caucasus proved to be influential for the evolution of the Russian Federation as a whole. Sakwa, in particular, examines the ironies of Chechenization.

On June 12, 2000, (in an echo of his own surprise appointment by Yeltsin) Putin tapped the Chechen mufti, Akhmed Kadyrov, to head the new loyalist Chechen administration, under a program that popularly was described as the Chechenization of the war. Putin's plan was gradually to turn the Chechen conflict over to the Kadyrov regime, which would be integrated as a local extension of federally centralized bureaucratic structures. The program effectively showcased the transfer of administrative power, since Kadyrov was allowed wide latitude for local operations and ample budgetary allocations, in exchange for his unswerving fealty to the federal center.[44]

The plan was feasible because Chechens like Kadyrov had been alienated by Islamists, who contributed to the lawless fragmentation of Chechen society during its period of de facto independence.[45] Kadyrov himself had fought against Russia in the first Chechen war, but was now prepared to align with old adversaries against his new Islamist enemies. Until his assassination in May 2004, Akhmed Kadyrov was a ruthless tactician, offering amnesties to Chechen militants at the same time that he made their operations more perilous. As more rebels switched sides, Kadyrov welcomed them into his administration, consolidated his power, and grew increasingly independent from Moscow.[46]

After Basaev's assassination of Akhmed Kadyrov in May 2004, power gradually passed to his son, Ramzan. Whether with Moscow's acquiescence or assistance, the last of Ramzan's Chechen rivals—Sulim Yamadaev—had been eliminated, and Ramzan had brought Chechnya ruthlessly under his control by 2008. In April 2009, Moscow declared an end to its counterterrorism campaign and withdrew most federal troops from Chechnya. Since then Ramzan has operated with almost complete independence from Moscow.

Ironically, as Sakwa notes, he has established an autonomous enclave not so different from that which Chechen separatists and Islamists fought for years to create—except that Kadyrov's Chechnya also enjoys massive federal subsidies. At least in its broader strokes, this seems to have been his father's vision. Before his death, Akhmed Kadyrov said, "We have been fighting for independence by military means for 400 years and have attained nothing. I am urging the Chechen people to spend at least 100 years trying to win independence by other means. We should demonstrate to the whole world that we are peaceful people. We will not impose an ideology alien to that of the Caucasus peoples brought in by all kinds of outsiders."[47]

Chechenization effectively meant that Putin and the Kadyrovs had followed one another in the centralization of authority over their respective spheres of power. Putin was able to work with the Kadyrovs because all three were prepared to compromise other objectives in order to advance centralized authority against those centrifugal forces they encountered in their respective political arenas. By cooperating in their reversal of centrifugal tendencies initiated in the Gorbachev–Yeltsin eras, Putin and the Kadyrovs achieved a compromise that significantly contributed to the recentralization of authority in the Russian Federation while allowing extensive autonomy to the bureaucratically-centralized Chechen administration.[48]

In terms of objectives for federal recentralization, Chechenization initially appeared to be an adaptation for the Federation's least integrated subject. Yet I shall argue that because of the role that the Chechen conflict played in Putin's rise to power, and because of its centrality to the initial years of his administration, the success of Putin's Chechenization program soon became the template for his recentralization of Russian administration with its characteristically top-down bureaucratic system. The fundamental premises of Putin's Chechenization policy were, in effect, subsequently elaborated for the administration of other North Caucasian republics. Under especially dramatic circumstances, these premises then were generalized to the reorganization of the Russian Federation itself.

During the month of August 2004, Shamil Basaev took credit for orchestrating explosions in the Moscow metro and on two of Russia's passenger aircraft. Then on September 1, a group of mostly Chechen and Ingush militants operating under Basev's direction commandeered School No. 1 in Beslan, North Ossetia. They held over 1,100 hostages under harsh conditions in the school gymnasium. Following events that remain controversial, at least 334 hostages died, including 156 children. The episode shocked the world, convulsed Russia, and altered the course of Islamist militancy in the North Caucasus. Though the hostage incident in Budenovsk (where he held over a thousand in a maternity hospital) and his invasions of Dagestan had not substantially discredited Basaev outside of Russia, the events in Beslan were condemned across the Muslim world, and he was blamed even by some of his militant Chechen supporters.[49] In his televised address on September 4, Putin announced that

> First, in the near future, a complex of measures aimed at strengthening the unity of our country will be prepared. Second, I consider it necessary to create a new system of forces and means for exercising control over the situation in the North Caucasus. Third, it is necessary to create an affective [sic] crisis management system, including entirely new approaches to the work of law enforcement agencies.[50]

Just one week later, in his speech at Beslan on September 13, 2004, Putin cited this security crisis in his call for a strongly centralized federal bureaucracy. He expressed support for a Central Election Commission proposal to eliminate the single mandate constituencies that accounted for half of the seats in the Russian State Duma, thereafter requiring that all Duma representatives should be seated from lists compiled by the national parties. This move effectively eliminated independent deputies in the Duma, strengthened party control of the body, and effectively reduced the number of viable federal parties. At the time of the announcement, the pro-Kremlin, United Russia Party enjoyed a two-thirds majority in the Duma, sufficient to initiate amendments to the constitution.[51]

In the same address, Putin announced plans to augment federal control by giving the Russian president power to nominate regional governors with the "endorsement" of regional legislatures, much as appointments previously had been made in Chechnya. He argued that these changes would reduce local corruption, streamline decision making, and strengthen government control in response to threats such as North Caucasian terrorism. Thus, in the immediate aftermath of the hostage tragedy in Beslan, Putin announced the effective extension of his Chechenization program to the Federation's other 88 subjects by means of the centralized appointment of local governors on terms essentially similar to those initially granted to Kadyrov four years earlier.

In fact this process had already begun in neighboring Ingushetia. In December 2001, Moscow forced the resignation of Ingushetia's popular President Ruslan Aushev, due partially to his criticism of Russia's campaign to prevent Chechen separatism on the eastern border of Ingushetia, while simultaneously enforcing the separation of the Prigorodny district from Ingushetia's western borders. In 2002, the Kremlin erred by replacing Aushev with Murat Zyazikov.

Essentially an appointee of the newly centralizing bureaucracy, Zyazikov lacked a local political base. Hence, Zyazikov could rely on nothing more than the allure of flagrant corruption and the muscle of the federal security services. By 2003 young men were disappearing at an alarming rate in sometimes-blatant abductions by law enforcement personnel.[52] Along with endemic poverty and rampant government corruption, these disappearances fueled a violent resistance with Islamist aspirations. On the night of June 21, 2004, Chechen and Ingush fighters launched well-coordinated attacks against law enforcement officials and civilians across Ingushetia. Thereafter these attacks became near-daily occurrences. The result was a rapid increase in repression, terrorism, and the corresponding decline of Ingush security from 2003 to 2008—along with the rise of the North Caucasus' only major peaceful opposition movement. By the summer of 2008, the opposition had grown to include well over 80 percent of the Ingush population. It was at this point that Russia's brief war with Georgia and its recognition of South Ossetian claims for independence from Tbilisi threatened to revive the smoldering conflict between Ingushetia and North Ossetia.[53]

As Stalin gave Prigorodny to North Ossetia, so he awarded South Ossetia to his Georgian homeland. Yet while Russia had defended Stalin's partition of Ingush land, it declined, in the aftermath of its war with Georgia in August 2008 to recognize Stalin's disposition of South Ossetia. Perceptions of Moscow's inconsistency added to the bitterness that Ingushes felt toward the Zyazikov regime. With a civil war already at hand in Ingushetia, Moscow faced the prospect of a massive popular uprising.[54]

In October 2008, these pressures culminated in the presidency of Yunus-Bek Yevkurov, whose Moscow supporters seemed to have learned from their preceding difficulties. The appointee clearly was the Kremlin's attempt to approximate Ruslan Aushev, but without Aushev's independent and outspoken political streak. As a Major-General in military intelligence (GRU), Yevkurov also signaled that Chechnya's autonomy would be exceptional if not evanescent, and that the Ministry of Defense would remain an influential force in the North Caucasus.[55]

Yevkurov himself seemed to have learned from Zyazikov's errors, embarking immediately upon a series of populist overtures. Yet near-daily militant attacks continued. In July 2009, Yevkurov was critically injured in a suicide attack that killed one of his relatives. Since that attack he has reduced his attempts to negotiate with opposition leaders.

One reason for Yevkurov's problems is that unlike the popularly elected Ruslan Aushev, Yevkurov is a bureaucratic appointee. Many Ingush—like other North Caucasians—distrust Moscow appointees, no matter how gifted and well-intentioned they may be. Any popular efficacy that they otherwise might have possessed is undermined by their appointment. A second cause of the Ingush insurgency is the sort of local grievances and economic disparities seen elsewhere in the region.

In Chechnya, Ramzan Kadyrov has sunk enormous federal subsidies into the security network through which he controls the republic, and into an ostentatious façade of reconstruction in the center of Grozny. Apart from its petroleum reserves, Kadyrov's hopes for economic development have hinged primarily on four industries: building construction, Electropult-Grozny, an Avtovaz auto factory producing Lada Priorias, and a woodworking plant. Though major construction projects have been subsidized largely by federal funds, and have been hampered by relentless corruption, they also have created jobs. Yet while the new stadium and central mosque are open to the public, the high-rise office suites and luxury hotel rooms that now dominate Grozny's skyline were not designed with most Chechens in mind. As a consequence of its protracted warfare and the exodus of ethnic-Russian specialists, Chechnya lacks an adequately educated workforce. Chechnya's official rate of unemployment remains well over 50 percent,[56] and since the lives of most Chechens are stubbornly impoverished, the beauty salons and sushi restaurants of central Grozny are an irritant for many and an incitement for an angry few.

Kadyrov has countered this resentment not only with brutal repression, but also with an officially sanctioned Islamic revival. The restriction of alcohol, the enforcement of the *hijab*, and the encouragement of polygamy are essentially alien practices for most North Caucasians, and yet they are becoming increasingly common in Chechnya as the republic drifts toward an approximation of *shariah* law. Kadyrov's support for Islam also serves his political objectives. By positioning himself as an Islamic leader, Kadyrov seeks to undermine the ideological base of the Islamist insurgency.

Yet in Chechnya, Islam provides the only alternative form of social organization to his own security structure. Having systematically eliminated rival Chechen warlords, the Kremlin has no one in Chechnya to rein in Kadyrov's caprices. Similarly, most Chechens are glad for whatever peace and stability they find. Despite their fears and resentments, they hope the rebirth of Grozny will sweep them along on the skirts of a new prosperity.

Although the administrative dynamics of their republic are in sharp contrast to those of Chechnya, many Dagestanis nurture similar hopes. In Dagestan, President Magomedsalam Magomedov lacks the military background and personal strength of his political cohorts in Chechnya and Ingushetia. While Akhmed and Ramzan Kadyrov were fighting Russian forces in the first Chechen war, and Islamist forces in the second, Magomedsalam and his father Magomedali were benefitting from a more peaceful Dagestan. The problem was that Magomedali amassed personal power instead of transferring political power in accord with the democratic constitution that Dagestan innovated from 1994 to 2003.

During the final years of the Union of Soviet Socialist Republics (USSR) and the first of Yeltsin's presidential terms, power devolved from Soviet verticality toward the ancient, and horizontally pluralistic, traditions of Dagestan's 34 ethno-linguistic groups. An intense but largely peaceful power struggle among a colorful multiplicity of Soviet elites, ethnic leaders, village elders, mountain clans, and emerging entrepreneurs culminated on July 26, 1994, in the adoption of an innovative democratic constitution.[57] In accord with its pluralistic traditions, Dagestan had the only collegial executive in the Russian Federation, and the only executive that was not chosen directly by popular vote. In a series of three referenda, Dagestanis rejected a popularly elected president for fear that the direct election of an individual leader would result in disproportionate power for a single ethnic group.[58]

Dagestan's State Council (*Gossovet*) consisted of one representative from each of its 14 principal ethnic groups. Yet while the Chair of the State Council was intended to rotate, it was monopolized by the representative from the Dargin ethnic group, Magomedali Magomedov. Dagestan also developed an ethnic electoral system that provided legislative representation nearly precisely proportionate to the population of most ethnic groups.[59] Thus as a natural result of local demographics and ancient traditions, Dagestan's constitution varied substantially from its federal counterpart.

In April 2000, almost immediately following Putin's election, federal officials requested that the attorney general of Dagestan, Imam Yaraliev, identify all articles of the Dagestani Constitution that did not match the Constitution of the Russian Federation. Yaraliev identified 45 points of variance. When Moscow rejected a series of proposed compromises, Dagestan's legislature made the requisite constitutional amendments. The following month Russia's Constitutional Court began a review of Dagestan's ethnic electoral system, thereby initiating a series of modifications that brought Dagestani elections into conformity with federal requirements over the next five years. Under federal pressure, Dagestan formally adopted a presidential system in 2003, nine years to the day after it had ratified its collegial executive.[60]

Most Dagestanis viewed these changes with ambivalence. Throughout its nine years of operation, Dagestan's innovative democratic system accomplished two primary objectives. It achieved ethnic proportionality, and it maintained political stability—even in those years when all surrounding territories were mired in protracted ethnic conflicts. Yet, Dagestan's economy remained stagnant, and available resources increasingly were monopolized by a shrinking circle of elites. Corruption was ubiquitous, economic disparities rankled traditionally egalitarian sensibilities, and Islamist extremism smoldered. Since the pluralism of Dagestan's political system mitigated against a bold and comprehensive approach to these problems, many Dagestanis hoped that the federal imposition of a centralized administration would alleviate some of these problems.[61]

Moscow would have been wiser to support Dagestan's incipient democracy against Magomedali's infringements, but instead the Kremlin appointed Dagestan's first president in February 2006. Since he was widely viewed as a principled leader without allegiance to any of Dagestan's clans or factions, Mukhu Aliev's appointment suggested that the Kremlin had learned from its disastrous installation of Murat Zyazikov in Ingushetia. Expectations rose following Aliev's early efforts to rationalize bureaucratic appointments and eliminate some corrupt local officials. These rising expectations culminated in a series of popular protests against local administrative abuses. Without warning, and with unprecedented brutality, some protests were suppressed by government forces. In defense of this suppression, Aliev stated that the government could not yield to popular protests because it would be a slippery slope to increasing demands and eventual chaos.[62]

This turn of events focused attention upon the fact that Aliev and other Dagestani administrators were no longer accountable to the local population, so much as to the central bureaucracy in Moscow. When this became evident, Aliev lost much of his popular support. Thereafter he proved to be no more effective at suppressing Islamist insurgency than at stimulating economic development. As leadership stalled, political power contracted into smaller circles. Protest was stifled, while economic disparities were ostentatiously flaunted. Corruption flourished in the increasingly malevolent social climate until it permeated all levels of public administration.[63]

Aliev's authority rested on nothing but the bureaucratic system that Putin was centralizing from Moscow downward through the regions. Since he had no personal basis for power in the republic, and since he was not the leader of an articulated political network, he could hope to govern only by extending the central bureaucracy downward to the local bosses who had always been key political players in Dagestan's *djamaat*-based political system. A Dagestani *djamaat* is a village, or a historically connected group of villages, and the surrounding countryside.[64] At this lower political stratum, the bureaucracy then applied the same regimen of sanctions and incentives—"sticks" and "carrots"—that had already secured administrative control when applied at the presidential level by the Kadyrovs in Chechnya.

The sanctions primarily take the form of brutalities committed by local police. Incentives are offered by means of political and financial corruption, extending downward to the level that is capable of exercising control of the local population. Whether in the ostentatious administrative style of Kadyrov's Chechnya or the divergent approaches of various *djamaat* leaders throughout Dagestan, one finds essentially the same system of sanctions and incentives—the same system that is found in slightly less vivid shades in Kabardino-Balkaria and Ingushetia. Because Dagestan's is ethnically a more segmented society than Chechnya's or Ingushetia's, and because it's central government is consequently weaker, effective administrative control occurs at a more local level in Dagestan than in the latter, and administrative styles are more variegated. One finds more repression in one *djamaat* and less in another. Salafism is quietly tolerated in one area and fiercely opposed elsewhere. Yet the role that these *djamaat* leaders play throughout Dagestan is essentially the same as that which is played on a grander—more-visible—scale by the Presidents of Chechnya, Ingushetia, or Kabardino-Balkaria. Like Kadyrov in Chechnya and Yevkurov in Ingushetia, Dagestan's *djamaat* leaders are the terminal nodes of the centralized bureaucracy that has been spreading and entrenching itself in Russia since May 2000. In accord with Putin's policy of gubernatorial appointments, this centralized bureaucratic administration extends outward from the center to each republic, and then downward into the inner sociopolitical structure as far as is necessary to ensure genuine control over the local population.

Wherever this bureaucratic system reaches one of its terminal nodes—whether it be Kadyrov's office in Grozny or the home of a village leader in Dagestan—the system strikes a similar deal: he who establishes himself as controlling any bureaucratic node enjoys opportunities to employ essentially similar carrots and sticks. Ironically, it is at each of these junctures that Moscow effectively hands over local autonomy and abandons micromanagement of affairs. At each of these bureaucratic nodes, Moscow exchanges administrative power and financial reward for local stability and loyalty to the federal center. Because of the prototypical role of Moscow's Chechenzation program in the subsequent development of this bureaucratic structure, which formally was extended throughout the Russian Federation in the aftermath of the 2004 Beslan hostage atrocity, I shall designate this centralized bureaucratic system as the "Chechenization Model" of Russian politics. The hallmarks of the Chechenization Model are:

- The formal-legal extension of the central bureaucracy down to terminal nodes at the level of Russian republics—such as Chechnya, Ingushetia, and Kabardino-Balkaria—or to further administrative substrata—such as Dagestani *raions* and *djamaats*.

- The institutionalization of arbitrary power at each of these terminal nodes, such that a more or less standard repertoire of sanctions and incentives yields local compliance with central bureaucratic policy.

- A terminal node of the bureaucratic structure occurs at the highest administrative stratum at which it is possible for the central bureaucracy effectively to exchange arbitrary power for local compliance. In Dagestan, for example, ethnic heterogeneity and weaker personal leadership requires that an effective exchange of arbitrary power for local compliance occurs at a lower administrative substratum than in neighboring Chechnya.

Frustrations for all parties are built into this federally Chechenized bureaucratic system. Kremlin leaders are exasperated to find that the local execution of their policies is ham-fisted, and that their budgetary subsidies line local pockets. At the bottom of the pyramid, local people are resentful because they are without opportunities for genuine political expression or opposition, other than those afforded by Islamist extremism.

This Chechenization Model of Russian politics differs from that of the Dual-state Model, as formulated initially by Ernest Fraenkel[65] in the context of fascist Germany, and as employed since then by political scientists to describe the divergence between formal-legal arrangements, and arbitrary-prerogative executive practices.[66] To one extent or another, this divergence can be found in any state, for as Bismark himself said, "Politics is the art of the possible." But Fraenkel was clearly correct about the extremity of this divergence in Nazi Germany, and the Dual-state Model may be applied usefully to Russia at least from Yeltsin's attack on the Russian Duma in October 1993 up to Putin's announcement of gubernatorial appointments in the aftermath of the Beslan tragedy of September 2004.

Nevertheless, an application of the Dual-state Model to Russia's regional politics during the period from September 2004 through the beginning of 2012 would appear to be less appropriate. In 2004 and 2005, Putin reconstituted Russia's formal-legal arrangements to allow presidential appointment of regional governors. He did so following the success of his Chechenization program. Fully to appreciate the importance of Caucasian events to the formal political changes that Putin proposed in 2004, it is helpful to review the following points in this context:

- Vladimir Putin may not have been appointed Prime Minister and subsequently elected to the Russian presidency were it not that the widespread instability in North Caucasus came to a crisis in the Chechnya-based invasion of Dagestan during August and September 1999.

- His response to the invasion of Dagestan, and the subsequent Russian invasion of Chechnya shaped Putin's leadership style from the first days of his administration.

- Putin's firm, militaristic approach to North Caucasian instabilities met with widespread popularity in Russia, and transformed Russia's normative political culture.

- Putin's military response in Dagestan and Chechnya was influential in his transformation of the Russian federal system on the model of the Russian military bureaucracy in 2000.

- The success of the Chechenization program in Chechnya from 2000 onward was influential in his replacement of Ruslan Aushev with Murat Zyazikov in Ingushetia during 2001 and 2002.

- In 2004—in the immediate aftermath of, and in direct response to, a series North Caucasian terrorist attacks—Putin's Chechenization program effectively became the template for his formal reconstitution of the Russian federal system, including the alteration of local electoral procedures and the centralized appointment of local governors.

- The centralized appointment of local governors was quickly implemented in the North Caucasus (as elsewhere in Russia) with the installation of Arsen Kanokov in Karardino-Balkaria in September 2005 and the appointment of Mukhu Aliev in Dagestan in March 2006. It was subsequently applied to the appointment of Yanus-bek Yevkurov in Ingushetia in 2008.

- Due to Aliev's political weakness, this same bureaucratic structure of centralized control was extended downward to the *djamaat* substratum of Dagestani politics.

- At all levels of this centralized bureaucratic structure, the same regime of sanctions and incentives essentially applied, and at all strata this regime crucially incorporated arbitrary executive action into the formal-legal bureaucratic structure.

- This administrative strategy was at least partially motivated by North Caucasian instabilities, and was strongly influenced by the success of the Chechenization program in Chechnya.

- After 2004, this centralized bureaucratic structure was extended throughout the Russian Federation on a formal-legal basis.

- The formal extension of its bureaucratic system in this manner did not undermine Russia's "power vertical," but rather enabled it to operate horizontally throughout its population base whenever it reached one of its terminal nodes, as required for governance.

For these reasons, one may go so far as to say that the Russian Federation has been Chechenized, both in formal-legal terms and in terms of its normative political culture.[67] Yet from 2004 to 2012, this did not increase the duality of Russian politics, but rather reduced duality in that prerogative rule received formal-legal incorporation into the Russian federal system. In direct response to Caucasian instabilities, prerogative rule was formally institutionalized throughout Russia, thereby at least partially reconciling Russia's formal-legal structure with the often-arbitrary practice of administrative decision-making in the localized terminal political nodes of the formal-bureaucratic structure.

It is helpful, first, to clarify the Chechenization Model of Russian politics by contrast to the Dual-state Model, and then to illustrate the Chechenization Model in terms of Walter Richmond's examination of preparations for the Sochi Olympics. In his application of the Dual-state Model, Richard Sakwa elsewhere has argued that Russian politics is characterized by two competing political orders. The first is the constitutional state, regulated by law and enshrining the normative values of the democratic movement of the late Soviet period and contemporary liberal democracies, populated by political parties, parliament, and representative movements and regulated by electoral and associated laws. The second is the administrative regime, which has emerged as a tutelary order standing outside the normative state although not repudiating its principles.[68]

By contrast, the Chechenization Model does not view Russian politics as characterized by two distinct and competitive political orders. Rather, it argues that in 2004 the Russian political system was transformed in order to institutionalize the localization of arbitrary administrative power within an over-arching, formal-legal framework. From 2004 to 2012 the Russian constitution purposefully did not "enshrine the normative values of the democratic movement of the late Soviet period and contemporary liberal democracies." Rather Vladimir Putin and Dmitry Medvedev led the Russian Federation in a new direction, which deviated formally as well as normatively from the values of both the late Soviet period and contemporary liberal democracies.

The Dual-state Model does indeed appear to apply to Russian politics from October 1993 (when the Yeltsin administration ordered the Russian military to attack the Russian legislature) to September 2004. Yet from the end of 2004 to the beginning of 2012, Putin and Medvedev fundamentally transformed and bureaucratized the Russian system. The Dual-state does not seem adequately to apply during this period.

This view offers a collegial counterpoint to Richard Sakwa's argument that the "highly centralized and personalized leadership exercised by Kadyrov is homologous to the power vertical strategy pursued by the federal leadership, but by definition undercuts the vertical power of the federal authorities."[69] The Chechenization Model shows that this kind of personalized leadership at the bottom is not contrary to federal authority, but is precisely what Russia's bureaucratic federal authority formally was founded on from 2004 to 2012.

From 2004 to 2012 there was not simply a split between a formal-legal ideal and arbitrary local practices. Rather a bureaucratic administrative structure that fundamentally incorporated arbitrary local practice was formally instituted. In short, the diversity and arbitrariness of local practices was built into the overarching formal-legal system adopted during those years.

This point may be neglected if one focuses upon a duality between formal ideals and local deviations. A dualistic approach also may miss subtleties in the operation of terminal bureaucratic nodes throughout the Federation, and it may overlook the fact that from 2004 to 2012 the Russian Federation formally switched from a democratic to an essentially bureaucratic administration. The Chechenization Model helps one to appreciate just how seminal Chechnya, along with Georgia, South Ossetia, Abkhazia, North Ossetia, Ingushetia, and Dagestan, has been in the evolution of the Russian Federation.

The Chechenization Model does not ignore the exceptional autonomy that has been established in Chechnya. On the contrary, the present analysis incorporates and underscores Chechen exceptionalism in that Chechenization is regarded as the template for Russian recentralization from 2004 to 2012.

At face value, Kadyrov's claim that "Chechnya saved Russia"[70] appears to be audaciously absurd. After all, Chechnya severely tested, and at times seemed close to destroying the Russian Federation. Yet when viewed from the context of the preceding analysis, there is meaning to be made from Kadyrov's claim. Chechnya, and the other Caucasian instabilities with which it has been connected, have transformed Russia in ways that are both deeply fundamental and broadly multifaceted. Since it rose from the Soviet ashes in 1991, the very survival of the Russian Federation has required that it undergo a fundamental and continuous process of transformation in order to survive—and in order to develop and prosper economically, politically, and spiritually. The Caucasus has—and still is—helping Russia to transform itself.

As cited in Sakwa's chapter,[71] Kadyrov is correct in placing his seemingly audacious claim into the context of six recent Caucasian wars—South Ossetia from 1991 to 1992, Abkhazia from 1992 to 1993, Chechnya from 1994 to 1996, Chechnya from 1999 to 2009,[72] Georgia in 2008, and the low-level civil war in the northeastern Caucasus from 1999 to the time of this writing. Taken together, in a maelstrom of dynamic, multidirectional causation, these and other directly related instabilities are the crucible that has melted Russia down, and recast it in a remarkably Caucasianized form.

As in any crucible, Russia's transformation has been rapid and difficult. Some of it has been regrettable, and some has been horrific. Yet it cannot be denied that as of ca. 1980, fundamental changes were required in Russia, and that Caucasian instabilities have played a substantial role in Russian transformation. That some of these transformations have been counterproductive means that further transformation is necessary. The Caucasus has been, and will be, a major cause of Russian transformation up to, and from this point forward.

Walter Richmond provides a helpful study of complex federal relationships in preparations for the 2014 Winter Olympic Games in Sochi. Richmond documents problems arising in the course of these preparations involving:

- center-periphery relations;
- constitutional and legal concerns;

- personal, civic, and infrastructural dislocations;
- ethnic frictions;
- environmental damage;
- financial problems.

Richmond explains that Presidential Order 848, which established an initial budget for the Games, was in violation of the Russian law "On the Federal Budget for 2007. Order 848 thereby created a formal-legal duality in the Russian Federal system. In order to remedy the violation the Duma passed Federal Law 310-F3 in January 2008, thereby creating a novel legal zone around Sochi, where the Olympic Committee formally was granted arbitrary power.[73] "The law was put in force retroactively from July 5, 2007," as Richmond notes, "so that Order 848 would be included. Furthermore, 310-F3 remains in effect until December 3, 2016; nearly three years after the Games are scheduled. There is speculation that this has to do with the law's reference to 'the development of Sochi as a mountain resort' in addition to preparations for the Games."[74] Thus in accord with the Chechenization Model, Moscow significantly has altered federal laws and constitutional arrangements in response to an extraordinary situation in the Caucasus. It is a point to which this analysis will shortly return.

Richmond makes other helpful points. Federal Law 310-F3 avoids legal duality, but it hardly solves local problems. First, there are a number of legal issues that have arisen as citizens and infrastructures are displaced. Citizens have been referred to the judicial system, but it seems that as 310-F3 has taken legal precedence, many people have been dissatisfied in ways that cannot be legally resolved.

Second, ethnic flames once again have been ignited as Circassian grievances and sensibilities have been ignored. If there were ever an opportunity for Moscow to make a gesture of reconciliation to the Circassian people, then it is the Sochi Olympics. Moscow has nothing to lose and everything to gain from, at the very least, building a monument and holding a ceremony (or opening an honest discussion) in honor of the Circassian people, and in honor of all Caucasian peoples, those who suffered or departed in the past, and those who remain Russian citizens today. At an event that symbolizes international aspirations for peace and good will, such a gesture would only add to Russia's stature. As Richmond suggests, Russia is diminished in the absence of conciliatory overtures.

Third, Olympic preparations have created serious problems for Sochi's fragile ecology. Again, Russian officials have attempted to address these problems in legalistic terms. The boundaries of a park, for example, have been adjusted conveniently. The recommendations of international organizations have been interpreted to fit Moscow's agenda. Protests have been repressed. Sochi's unique ecology has been damaged.

Arising in the case of Olympic preparations, these three problem sets may be conceived as types of inner conflict or duality in Russian society. Yet from Richmond's discussion, it appears that Sochi Olympic preparations provide evidence in support of the Chechenization Model. That is, the formal-legalistic features of this duality are, at least superficially, addressed by Federal Law 310-F3, as well as by the Russian courts and other local legal procedures. By these formal means, the central bureaucracy has been extended to localized terminal nodes in the Sochi region. From these terminal nodes, bureaucrats and administrators apply their standard repertoire of sanctions and incentives in efforts to obtain local compliance with central policy.

Moscow has made other formal arrangements in its efforts to address tensions in this region. As discussed by Foxall and Richmond, Russia's Southern Federal District was divided into the Southern District and the North Caucasian District on January 20, 2010. The announcement was made by Russia's President, Dmitry Medvedev, who appointed Alexander Khloponin both as Presidential Envoy to the new Federal District, and as a Deputy Prime Minister. This meant that Khloponin reported both to Medvedev and to Putin, who was serving then as Russian prime minister.

The move signaled Moscow's recognition that conflict in the North Caucasus was spinning out of control, and that a new approach was required. Medvedev's announcement effectively divided the Southern Federal District into two parts. The regions remaining in the Southern District were Krasnodar, Astrakhan, Rostov, Volgograd, Adygeya, and Kalmykiya. The new North Caucasus District included the republics of Dagestan, Chechnya, Ingushetia, North Ossetia, Kabardino-Balkaria, Karachayveo-Cherkessia, and Stavropol'skii *krai*. The new district would be administered from the Stavropol'skii resort town of Pyatigorsk.

To this position Khloponin brought a set of useful skills. After establishing a successful financial firm, he moved into the metals industry, and in 1996 became the head of the Norilsk Nickel corporation. Khloponin entered politics in 2001, becoming governor of the resource-rich Taimyr Autonomous District. In 2002 Khloponin was elected to govern the Krasnoyarsk Region, where he presided over impressive economic expansion. In 2007, Krasnoyarsk grew faster than either Moscow or St. Petersburg. Khloponin was appointed with the support of Dagestani billionaire, Suleiman Kerimov, who has shown particular interest in attracting outside invesment into Dagestan's economy.

Khloponin's biography, along with a series of statements that Medvedev issued around the time of this appointment, indicated that the portfolio of the new presidential envoy prominently included the socioeconomic development of the North Caucasus. This already marked a partial shift in focus from Putin's security-oriented approach to the North Caucasus—in accord with the Chechenization Model—to a new approach that also viewed the stabilization of the region in terms of socioeconomic development. The origins of this new approach can be traced to the 117-page 2005 "Report on Conditions in Dagestan and Measures for Its Stabilization," prepared by Alexander Pochinok and authored, in large part, by Enver Kisriev, the Dagestani sociologist.[75]

As Foxall and Richmond observe, the creation of the North Caucasus Federal District was important in its separation of the North Caucasus region between two Federal Districts. Just as Khlponin's appointment signaled that the North Caucasus District—in the eastern part of this region—was being prepared for socioeconomic development with Stavropol'skii *krai* at its head, so the western portion of the North Caucasus, the portion that remained in the Southern Federal District, was—as Richmond describes—already embarked on an even more dramatic course of economic development.

Though Khloponin's appointment represented a long-overdue shift from the Kremlin's narrow focus on security, and a new commitment to regional economic development, it is unlikely that this structural alteration will prove sufficient to solve the problems of the North Caucasus republics. In order to improve the republic's chronically dismal investment climate, and achieve genuine economic development Khloponin would have to focus first on political problems at the root of the insurgency: government incompetence and corruption, combined with police brutality. Moreover, unless corruption is effectively addressed, any economic development is likely to add to already-destabilizing economic disparities. Ironically, these objectives are at odds with Khloponin's own appointment.

Khloponin had the ability to succeed in Krasnoyarsk, but his success was partly due to the political legitimacy that he gained through popular election. By way of his Kremlin appointment, he was denied that same legitimacy in the North Caucasus. Like most Kremlin appointees, Khloponin lacked a popular political base in the region. Moreover, those appointees who began with some proportion of a popular base—like Kadyrov in Chechnya, Aliev in Dagestan, or Yevkurov in Ingushetia—were delegitimized in the eyes of some locals by means of their appointment. This was because Kremlin selection denied genuine political expression and accountability to the local populous and precluded the formation of legitimate political opposition. As a result of the system of centralized appointment, the only possible opposition was illegitimate opposition, and the only functioning political opposition in the North Caucasus was that of Islamist extremism.

Yet despite all of this, and despite the difficulties in their preparations, the probable success of the Sochi Olympics will highlight Russia's leadership in the emergence of a Black Sea Economic Zone. Olympic preparations are creating jobs and stimulating the development of Russia's Black Sea region. For example, at the time of this writing, the Russian oil company Rosneft has reached promising Black Sea exploration deals with Exxon and

Italian Eni in the Western Chernomorsky field off the Romanian coast. At the same time, Ukraine has announced that it will increase Black Sea oil production. In 2011, the Russian techno-engineering company, ScanEx, and the Shirshov Institute of Oceanography announced the discovery of a Black Sea oilfield near the Georgian town of Poti, just south of Abkhazia.

In preparation for this regional development, Russia's Black Sea coast has been doubly distanced from the chronic problems of the North Caucasus by the creation of two administrative barriers: first Federal Law 310-F3 creating an extra-constitutional zone around Sochi; and second, its inclusion— along with the rest of Krasnodar—in the Southern Federal District. Part of the point of the Sochi Olympics is the further distinction and development of the emergent Black Sea Economic Zone.

This is also evident in Moscow's appointment of Alexander Tkachev to its newly-created position[76] as envoy to Abkhazia, a post that Moscow has linked to the Sochi Olympics. Sochi is immediately adjacent to Abkhazia, and Tkachev is not only a popular leader in Krasnodar but also a successful businessman. His appointment has been welcomed by Abkhazia's separatist government in Sukhumi, which quickly made Tkachev an honorary Abkhazian citizen.

Since 2008, Russia has prevented Georgian intervention in Abkhazian sea trade, and Sukhumi has enjoyed visits from vessels flying foreign flags. While Abkhazian exports have been primarily timber and other raw materials, Sukhumi has been courting light manufacturing enterprises, and it is likely that Tkachev will work behind the scenes to encourage foreign investment, while quietly integrating Abkhazian businesses into Olympic preparations.

Thus Abkhazia has viable claims for independence. Yet while Abkhazian elites favor this path, they are economically and militarily beholden to Moscow. Coming years probably will see bureaucratic innovations that allow Abkhazia's nominal independence, while consolidating its de facto dependency. Moscow thus retains options to first announce the redundancy of both an envoy and a separate ambassador to Abkhazia, and then to recall its ambassador. Then, second, to appoint Tkachev (or his successor) as Moscow's Presidential Envoy to its Southern Federal District.

In such a manner, Abkhazia may be annexed informally to Russia's Southern Federal District while continuing to claim independence. This process further may be eased by an extension and expansion of Federal Law 310-F3, to include Abkhazia along with Sochi in an extra-constitutional zone, allowing Moscow and Sukhumi to argue that Abkhazia was not being annexed politically so much as being economically assisted.

A similar bureaucratic process may allow for the informal, yet, effective annexation of South Ossitia into the Russian Federation. In March 2012, Taymuraz Mamsurov was appointed as the Russian envoy to South Ossetia. As president of North Ossetia, Mamsurov has advocated the retention of Prigorodny and the annexation of South Ossetia.[77]

It is in accord with the preferences of South Ossetians that South Ossetia has been incorporated bureaucratically into the Russian Federation. South Ossetians fear Tbilisi, and will neither consider nor accept reintegration into Georgia. From a South Ossetian perspective, South Ossetia was never a legitimate part of Georgia, and Soviet boundaries were due to little more than Stalin's personal whims backed by Soviet military force. In their view, South Ossetians liberated themselves from Soviet oppression at their first opportunity. Yet South Ossetians know that contemporary Russians, unlike Georgians, will not occupy their homes and villages. Instead Russia will subsidize their local budget while providing genuine security. The gradual integration of South Ossetia into the Federation is a bureaucratic extension that serves Russian interests:

- by providing a new pro-Moscow, southern tier cementing Ingushetia and Chechnya as federal subjects;

- by supporting a Caucasian population that visibly wishes to belong to the Federation;

- by providing Russia with strategic access to the South Caucasus.

As South Ossetia continues to stabilize in coming years, Moscow may relieve the situation in Prigorodny by resettling some of the South Ossetian refugees whose northward migration precipitated the Ingush-Ossetian conflict. Such a move might help to relieve tensions in Ingushetia.

A hallmark of the Chechenization Model is the extension of Russia's central bureaucratic hierarchy downward into locally-administrative terminal nodes, where various forms of autonomous and arbitrary power involve the application of similar repertoires of sanctions and incentives. The incorporation of Abkhazia and South Ossetia into this centralized bureaucratic structure is in accord with the Chechenization Model, regardless of how much autonomy or other localized features Abkhazia and South Ossetia may retain. By these federal arrangements, Moscow has extended its Chechenized approach.

Yet, as we have seen, this Chechenized approach is inconsistent with its own objectives. By means of the Sochi Olympic development and by means of Kholoponin's socioeconomic programs, the Kremlin has sought to relieve tensions resulting from this inconsistency. Yet until there is an end to corruption, economic development will only add to the disparities that are at the base of these tensions. The Chechenized political system cannot eliminate corruption because corruption plays a key role in the system of local sanctions and incentives that is key to Chechenization.

As of the beginning of 2012, this fundamental contradiction had begun to alter Russian politics in new ways. For example, in July 2012, the Russian Duma responded to Moscow's nascent democratic opposition, and to the Kremlin's frustrations in the Caucasus, by instituting new, notably complex and restrictive, procedures for the election of local governors. Under the new law, political parties will nominate gubernatorial candidates after "consultation" with the Russian president. Individuals may stand for election after their petitions gather sufficient signatures.[78]

The new law also specifies that governors may be removed either from above or from below. On the one hand, the Russian president is now empowered to dismiss governors convicted of corruption or other misconduct, including "conflicts of interests." On the other hand, a governor will be dismissed if 25 percent of local residents vote for his removal in a referendum organized by the local legislature. Other reforms ease the way for new political parties to register and to participate in elections.[79]

These reforms alter formal administrative arrangements, initially introduced by Putin in his Beslan address on September 13, 2004. At least ostensibly, governors now will be elected locally and will have greater local accountability. Local electoral procedures also have become somewhat more accessible. In these ways, the Russian political system appears to have begun responding to contradictions inherent in the Chechenized approach. Sooner or later these inherent contradictions will require that Russian politics develop beyond the Chechenization Model.

In the next section, I shall describe this dialectically transcendent approach as a Causal Reciprocity (CR) Model of relations among Caucasians and Russians. Thus, I understand the Dual-state Model as applying to Russian politics at least from October 1993 to September 2004. I understand the Chechenization Model as applying from September 2004 to July 2012. I anticipate the CR Model as applying from July 2012 onward.

In retrospect, the CR approach seems to have been foreshadowed in contributions throughout this volume. Patrick Armstrong views Russia both as being affected by, and reacting to, Caucasian instabilities. Domitilla Sagramoso and Akhmet Yarlykapov consider causal influences as moving northward toward Moscow, and also southward from the bureaucratic center to the North Caucasus in causal feedback loops. Robert Schaefer and Andrei Doohovskoy suggest a "network-centric" meta-systemic model, which incorporates features of self-organization and self-development. Andrew Foxall describes Stavropol'skii *krai* not only as being affected by instabilities flowing upward from the North Caucasus but also as being enhanced by its new status as a regional economic and political center. Ricahrd Sakwa argues that Chechenization has undermined Moscow normatively at the same time that it has transformed Chechnya. Nicolai Petro finds constructive changes in religious culture moving in both northward and southward directions. Anna Mateeva's description suggests prospects for further transformative interface between Russia and the Caucasus. Indeed, from the standpoint of causal reciprocity it is interesting that Armstrong and Foxall respectively view Georgia and Stavropol'skii *krai* as "a canary in the coal mine," the former for toxic influences moving southward and the latter for toxic influences moving northward.

In the first section, we saw that how tensions in Georgia led to southern conflicts in Abkhazia and South Ossetia, which in turn, influenced northern conflicts in Prigorodny and Chechnya. We saw how Islamist influences from the South and East culminated in the second conflict in Chechnya, and we examined the transformation of the Russian military that resulted from the Chechen conflicts. In this second section, we have seen how instabilities rising northward from Caucasian conflagrations, such as those that Foxall describes, resulted in fundamental transformations of the Russian Federation. Because conflicts in Chechnya have played such a formative role in these transformations, and because the Putin-Kadyrov program served essentially as a template for these transformations, they cumulatively have been described as the Chechenization Model of Russian politics. While the Chechenization Model seems to go beyond Dual-state Models in some respects, the former Model is supported through its application to an analysis of Sochi Olympic preparations. The Chechenization Model also has been extended to the cases of Abkhazia and South Ossetia.

Yet recent developments in Russian politics suggest a need for a CR Model. The next section shows how a CR Model allows for further modification in response to normative tensions and ongoing political influences by way of nonlinear, causal feedback loops to meta-systemic self-organization.

Caucasian crosscurrents

In the third section of the book, Nicolai Petro and Anna Matveeva explore normative tensions in Russia and the Caucasus. Petro argues that Islamic and Orthodox faiths are joining with the state to implement a "Russian Model" for the development of a multicultural normative order. The Russian Model displays the normative influence of the Caucasus on Russia, illustrates the interaction of normative and political factors, and demonstrates the potential for fruitful syntheses of Caucasian with Russian influences. Clearly, it is hopeful that Russian Islamic and Russian Orthodox (ROC) officials have recognized their common foundation in shared values. Yet the efficacy of the Russian Model would seem to be challenged by ongoing religious alienation and violence in the North Caucasus—such as that which Sagramoso, Yarlykapov, and Matveeva describe. It is particularly alarming that there have been high profile attacks against moderate Islamic officials, especially in Tatarstan and Dagestan.[80]

As this volume goes to print, there are some who have expressed concerns about cooperation between the ROC and the Russian state. A catalyst for some of these concerns has come from three members of a feminist collective who were arrested and convicted for a protest performance on the main alter of Russia's principal Orthodox site, the Christ the Savior Cathedral, in the center of Moscow.[81] "Holy Mother, Blessed Virgin, drive Putin away," screamed members of the band in February 2012, just weeks before Russia's presidential election.[82] The women said that they were protesting cooperation between the Orthodox Church particularly with regard to Vladimir Putin's election campaign. The band also belted out coarsely antireligious lyrics during a commemorative service in the sanctuary. In the context of Petro's chapter, the band may be understood as protesting the "Russian Model" of cooperation among religious and government authorities.

Prior to sentencing of the band members, Putin called for leniency; ROC officials appealed for mercy on behalf of the group.[83] Yet many critics linked the band's conviction to repressive tactics that Russian authorities brought to bear against a series of democratic protests that occurred in the months following irregularities in legislative elections in December 2011. Outside of Russia, the band's two-year sentence was condemned as disproportionate by celebrities, journalists, and policy makers, but Russians were surveyed as approving the sentence by a margin of 53 to 27 percent.[84] Whereas Western critics tended to view the case in terms of Putin's leadership style, many Russians saw the stunt as an offensive attack on legally protected religious freedoms.

At the outset, it must be observed that cooperation between religious and political orders has occurred in most civilizations throughout human history. Today, nations such as Denmark and Norway have state churches, responsible for cooperation with public authorities in the promotion of moral order. At least since Augustine, many political philosophers have given compelling reasons for this cooperation. Closer to Russia's modern history, G. W. F. Hegel viewed religion as the moral foundation of the state, and saw the state as giving worldly expression to religious principles. For Hegel, church and state have reciprocal roles to play in an ongoing and dialectical moral development.[85] A dialectical development allowing a synthesis of moral and cultural values would seem to be exactly what Russia and the Caucasus need.

Hegel was particularly interested in this ongoing, meta-systemic moral development as an antidote to vacuity and fragmentation of modern society. Petro describes how Orthodox and Islamic leaders have united in the face of similar problems that they view in terms of "secularism." This would seem to be precisely what concerns some secularists. Petro notes the opposition of ROC leaders to extreme forms of state-sponsored secularism, such as those that occurred under totalitarian regimes of the mid-twentieth century. But this does not seem to address concerns of contemporary rationalist[86] and moderate secularists, such as typically found among the educated classes of Russia and the West.

Yet at the time of this writing, Russia had taken no steps that were clearly anti-secularist. The conviction and suprisingly harsh sentencing of the feminist band alarmed secularists worldwide. Still the trial was in accord with legal procedures that had been on the books for considerable time. Some of those who criticized Russia for adhering to its laws in this case were the same who criticize Russia for skirting its laws in other cases. Armstrong's point about Russophobic memes was recalled by the hundreds of Western media reports that reveled in anti-Putin rhetoric while ignoring the fact that the bands performance was illegal and offensive to millions of people. Christ the Savior Cathedral is surrounded on all sides by broad plazas. Immediately adjacent to those plazas are three broad boulevards and two public parks. Why was the performance not staged in any of these outdoor areas instead of on the altar of the church, and near a commemorative service? The band had performed protests in the streets of Moscow without serious incident or arrest. Their brief detention and release after their unsanctioned performance in Red Square was consistent with legal practices in many countries that pride themselves on democratic rights and freedom of speech. Since the band had not been repressed when they protested in the streets, why was their conviction a sign of political repression? (See the Appendix for an analysis of this case in connection with Armstrong's discussion of memes.)

Yet, rightly or wrongly, the case of the feminist band plays a role in normative cleavages that indisputably are developing in Russian society. Whether or not this particular case has any real relevance to their concerns, critics were correct in stressing that some democratic protests were repressed beginning in December 2011. A significant feature of the Chechenization Model is that it views Russia's democratic protest movement from 2011 onward not as a reformist attempt to reconcile institutionalized norms with political practice, but rather as a revolutionary movement aimed at subverting what had become an institutionally bureaucratic—that is, a fundamentally nondemocratic—political system.

With her excellent fieldwork, Anna Matveeva shows how deep some of these normative divisions have become in a portrait of Ingushetia, Chechnya, and Dagestan. She notes that this divergence is occurring in all three republics and not in Chechnya alone, lending support to the Chechenization Model. Wherever the bureaucratic structure arrives at a terminal node, we find the same application of arbitrary sanctions and incentives. Along with Andrew Foxall, Domitilla Sagramoso, and Akhmet Yarlykapov, Anna Matveeva examines the discourse of this divergence both in these republics and in the Russian Federation as a whole. Her discussion is particularly notable in that she is able to present issues of Russian and Caucasian identity both from northern and from southern perspectives. This is daunting insofar as her presentation allows us to see just how different each of these perspectives is from the other, and how little of the other each of these two perspectives seems to understand. Yet while some Russians do not want Caucasians coming northward, it seems that many North Caucasian want Russians to come back to the Caucasus. As these republics veer away from Russia, they still seek Russian influence and Russian funding. Matveeva's study raises many questions: if these republics diverge so far as to constitute an "inner abroad," will that still be tolerable to the Kremlin and to the people of Russia? What choices does anyone have? What would become of Ingushetia, Chechnya, or Dagestan if they really were to separate from Russia? Would they repeat the trajectory of Chechnya from 1997 to 1999, as Putin says he fears? However they eventually may be answered, questions such as these ensure that the Caucasus will continue to shape Russia.

Matveeva's account returns us to the contemporary Islamist insurgency, as examined in depth by Domitilla Sagramoso and Akhmet Yarlykapov. It is interesting that the insurgency has developed a hierarchical structure analogous with Russia's bureaucratic administration of the North Caucasus. Because Russia's bureaucratic centralization has imposed similar circumstances, and similar problems, across the region, the insurgency opportunistically attacks its most vulnerable bureaucratic nodes.

Yet it must be recalled that the North Caucasian insurgency remains an ungainly convergence of a global ideology with local frustrations and grievances. While some extremist attacks are regionally coordinated, while tactics often resemble those in other Muslim areas of the globe, and while local extremist leaders often are endorsed by Doku Umarov it is nonetheless instructive to consider that if conditions for ordinary people in any one of these republics were dramatically improved, then the local attacks would decline regardless of events in other parts of the region.

Though Salafism is fundamentally and violently at odds with traditional Sufism, Islamist resistance affords Dagestanis, Chechens, and some Ingushes with their only viable means of political opposition to Moscow's corrupted bureaucratic octopus. Not unlike Grozny or Vladikavkaz, Dagestan's urban areas—such as Makhachkala, Kaspiysk, and Khasavyurt—are bristling with construction projects. Yet the fruits of this rapid development are hung so high that only a few can reach them, while they remain visible inspirations for festering resentments on the part of many people stranded at lower social strata. When these frustrations are expressed, the indiscriminate and brutal responses of beleaguered and fearful policemen lead to new rounds of resentment and anger in further cycles of causal reciprocity. Caught in this vortex, Dagestan now sees more violence than any other region—and conditions are deteriorating.

Yet while Dagestan, Chechnya, and Ingushetia are veering away from the Federation, Georgia nonetheless seems to be edging awkwardly and tentatively closer. Georgians remain uncomfortable with the rapid expansion of Russia's influence in the emergence of the Black Sea Economic Zone. Georgian leaders are struggling to arrive at a new strategy that balances

Russia's growing presence in the South Caucasus with that of the West and China.

In 2011 and 2012, this new strategy took the form of a series of economic overtures toward Russia and China. Tbilisi finally agreed to Russia's admission to the World Trade Organization (WTO), and relaxed visa requirements for Russian citizens. While Moscow accepted Georgian mineral water—following improvements by Georgian bottlers—and while it will resume imports of Georgian wines, Russia's reception of these overtures has been reserved.

From Tbilisi's standpoint, this reluctant rapprochement was nonetheless a sound strategy. In announcing the new visa regime, Georgia's President Mikheil Saakashvili reaffirmed his antipathy toward the Kremlin while appealing directly for warmer relations with Russian citizens. His strategy was to sidestep the political problems surrounding South Ossetia and Abkhazia, along with his personally poor relationship with Vladimir Putin, while gradually strengthening Georgia's position through relationships built on business and tourism. Without wishing to lose face, or to alienate Georgia's Western sponsors, Sakashavili sought marginally to improve relations with Russia.

Meanwhile Chinese investment in Georgia was increasing sharply. For example, the USD630 million Neskra 210-megawatt hydropower plant was constructed by Sinohydro Group as part of Tbilisi's USD2.5 billion investment in hydropower projects that reduced Georgia's dependence on Russian fossil fuels.[87] The Kodori hydropower plant was completed by China's Sichuan Electric Power Corporation (SEPC) at the confluence of the Alazani and Samkura Rivers, not far south of Russia's border in the Pankisi Valley (a home to anti-Russian *jihadists* ten years earlier). Built at a cost of USD34 million, the plant was 93 percent owned by SEPC, a subsidiary of China's State Grid Corporation. Georgia's biggest Chinese investor was (at the time of this writing) the Xinjiang Group, which mines marble, granite, and gold, and which converts Georgian timber into furniture and cabinets for world markets. The same company also constructed facilities for Tilbisi's answer to Sochi, the 2015 European Youth Olympics. In another mining project, China's Chong Qing Wan Li Lian Xing Group invested USD3.5 of a projected 200 million.[88]

Foreign investment in Georgia increased from USD658.4 million in 2009, to 814.5 million in 2010, to 918 million in 2011—including a Trump Tower in Batumi.[89] Saakashvili signaled his recognition of shifting Black Sea economic parameters, when he sought foreign investors for the construction—Chinese style—of a completely new city, called Lazika, in the protected Kolkheti coastal wetlands just north of Batumi.[90]

Recognizing Western economic weakness in an increasingly foreboding regional climate, Tbilisi has sought to improve relations with Russia by making economic overtures in lieu of political concessions. Over the longer term, Russia will engage economically with Georgia because every investment that it fails to make will be made by China, and Kremlin officials want the Chinese economic juggernaut on their southern border no more than they want NATO. Thus, the United States armed and trained Georgian troops to chase anti-Russian *jihadists* out of Georgia's Pankisi Valley so that Chinese companies could build and benefit from it. While the United States spent money that it borrowed from China in creating greater Russian animosity, Chinese profits rendered twentieth-century rivalries among Georgia, Russia, Europe, and the United States more anachronistic than they had already become by 1992.

Both Russia and Georgia are acting with anticipation of declining Western influence.[91] One way or another, this new reality will bring them closer together. In years ahead, it is likely that Russia will become increasingly overt in its administration of Abkhazia and South Ossetia, until gradually improving economic ties between Russia and Georgia finally render these territorial disputes irrelevant.

Causal reciprocity in Russia and the Caucasus

How has the Caucasus shaped Russia?

This volume has traced a series of events that developed causally northward from Tbilisi through South Caucasian conflicts in Abkhazia and South Ossetia, to influence conflicts in Prigorodny and Chechnya. We have seen how these instabilities were interwoven with Islamic influences arriving in Dagestan and Chechnya from Central Asia and the Middle East. Then we saw how resulting North Caucasian conflicts led to effects further northward in the Russian Federation. We reviewed the ongoing and fundamental transformation of the Russian military that followed from conflicts in Chechnya, and considered changes wrought in Chechnya by the new Russian military, especially after 1999. We saw how these conflicts contributed to the origins and substance of the presidency of Vladimir Putin, and how it influenced his recentralization of Russian politics within the parameters of a federal model based upon the bureaucratic structure of Russia's military districts.

Then we saw how political policies associated with the Chechenization program altered the Russian political system. Whereas Richard Sakwa cogently argued that Chechenization contributed to the duality of the Russian system, I have argued, that Chechenizaton became the model for an over-arching system of Russian government from 2004 to 2012. Applying this Chechenization Model to Walter Richmond's analysis of preparations for the Sochi Olympics, I have argued that this system included fundamental normative and political problems that have led to the ongoing development of the Russian politics and culture.

For example, Nicolai Petro showed how Russian and Caucasian norms are synthesized in the Russian Model of cooperation among Orthodox, Islamic, and government officials. And in Anna Matveeva's discussion of a northeastern Caucasus transformed beyond traditional Russian norms we see how far this synthetic cultural and political development may carry Russia and the Caucasus. The Caucasus has done much to shape Russia, and will continue to transform it, in all of these ways and more.

Notes

1 An exception is Peter Reddaway Gail Lapidus, Barry Ickes, Carol Saivetz, and George Breslauer., "Russia in the Year 2003," *Post- Soviet Affairs*, 20(1) (2004): 1–45. Yet even this study was published prior to the changes in Russia's federal government that took place after September 2004.
2 The latter question is implicit in most stories that the Western media have told about Russia and the Caucasus for the last 20 years. The scholarly studies that presuppose this question are also numerous. A brief sampler might include works such as John Dunlop, *Russia Confronts Chechnya: Roots of a Separatist Conflict* (Cambridge: Cambridge University Press, 1998); Matthew Evangelista, *The Chechen Wars: Will Russia Go the Way of the Soviet Union* (Washington, DC: Brookings Institution Press, 2002); Carlotta Gall and Thomas de Waal, *Chechnya: Calamity in the Caucasus* (New York: NYU Press, 1999); James Hughes, *Chechnya: From Nationalism to Jihad* (Philadelphia: University of Pennsylvania Press, 2007); Anatol Levin, *Chechnya: Tombstone of Russian Power* (New Haven: Yale University Press, 1999); and Tony Wood, *Chechnya: The Case for Independence* (London: Verso, 2007).
3 Robert Ware and Enver Kisriev, *Dagestan: Russian Hegemony and Islamic Resistance in the North Caucasus* (Armonk, NY: M. E. Sharpe, 2010), 127, 150.
4 *Russia: The Ingush-Ossetian Conflict in the Prigorodnyi Region* (Paperback) by Human Rights Watch, Helsinki Human Rights Watch (April 1996), ISBN 1–56432–165–7. Similar problems occur elsewhere in the region, such as Dagestan's Novolakskii raion, which was the eastern end of the Checheno-Ingush ASSR up to 1944. Ethnic Laks were forcibly resettled into the homes of Chechens. Smoldering resentments nearly flared into ethnic conflict in the early 1990s. A series of negotiations have attempted to address the problem, without yet fully resolving it. See Ware and Kisriev, *Dagestan*, 124–8,145–54.
5 *Russia: The Ingush-Ossetian Conflict in the Prigorodnyi Region.*
6 Ibid.
7 As revealed when a *Wall Street Journal* reporter obtained a laptop computer with crucial information following the invasion of Afghanistan. See Allen Cullison, "Saga of Dr. Zawahri Sheds Light On the Roots of al Qaeda Terror," *Wall Street Journal*, 2002; Ayman al-Zawahri, http://en.wikipedia.org/wiki/Ayman_al-Zawahiri; "Bin Laden No. 2 Sat in a Jail in Dagestan" www.freerepublic.com/focus/news/710803/posts

8 Ware and Kisriev, *Dagestan*, 96.
9 Ibid.
10 Ibid.
11 Ibid.
12 Ibid., 97–104.
13 *Djamaat* will be used in reference to the political structures traditionally associated with Dagestani village life. *Jamaat* will be used to designate Islamist organizations.
14 Ware and Kisriev, *Dagestan*, 96.
15 Ibid. See also, Hilary Pilkington and Galina Yemelianova, *Islam in Post-Soviet Russia* (London: Routledge, 2003), 154.
16 Ware and Kisriev, *Dagestan*, 100–1.
17 It was Raduyev who led the January 9, 1996 raid on the Dagestani city of Kizliar, resulting in his detainment of 3,500 hostages and a bombardment of the Dagestani village of Pervomayskoyae by Russian Federal troops, during which more than 100 of the hostages died.
18 Ware and Kisriev, *Dagestan*, 103–4.
19 Ibid.
20 Ibid.
21 Ibid.
22 *Novoje Delo*, 28, July 10, 1998.
23 Ware and Kisriev, *Dagestan*, 105–6.
24 Reporting on the Congress is due largely to E. Kozhaeva's article "Vainakhs and Us," *Molodezh Dagestana*, no. 17, April 23, 1999. The quotations in this paragraph are from that article. See Ware and Kisriev, *Dagestan*, 121–3.
25 I first learned of the invasion at the moment that I boarded a flight from New York to Moscow for purposes of travel to Dagestan to initiate survey research. The survey was delayed for six months as a consequence of fighting and instability in Dagestan. See Ware and Kisriev, *Dagestan*, 88–120 for results of the survey in the context of Islam and Islamism in Dagestan.
26 Ware and Kisriev, *Dagestan*, 123.
27 Ibid.
28 Ibid.
29 Many writers have argued that these bombs were the work of Russian security services bent on mobilizing Russian citizens for an invasion of Chechnya. In part, these arguments are based upon disturbing-but-inconclusive evidence that the security services were responsible for an unexploded bomb discovered in an apartment block in Ryazan on September 22. However, I have argued that the explosions more likely were the work of Khattab and the Islamists in Karamakhi. See Robert Ware, "Revisiting Russia's Apartment Block Blasts," *Journal of Slavic Military Studies*, 18(4) (December 2005); Robert Ware, "A Multitude of Evils," in *Chechnya: From Past to Future*, (pp. 79–115), R. Sakwa, ed., 90–6. (London: Anthem, 2005). Also see Ware and Kisriev, *Dagestan*, 124–8.
30 Evangelista, *The Chechen Wars*, 69.
31 For example, see, Robyn Dixon, "Chechnya's Grimmest Industry," *Los Angeles Times*, September 18, 2000, http://articles.latimes.com/2000/sep/18/news/mn-23005; Dimitry Nepomnyaschy, "Hostages Relive Chechen

Ordeal," Institute of War and Peace Reporting, http://iwpr.net/report-news/hostages-relive-chechen-ordeal

32 Ibid.

33 Ibid.

34 Alessandra Stanley, "6 Red Cross Aides Slain in Chechnya, Imperiling the Peace, *New York Times*, December 18, 1996; www.nytimes.com/1996/12/18/world/6-red-cross-aides-slain-in-chechnya-imperiling-the-peace.html?pagewanted=all&src=pm

35 For example, see Jim Heintz, "Kidnappers in Chechnya Free American Hostage," *ABC News*, http://abcnews.go.com/International/story?id=81551&page=1

36 The first major relief organization to assist the northeastern Caucasus was the World Food Program, which dispatched a convoy of trucks to Dagestan in April 2000. The drivers and staff for that operation were entirely local people. Many more months went by before Western NGO staffers attempted to visit the northeastern Caucasus. They did so in small numbers, with generally restricted mobility. Further kidnapping of NGO staff subsequently occurred. For example, see www.doctorswithoutborders.org/publications/alert/article.cfm?id=3316&cat=alert-article, or www.doctorswithoutborders.org/news/article.cfm?id=711%20&cat=field-news

37 To the best of my knowledge.

38 Exceptions included the courageous Anna Politkovskaya and Anne Nivat. See Anna Politkovskaya, *A Dirty War: A Russian Reporter in Chechnya* (London: Harvill, 2001); Anna Politkovskaya, *A Small Corner of Hell: Dispatches from Chechnya*, translation of *Vtoraya chechenskaya* (Chicago: The University of Chicago Press, 2003); Anna Politkovskaya, *Putin's Russia* (London: Harvill, 2004). Also see Anne Nivat, *Chienne de Guerre: A Woman Reporter Behind the Lines of the War in Chechnya* (New York, Perseus, 2001). I must add that while I deeply admire Anna Politkovskaya's courageous and path-breaking work, and while I inevitably must defer to her extensive experience, the United States Congressional Commission on Security and Cooperation in Europe once gave us the opportunity respectfully to diverge in our interpretations of some events (September 16, 2003).

39 This trend was so inclusive that there is little point in singling out a few reporters. Instead the reader is invited to consult nearly any of the reports in the popular Western media from this period. The searchable archive of *Johnson's Russia List* for these years provides a helpful sample. See http://archive.constantcontact.com/fs053/1102820649387/archive/1102911694293.html

40 Robert Ware, "Revisiting Russia's Apartment Block Blasts," *Journal of Slavic Military Studies*, 18(4) (December 2005) pp. 599–606; Ware, "A Multitude of Evils." Also see Ware and Kisriev, *Dagestan*, 124–8.

41 Robert Ware, "Has the Russian Federation Been Chechenised?" *Europe-Asia Studies*, 63(3) (May 2011) pp. 493–508.

42 Ibid. As of July 2009, Putin's famous toast was recalled by a billboard near government buildings on Makhachkala's main square.

43 Ibid.

44 Ibid.

45 Ware, "A Multitude of Evils."

46 Ware, "Has the Russian Federation Been Chechenised?"
47 Mufti Akhmad-Khadzhi Abdul Kadyrov GUDERMES, March 18, 2008, Interfax.
48 Ware, "Has the Russian Federation Been Chechenised?"
49 Ibid. Also see http://news.bbc.co.uk/2/hi/europe/3665136.stm
50 "Putin Tells Russia: We Shall Be Stronger," *New York Times,* www.nytimes.com/2004/09/05/international/europe/05rtext.html
51 Ware, "Has the Russian Federation Been Chechenised?"
52 "Zyazikov Frets over Ingush Abductions," *The Moscow Times (Associated Press)*, July 4, 2004, www.themoscowtimes.com/news/article/zyazikov-frets-over-ingush-abductions/229791.html; http://en.wikipedia.org/wiki/Murat_Zyazikov
53 Ibid.
54 Ibid.
55 Ibid.
56 The grey economy provides additional income to some.
57 Robert Ware and Enver Kisriev, "Ethnic Parity and Political Stability in Dagestan: A Consociational Approach," *Europe-Asia Studies*, 53(1) (January 2001): pp. 105–31; Ware and Kisriev, *Dagestan*.
58 Ibid.
59 Ibid.
60 Robert Ware and Enver Kisriev, "Russian Recentralization Arrives in the Republic of Dagestan: Implications for Institutional Integrity and Political Stability," *Eastern European Constitutional Review*, 10(1) (Winter, 2001): pp. 68–75; Ware and Kisriev, *Dagestan*.
61 Ware, "Has the Russian Federation Been Chechenised?"
62 Ware and Kisriev, *Dagestan*, 217–25.
63 Ware, "Has the Russian Federation Been Chechenised?"
64 Ware and Kisriev, *Dagestan*.
65 Ernst Fraenkel, *The Dual State: A Contribution to the Theory of Dictatorship*, translated from the German by E. A. Shils, in collaboration with Edith Lowenstein and Klaus Knorr (New York: Oxford University Press, 1941), reprinted by The Lawbook Exchange, Ltd, 2006.
66 See Richard Sakwa's discussion in this volume.
67 Ware, "Has the Russian Federation Been Chechenised?"
68 Richard Sakwa, "The Dual State in Russia," *Post-Soviet Affairs*, 2010, 26(3) pp. 185–206.
69 Richard Sakwa, "Blowback? Chechnya and the Challenges of Russian Politics," page 175 of this volume.
70 Ibid., 187.
71 Ibid., 188.
72 Instead of 2002, when Putin declared an end to the second war in Chechnya, the date here is taken to be the formal end of the Counter-terrorist Operation (KTO) in April 2009. As several contributors note, hostilities continue in Chechnya at the time of this writing; so any date for the end of the war will be equivocal.
73 "Federal'nyi Zakon 310-F3," *Departament Krasnodarskogo kraia po Realizatsii Polnomochii pri Podgotovke Zimnikh Olimpiiskikh Igr 2014 goda*, www.olympdep.ru/docs/ofdoc31

74 Walter Richmond, "Preparations for the Sochi Olympics," pages 205–6 of this volume.

75 See Ware and Kisriev, *Dagestan*, 191–2.

76 March 2012.

77 His appointment came little more than a week before the election of Leonid Tibilov as president of South Ossetia.

78 "Medvedev submits bill to reinstate governor elections," *Ria Novosti,* January 16, 2012, http://en.rian.ru/russia/20120116/170780108.html; "Bill on governor elections passes upper house," *RT,* http://rt.com/politics/governor-elections-upper-house-121/, "Russia returns to direct election of governors," *Russia Beyond the Headlines,* May 2, 2012. http://rbth.ru/articles/2012/05/02/russia_has_the_direct_gubernatorial_Elections_returned_15558.html

79 Ibid.

80 "Sheikh Murdered over Religious Split Say Analysts," http://en.ria.ru/russia/20120830/175517955.html; "The End of Peaceful Co-existence," *The Economist,* www.economist.com/node/21561947

81 See Nicolai Petro, "Some Orthodox Reflections on the (P)ussy (R)iot Case," *OEN,* www.opednews.com/articles/Some-Orthodox-Reflections-by-Nicolai-Petro-120821-35.html

82 "Pussy Riot Jail Term Rated Fair by Most Russians," *Bloomberg Businessweek*, www.businessweek.com/news/2012–08–29/pussy-riot-jail-term-rated-fair-by-most-russians-poll-shows. Numerous Western reports cited the band's performance as referencing Putin. The appendix refers to eye-witness accounts that Putin was not mentioned.

83 "Putin calls for leniency in sentencing in Pussy Riot trial," CNN, http://articles.cnn.com/2012–08–03/world/world_europe_russia-pussy-riot-trial_1_russian-president-vladimir-putin-show-leniency-kangaroo-court, www.irishtimes.com/newspaper/breaking/2012/0817/breaking11.html; "Church Urged Mercy for Pussy Riot," *Irish Times*, www.irishtimes.com/newspaper/breaking/2012/0817/breaking11.html

84 "Pussy Riot Jail Term Rated Fair By Most Russians, Poll Shows," *Bloomberg News*, www.bloomberg.com/news/2012–08–29/pussy-riot-jail-term-rated-fair-by-most-russians-poll-shows.html

85 See the following works by G. W. F. Hegel, *Lectures on the Philosophy of World History: Introduction* (Cambridge: Cambridge University Press, 1995), 105, 107, 108, 110; G. W. F. Hegel, *Lectures on the Philosophy of Religion* (Berkeley: University of California Press, 1984), 452–5, 472; G. W. F. Hegel, *Philosophy of Mind* §552 and *Philosophy of Right* §270.

86 For example, see Richard Dawkins, *The God Delusion* (New York: Houghton Mifflin, 2006).

87 "Georgia Says China to Construct $630 Million Hydropower Plant," *Bloomberg News*, www.businessweek.com/news/2012–04–17/georgia-says-china-to-construct-630-million-hydropower-plant

88 "China Will Invest up to 1.7 Billion USD in Next Five Years," *The Financial*, http://finchannel.com/Main_News/Geo/107064_Chinese_will_Invest_up_to_1.7_Billion_USD_in_Georgia_in_Next_5_Years/

89   Margarita Antidze, "Trump Flies into ex-Soviet Georgia for Tower Project," *Reuters*, April 21, 2012, www.reuters.com/article/2012/04/21/us-georgia-trum p-idUSBRE83K0D220120421

90   Ellen Barry, "On Black Sea Swamp, Big Plans for Instant City," *New York Times*, April 21, 2012, www.nytimes.com/2012/04/22/world/europe/in-georgia-plans-for-an-instant-city.html

91   Robert Ware, "Iran Attack May Spark Caucasus War and Economic Turmoil," *antiwar.com*, http://original.antiwar.com/robert-bruce-ware/2012/09/12/iran-attack-could-spark-caucasus-war-and-economic-trouble/; Reprinted *Johnson's Russia List*. Accessed September 13, 2012.

Bibliography

Antidze, Margarita, "Trump Flies into ex-Soviet Georgia for Tower Project," *Reuters*, April 21, 2012, www.reuters.com/article/2012/04/21/us-georgia-trump-idUSBRE83K0D220120421

Augustine of Hippo, *City of God*. London: Penguin, 2003.

Barry, Ellen, "On Black Sea Swamp, Big Plans for Instant City," *New York Times*, April 21, 2012. www.nytimes.com/2012/04/22/world/europe/in-georgia-plans-for-an-instant-city.html

Dixon, Robyn, "Chechnya's Grimmest Industry," *Los Angeles Times*, September 18, 2000, http://articles.latimes.com/2000/sep/18/news/mn-23005

Dunlop, *Russia Confronts Chechnya: Roots of a Separatist Conflict*. Cambridge: Cambridge University Press, 1998.

Gall, Carlotta, and de Waal, *Chechnya: Calamity in the Caucasus*. New York: New York University Press, 1999.

Gammer, Moshe, *Muslim Resistance to the Tsar: Shamil and the Conquest of Chechnia and Daghestan*. Abingdon, UK: Frank Cass and Company, 1994.

Griffin, Nicholas, *Caucasus*. New York: St Martin's Press, 2001.

Hahn, Gordon M., "The *Jihadi* Insurgency and the Russian Counterinsurgency in the North Caucasus," *Post-Soviet Affairs*, 24(1) (January–March 2008): 1–39.

— *Russia's Islamic Threat*. New Haven and London: Yale University Press, 2007.

Hegel, G. W. F., *Lectures on the Philosophy of Religion*. Berkeley: University of California Press, 1984.

— *Lectures on the Philosophy of World History: Introduction*. Cambridge: Cambridge University Press, 1995.

— *Philosophy of Mind*. Oxford: Oxford University Press, 1968.

— *Philosophy of Right*. Oxford: Oxford University Press, 1988.

Heintz, Jim, "Kidnappers in Chechnya Free American Hostage," *ABC News*, February 4, 2002; http://abcnews.go.com/International/story?id=81551&page=1

Hughes, James, *Chechnya: From Nationalism to Jihad*. Philadelphia: University of Pennsylvania Press, 2007.

Human Rights Watch, "Russia: The Ingush-Ossetian Conflict in the Prigorodnyi Region," Human Rights Watch Helsinki Human Rights Watch, April 1996 (Paperback). ISBN 1–56432–165–7.

King, Charles, *The Ghost of Freedom: A History of the Caucasus*. Oxford: Oxford University Press, 2008.

Kisriev, Enver and Robert Bruce Ware, "Russian Hegemony in Dagestan," *Post-Soviet Affairs*, 21(1) (2005) pp. 26–55.

Levin, Anatol, *Chechnya: Tombstone of Russian Power*. New Haven: Yale University Press, 1999.

Matveeva, Anna, *North Caucasus: Views From Within*. London: Saferworld, March 2012.

— "The North Caucasus: The Russian Inner Abroad," in *Borderlands in Transition*. Moscow: Moscow Carnegie Center, 2000.

Owens, Admiral William, "The Emerging US System of Systems," *National Strategic Forum*, 63 (February 1996); www.dtic.mil/cgi-bin/ GetTRDoc?AD=ADA394313

Pilkington, Hilary and Galina Yemelianova, *Islam in Post-Soviet Russia*. London: Routledge, 2003.

Politkovskaya, Anna, *A Dirty War: A Russian Reporter in Chechnya*. Harvill: London, 2001.

— *A Small Corner of Hell: Dispatches from Chechnya*, translation of *Vtoraya chechenskaya*. Chicago: The University of Chicago Press, 2003.

— *Putin's Russia*. London, Harvill, 2004.

Russell, John, *Chechnya: Russia's "War on Terror."* London, Routledge, 2007.

Reddaway, Peter, Gail Lapidus, Barry Ickes, Carol Saivetz, and George Breslauer., "Russia in the Year 2003," *Post-Soviet Affairs*, 20(1) (2004): 1–45.

Sagramoso, Domitilla, "The Radicalization of Islamic Salafi *Jamaats* in the North Caucasus: Moving Closer to the Global *Jihad*ist Movement?" *Europe-Asia Studies*, 64(3) (May 2012): 561–95.

Sakwa, Richard, *The Crisis of Russian Democracy: The Dual State, Factionalism and the Medvedev Succession*. Cambridge, Cambridge University Press, 2011.

— "The Dual State in Russia," *Post-Soviet Affairs*, 26(3) (July–September 2010): 185–206.

— "The Revenge of the Caucasus: Chechenization and the Dual State in Russia," *Nationalities Papers*, 38(5) (September 2010): 601–22.

Sakwa, Richard (ed.), *Chechnya: From Past to Future*. London: Anthem, 2005.

Schaefer, Robert W., *The Insurgency in Chechnya and the North Caucasus: From Gazavat to Jihad*. Santa Barbara: Praeger Security International, 2011.

Stanley, Alessandra, "6 Red Cross Aides Slain in Chechnya, Imperiling the Peace," *New York Times*, December 18, 1996. www.nytimes.com/1996/12/18/ world/6-red-cross-aides-slain-in-chechnya-imperiling-the-peace. html?pagewanted=all&src=pm

Ware, Robert Bruce, "Has the Russian Federation Been Chechenised?" *Europe-Asia Studies*, 63(3) (2011): 493–508.

— "Iran Attack May Spark Caucasus War and Economic Turmoil," *antiwar.com*l September 13, 2012. http://original.antiwar.com/robert-bruce-ware/2012/09/12/ iran-attack-could-spark-caucasus-war-and-economic-trouble/; Reprinted *Johnson's Russia List*, September 13, 2012.

— "A Multitude of Evils: Mythology and Political Failure in Chechnya," in *Chechnya: From Past to Future*, R. Sakwa (ed.), 79–116. London: Anthem, 2005.

— "Revisiting Russia's Apartment Block Blasts," *Journal of Slavic Military Studies*, 18(4) (December 2005): pp. 599–606.

Ware, Robert Bruce and Enver Kisriev, *Dagestan: Russian Hegemony and Islamic Resistance in the North Caucasus.* Armonk, NY: M. E. Sharpe, 2010, 124–8.

— "Ethnic Parity and Democratic Pluralism in Dagestan: A Consociational Aproach," *Europe-Asia Studies*, 53(1) (2001): 105–32.

— "Political Islam in Dagestan," *Europe-Asia Studies*, 55(2) (2003): 287–302.

— "Russian Recentralization Arrives in the Republic of Dagestan: Implications for Institutional Integrity and Political Stability," *Eastern European Constitutional Review*, 10(1) (Winter 2001): pp. 68–75.

Ware, Robert Bruce, Enver Kisriev, Werner Patzelt, and Ute Roericht, "Dagestani Perspectives on Russia and Chechnya," *Post-Soviet Affairs*, 18(4) (2002): 306–31.

Wood, Tony, *Chechnya: The Case for Independence.* London: Verso, 2007.

APPENDIX

A Case Study of Western Memes: The Pussy Riot Conviction

Nicolai N. Petro

In September 2011, a group of women who had been active in a variety of performance-protest events established a band called "Pussy Riot"—henceforth "PR." It was not a musical band in the traditional sense, as members declined to advertise their performances, famously wore masks to hide their identities, and plainly stated that the purpose of their performances was to provoke political change, and ultimately "a revolution in Russia."[1] Public acts of defiance were at the heart of the group's mission since, in the words of their chief spokesperson Nadezhda Tolokonnikova, the media attention they attracted was intended to "stir up that part of society which (was) . . . politically apathetic."[2]

PR attracted attention on January 20, 2012, when they staged an unsanctioned concert with smoke bombs in Red Square. Eight members of the band were taken into custody and released after paying small fines.[3] On February 19 they staged a spontaneous protest performance in Moscow's Elokhov Cathedral, afterward painting graffiti on the Cathedral gates.

Three members of the band were arrested for an incident that took place on February 21, 2012. While some 50 people were attending commemorative services in the Cathedral of Christ the Savior, three women stormed the altar and began to enact a parody of the liturgy. Attired in bright colors and balaclavas, the style of the parody was that of a punk band, belting out a song titled "Holy Shit"[4] with guitars and amplification.

The lyrics referred to the Patriarch of Moscow as a "bitch," told the Orthodox faithful that they "crawl and bow" to "their chief saint—the head of the KGB," and described the liturgy as "God shit." According to eye witnesses who later testified at the trial, there was no mention of either Putin or politics during this performance,[5] although Western reports commonly claimed such references.[6]

Their performance lasted about one minute, before it was interrupted by security guards, and the women were escorted out of the cathedral. They later posted a montage of their performance on YouTube. In March the three women were arrested and charged under Article 213 of the Criminal Code of the Russian Federation ("Hooliganism"), aggravated, in this instance, by conspiracy, and by Article 3, Paragraph 6 of the Law on Freedom of Conscience, Religion and Religious Association that prohibits "calculated insults of the feelings of citizens in connection with their attitudes toward religion" when these take place "immediately adjacent to objects of religious veneration." Conspiracy carries a harsher sentence, namely jail time. Prosecution under the Law on Freedom of Conscience, Religion and Religious Association provides for criminal liability. On August 17, 2012 the three were sentenced to two years of imprisonment, less time already served.

According to BBC Monitoring, condemnation of the trial was "almost universal" in the European and American press.[7] Western reporting and commentary tended to see the incident as a harmless prank that, in the words of the Washington Post's editorial board, "may have upset some Russians, as it may have amused others."[8] The Western media framed the issue as one of free speech, under threat by an increasingly authoritarian political system headed by Vladimir Putin. The trial itself was frequently described as a "farce," and the Russian Orthodox Church, instead of being the victim, was chastised for being a party to oppression.

The view in Russia, where transcripts of the trial were readily available on various media websites, was different. While a minority shared the Western media's view that the issue was one of free speech, a majority accepted the court's judgment that it was a hate crime. Of those who said that they had followed the case, 86 percent favored some form of punishment.[9]

The difference in interpretation centered on the trial itself. The state argued that this was a hate crime. Such a crime, in Russia as elsewhere, must display two characteristics. First, an identifiable group must be targeted—in this case Orthodox Christians. Second, members of this group must be able to demonstrate how they were injured. The prosecution did so methodically, calling on eyewitnesses to the event who testified to their victimization. In this context, it is worth noting that the Cathedral of Christ the Savior is Russia's preeminent cathedral. It was consecrated to the victory over Napoleon, and destroyed by Stalin in 1931 to demonstrate the Soviet system's devotion to the abolition of religion. It was rebuilt in the 1990s in a national campaign that many see as the true end of religious persecution by the state. The prosecution's case made no reference to violations of canon law. Indeed, the judge denied all requests by the defense to introduce experts on religion, and in her closing remarks she reiterated her argument that any appeals on religious grounds, or to religious authority, were beyond the court's jurisdiction.[10]

In addition to trying to "put religion on trial," the PR defense sought to incriminate the political system, as well argue that The Church of Christ the Savior was not really a church, since commercial activity, such as the sale of votive candles, took place throughout the premises. Given oblique defense strategies, and the defendants' admission at the trial that they had intentionally and knowingly violated the law, an acquittal seemed unlikely. In addition, there were aggravating circumstances: the defendants fled the scene, lied to authorities, showed no remorse, insisted that they did nothing wrong, and asserted that if released they would commit similar actions. While the length of their sentence was controversial, any realistic observer would have anticipated jail time.

Given the "memes" that predominate in Russian–American relations, it was not surprising that Western media coverage of these events was selective. There are decades of Cold War animosity, as well as centuries of ignorance about Orthodox Christianity, to overcome. Most media outlets have neither the time nor the expertise to challenge these deeply entrenched stereotypes. The results were evident in the coverage of this case.

Note: As this appendix was being edited, the *New York Times* posted the following:

> The executive director of Amnesty International USA, Suzanne Nossel, said that Pussy Riot had been a galvanizing force for young activists, especially after Amnesty International labeled its members "prisoners of conscience" when they were arrested in March. "It's partly because they're young and their medium is artistic," she said. "They defy the stereotype of 'prisoner of conscience' of yore, at least in how they look." ("An Award and More Support for Pussy Riot," *New York Times*, September 21, 2012. http://artsbeat.blogs.nytimes.com/2012/09/21/an-award-and-more-support-for-pussy-riot/)

RBW

Notes

1 "Pussy Riot: 'Wir wollen eine Revolution," *Der Spiegel*, September 2, 2012. www.spiegel.de/spiegel/vorab/russland-pussy-riot-wollen-eine-revolution-a-853358.html

2 "Nadezhda Tolokonnikova: ya sklonna proshchat'," *Radio Svoboda*, September 3, 2012. www.svobodanews.ru/content/article/24696521.html

3   Ryan Cooper, "Who is Pussy Riot?" 2012, http://punkmusic.about.com/
od/punkinthenews/a/Who-Is-Pussy-Riot.htm; http://grani.ru/blogs/free/
entries/195012.html

4   Ibid.

5   "Pussy Riot Jailed for Two Years," *RIA Novosti*, August 17, 2012.
http://en.rian.ru/russia/20120817/175268773.html

6   "Pussy Riot Jail Term Rated Fair by Most Russians," *Bloomberg Businessweek*,
August 29, 2012 www.businessweek.com/news/2012–08–29/pussy-riot-jail-
term-rated-fair-by-most-russians-poll-shows. David Remnick, "Married to
Pussy Riot," *The New Yorker*, September 21, 2012 www.newyorker.com/online/
blogs/newsdesk/2012/09/pussy-riot-receives-lennonono-grant-for-peace.html

7   "Press aghast at Pussy Riot Verdict," *BBC News*, August 18, 2012.
www.bbc.co.uk/news/world-europe-19307077

8   "A Russian Farce over punk rock band," *Washington Post*, August 17, 2012.
www.washingtonpost.com/opinions/pussy-riot-sentence-echoes-russias-bad-
old-days/2012/08/17/380354bc-e8a6–11e1-a3d2–2a05679928ef_story.html

9   "Rossiyane o dele Pussy Riot," Levada Center, August 31, 2012. www.levada.
ru/31–07–2012/rossiyane-o-dele-pussy-riot

10   Alex Mercouris provides a very detailed analysis of the legal case in
two postings on his blog: "Pussy Riot" at http://mercouris.wordpress.
com/2012/08/07/pussy-riot-2/ (August 7, 2012); and "Pussy Riot—
After the Judgment" at http://mercouris.wordpress.com/2012/08/28/
pussy-riot-after-the-judgment/ (August 28, 2012).

INDEX